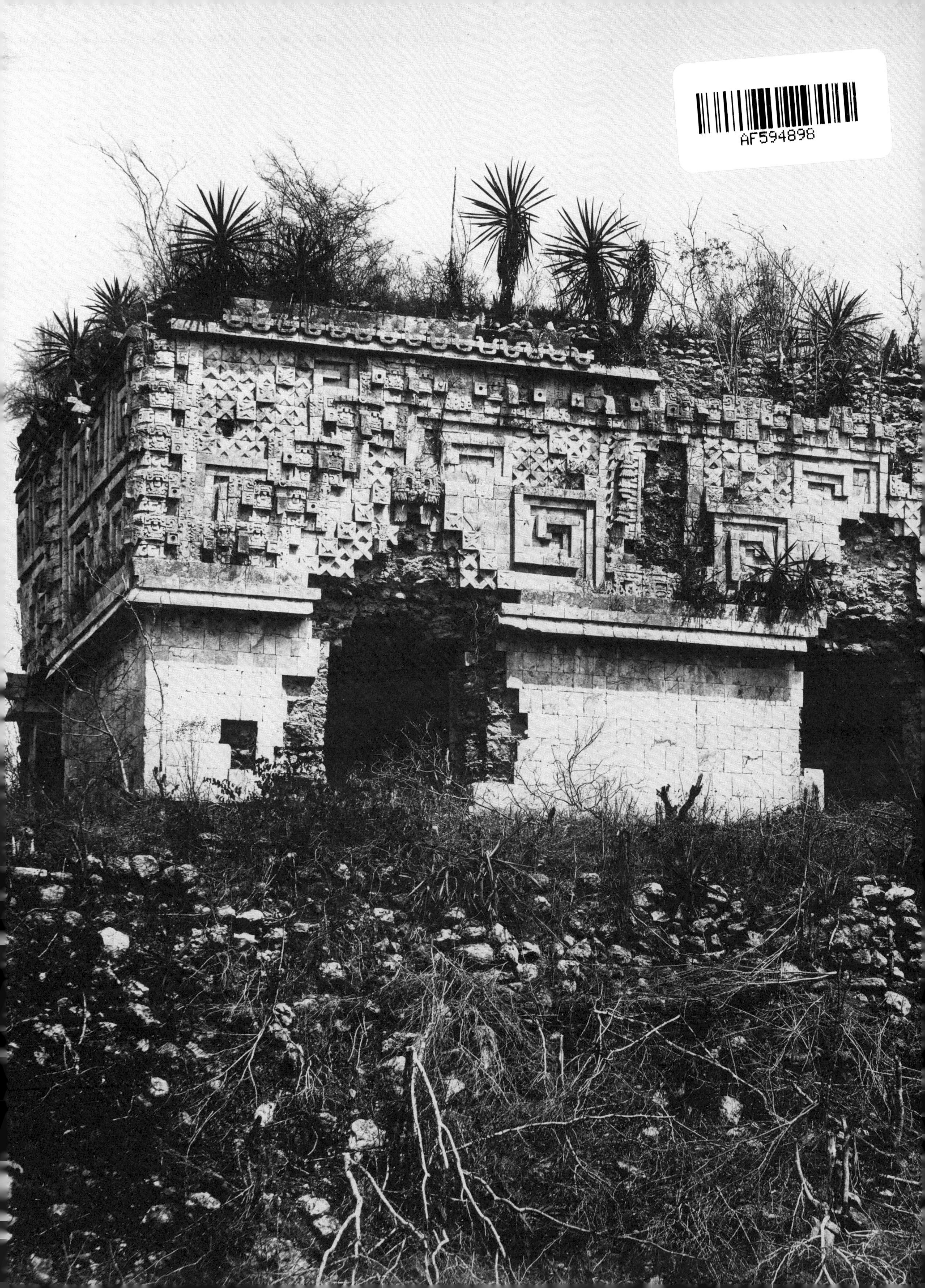

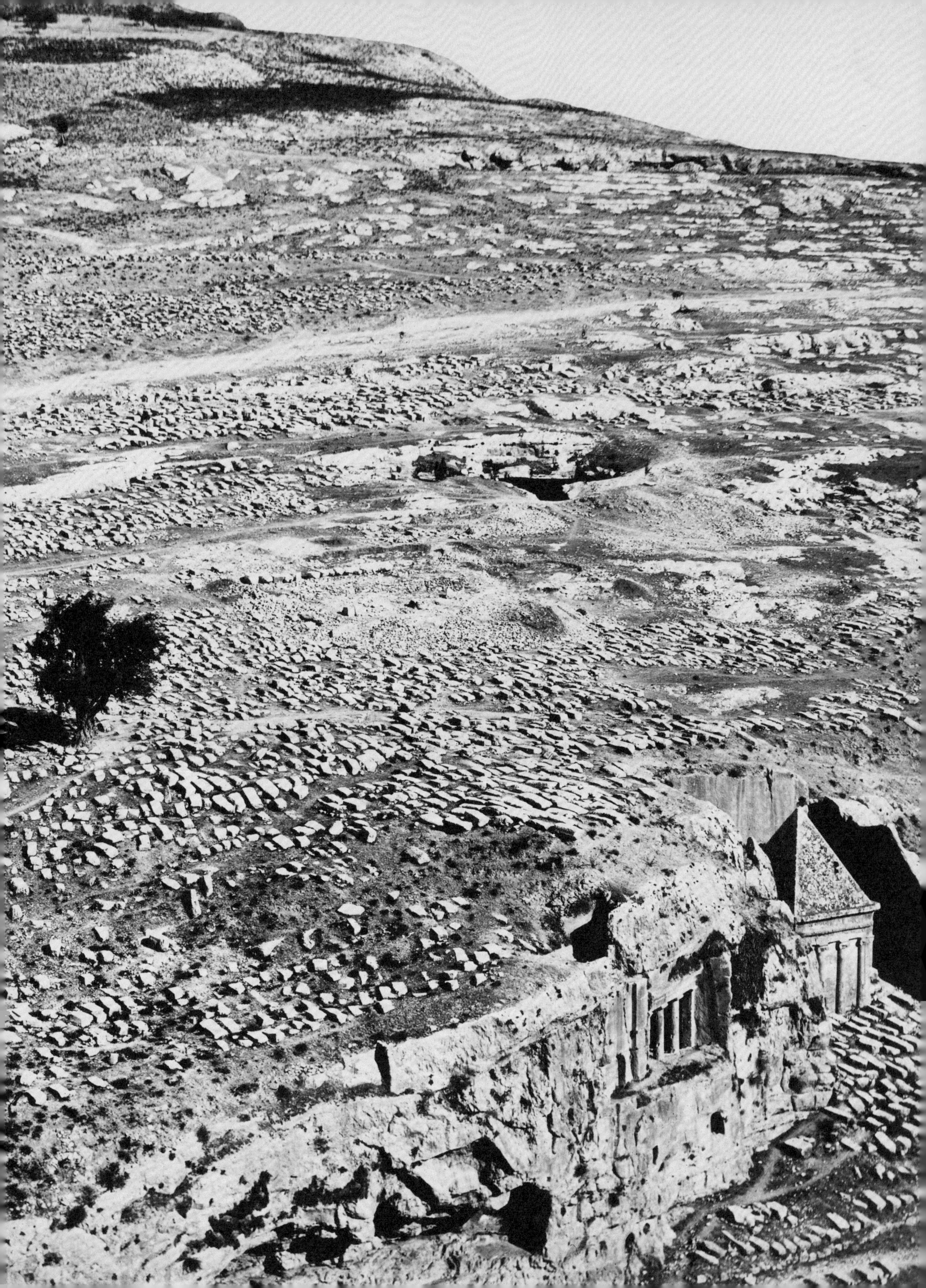

Terraforming

OLANA'S HISTORIC PHOTOGRAPHY
COLLECTION UNEARTHED

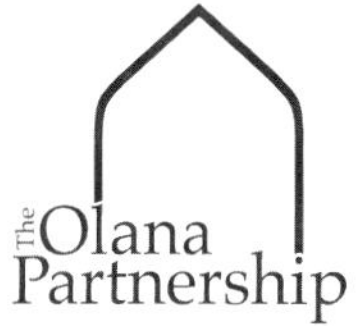

FOREWORD

At every turn, scholars, curators, and artists who delve into the collections of Olana State Historic Site. With over 90,000 items, the collections contain hidden depths. It is not that the objects themselves are unknown to our staff or that of the New York State Bureau of Historic Sites, in whose prudent care they lie. Rather, that, like ingredients on the pantry shelves, they stand inert until the human intellect plays upon them, reconstituting the webs of historical, social, and economic relationships that they express or have the potential to express to contemporary audiences. To this end, The Olana Partnership organizes and funds special exhibitions.

This year's project, led by guest curator David Hartt, working in collaboration with our curatorial staff, focuses on the nineteenth-century photography collected by Frederic Church between 1850 and 1900. Accompanied by able guides in Will Coleman, The Olana Partnership's former Director of Collections & Exhibitions, and Michele Phillips, New York State Paper Conservator at the Division for Historic Preservation, Hartt plunged into this collection of 5,000 images to make a selection of 137 photographic prints. They reveal a rich seam connecting his and Church's interest in the shaping of the earth's surface through both natural and human forces. Our engagement with historian of photography Corey Keller has clarified that Olana's photography collection is one of the largest assembled during the nineteenth century in the United States and is particularly remarkable for remaining intact at its artist-collector's home. Yet it remains mysterious, with about half the photographs unattributed, as of yet, and most never having been publicly exhibited. It is my hope that this publication will help to develop the interest and resources to undertake further research and digitize the collection for scholarly and public access.

In addition to those mentioned above, I want to express The Olana Partnership's appreciation to our New York State Office of Parks, Recreation and Historic Preservation collaborative partners, including Amy Hausmann, Director, Olana State Historic Site, and Gregory Smith, Director of the New York State Bureau of Historic Sites, and his remarkable team at the Peebles Island Resource Center. I also thank the Wyeth Foundation for American Art for generously funding this publication. The exhibition itself has been made possible by support from The Olana Partnership's Novak-Ferber Exhibitions Fund and The Henry Luce Foundation as well as the New York State Council on the Arts with the support of the Office of the Governor and the New York State Legislature. Finally, I express my appreciation to Mark Prezorski, Senior Vice President & Landscape Curator and Ida Brier, our Librarian and Archivist, and my deepest admiration and gratitude for the contributions of Allegra Davis, Associate Curator, in bringing this project to fruition.

Sean E. Sawyer, PhD
Washburn & Susan Oberwager President
The Olana Partnership

WHAT WAS PHOTOGRAPHY TO FREDERIC CHURCH?

William L. Coleman

The more than 5,000 nineteenth-century photographic prints that were acquired by the artist Frederic Edwin Church and survive in Olana's collection have been a secret too well kept: little documented, little known, and rarely seen apart from a small highlights show at the Dahesh Museum of Art in New York over twenty years ago.[1] A fundamental problem in tackling this remarkable trove of historic visual culture, which ranges from iconic works by leading names of early photography to amateur images of Olana itself, has been the scanty evidence of its circumstances of acquisition or use. For this reason, the holdings in this area have been known only to insiders: precious traces of a past encounter between traditional and new media awaiting their time in the spotlight.

With *Terraforming: Olana's Historic Photography Collection Unearthed,* that moment has arrived at last. By combining the perspectives of an artist who has uncommon expertise in the history of photography, with that of an historian of American landscape painting, the result has been a project rooted in the close looking and visual juxtaposition for which Olana's photographs are their own best evidence. This rich collaboration with David Hartt is founded upon a period of deep immersion in the collection. We went side-by-side, print-by-print, through what has been revealed to be one of the most important collections of nineteenth-century landscape photography in the country. We found a strong throughline in the subjects that spoke to Church as an artist-collector, as well as the complementary roles we could each play in this project. While David brought an acute visual sensitivity and broad material-historical understanding to the process of reflection and selection, my self-appointed position was to ask one deceptively simple question that underlies the exhibition, and to which this essay proposes some answers: what was photography to Frederic Church?

Among Olana's photography holdings is a fascinating print that both in its content and reception history crystallizes the issues of the collection as a whole. A church of European design appears atop an incline that is thick with vegetation. An early cataloguer has recorded the object in pencil on the archival folder as "Photograph—Mexico. Church on hill". On a 1995 research visit, the late critic Olivier Debroise and scholar of Latin American art James Oles have written in a colophonic correction "Not a hill! The building is atop a Pre-Columbian pyramid!" Indeed, the unknown colleague who catalogued the object, after Olana and its collection came into the ownership of the people of New York in 1966, overlooked this clear indication on the print itself from the Mexico City photography firm of Gove & North. The subject is in fact a classic case of the conflicted meeting of faith and culture in the natural world: the 1575 Church of Our Lady of the Remedies planted atop the Great Pyramid of Cholula, the largest pyramid in the world, dating to the first millennium of the common era.

The layered transformation of land for human uses, or "terraforming," in this rich photograph is characteristic of the compositions and subjects that captured this artist's imagination, both in forming a photography collection and in his own practice of painting and land art on a monumental scale. Just as the church sits atop an ancient temple site in Cholula, so does Olana's main house sit atop a designed landscape with a deep history of human use long before Church began his forty-year engagement with the property. The sheer number of photographic materials of this kind, accumulated during the same period in which he was making creative work with strong relationships to the prints he owned, presents a preponderance of evidence for the conclusion that photography was an important tool of Church's artistic practice across media. It was one more new visual technology that he

1 Thomas Weston Fels et al., *Fire and Ice: Treasures from the Photographic Collection of Frederic Church at Olana* (New York: Dahesh Museum of Art; Ithaca: Cornell University Press, 2002).

welcomed into his work in the course of a global career that engaged many others. Certain prints in the collection present compelling parallels, and physical evidence of use, which suggest Church's embrace of photography as a compositional tool for his major paintings.[2]

Beyond the content of the collection itself, Church's own comments on the uses of photography are infrequent. An 1860 letter from Church to Samuel Putnam Avery—an art dealer, collector, and later a fellow trustee of New York's Metropolitan Museum of Art with Church—acknowledges receipt of some photographs and a request to acquire a few of them, subjects unspecified.[3] Church told an inquirer in 1865 that he could not provide a portrait photograph of himself, "intending to sit [for such a photograph] all winter but have not done so."[4] This is intriguing evidence that he saw the potential value of photography in building his brand, as well as valuing the visual information it could transmit for his work. Even more useful is a note in which Church indicated that an unnamed photographer would accompany the Churches on their journey from Beirut to Palmyra, evidence of a painting practice for which photography was not a threat but a welcome fellow traveler in the transmission of useful information and inspiration.[5] Preparing to return to New York from London with "heaps of sketches and photographs," Church suggests that he has been collecting photographs on his travels.[6] We see also rare evidence of the direct commissioning of photographs, and their role in the making of Olana itself, in a letter of 1881 in which he tells a regular correspondent that "I expect in August a Photographer to come here and take a series of views including the House so I wish to have a few details finished—such as enclosed verandah by the Nursery."[7]

These valuable pieces of documentary evidence join a substantial existing body of scholarship connecting Church and kindred painters of his generation to the rise of photography and the nineteenth-century urban culture of popular visual entertainments. These technologies became a legitimate tool of a painter's art. Church made creative use of reproductive media to further his work, including instances of applying paint over photographic and lithographic prints, the use of a magic lantern image projector and hundreds of examples of the early three-dimensional viewing technology known as the stereograph. They combine to present an image of an artist who welcomed new media as an inspiration and tool for his multidisciplinary practice of landscape art.[8]

In this context, David's groundbreaking, research-informed practice, which bridges traditional and new media, finds an uncannily apt home. He has been substantively engaged with Church's ideologically complex travels in Jamaica and the Canadian Maritimes for years as part of a larger practice grounded in the critical interrogation of photography. The new work David has made for *Terraforming* as well as the overarching eye and insight he has brought to the curatorial operation make for a unique project that, we hope, will reveal some of the operations, assumptions, and questions that drove the practice of an artist who was once contemporary, not so long ago.

2 For example, a photograph by Dimitrios Konstantinou (OL.1982.1454), showing the Parthenon from the same vantage point of Church's *The Parthenon* of 1871, bears intersecting guidelines in pencil marking the center of the composition. See Kevin J. Avery, "'The Finest Edifice on the Finest Site in the World': Church's *Parthenon*," in *Frederic Church: A Painter's Pilgrimage* (Detroit: Detroit Institute of Arts, 2017): 166-169. I thank Allegra Davis for this reference.

3 Frederic Church to Samuel P. Avery, 21 November 1861. Collection of the Metropolitan Museum of Art, Gift, Samuel P. Avery, Jr., 1914. Transcript in the Olana archives.

4 Frederic Church to Charles Hart, 31 March 1865. Archives of American Art, Smithsonian Institution. Transcript in the Olana archives.

5 Frederic Church to William H. Osborn, 18 April 1868. Collection of Olana State Historic State, New York Office of Parks, Recreation and Historic Preservation, OL.2003.11.A-H

6 Frederic Church to Edward Weeks, 7 June 1869. Collection of Olana State Historic State, New York Office of Parks, Recreation and Historic Preservation, OL.1989.281.3.

7 Frederic Church to Erastus Dow Palmer, 15 July 1881. McKinney Library, Albany Institute of History and Art. Transcript in the Olana archives.

8 For example Jennifer Raab, "Narrative Luxury" in *Frederic Church: The Art and Science of Detail* (New Haven: Yale University Press, 2005): 65-85. See also in relation to Church's teacher, Wendy Ikemoto, "A 'Higher Style' of Looking: Thomas Cole and Popular Media," *The Burlington Magazine* vol. 156, no. 1335 (June 2014): 385-390. Maura Lyons is at work on a book on Church's hybrid media that will be the definitive resource on this topic. Her recorded lecture in Olana's 'Subject Specialists' series, now on YouTube, offers a preview of things to come: "Below the Surface: What Scientific Imaging Reveals about Church's Artistic Process," 18 May 2021. The collection of Olana State Historic Site includes 510 stereographs and 7 broken pieces of magic lantern slides (OL.2004.1144.A-.G). The diary of Emma Carnes, Church's mother-in-law, notes that she sent her grandson Louis "a new kind of Magic Lantern a Pollyopticon [sic]" as a gift (December 27, 1884, Emma Carnes Diary, 1884-January 1886, Collection of Olana State Historic Site, New York State Office of Parks, Recreation and Historic Preservation, OL.2000.285).

TO BRING THE WORLD HOME: FREDERIC CHURCH AND PHOTOGRAPHY

Corey Keller

Frederic Edwin Church was enormously curious and keenly attuned to the issues of his time. It is therefore not surprising that he would have been interested in photography, which was invented during his lifetime and revolutionized picture-making in the nineteenth century. Photography's entrance onto the scene intensified existing debates (and introduced several new ones) about the proper relationships between art and science, nature and representation, detail and overall effect; all issues that were central to Church's painting. What is surprising, however, is that despite these obvious points of intersection, little historical attention has been paid to either Church's substantial collection of photography, or to what the medium might have signified for the painter. The size and scope of this collection provides incontrovertible evidence of Church's interest in the medium, yet the character of his engagement remains poorly understood. However, the examination of Church's photography collection offers a new perspective from which to consider the place of his work, and the trajectory of his career, within the debates that shaped nineteenth-century landscape painting. Thinking about Church as a consumer of images profitably enlarges and complicates our understanding of him as a producer of them.

Any visitor to Olana can testify to Church's exuberant passion for collecting. He and his wife shipped home hundreds of objects acquired during their extensive travels, transforming their home—its architecture, décor, and landscape—into a Gesamtkunstwerk. "The whole house," wrote an awestruck journalist in 1884, "is a museum of fine arts, rich in bronzes, paintings, sculptures, and antique and artistic specimens from all over the world."[1] Church's collection of photographs depicting foreign places, architecture, and people, though rarely mentioned in such reports, clearly represents an extension of this impulse to bring home the world for the purposes of edification and delight. Such travel photographs represent a significant concentration within his overall photography collection.[2] They range from the unique (the earliest works in the collection are one-of-a-kind daguerreotypes of Niagara Falls by Platt D. Babbitt, taken in the early 1850s) to the mass-produced (such as stereoviews that were produced in the thousands), and they describe a considerable part of the globe, from the icebergs of the Arctic to the jungles of India. The collection includes works by the most acclaimed practitioners of the medium, as well as by those whose names are now lost to history.

Given the overlap in subject matter between many of Church's paintings and the photographs he owned, the most obvious motivation for such a collection is the amassing of pictorial source material for future paintings. He would certainly not be the only artist to use photographs as supplements to or substitutes for preparatory sketches. Eugène Delacroix, Alfred Bierstadt, Thomas Eakins, and John Singer Sargent are just a few of the celebrated nineteenth-century painters known to collect, commission, or even make their own photographs as studies. However, few direct correlations can be drawn between specific photographs in the collection and Church's completed paintings, suggesting that the photographs may have served other purposes. Perhaps they supplied an inventory of details and local color to fire the imagination rather than serve as direct models. Though the iconographic content of Church's photographs is certainly important, the collection should also be seen as the reflection of a particular philosophical orientation: a manifestation of the age's breathtaking optimism that the world was collectible and, consequently, knowable. Collecting became a passion in the nineteenth century, undertaken at scales that ranged from the individual curio-hunter to national programs of colonialism and

1 F.N. Zabriskie, "Old Colony Papers: 'An Artist's Castle and our Ride Thereto,'" *New York Christian Intelligencer,* September 10, 1884, 2. Cited in James Anthony Ryan, "Olana: Architecture and Landscape as Art," in *Frederic Edwin Church,* ed. Franklin Kelly (Washington, DC: National Gallery of Art, 1989), 143.

2 The total collection comprises nearly 7,000 photographs and includes views Church commissioned of Olana and its surroundings, family photographs, and pictures collected by the artist's sons, one of whom went on to become a photographer himself. My sincere thanks go to Allegra Davis, Associate Curator, and Ida Brier, Archivist for their patience and generosity in answering my queries about the collection.

empire building. Scientific studies such as Charles Darwin's research in the Galapagos, or Alexander von Humboldt's wildly popular multi-volume *Cosmos: A Sketch of the Physical Description of the Universe* (1845–62, the final book published posthumously) profoundly influenced Church's approach to the landscape and were also characterized by the amassing of observations, measurements, and specimens. This was in an effort to draw connections between seemingly disparate details and discern the larger patterns governing the universe. Whether in the service of personal curiosity, scientific knowledge, or geopolitics, collections offered a matrix through which the world could be seen, sorted, and mastered.

Many of the photographs in Church's collection were acquired as he traveled. Church was participating in a longstanding tradition: by the nineteenth century, travel and the consumption of images were inextricably intertwined. Generations of wealthy Europeans and Americans had sketched along the Grand Tour, creating visual records of their peregrinations. By the beginning of the eighteenth century, such tourists could also purchase etchings and engravings as souvenirs of the landscapes, monuments, and famous artworks they visited. Predictably, when photography was invented in 1839, the documentation of distant places was one of the first applications envisioned for the new medium. (William Henry Fox Talbot, the English inventor of photography on paper, went so far as to attribute the motivation for his early experiments to the frustration he experienced sketching at Lake Como.) Enterprising photographers established studios all along the tourist trail, from London to Egypt and beyond, to meet the ever-growing demand for views. Their activities were not only an extension of established practices, but also a response to changes in the very nature of travel itself. The year before photography's invention, the first transatlantic steamship docked in New York after a record-breaking sixteen-day journey from England. By the late 1870s, the average trip from the United States to Europe had been nearly cut in half, to only a week. As travel became less physically and (to some extent) financially demanding, it also became available to a broader class of tourist whose tastes tended not to traditional forms of art, but to photography.

The acquisition of prints and photographs became so integral a part of traveling that merchants were regularly featured in travel guidebooks. As travel became increasingly accessible, these books became essential companions and helped establish itineraries—especially in Europe and the Middle East—that became almost completely standardized. They also influenced and even homogenized the way these itineraries were represented. Guides listed such practicalities as hotels, restaurants, and English-speaking pharmacies. As nineteenth-century travelers tended to linger in one spot much longer than tourists now do—Church and his wife, for example, spent nearly six months in Rome during their two-year sojourn of Europe and the Middle East—they might also name more esoteric resources, including local fencing masters, language instructors, and dance teachers. But every guide had information on vendors of maps, engravings, and photographs, and often identified particular practitioners by name. The recommendations for Rome made by John Murray's very popular *Handbook for Travelers,* for example, were quite specific:

> The most eminent artists in photography at Rome are Sig. Cuccioni, an Italian, at 18, Via Condotti, and Mr. Anderson, an Englishman. Cuccioni's photographs are excellent, and the large ones of the Coliseum, the Roman Forum, St. Peter's, St. Paul's, the Castle of St. Angelo, the Fontana di Trevi, &c., are *chefs-d'oeuvres,* unique for their size and execution; his reproductions of the ancient sculptures in the museums of the Capitol and Vatican are also extremely good. Mr. Anderson's photographs, the best we have seen, are extremely faithful and good, and of different sizes to suit all purses and purchasers....[3]

3 *Handbook of Rome and its Environs* [Seventh Edition] (London: John Murray, 1864): xxii.

Church, too, seems to have followed the recommendations of his guidebook. The inventory of his library at Olana suggests that in Rome he consulted the equally popular Baedeker guide. Unlike Murray, who highlighted the group of foreign photographers known as the Circle of the Caffè Greco, Baedeker praised the work of Carlo Baldessare Simelli.[4] Church acquired a substantial group of Simelli's work while in Rome.

If collecting photographs became a common touristic practice, the scale of Church's holdings puts him in a rarefied class of collector. Few collections of this size remain intact today; those that do give a vivid picture of the enormity and global distribution of the industry that catered to travelers' appetites for photographs. The typical destination for such pictures was an album, either assembled by hand or by a professional album-maker. Lady Annie Brassey, for example, an English aristocrat who traveled extensively on a series of private yachts (one of which was equipped with a darkroom to accommodate her own efforts in photography), assembled the photographs she collected into some 70 albums.[5] Isabella Stewart Gardner, best known today for her eponymous museum in Boston, was also an avid traveler and photograph album-maker, and offers a useful parallel to Church in that her photography collection was also symptomatic of a grander collecting strategy.[6] She collected her photographs into albums that serve as a visual diary of her travels and that she shared with friends, and later, visitors to her museum.

Rather than organize his photographs chronologically into albums that reflect a personal experience of moving through time and space, Church seems to have grouped most of them into unbound portfolios, sorted by geographic subject. In this respect, his collection more closely resembles a pictorial atlas. It also mimics the kinds of reference collections assembled at that time by museums and libraries. As photography became increasingly incorporated into archaeological research, scientific practice, and art history, among other fields of study, photographs offered a compact and convenient way of cataloguing, organizing, and comparing diverse materials by bridging discrepancies of scale, era, and geography. Church may well have been familiar with the picture collection assembled by the Boston Athenaeum (where he exhibited his paintings on more than one occasion), one of the earliest American institutions to collect photography. Founded in 1807, the Athenaeum maintained an impressive repository of maps, charts, prints, models, and books of engravings intended as a visual resource for engineers, artists, and the interested public. In 1859, they began adding photographs, which were similarly sorted by topic. A good number of the photographs in the Athenaeum's collection were reproductions of works of art or architecture, but many others represented contemporary subjects, especially the American Civil War.[7] In 1931, Walter Benjamin famously commented on the impact of photography on works of art, remarking, "Anybody will be able to observe how much more easily a painting, and above all sculpture or architecture can be grasped in photographs than in reality."[8] Though Benjamin was here specifically concerned with the status of the artistic original, his assessment that the mechanical reproduction of the world resulted in a kind of intellectual mastery over it had far-reaching consequences. Within the context of the archive, photographs assumed the status of information: the photograph of the thing, elided with the thing itself.

By conflating representation with the subject represented, photography was also frequently understood as a substitute for experience. As the possibility of travel grew in the nineteenth century, so did the desire to do so. But not everyone who wanted to experience distant lands wished, or could afford, to do so in person. A flourishing industry catered to the desires of armchair travelers, offering a variety of travel substitutes, ranging from descriptive written accounts to immersive environments such as panoramas that simulated the physical experience of being somewhere else. Photography played an important role in this. Unlike travel narratives, which recorded a

4 Karl Baedeker, *Italy: Handbook for Travelers. Second Part: Central Italy and Rome* (Coblenz: Verlag K. Baedeker, 1867): 103.

5 The albums are in the Lady Annie Brassey Photograph Collection at The Huntington Library, San Marino, CA.

6 For a more nuanced analysis of Gardner's album-making in relationship to her museum-building efforts than can possibly be summarized here, see Casey K. Riley, "From Page to Stage: Isabella Stewart Gardner's Photograph Albums and the Development of her Museum, 1874-1924," PhD dissertation, Boston University, 2015. I am grateful to Dr. Riley for making her unpublished dissertation available.

7 Sally Pierce, "Prints and Photographs at the Boston Athenaeum," in *The Boston Athenaeum Bicentennial Essays*, ed. Richard Wendorf (Boston: The Boston Athenaeum, 2009): 149-191. My thanks to Christina Michelon, Special Collections, Boston Athenaeum, for her research assistance.

8 Walter Benjamin, "A Short History of Photography" (1931), trans. Phil Patton, *Artforum* 15, no. 6 (February 1977): 50.

singular experience from a particular point of view, photographs offered the illusion of objectivity. At once specific and generic, photographs seemed to present the facts as they were, uninflected by personal perspective, just as they would be discovered by anyone who stood on that same spot. The experiences photographs offered were not viewed as poor substitutes either: many commentators remarked that in a photograph, an observer might see details they would have been physically incapable of perceiving or too preoccupied to remark on while visiting. This effect of immediacy was heightened by the inception of the stereoview: a pair of nearly identical photographs examined through a specialized viewer, producing the illusion of three-dimensionality. Oliver Wendell Holmes took this logic of substitution to the extreme when he famously suggested in 1859 that stereoviews could replace the original objects altogether: "Give us a few negatives of a thing worth seeing, taken from different points of view, and that is all we want of it. Pull it down or burn it up, if you please."[9] Stereoview companies developed extensive "tours" of foreign lands to be undertaken entirely from the comfort of one's own home.

Not all the travel photographs Church collected were bought on site; many depict locales he never visited. The exquisite portfolio of photographs by Claude-Joseph Desiré Charnay in the Olana collection is a case in point.[10] Carrying some 1500 pounds of photographic equipment over inhospitable terrain, Charnay, a former schoolteacher, photographed key archaeological sites across Mexico, including Mitla, Chichén-Itza, and Uxmal, between 1858 and 1860. Unlike the monuments of Europe that were easily seen by any visitor and routinely commemorated by artists, the Mayan ruins Charnay depicted were engulfed in dense overgrowth and essentially inaccessible. Such photographs were not supplements to experience but replacements for it, as the ruins had been previously unknown to most Europeans, and few would ever see them in person. Many of the photographs in Church's collection—those of India, for example, or Persia—functioned similarly for the painter; his farflung adventuring was largely curtailed by the 1870s due to his health, though he wintered regularly in Mexico throughout the 1880s and 1890s. It is worth noting that Church's hero, Alexander von Humboldt—an early proponent of the daguerreotype—also surrounded himself with photographs of faraway places when he became too old and frail to travel.

The years covered by Church's photography collection, approximately 1850 to 1900, also map onto critical technological shifts within photography itself. These changes not only affected the kinds of pictures photographers made, but also profoundly shaped the broader visual culture. The 1850s were still early days for the medium, and the practice encompassed a broad range of techniques, from the mirror-like daguerreotype to the textured, soft-edged calotype (photographs made using paper negatives) to the nascent wet collodion on glass that produced sharp, precise negatives. Who made photographs was also shifting during this period; as photography evolved from a craft to an industry, a schism opened up between amateur and commercial photographers, with the former embracing atmospheric effects they deemed more artistic, and the latter catering to the public's burgeoning appetite for finely detailed imagery on glossy paper.[11] So although we may speak of "photography" as a monolithic medium, in the nineteenth century its methods of production and aesthetic properties were very much in flux, and the medium's relationship to both science and art was being constantly re-negotiated. Over the course of the 1860s, albumen prints produced from glass negatives came to dominate the market, in part due to the industrialization of photographic materials, and in part due to popular taste. In the latter decades of the nineteenth century, photography became increasingly synonymous with exactitude, facticity, and above all, detail.

In her excellent study, *Frederic Church: The Art and Science of Detail,* Jennifer Raab has pointed to the centrality of the detail as both a feature

9 Oliver Wendell Holmes, "The Stereoscope and the Stereograph," *The Atlantic,* June 1859, 747.

10 Church's collection includes a rare complete set of Charnay's portfolio *Cités et ruines américaines: Mitla, Palenqué, Izamal, Chichen-Itza, Uxmal* (1862–63).

11 See Grace Seiberling, *Amateurs, Photography, and the Mid-Victorian Imagination* (Chicago: The University of Chicago Press, 1986): 18-45.

and problem within Church's paintings, as well as in their critical reception. "Nineteenth-century viewers expected landscape paintings to balance precision and generality, detail and effect, but Church's works often seemed to upset this balance, especially as his career progressed."[12] She argues that the profusion of detail in his work—and the increasingly negative reactions to it—illustrates the expectations viewers had for landscape painting: that such details would exceed mere scientific empiricism, and imbue the material world with grander symbolic meanings. But if the detail became associated with the scientific and the material during this period, it was also inextricably aligned with the photographic. Photography's perceived fidelity to the real, or, in the language of the day, its "truth to nature," necessarily put it into both conflict and conversation with dominant theories of art, particularly those that governed landscape painting. Another possible reading for the negative critical response to Church's later paintings is a reaction against the populist cult of the detail engendered and popularized by photography by the 1870s. One of the most withering critiques of Church's work, from William James Stillman, an ardent champion of John Ruskin's creed that art be faithful to nature, makes this connection clear. Stillman's central criticism of Church is that he fails to differentiate between mere description and art. But the metaphors he uses are drawn directly from photography, comparing Church's mind to a "camera obscura in which everything that passed before it was recorded permanently," and his rendering of details "as clear as that of a photographic lens."[13] Church's error lay in recording the material world as it was, like a camera, rather than elevating it to the level of symbol, the job of an artist.

Writings across nineteenth-century art theory betray an ambivalence about photography's role in naturalism even as photography helped set the very terms of the debate. John Ruskin's writings are in fact wonderfully complex, even contradictory, and demonstrate (perhaps accidentally) the ways in which photography, painting, and theories on the interpretation of nature were mutually inflecting, bound together in a Gordian knot.[14] Rather than representing opposite poles of a debate, photography and painting were interconnected in ways that reveal a great deal about how knowledge was then gleaned about the world, and about the roles both science and art had in organizing and presenting it. An examination of Church's collection of photography is much more than a simple exercise in iconographic influence. Photography may well have inspired the subjects of Church's paintings, but more importantly, it indelibly shaped the visual culture within which his work was both produced and received.

12 Jennifer Raab, *Frederic Church: The Art and Science of Detail* (New Haven: Yale University Press, 2015): 1.

13 William James Stillman, *Autobiography of a Journalist,* vol. 1 (Boston and New York: Houghton, Mifflin, 1901): 96. Ironically, Stillman had studied painting with Church and later became a noted photographer in Greece. Stillman's extraordinary photographs of the Acropolis from 1870 are well represented in Church's collection.

14 See Tim Barringer, "An Antidote to Mechanical Poison: John Ruskin, Photography, and Early Pre-Raphaelite Painting," in *The Pre-Raphaelite Lens: British Photography and Painting, 1848-1875,* ed. Diane Waggoner (Washington, DC: National Gallery of Art, 2010): 18-31.

OLANA'S HISTORIC PHOTOGRAPHY COLLECTION UNEARTHED

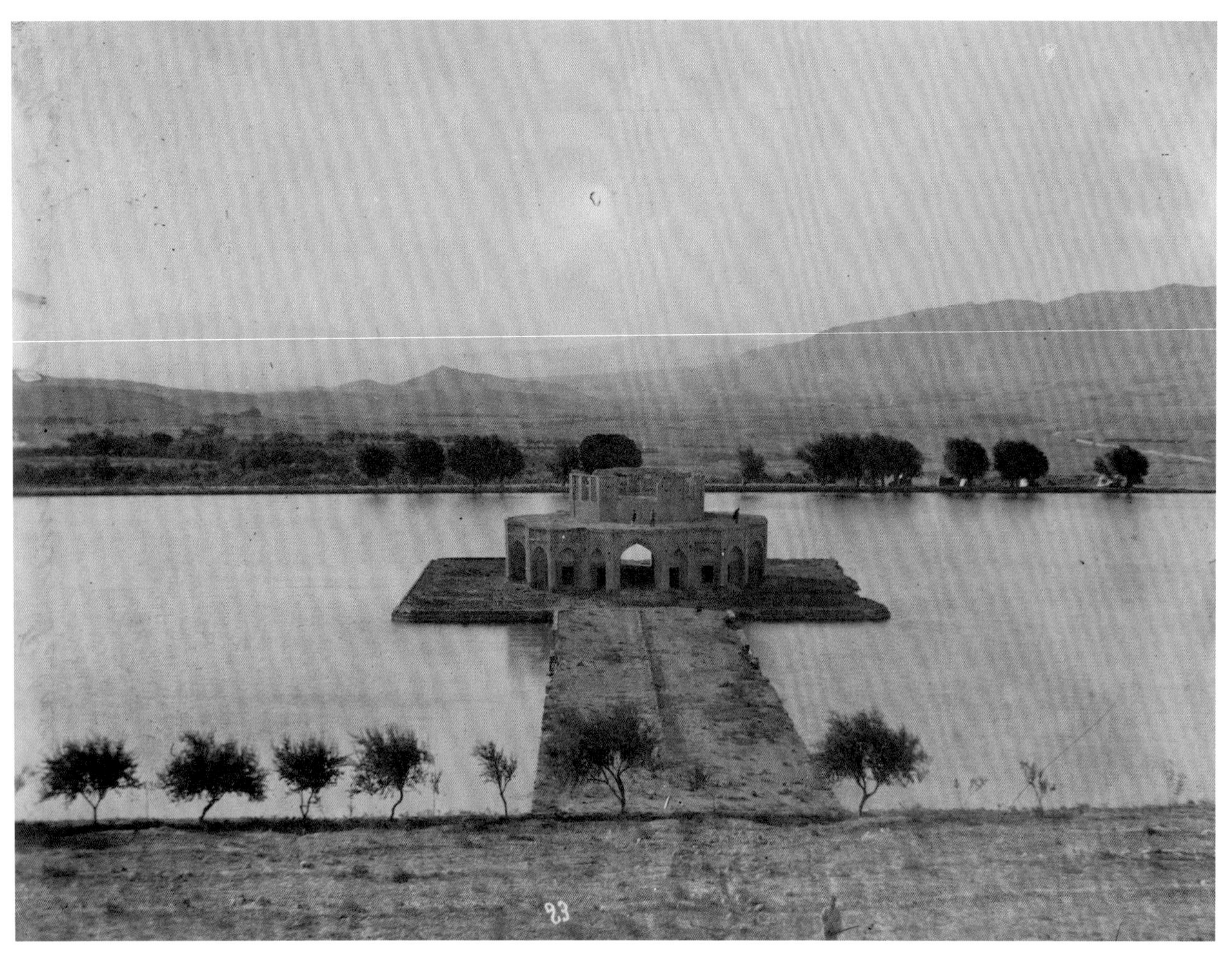

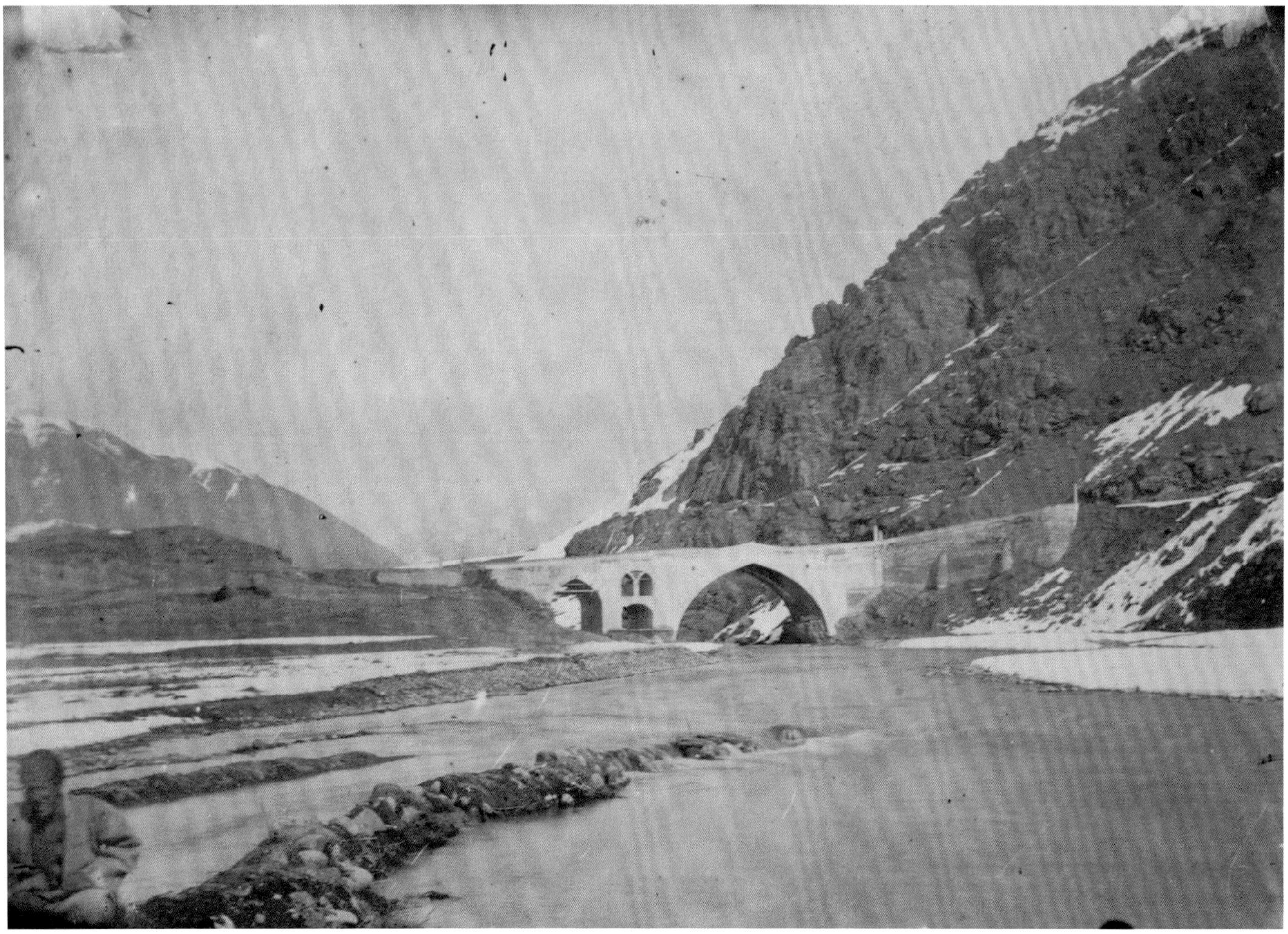

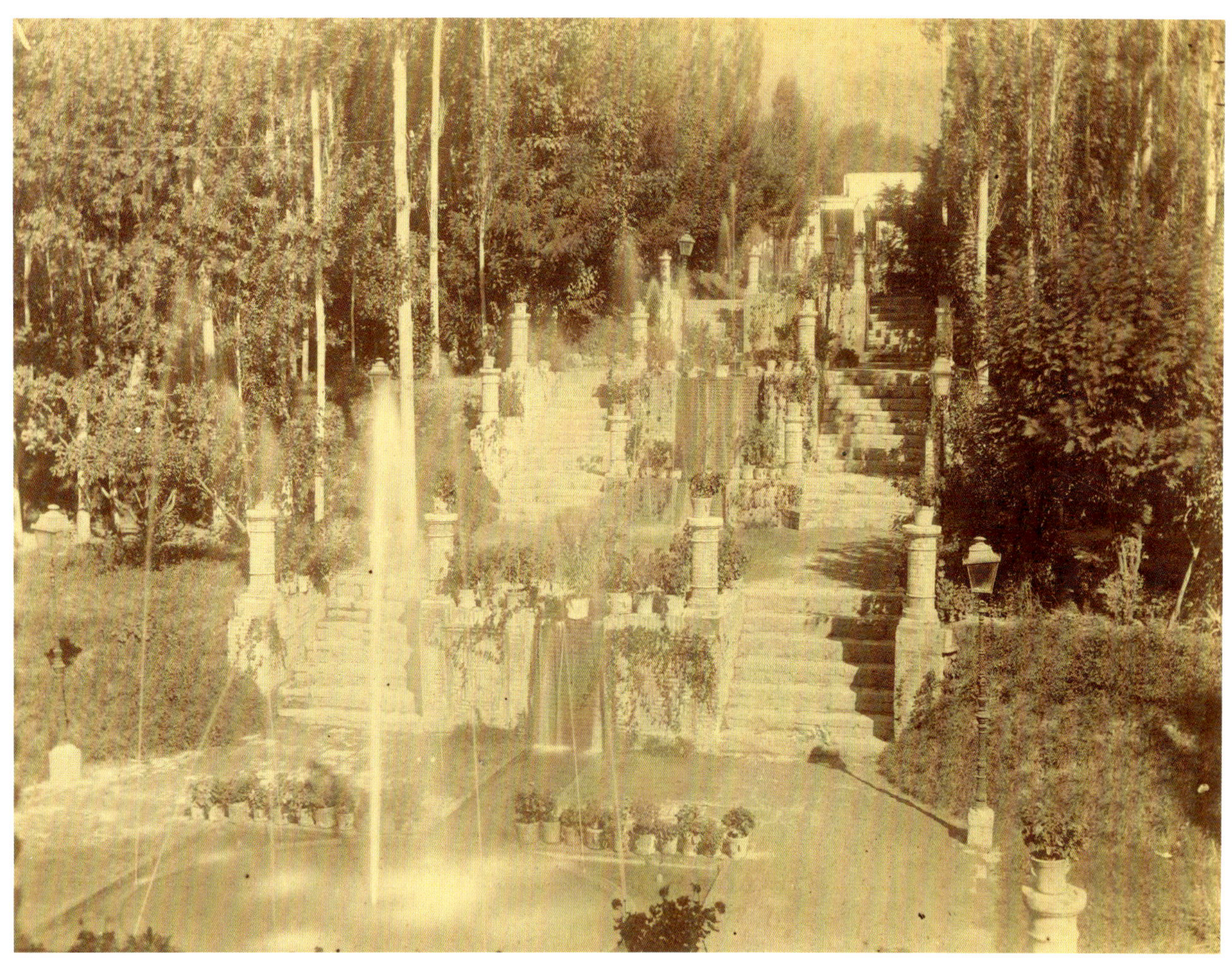

Photographer Unknown
Part of an Old Summer Palace (Tabreez),
late 19th century
19th-century photographic print,
image size: 6 7/16 × 8 ½ inches
OL.1981.590.3

Photographer Unknown
Bridge Across the Kizzil Oozoon, Near Koflon Koo, On the Way to Tehran,
late 19th century
19th-century photographic print,
image size: 5 ½ × 8 ½ inches
OL.1981.594

Photographer Unknown
Views of Tehran, A Summer Palace in Isfahan,
late 19th century
19th-century photographic print,
image size: 6 ⅞ × 9 ⅛ inches,
historic mount: 10 × 12 inches
OL.1981.494.90

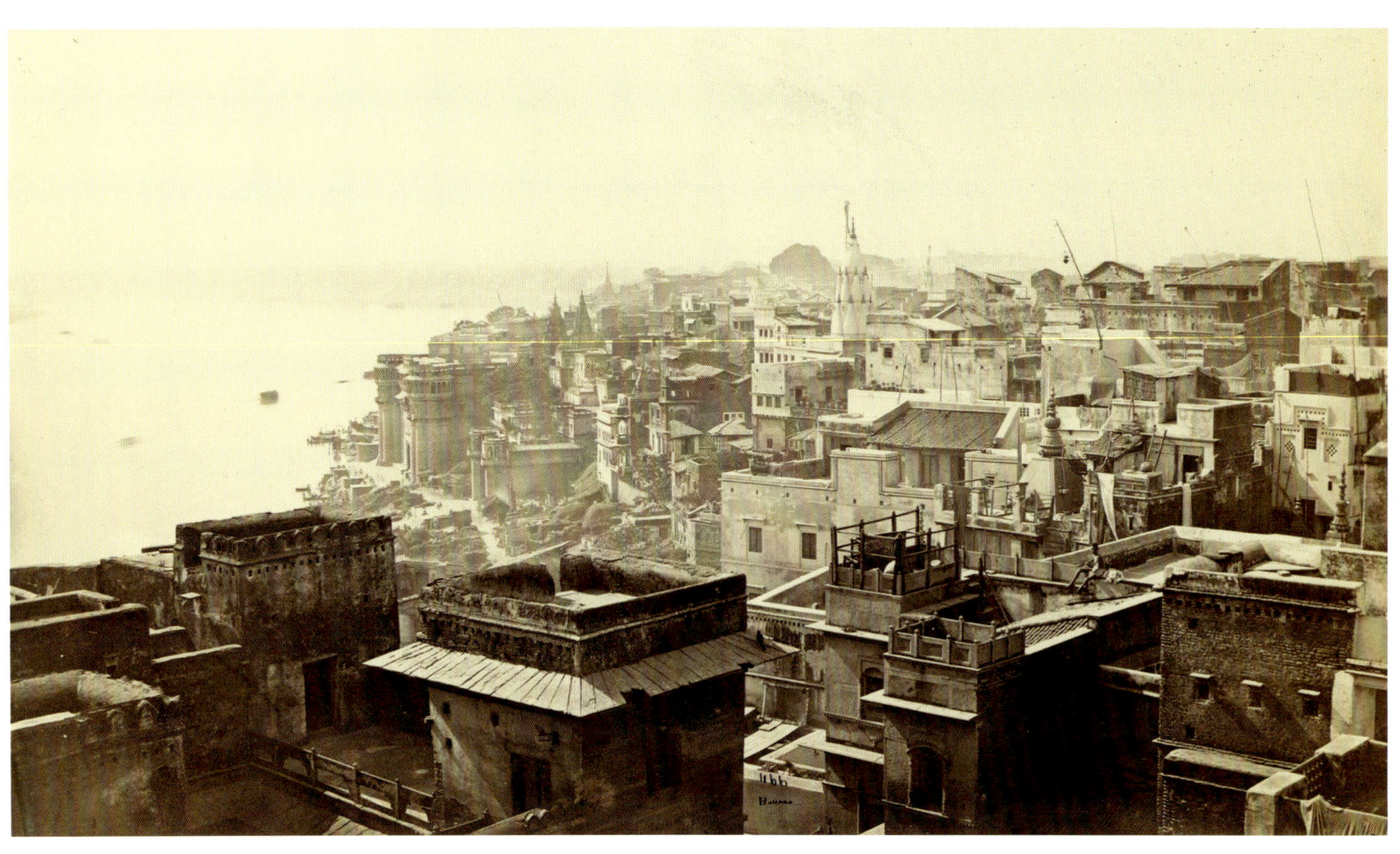
1166

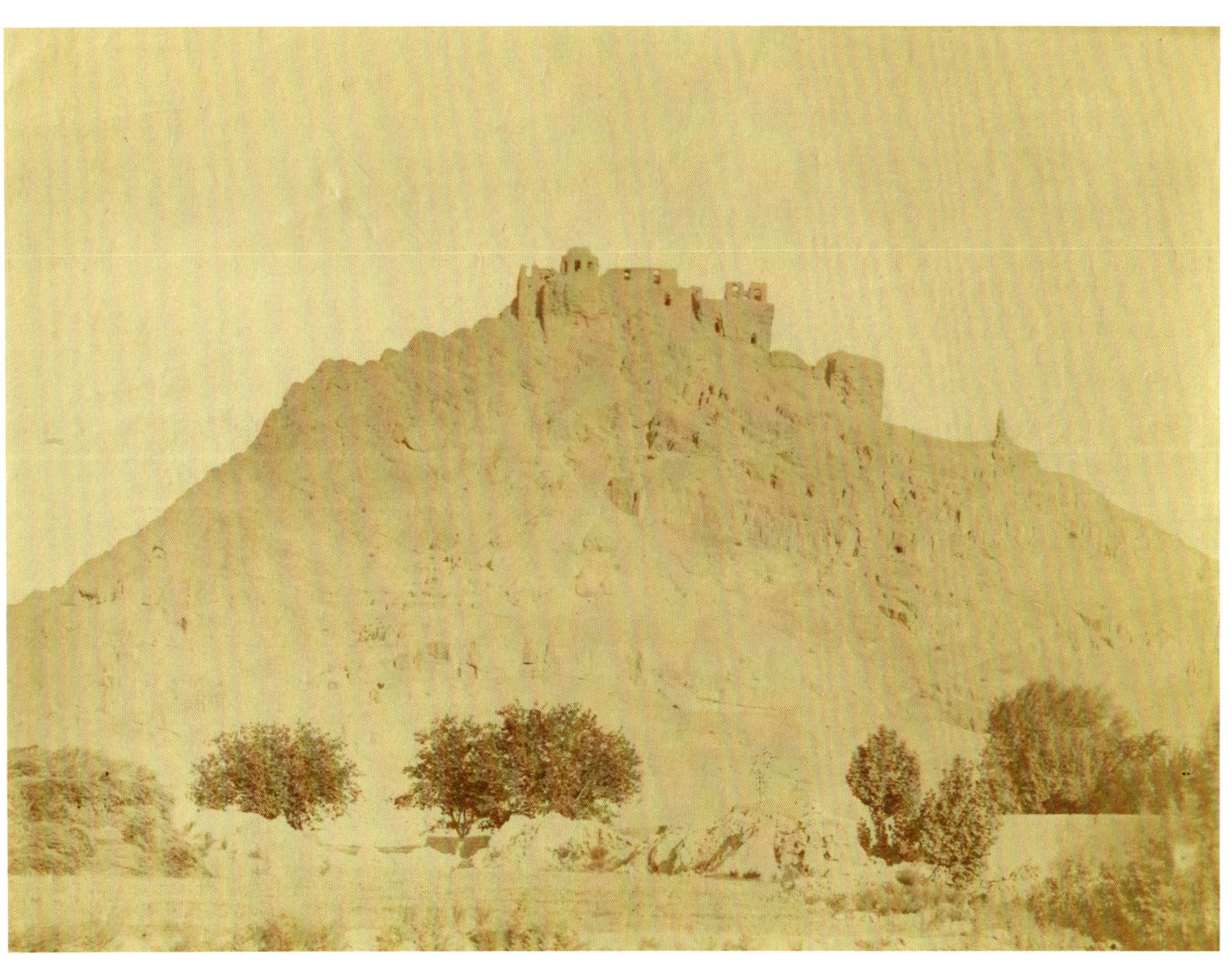

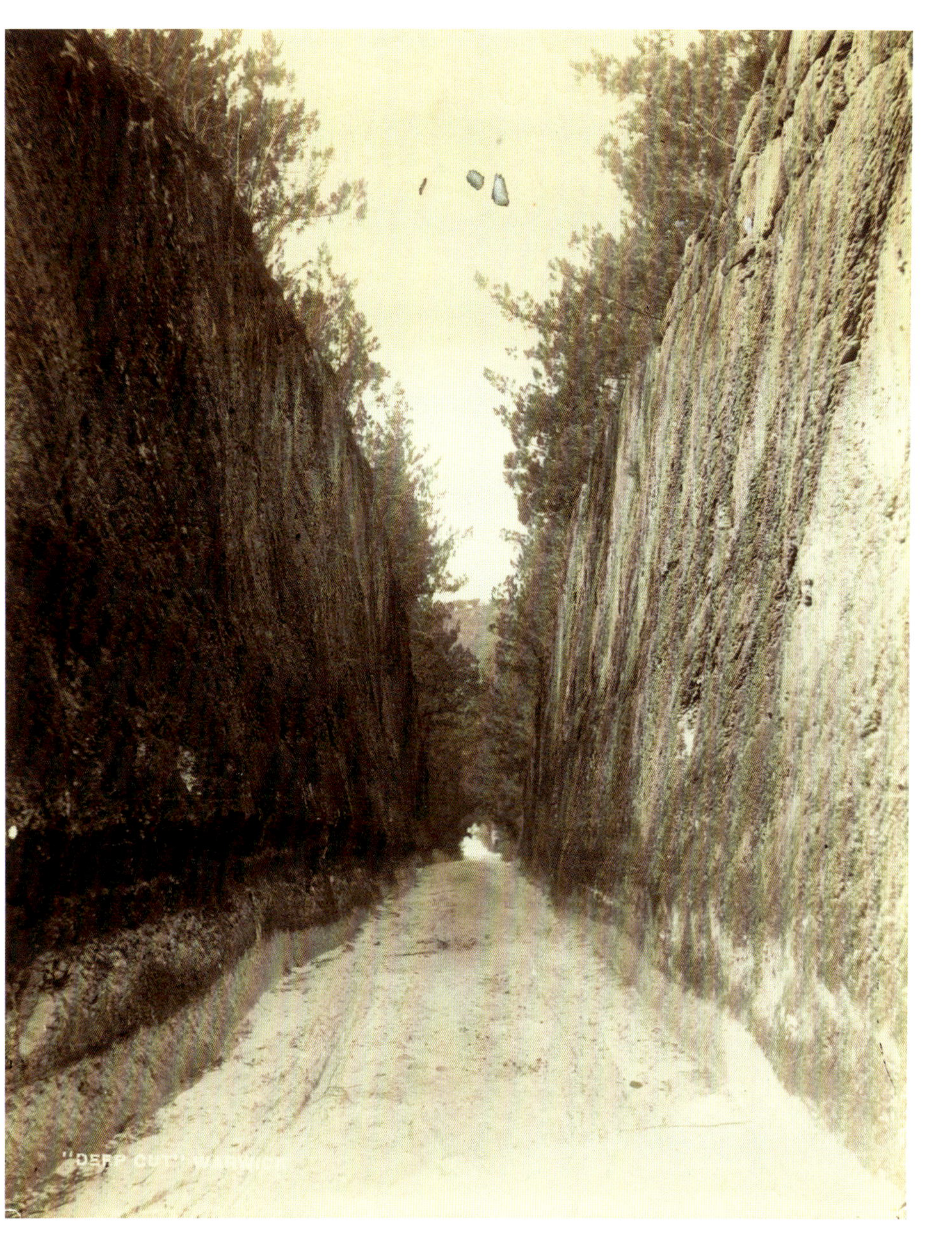

Samuel Bourne (1834–1912)
The City and Ghats, from the Top of the Great Mosque, Benares,
ca. 1865–66
19th-century photographic print,
image size: 7 7⁄16 × 12 5⁄8 inches,
historic mount: 14 × 17 inches
OL.1982.1400

Photographer Unknown
Dester, Citadel Ruins,
late 19th century
19th-century photographic print,
image size: 6 ¼ × 8 ½ inches
OL.1981.600

Photographer Unknown
Deep Cut, Warwick, or *Khyber Pass,*
late 19th century
19th-century photographic print,
image size: 9 5⁄16 × 7 ¼ inches
OL.1981.619

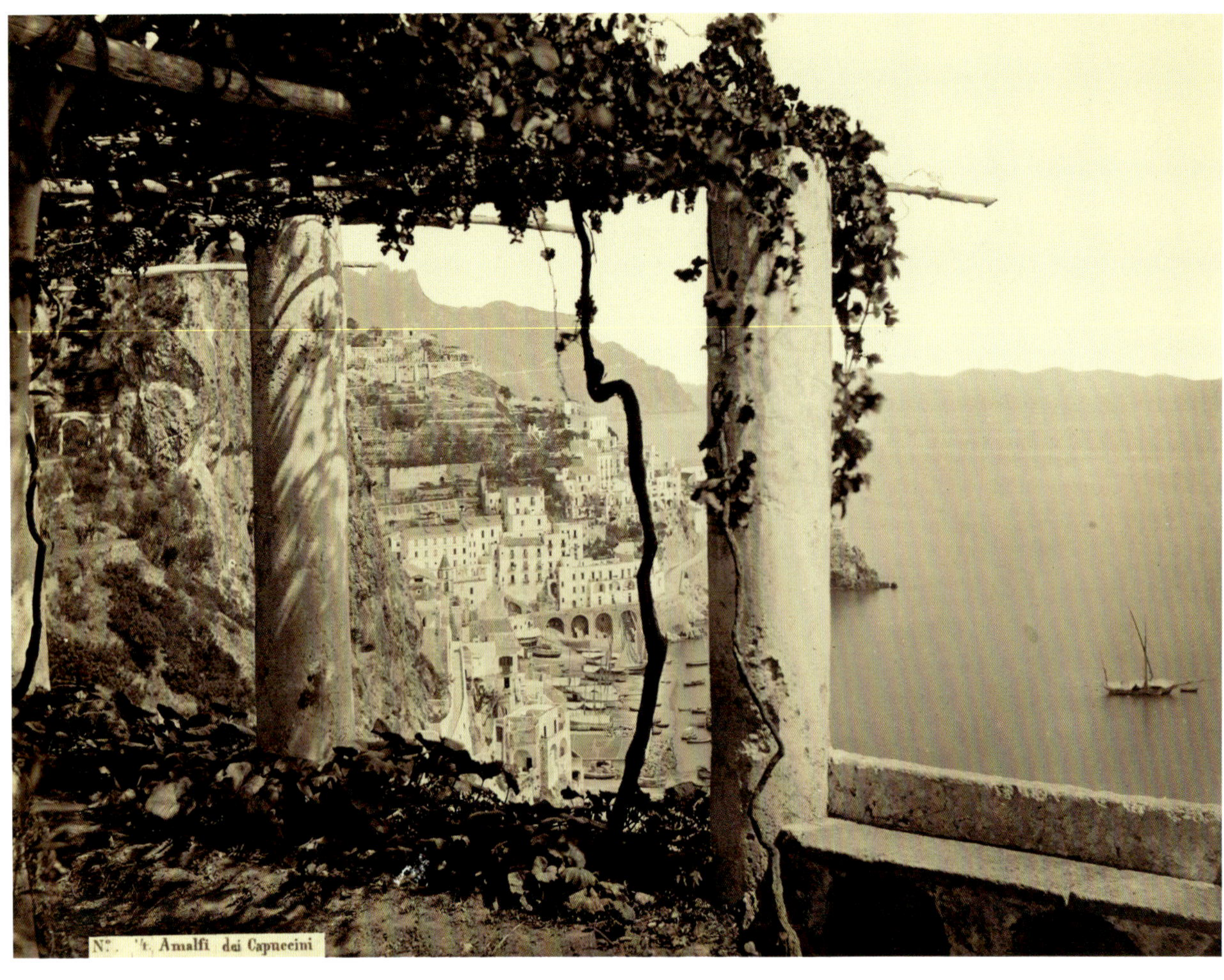

Robert Rive (active 1860s–1880s)
Amalfi dai Capuccini,
ca. 1860s–1880s
19th-century photographic print,
image size: 7 ¾ × 10 ¼ inches,
historic mount: 9 ½ × 12 ¹¹⁄₁₆ inches
OL.1981.338

Photographer Unknown
Night Blooming Cereus,
late 19th century
19th-century photographic print,
image size: 7 ¹⁵⁄₁₆ × 10 inches
OL.1981.391.1

Carlo Baldassare Simelli (1811–ca. 1877)
Cactus Growing on Stone Wall, Rome, Italy,
ca. 1864–1871
19th-century photographic print,
image size: 7 ⅝ × 10 ³⁄₁₆ inches,
historic mount: 9 ⁹⁄₁₆ × 12 ½ inches
OL.1981.613.53

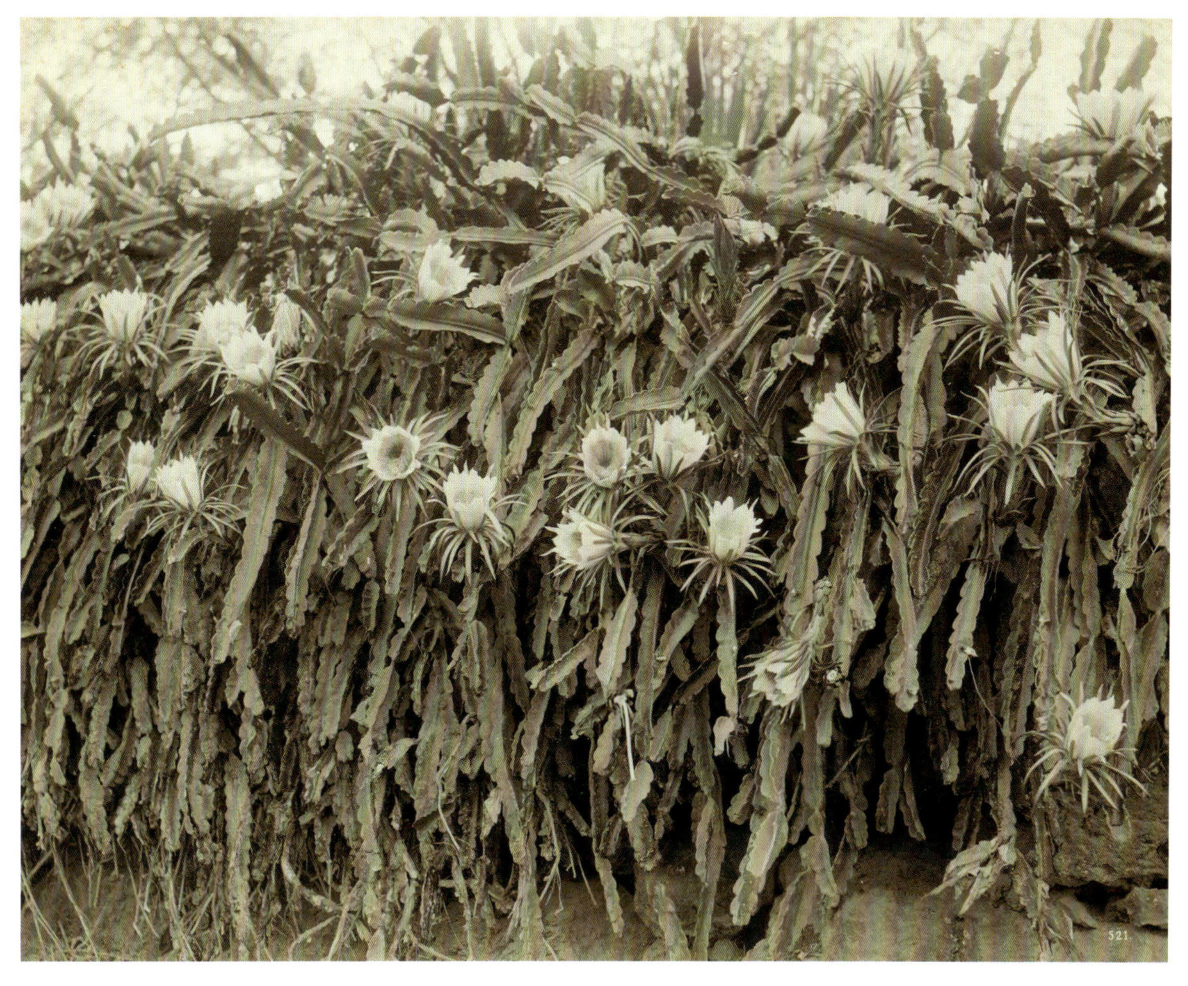
521.

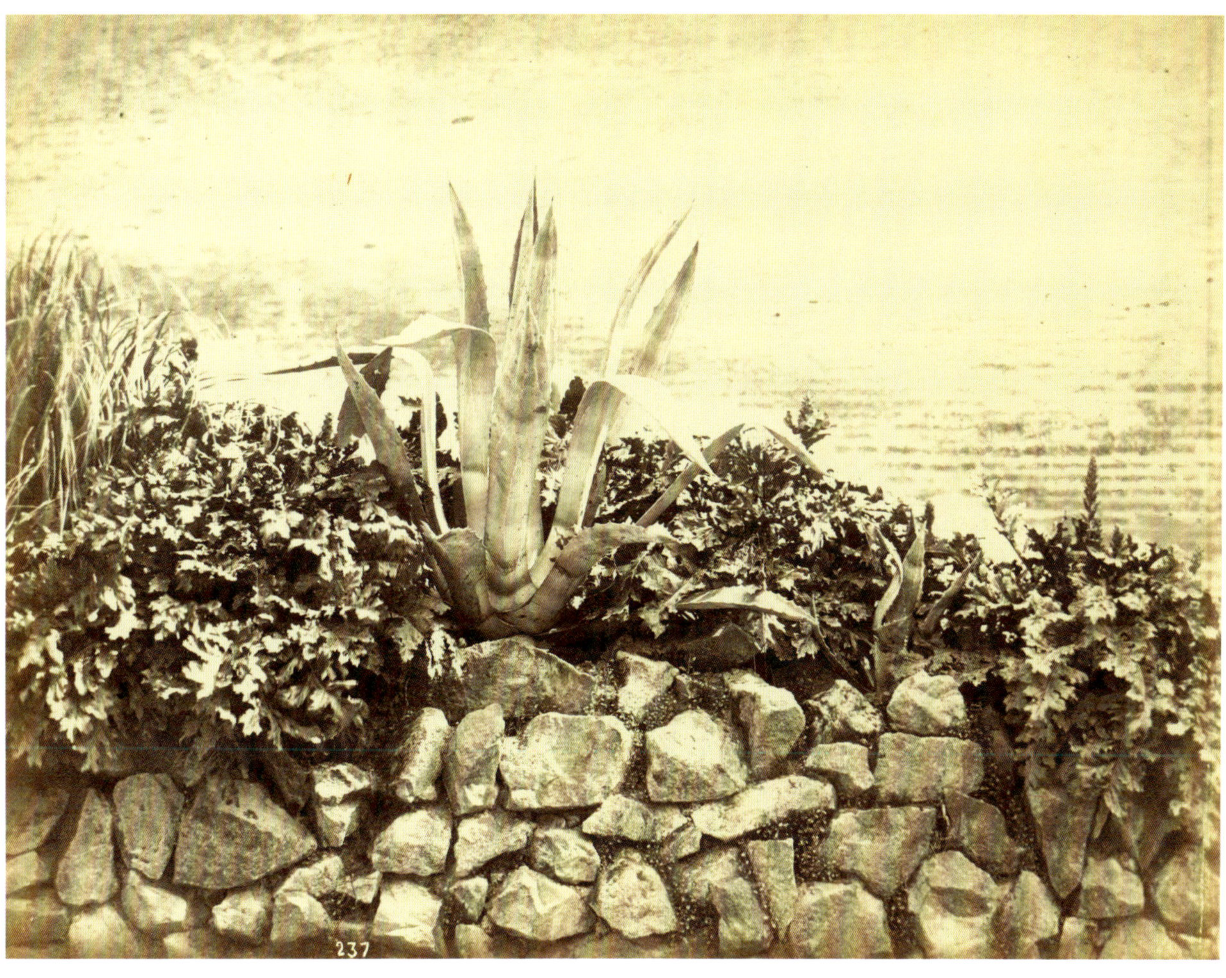
237

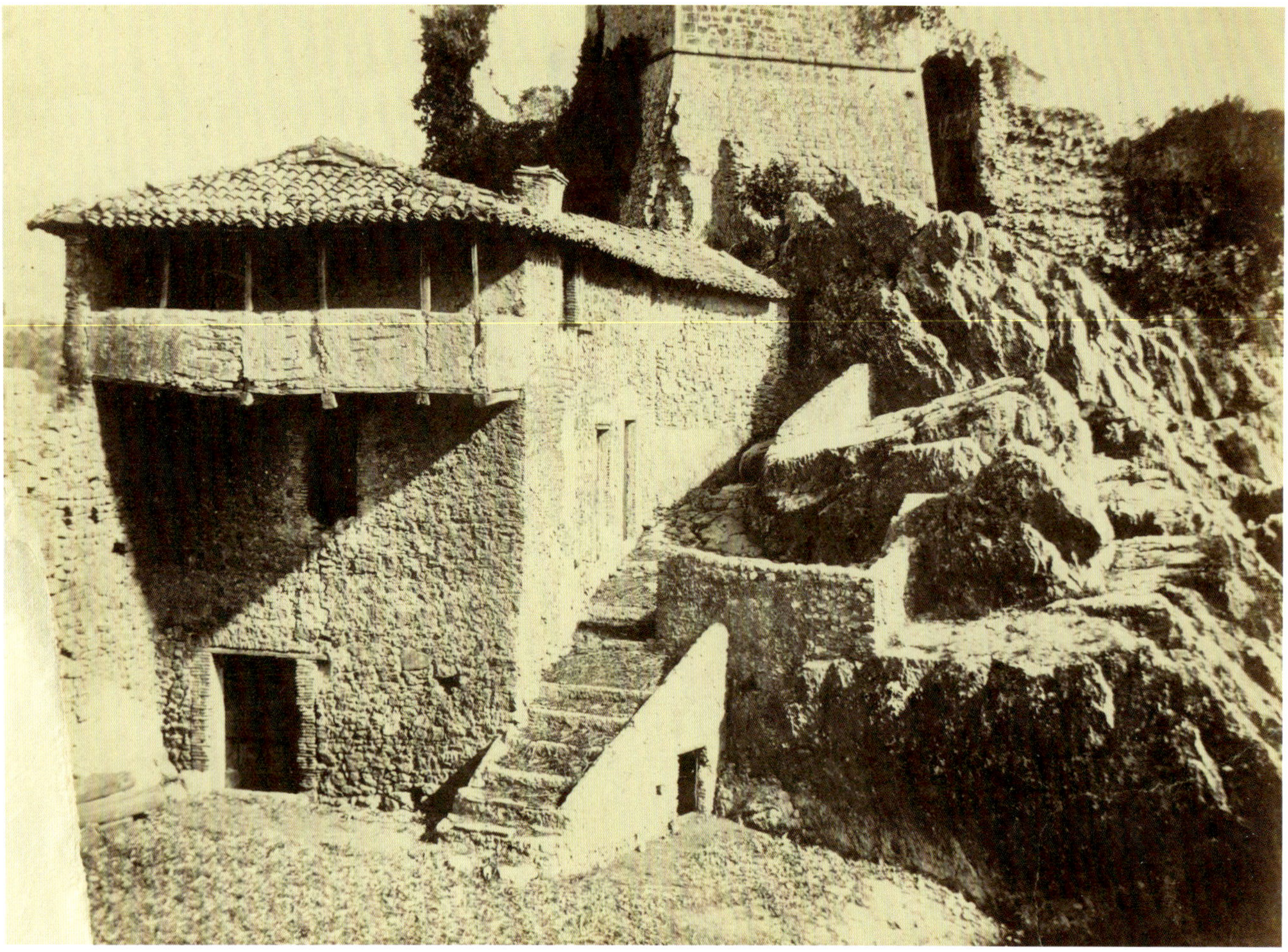

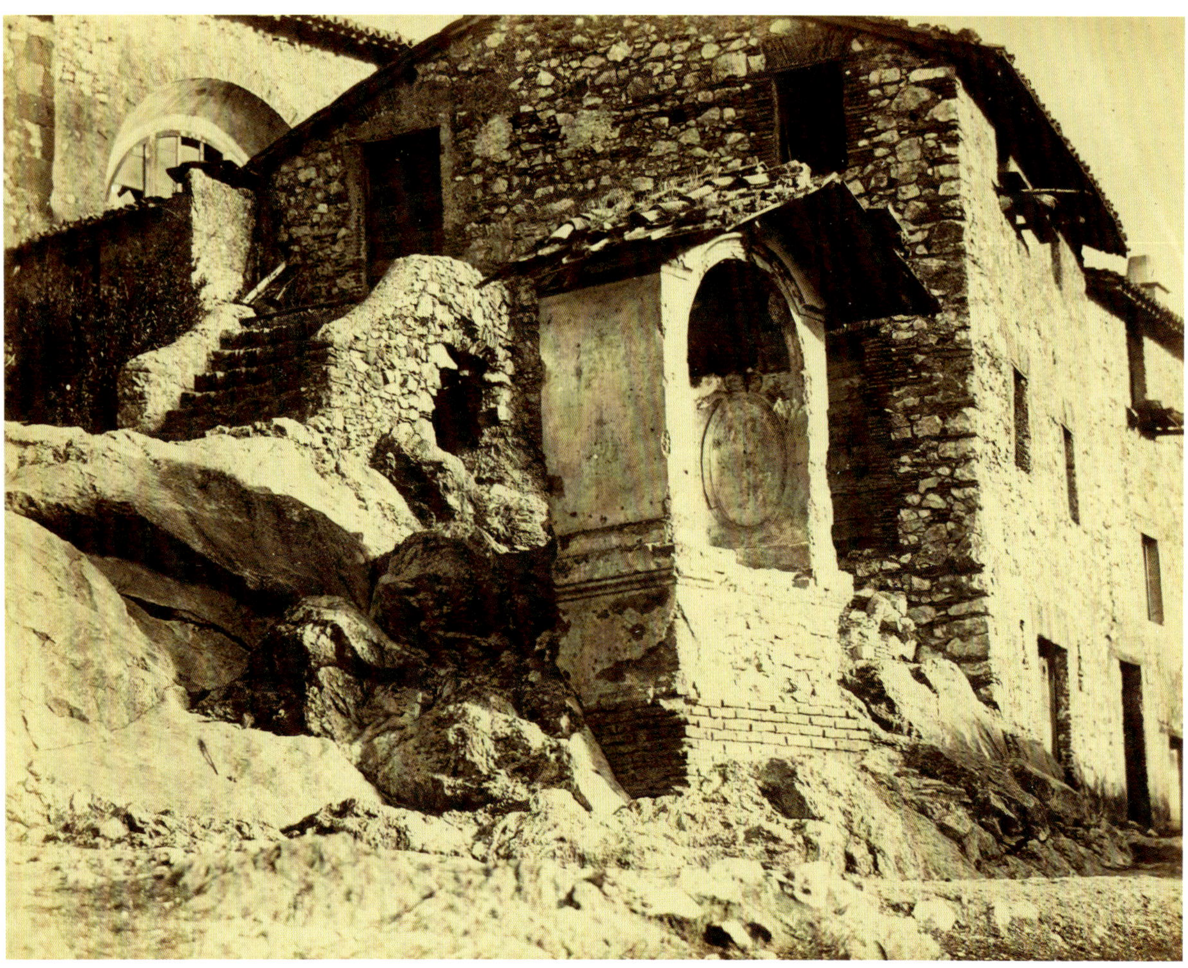

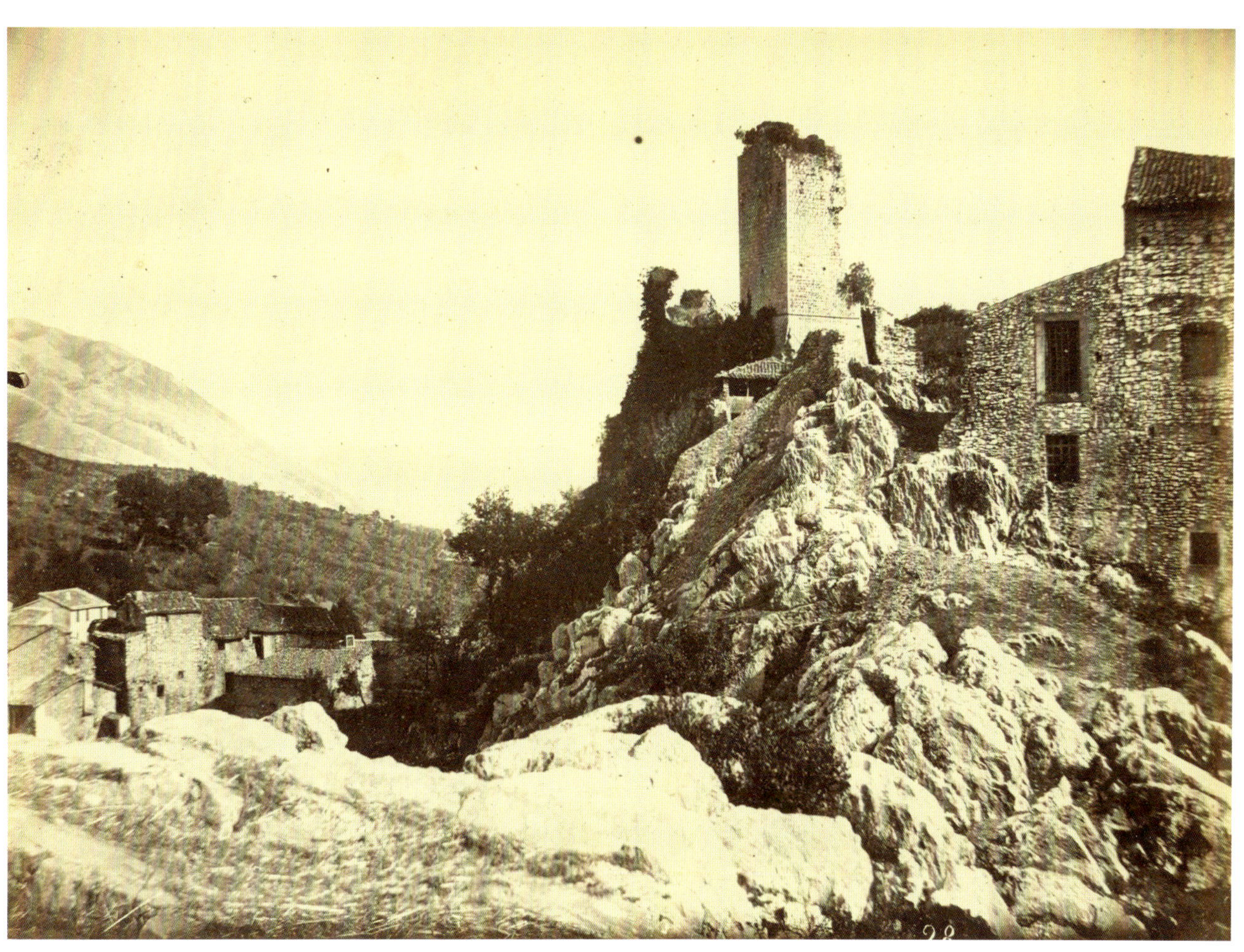

Carlo Baldassare Simelli (1811–ca. 1877)
Stone House, Rome, Italy,
ca. 1864–1871
19th-century photographic print,
image size: 7 3⁄16 × 9 7⁄8 inches,
historic mount: 9 5⁄8 × 12 1⁄2 inches
OL.1981.613.1

Carlo Baldassare Simelli (1811–ca. 1877)
Stone Building, Rome, Italy,
ca. 1864–1871
19th-century photographic print,
image size: 7 7⁄8 × 10 5⁄16 inches,
historic mount: 9 11⁄16 × 12 9⁄16 inches
OL.1981.613.2

Carlo Baldassare Simelli (1811–ca. 1877)
Village on Hillside, Rome, Italy,
ca. 1864–1871
19th-century photographic print,
image size: 7 1⁄2 × 10 5⁄16 inches,
historic mount: 9 11⁄16 × 12 11⁄16 inches
OL.1981.613.3

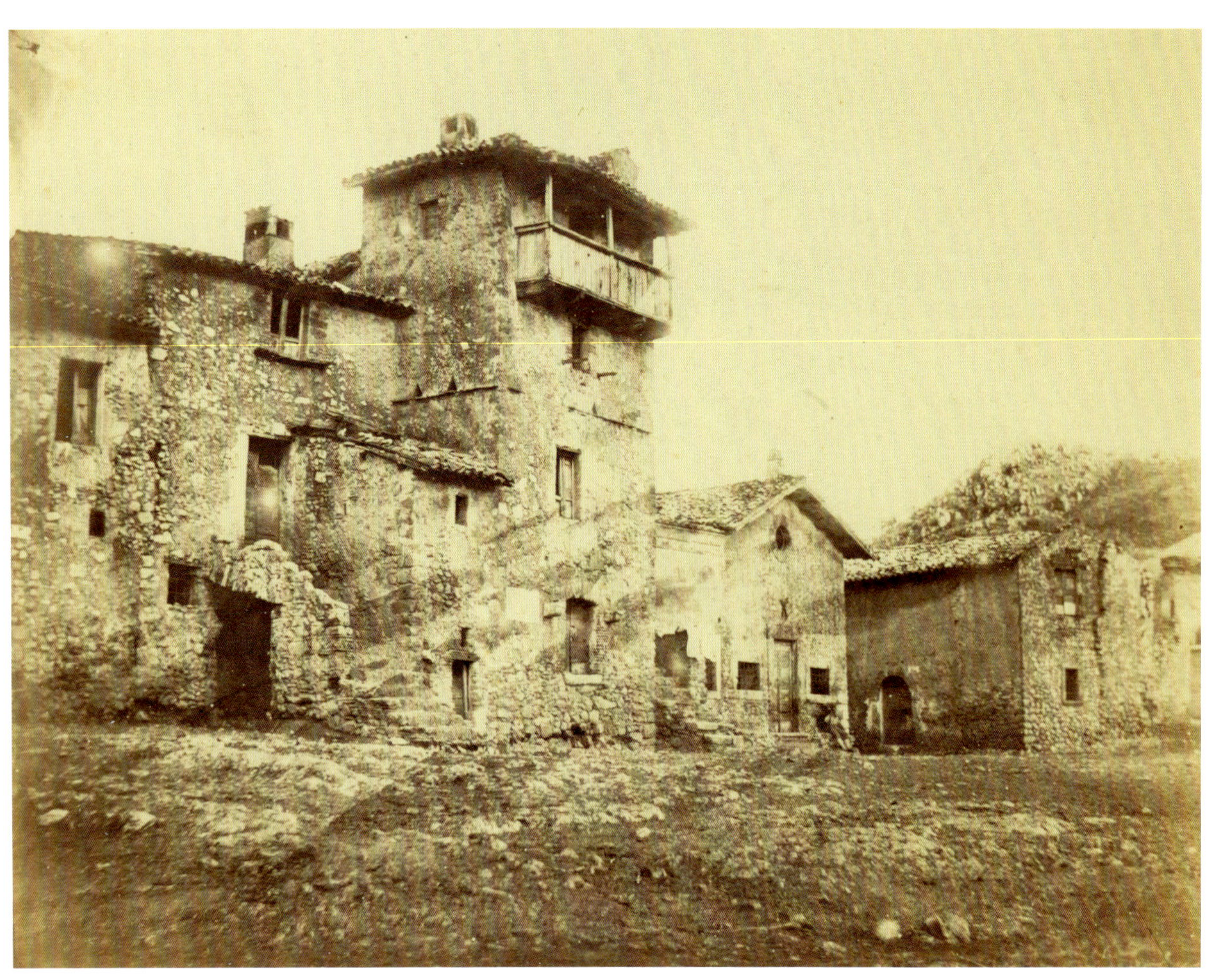

Carlo Baldassare Simelli (1811–ca. 1877)
Stone Building with Mountain Peak, Rome, Italy,
ca. 1864–1871
19th-century photographic print,
image size: 7 5⁄16 × 9 13⁄16 inches,
historic mount: 9 ¾ × 12 11⁄16 inches
OL.1981.613.7

Carlo Baldassare Simelli (1811–ca. 1877)
Stone Building, Rome, Italy,
ca. 1864–1871
19th-century photographic print,
image size: 7 13⁄16 × 10 ⅛ inches,
historic mount: 9 ⅝ × 12 ⅝ inches
OL.1981.613.31

Carlo Baldassare Simelli (1811–ca. 1877)
Stone Steps, Rome, Italy,
ca. 1864–1871
19th-century photographic print,
image size: 7 ⅞ × 10 7⁄16 inches,
historic mount: 9 ⅝ × 12 ⅝ inches
OL.1981.613.32

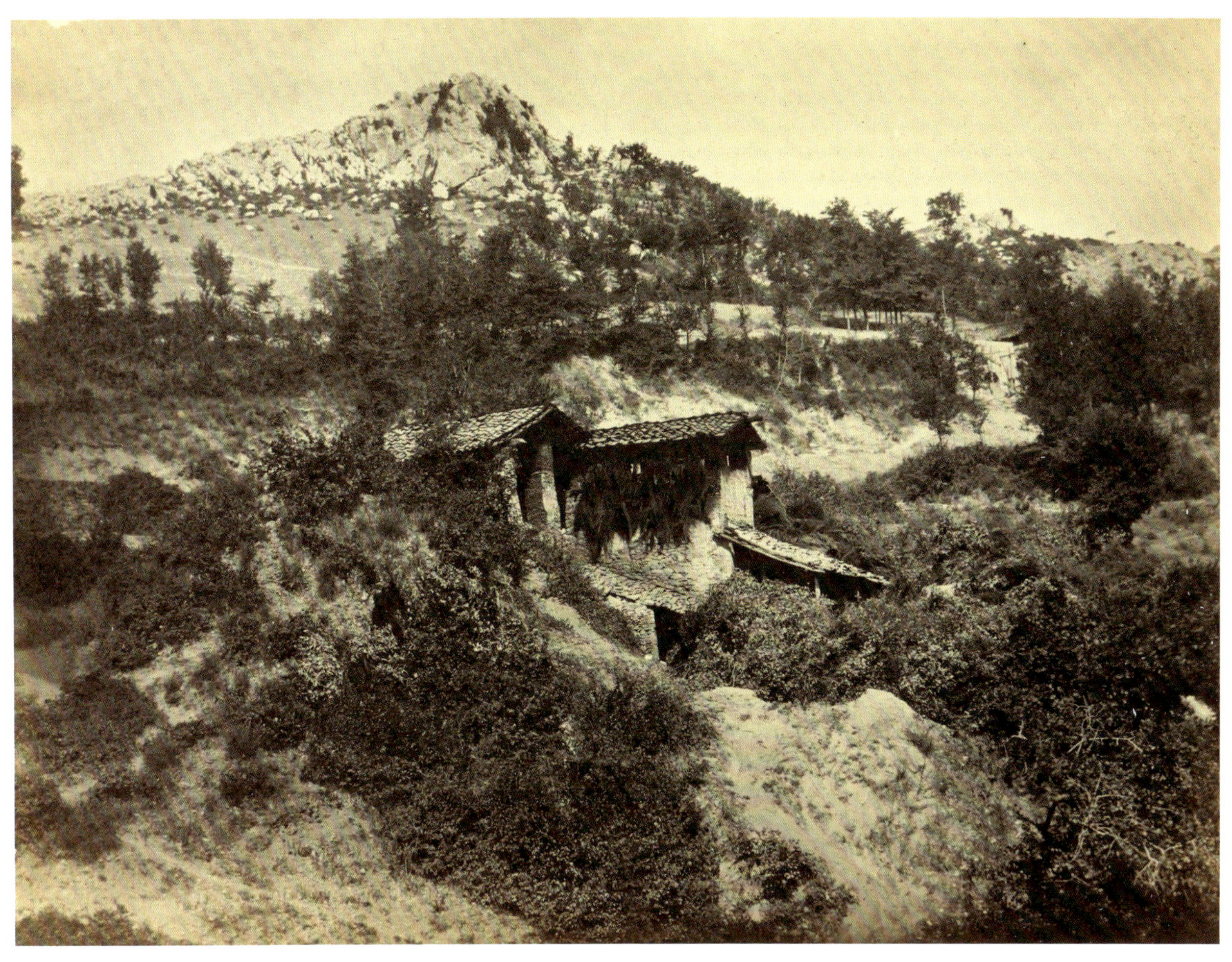

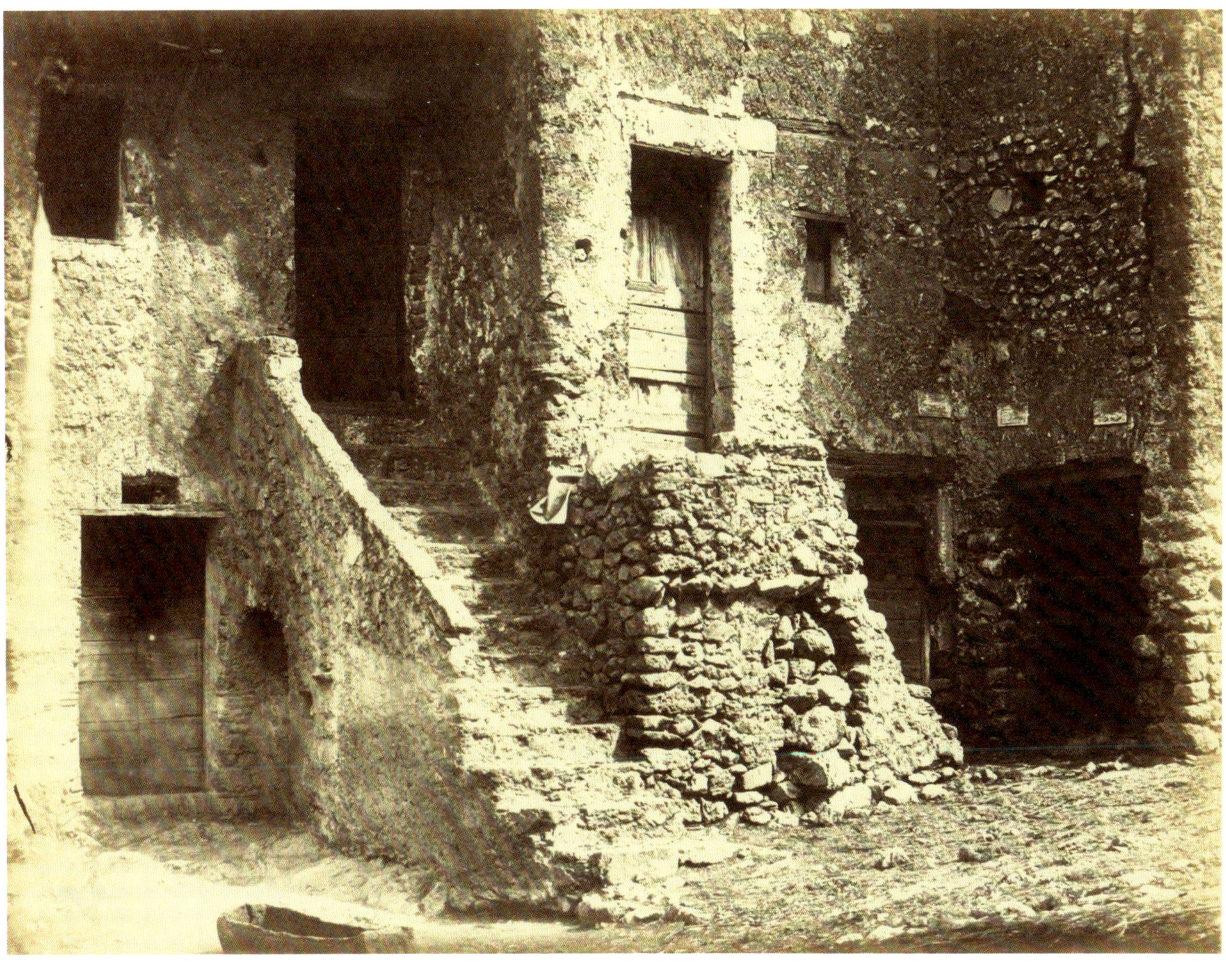

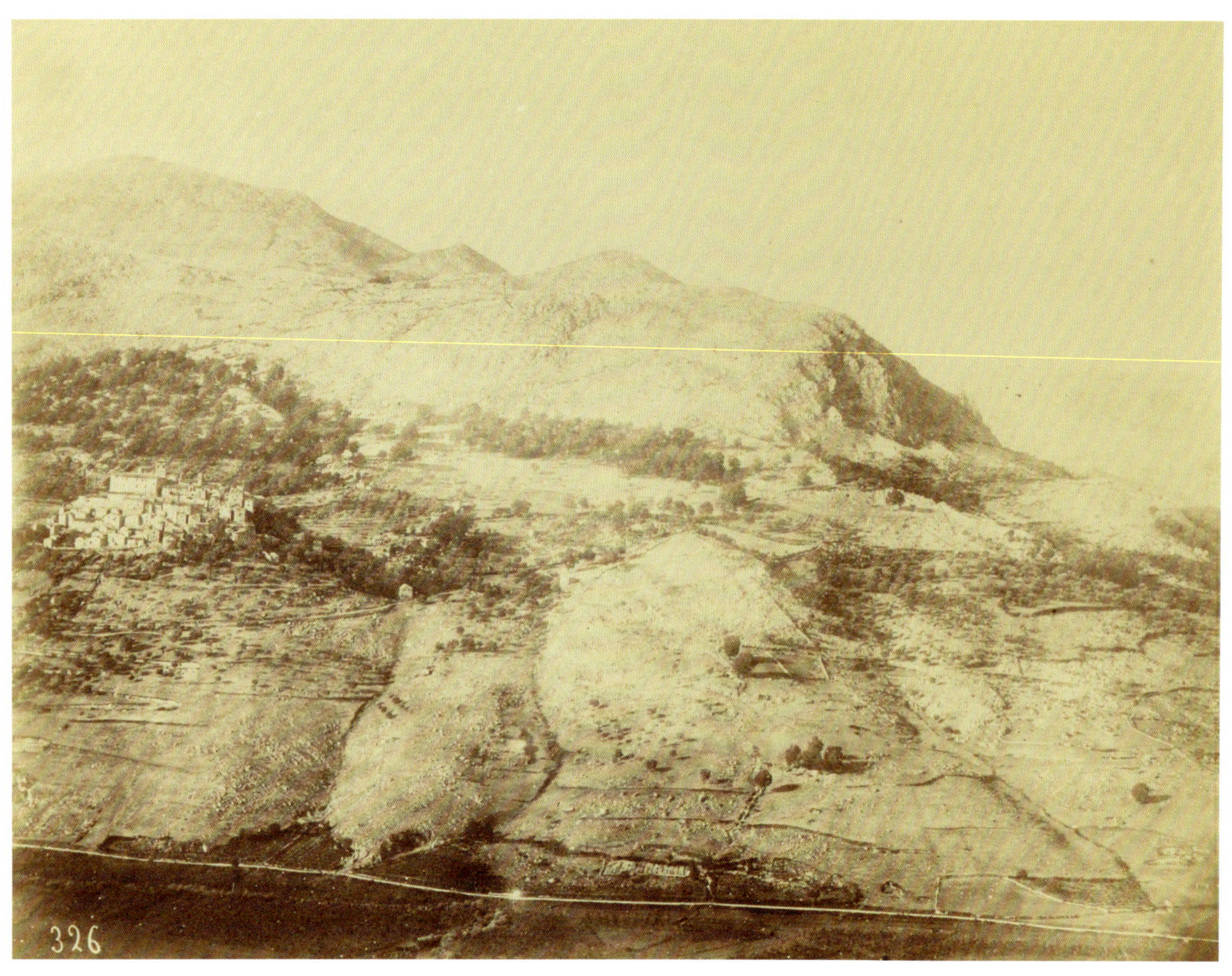
326

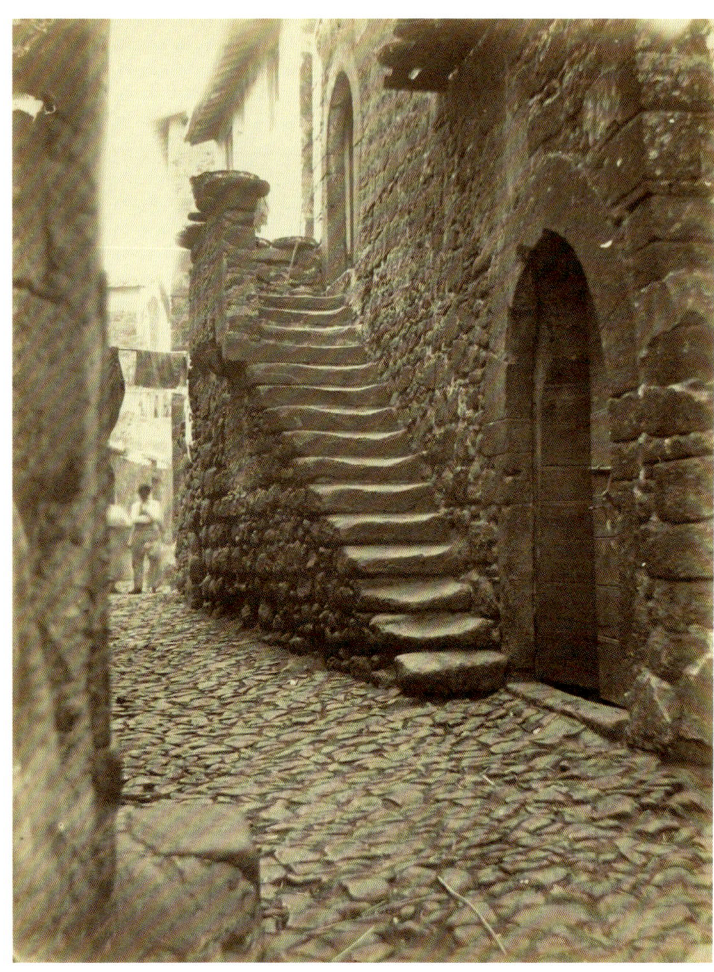

Carlo Baldassare Simelli (1811–ca. 1877)
Aerial Landscape, Rome, Italy,
ca. 1864–1871
19th-century photographic print,
image size: 7 13/16 × 10 3/16 inches,
historic mount: 9 11/16 × 12 11/16 inches
OL.1981.613.36

Carlo Baldassare Simelli (1811–ca. 1877)
Street Scene, Man and Laundry in Backyard, Rome, Italy,
ca. 1864–1871
19th-century photographic print,
image size: 10 1/4 × 7 7/8 inches,
historic mount: 12 11/16 × 9 11/16 inches
OL.1981.613.51

Photographer Unknown
Parte di un Corridoio del Colosseo,
late 19th century
19th-century photographic print,
image size: 10 1/16 × 7 3/8 inches,
historic mount: 12 3/4 × 9 3/4 inches
OL.1981.290

Carlo Baldassare Simelli (1811–ca. 1877)
Two Roads Converging, or *Dry Riverbed, Rome, Italy,*
ca. 1864–1871
19th-century photographic print,
image size: 7 11/16 × 10 1/4 inches,
historic mount: 9 7/16 × 12 5/8 inches
OL.1981.613.41

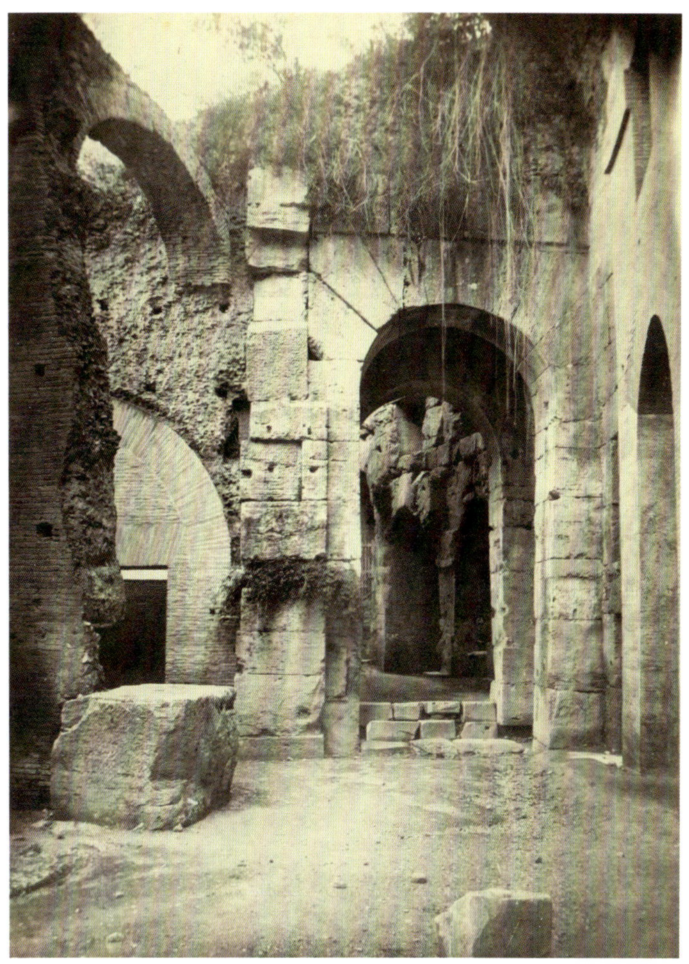

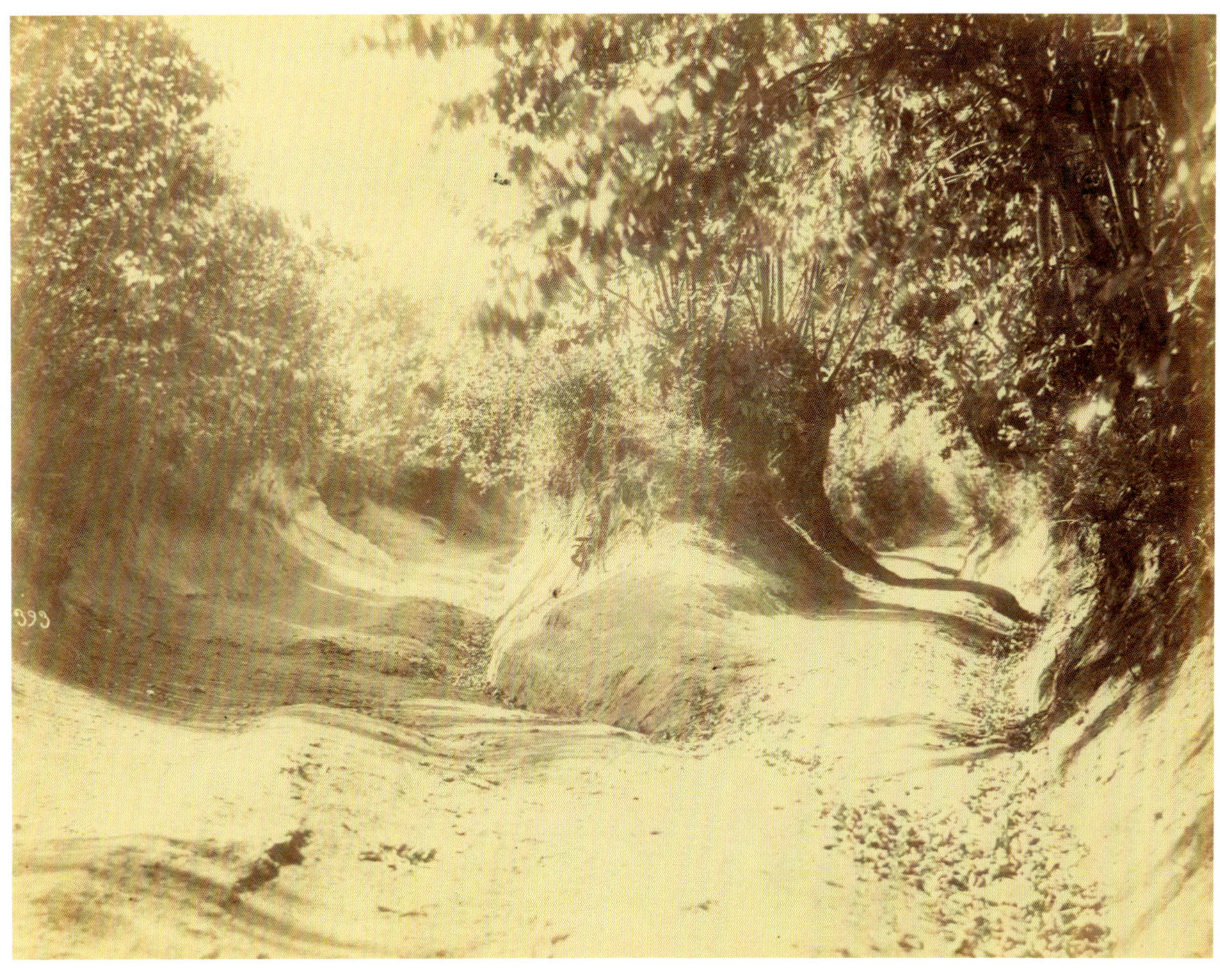

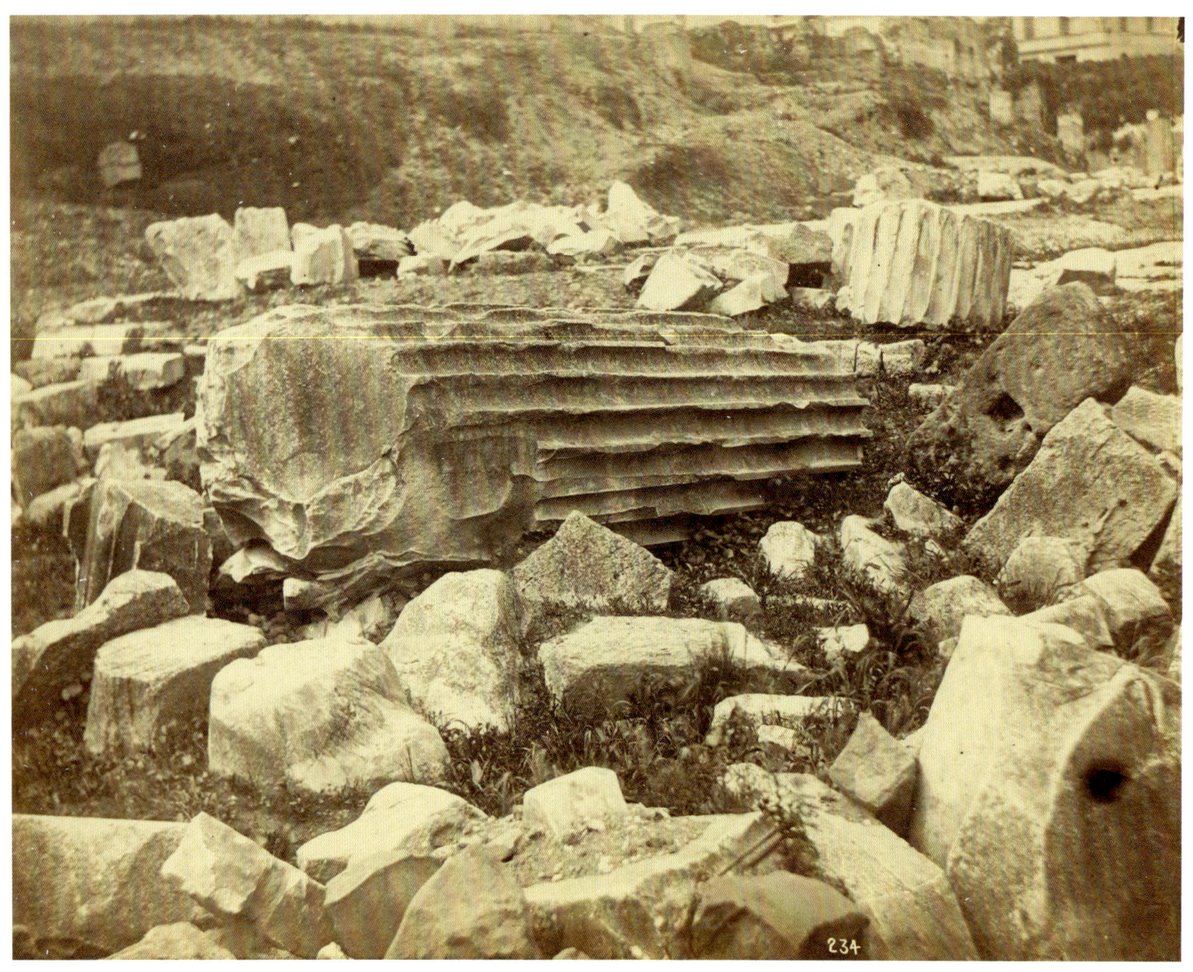
234

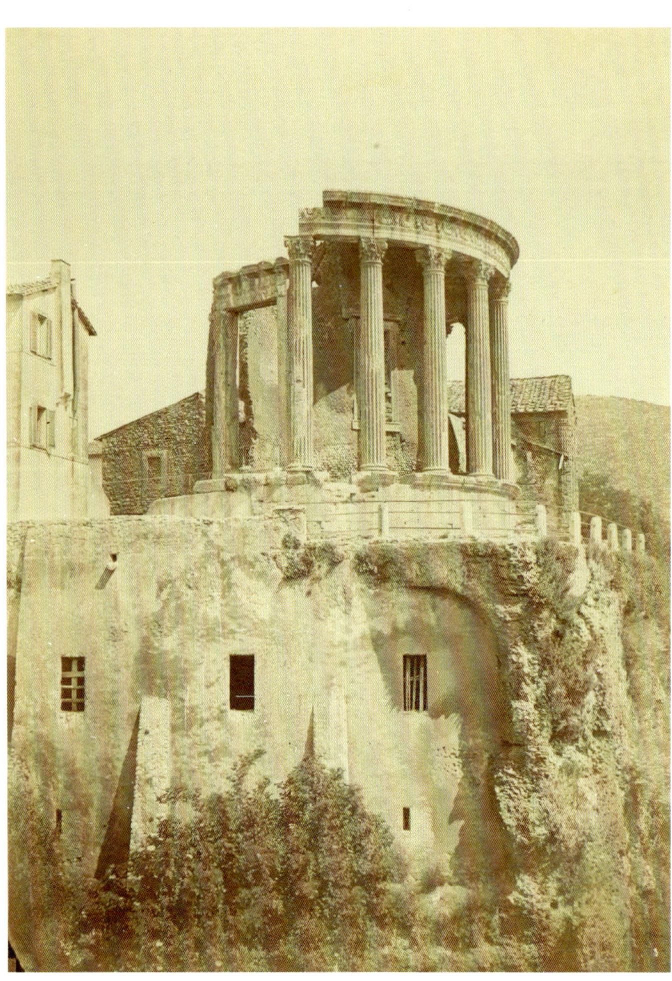

Carlo Baldassare Simelli (1811–ca. 1877)
Ruins, Rome, Italy,
ca. 1864–1871
19th-century photographic print,
image size: 7 ⅞ × 10 1/16 inches,
historic mount: 9 ¼ × 12 ½ inches
OL.1981.613.24

Photographer Unknown
Temple of Vesta, Tivoli, Italy,
late 19th century
19th-century photographic print,
image size: 14 ⅝ × 10 ⅝ inches,
historic mount: 20 15/16 × 15 ½ inches
OL.1983.442

Unknown Photographer
Temple of Minerva, Forum of Nerva, Rome,
late 19th century
19th-century photographic print,
image size: 14 ½ × 11 5/16 inches,
historic mount: 20 ½ × 15 ½ inches
OL.1983.478

Carlo Baldassare Simelli (1811–ca. 1877)
Landscape with Ruins, Rome, Italy,
ca. 1864–1871
19th-century photographic print,
image size: 7 ⅜ × 9 ¾ inches,
historic mount: 9 ⅝ × 12 9/16 inches
OL.1981.613.54

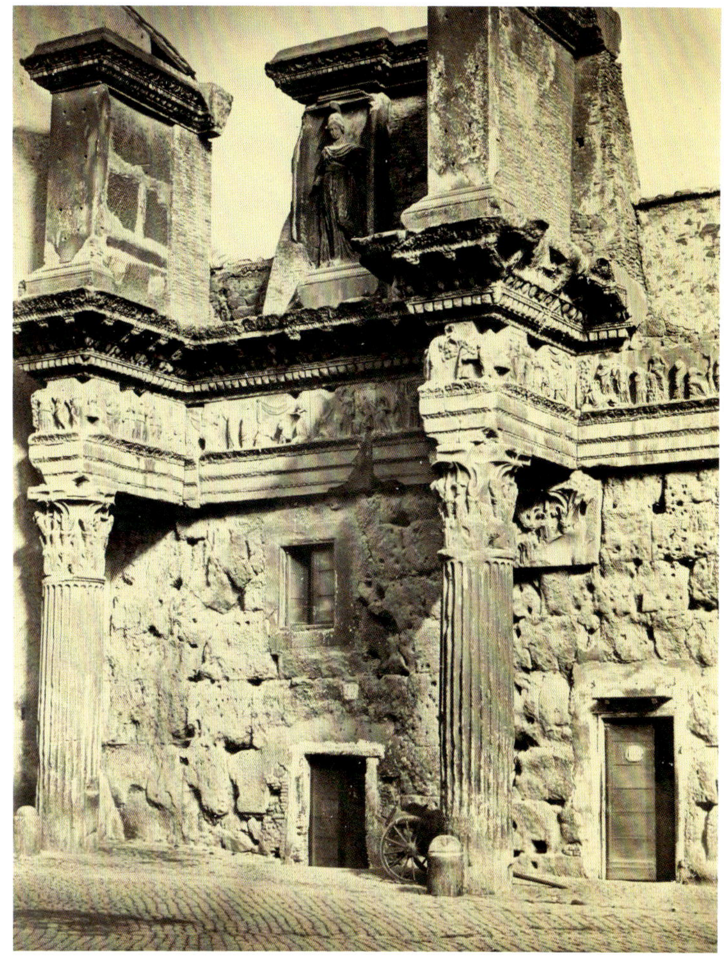

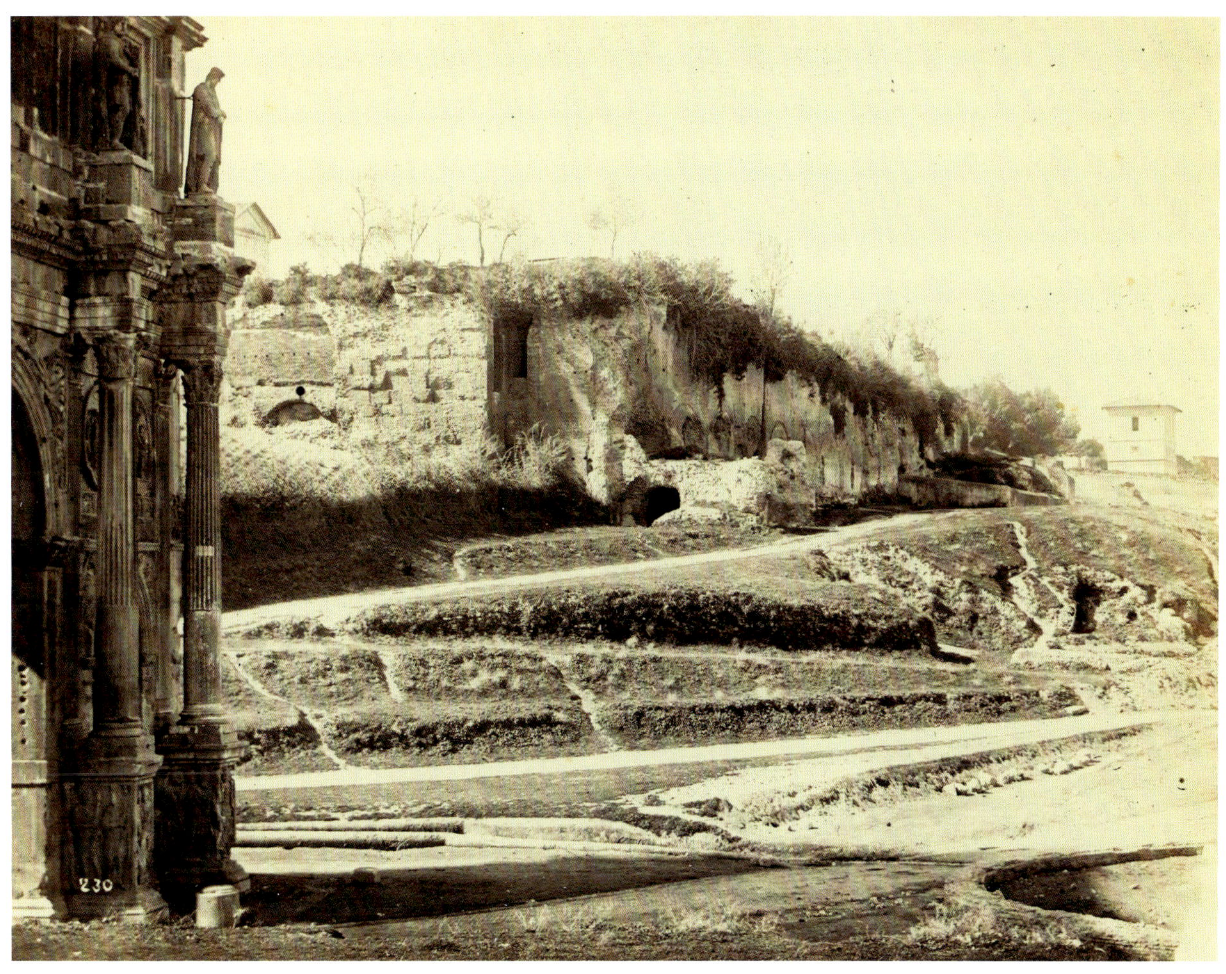

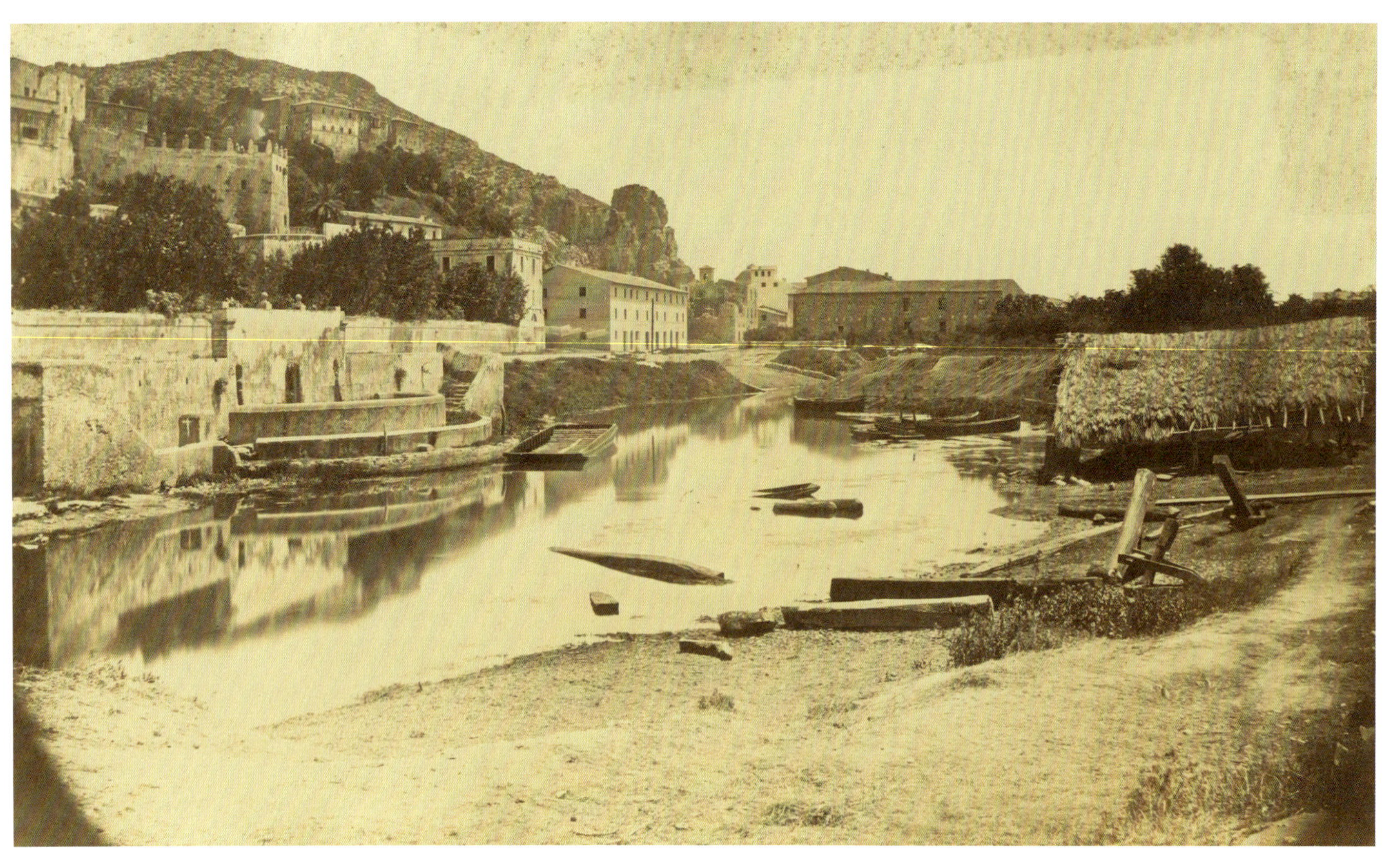

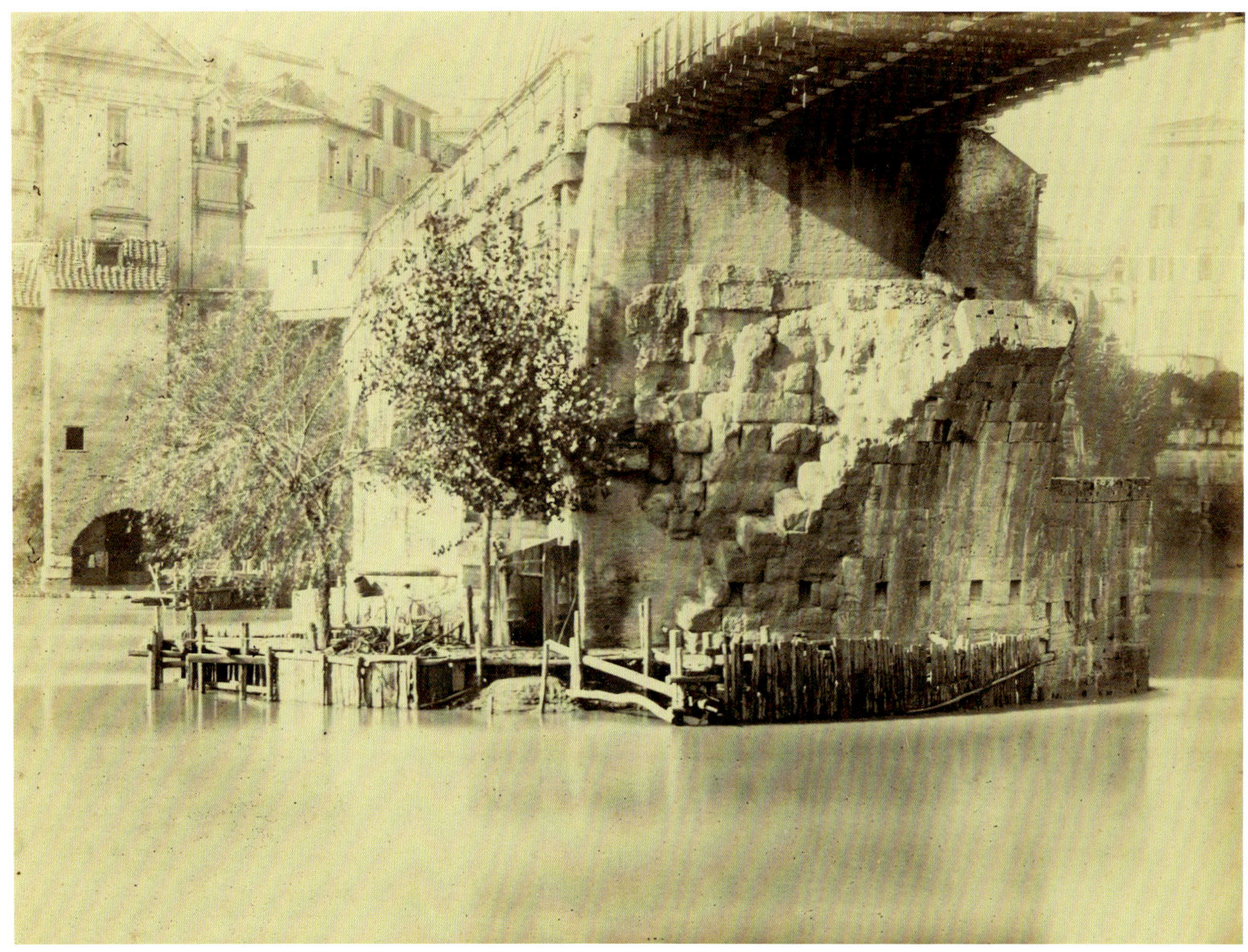

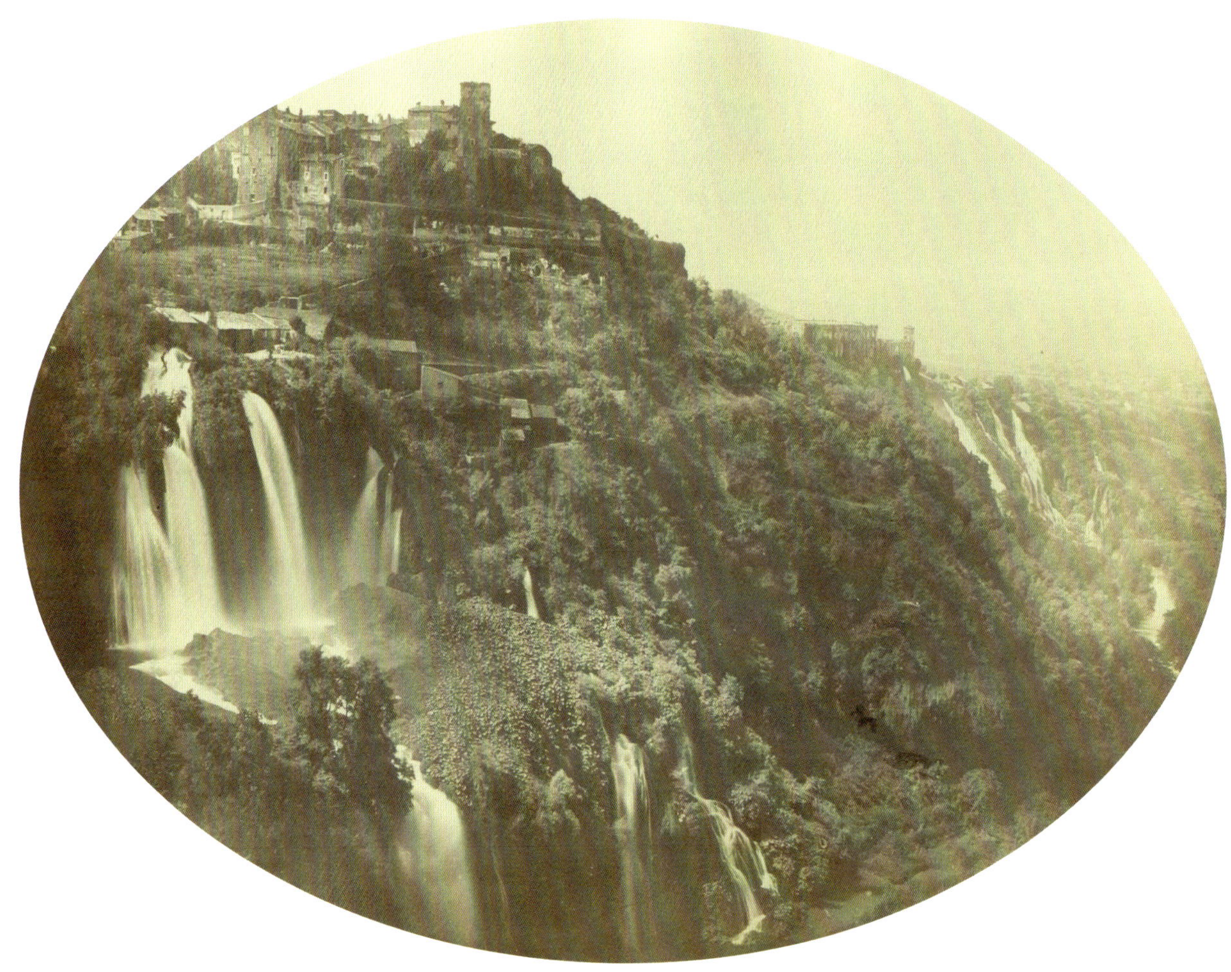

Photographer Unknown
Terracina, Italy,
late 19th century
19th-century photographic print,
image size: 9 7⁄16 × 15 3⁄4 inches,
historic mount: 16 11⁄16 × 21 7⁄8 inches
OL.1983.444

Carlo Baldassare Simelli (1811–ca. 1877)
Underside of Bridge, Rome, Italy,
ca. 1864–1871
19th-century photographic print,
image size: 7 3⁄4 × 10 7⁄16 inches,
historic mount: 9 11⁄16 × 12 11⁄16 inches
OL.1981.613.15

Photographer Unknown
Tivoli, Italy,
late 19th century
19th-century photographic print,
image size: 12 1⁄8 × 15 7⁄8 inches,
historic mount: 15 1⁄16 × 18 11⁄16 inches
OL.1983.420

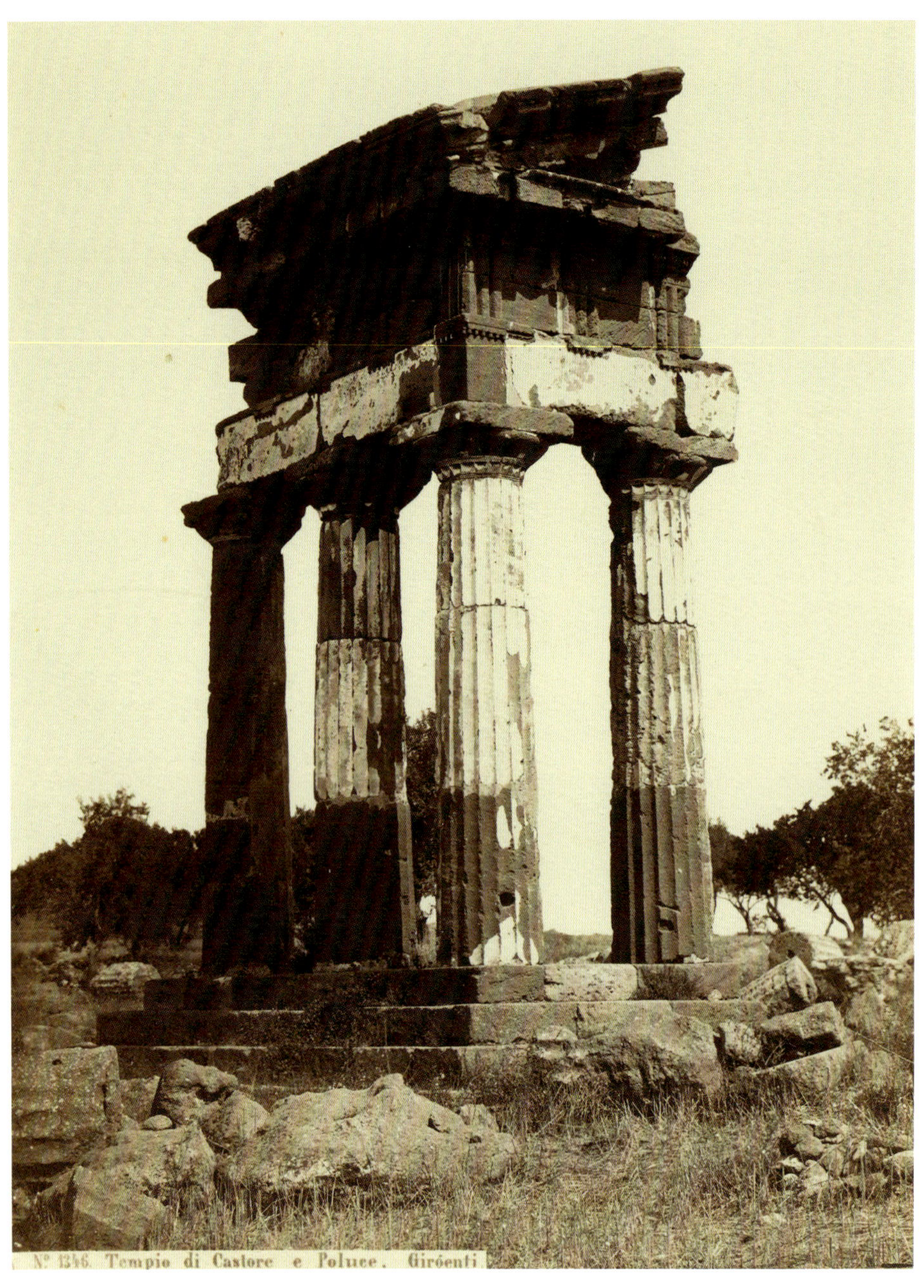

Giorgio Sommer (1834–1914) and Edmund Behles (1841–1921)
Tempio di Castore e Poluce, Girgenti,
ca. 1860s–1870s
19th-century photographic print,
image size: 9 ⁹⁄₁₆ × 7 ¹⁄₁₆ inches,
historic mount: 15 ¾ × 12 inches
OL.1983.492

Robert Rive (active 1860s–1880s)
Tempio di Cerere a Paestum,
ca. 1860s–1880s
19th-century photographic print,
image size: 7 ½ × 9 ⅝ inches,
historic mount: 12 ⅜ × 15 inches
OL.1983.502

Photographer Unknown
Italy, Flock of Sheep Grazing in Field, Ruins of Claudian Aqueduct Extending into Distance,
late 19th century
19th-century photographic print,
image size: 6 ¹⁵⁄₁₆ × 9 ¹¹⁄₁₆ inches,
historic mount: 11 ¹⁵⁄₁₆ × 15 ¹¹⁄₁₆ inches
OL.1983.417

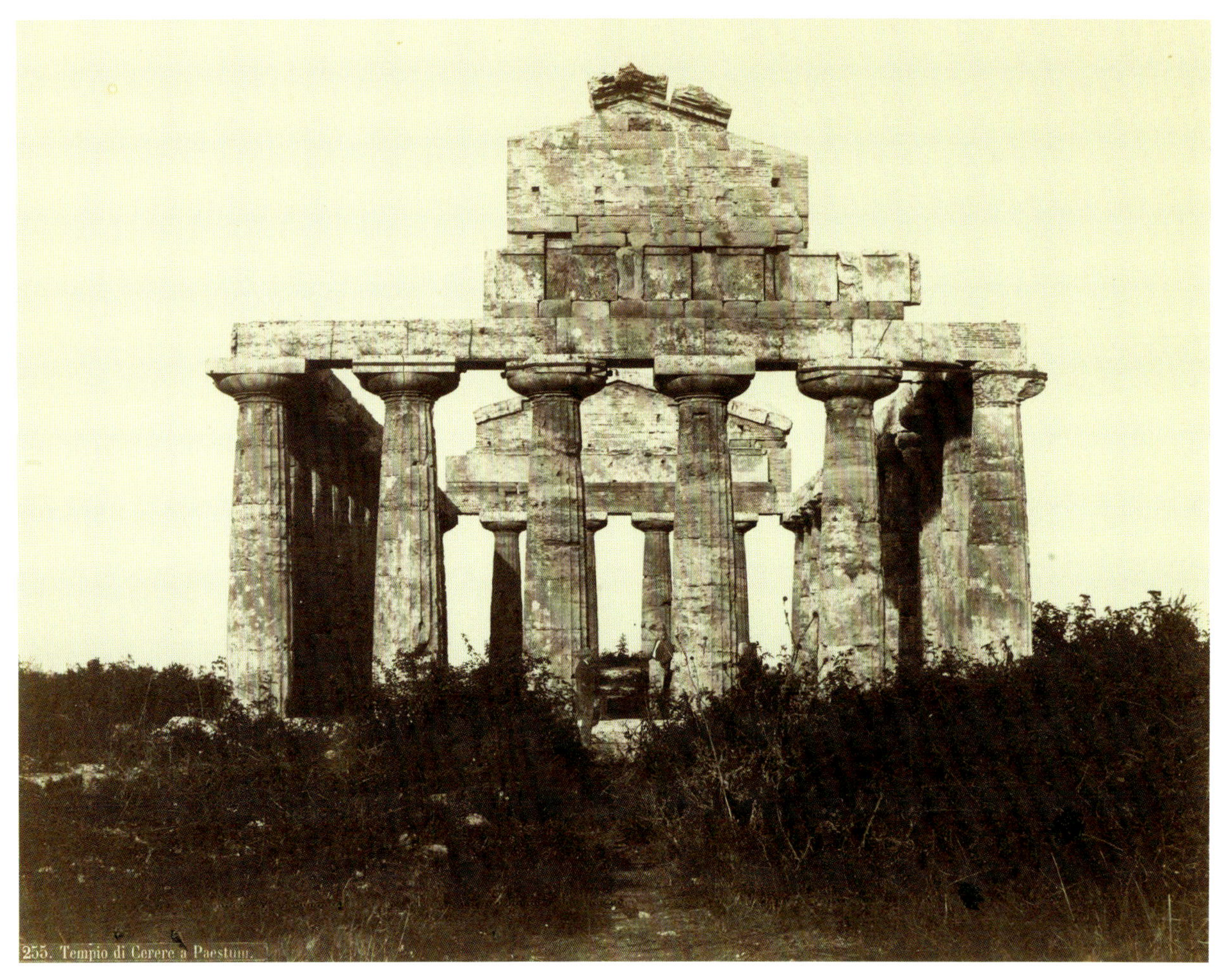
255. Tempio di Cerere a Paestum.

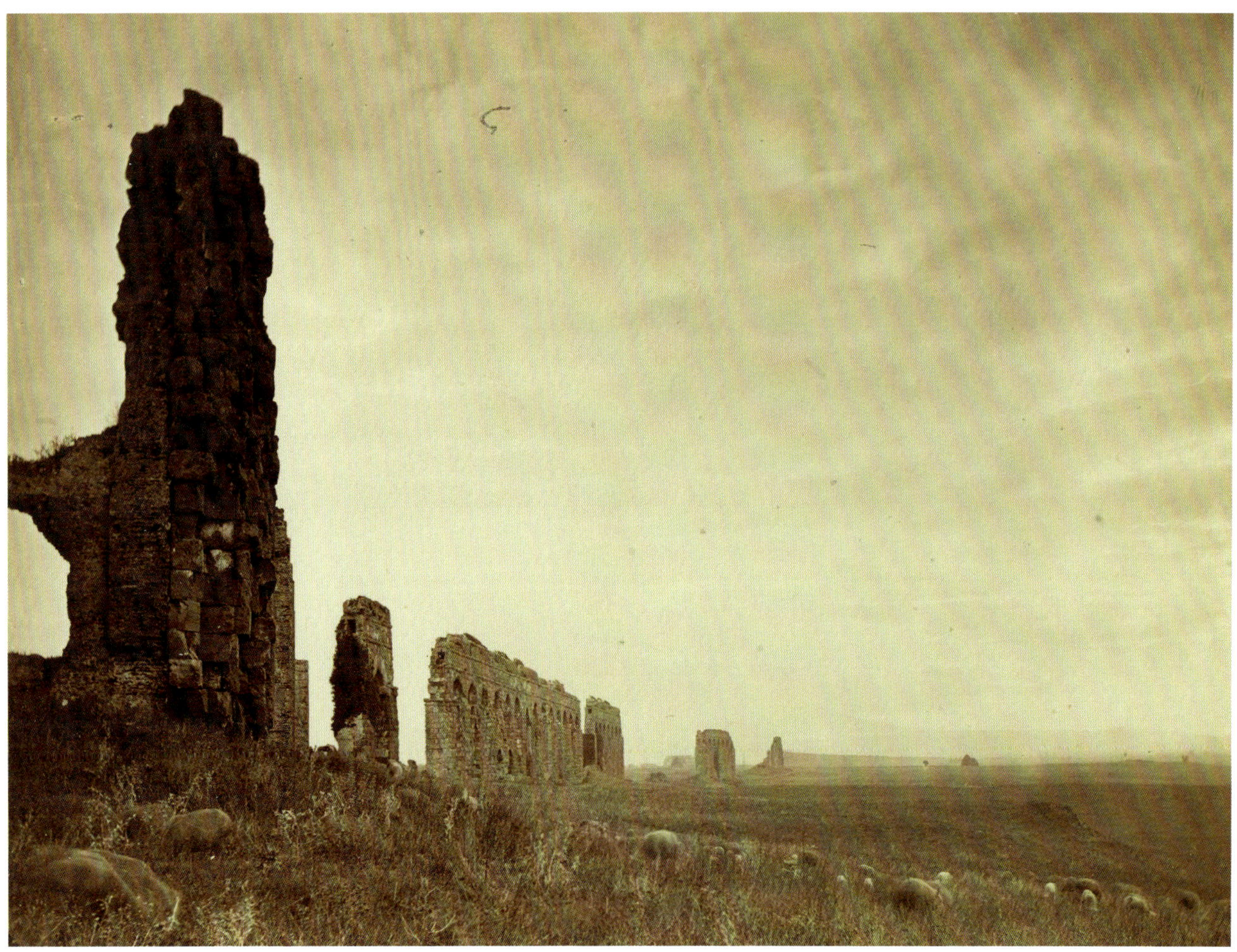

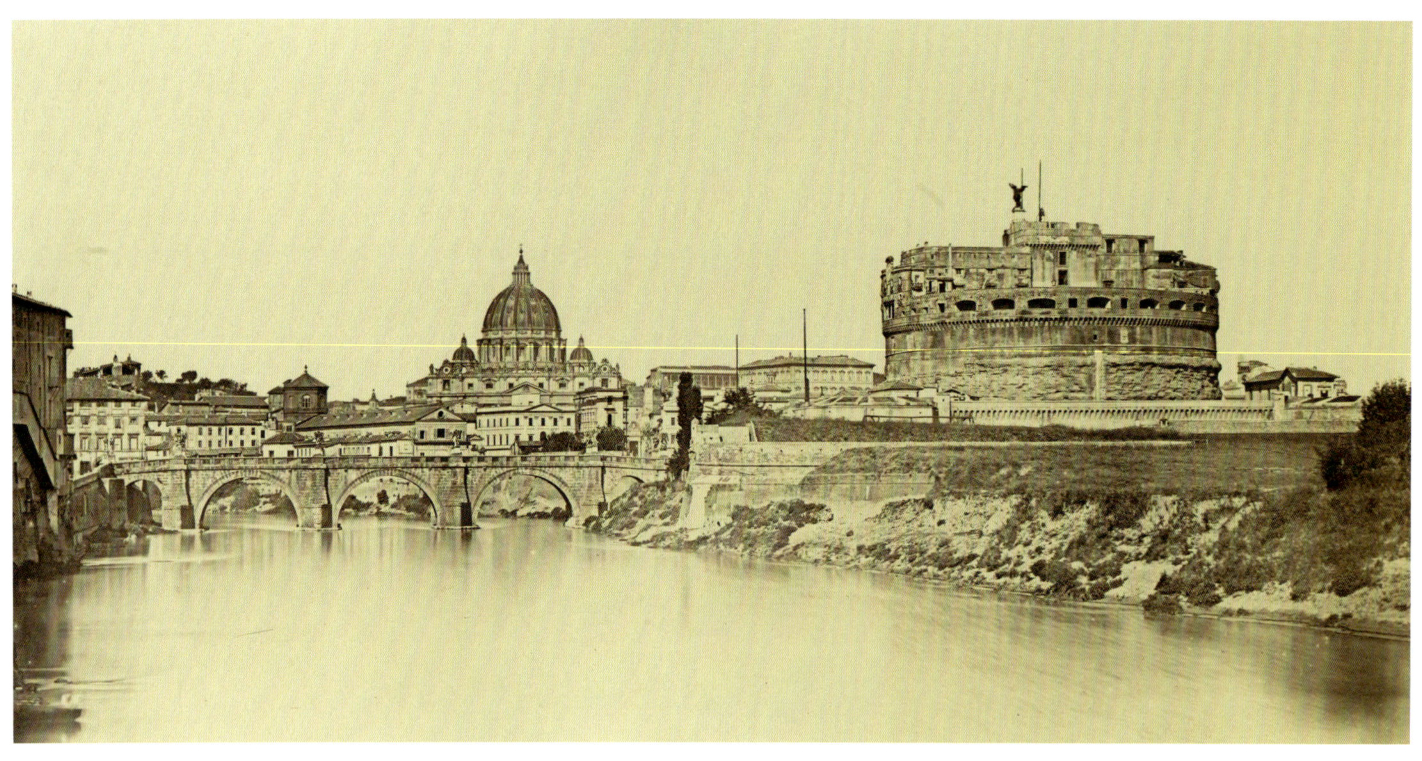

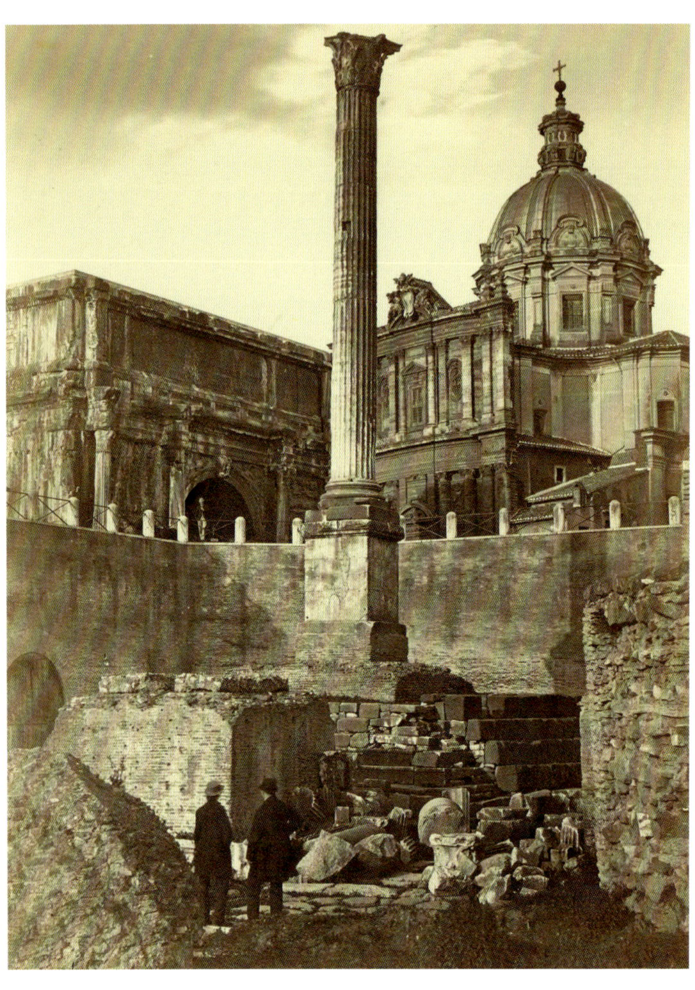

Photographer Unknown
Panoramic View of Rome, Italy,
late 19th century
19th-century photographic print,
image size: 7 9⁄16 × 14 7⁄16 inches,
historic mount: 16 13⁄16 × 21 7⁄8 inches
OL.1983.488

Photographer Unknown
Forum and Church of St. Martina e Luca and Arch of Septimius Severus, Rome, Italy,
late 19th century
19th-century photographic print,
image size: 14 13⁄16 × 11 11⁄16 inches,
historic mount: 21 7⁄8 × 18 3⁄8 inches
OL.1983.440

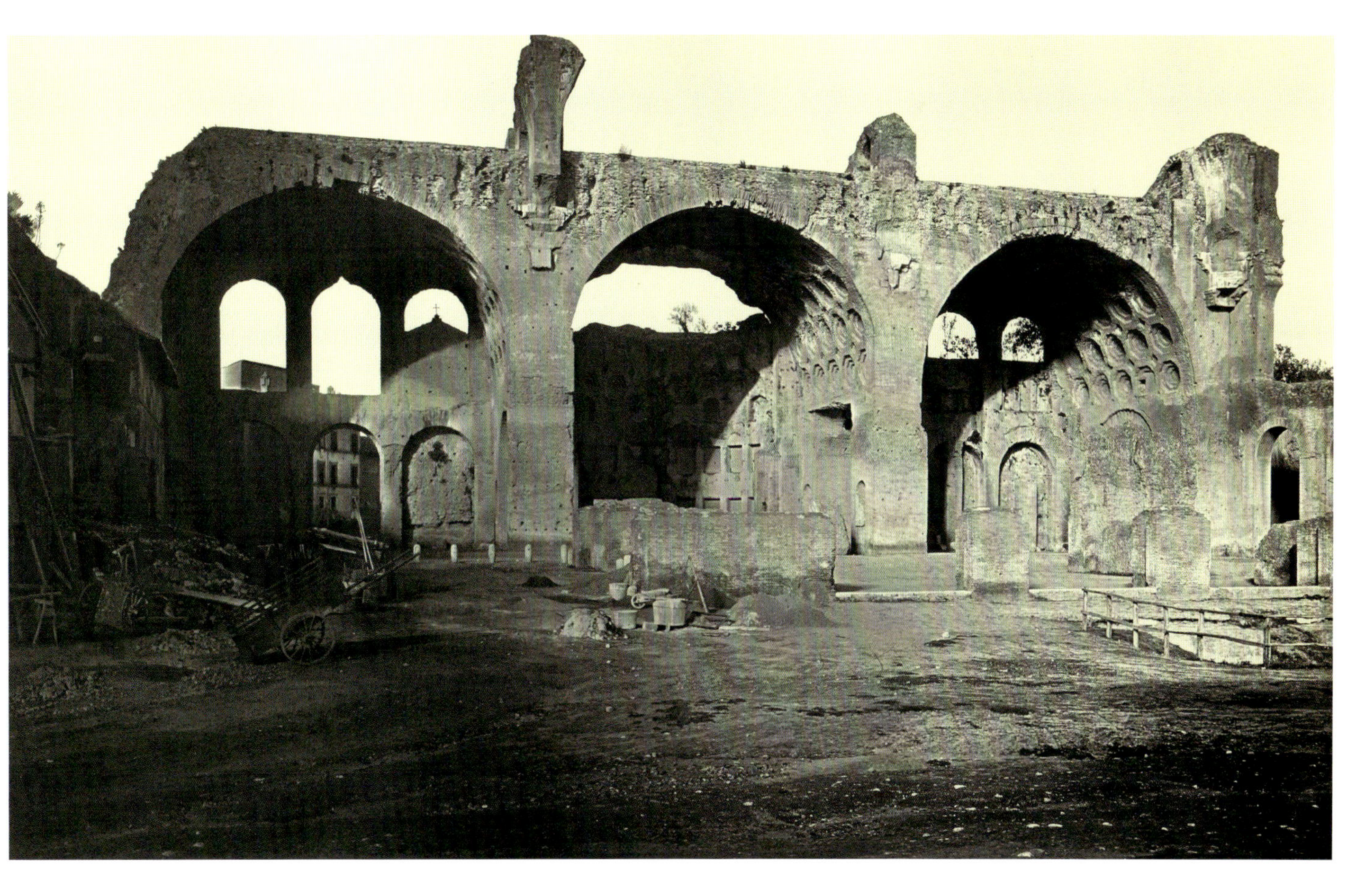

Photographer Unknown
Basilica of Maxentius and Constantine, Rome, Italy,
late 19th century
19th-century photographic print,
image size: 10 × 16 1⁄16 inches,
historic mount: 16 13⁄16 × 21 13⁄16 inches
OL.1983.426

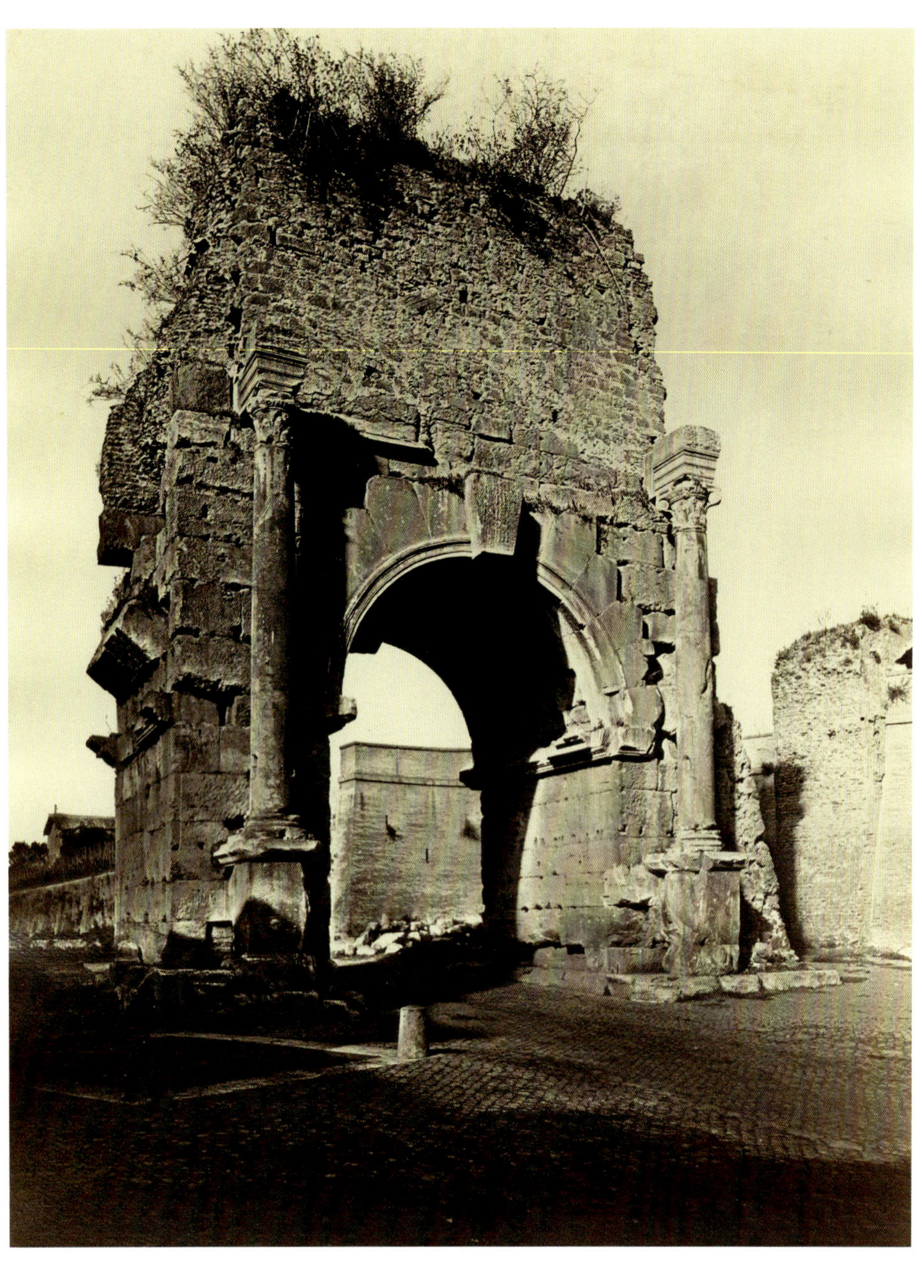

Photographer Unknown
Ruins, Italy,
late 19th century
19th-century photographic print,
image size: 6 ⅜ × 11 ⅜ inches,
historic mount: 11 15/16 × 15 13/16 inches
OL.1983.411

Unknown Photographer
Arch of Drusus, Via Appia, Rome,
late 19th century
19th-century photographic print,
image size: 16 ¼ × 12 inches,
historic mount: 21 ⅞ × 18 ⅞ inches
OL.1983.475

Photographer Unknown
Arch of Constantine, Rome, Italy,
late 19th century
19th-century photographic print,
image size: 10 ⅝ × 14 11/16 inches,
historic mount: 18 7/16 × 22 inches
OL.1983.445

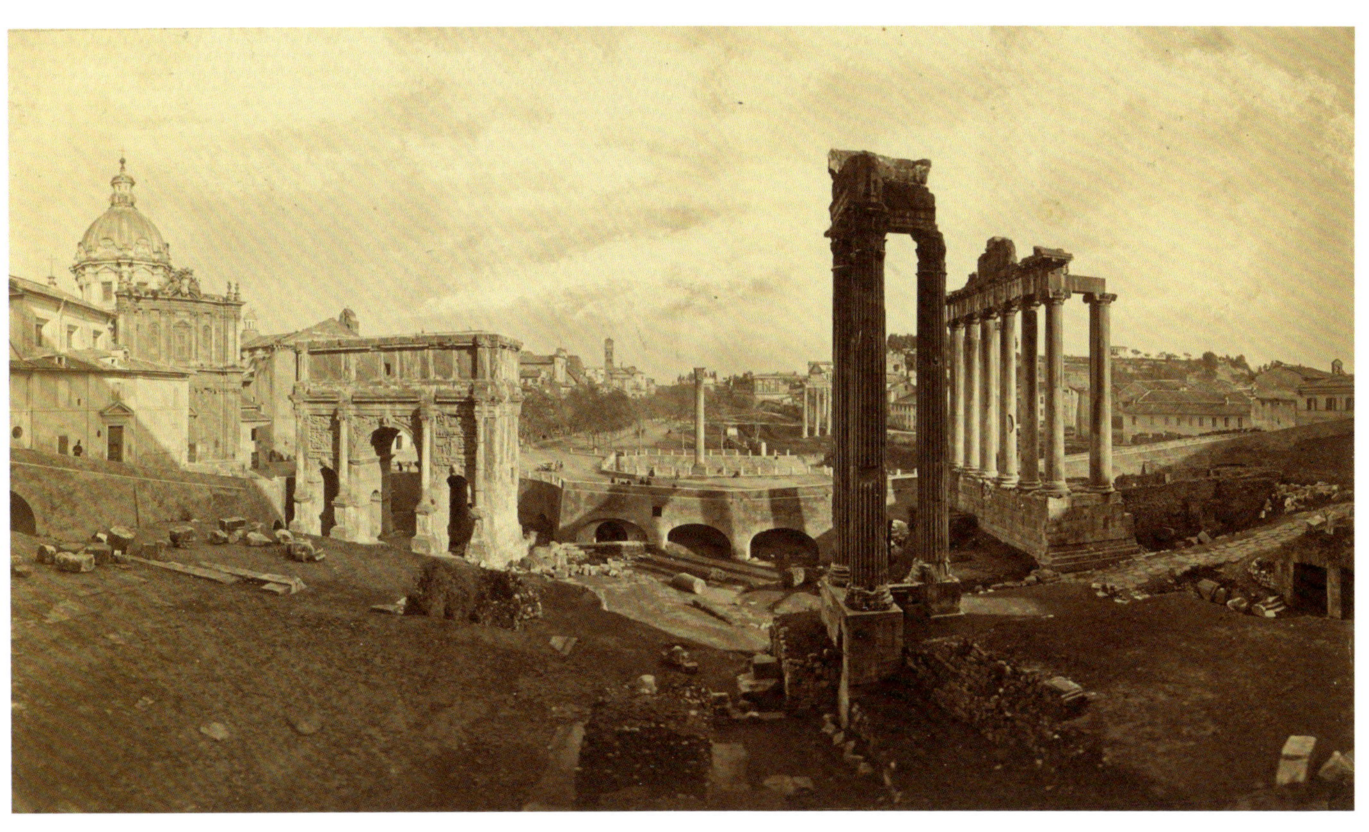

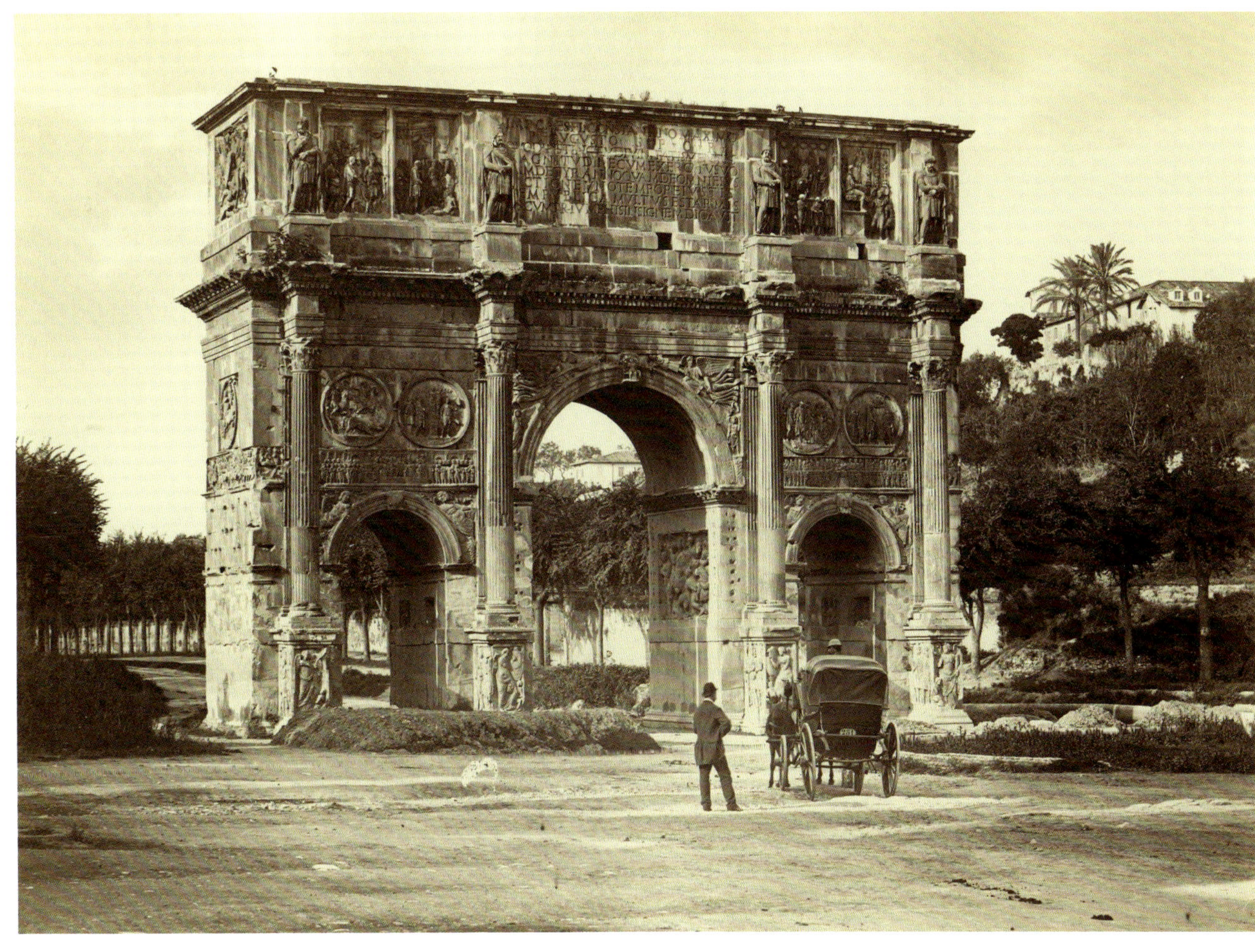

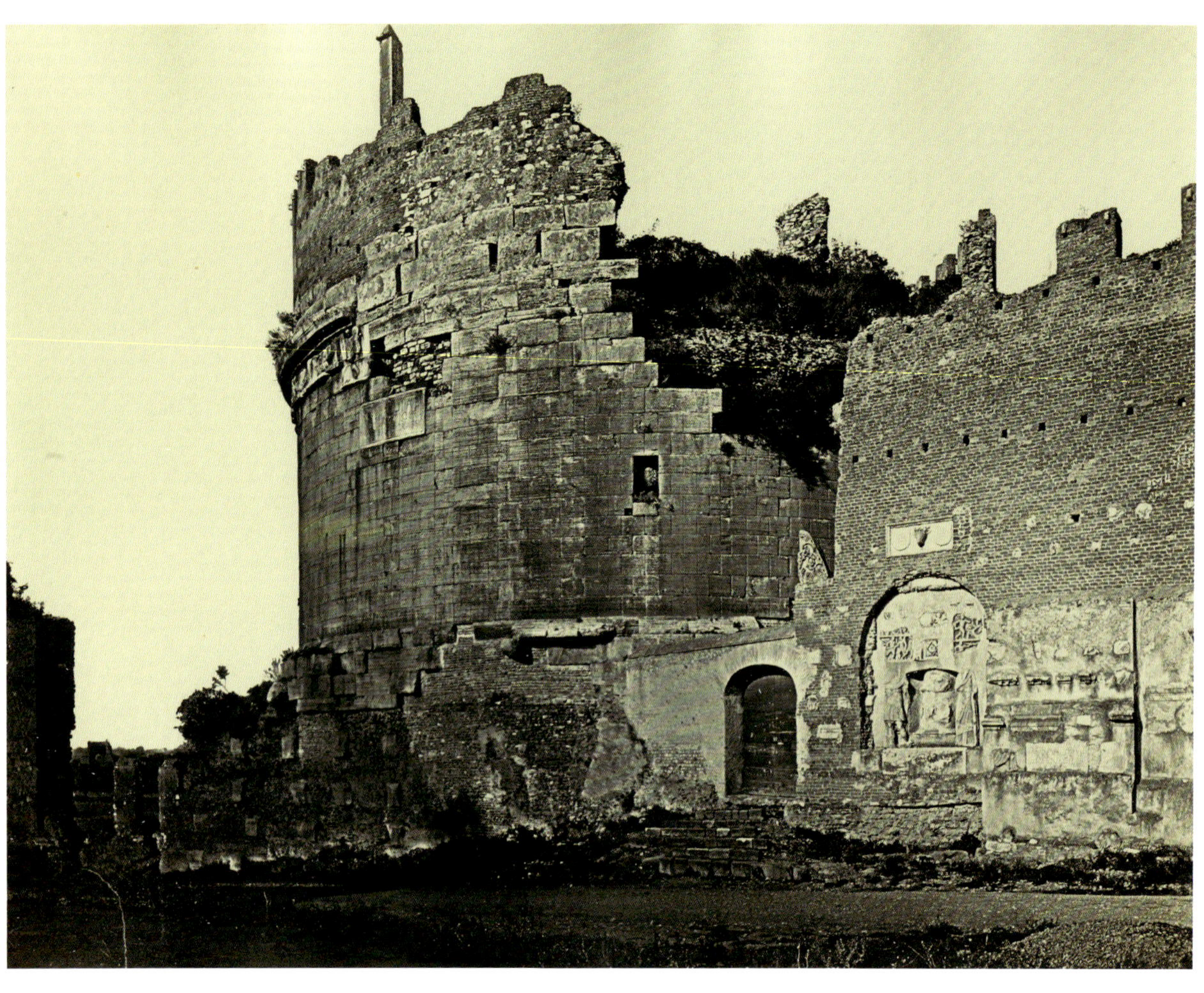

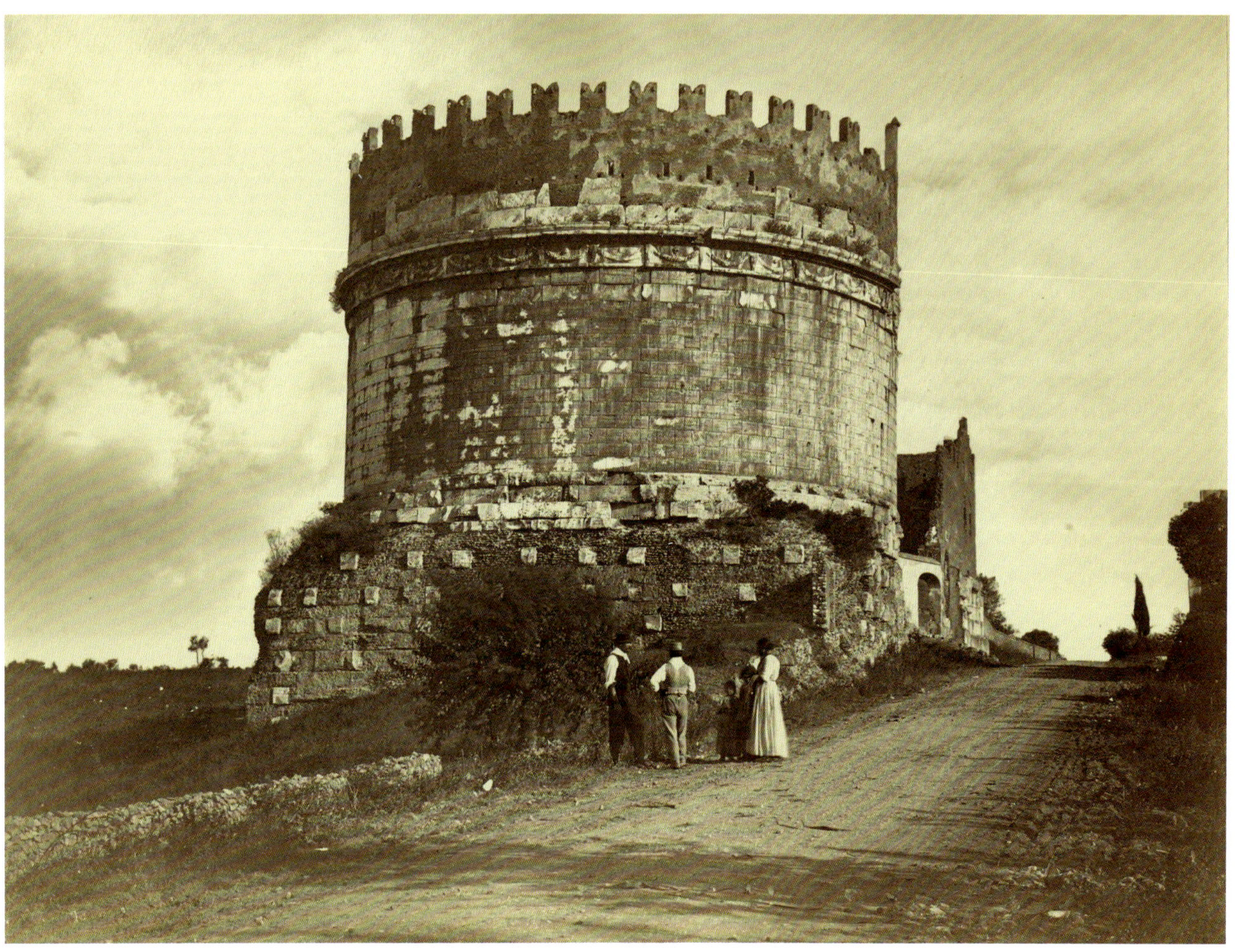

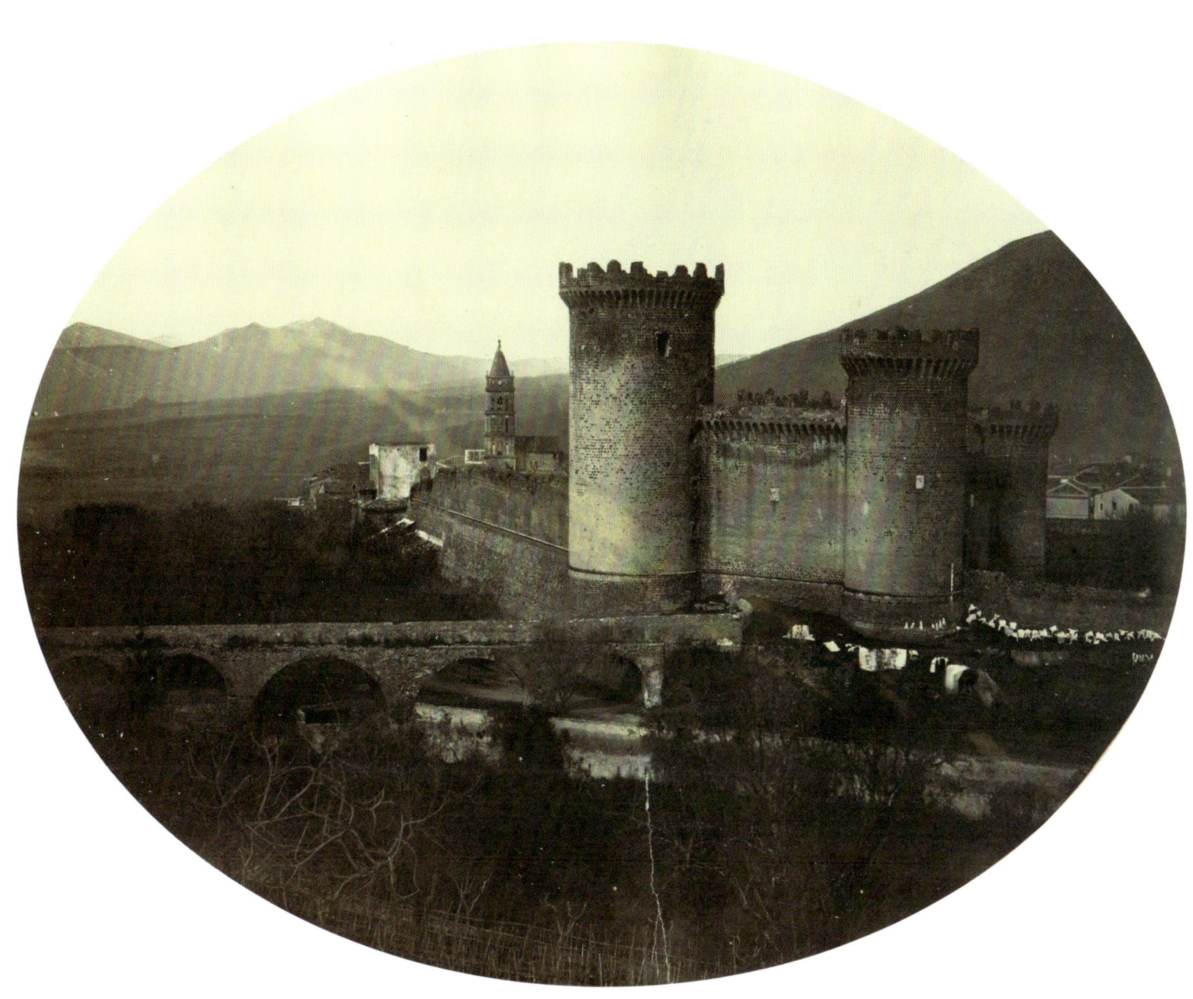

Photographer Unknown
Tomb of Caesar Metellius (Cecilia Metella),
late 19th century
19th-century photographic print,
image size: 12 3⁄16 × 15 9⁄16 inches,
historic mount: 18 3⁄8 × 21 7⁄8 inches
OL.1983.485

Photographer Unknown
Appian Way, Tomb of Cecilia Metella, Italy,
late 19th century
19th-century photographic print,
image size: 10 9⁄16 × 14 5⁄8 inches,
historic mount: 18 3⁄8 × 22 inches
OL.1983.421

Robert Macpherson (1811–1872)
Rocca Pia, Tivoli,
ca. 1860
19th-century photographic print,
image size: 12 1⁄8 × 15 9⁄16 inches,
historic mount: 15 1⁄8 × 18 3⁄4 inches
OL.1983.474

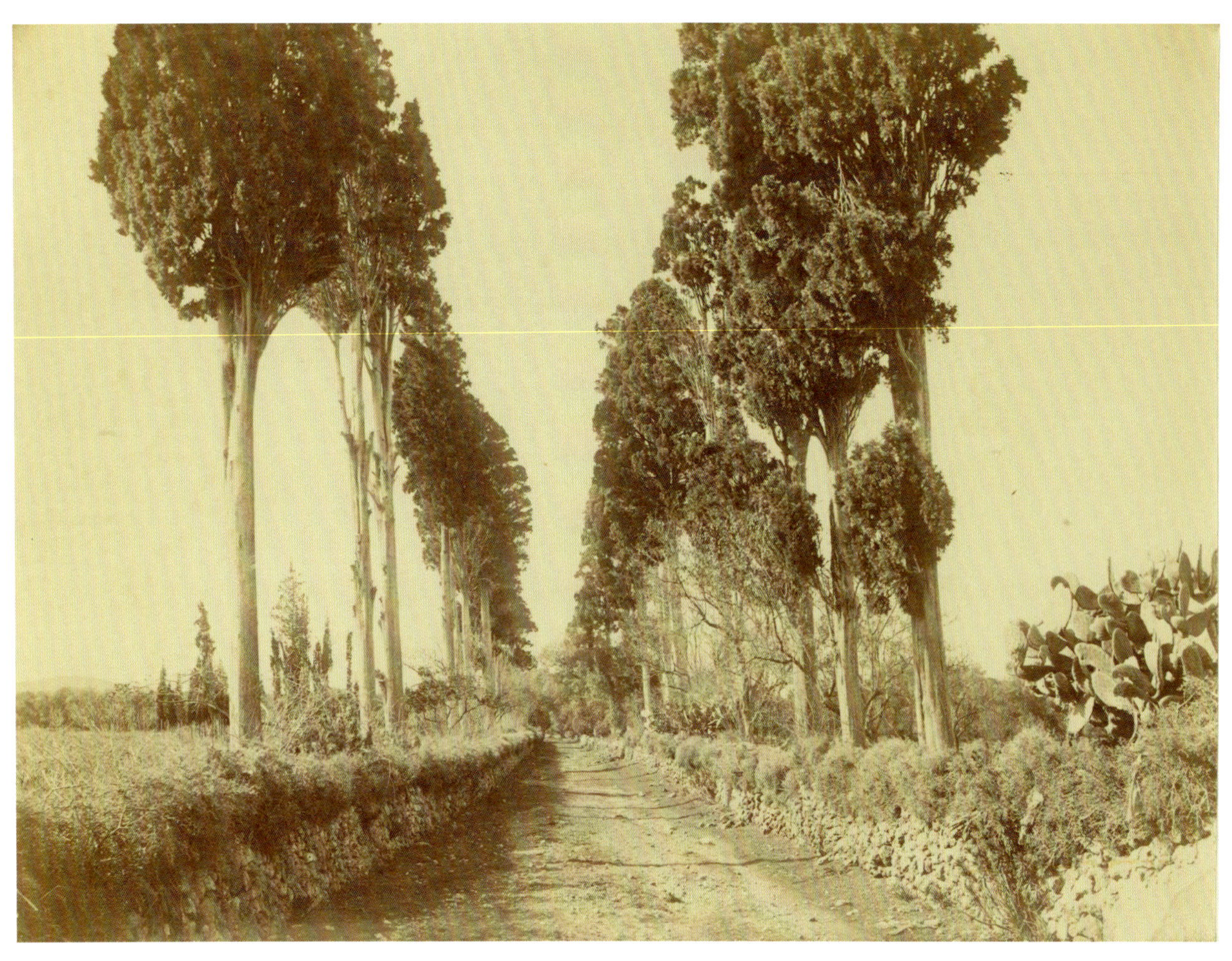

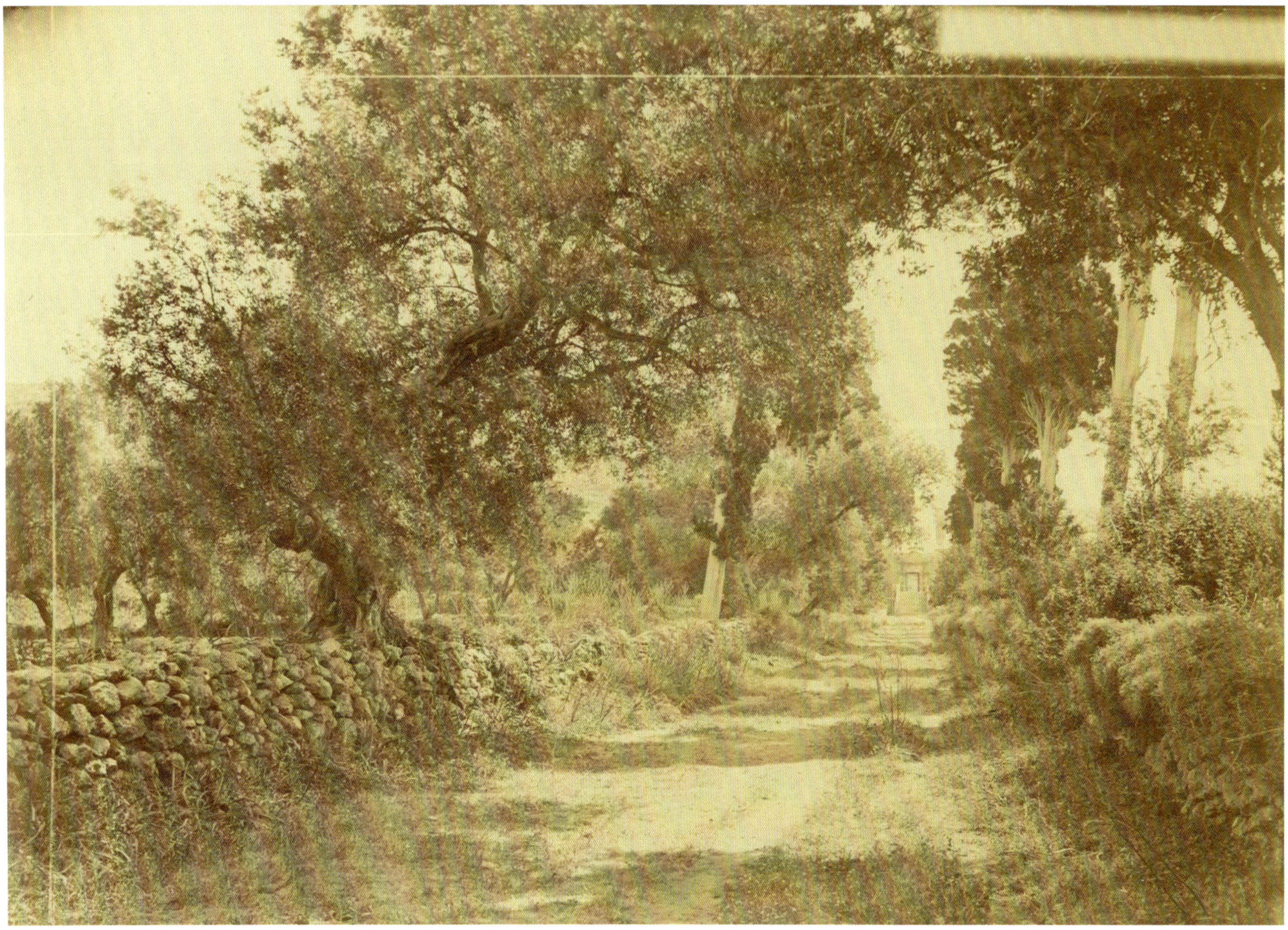

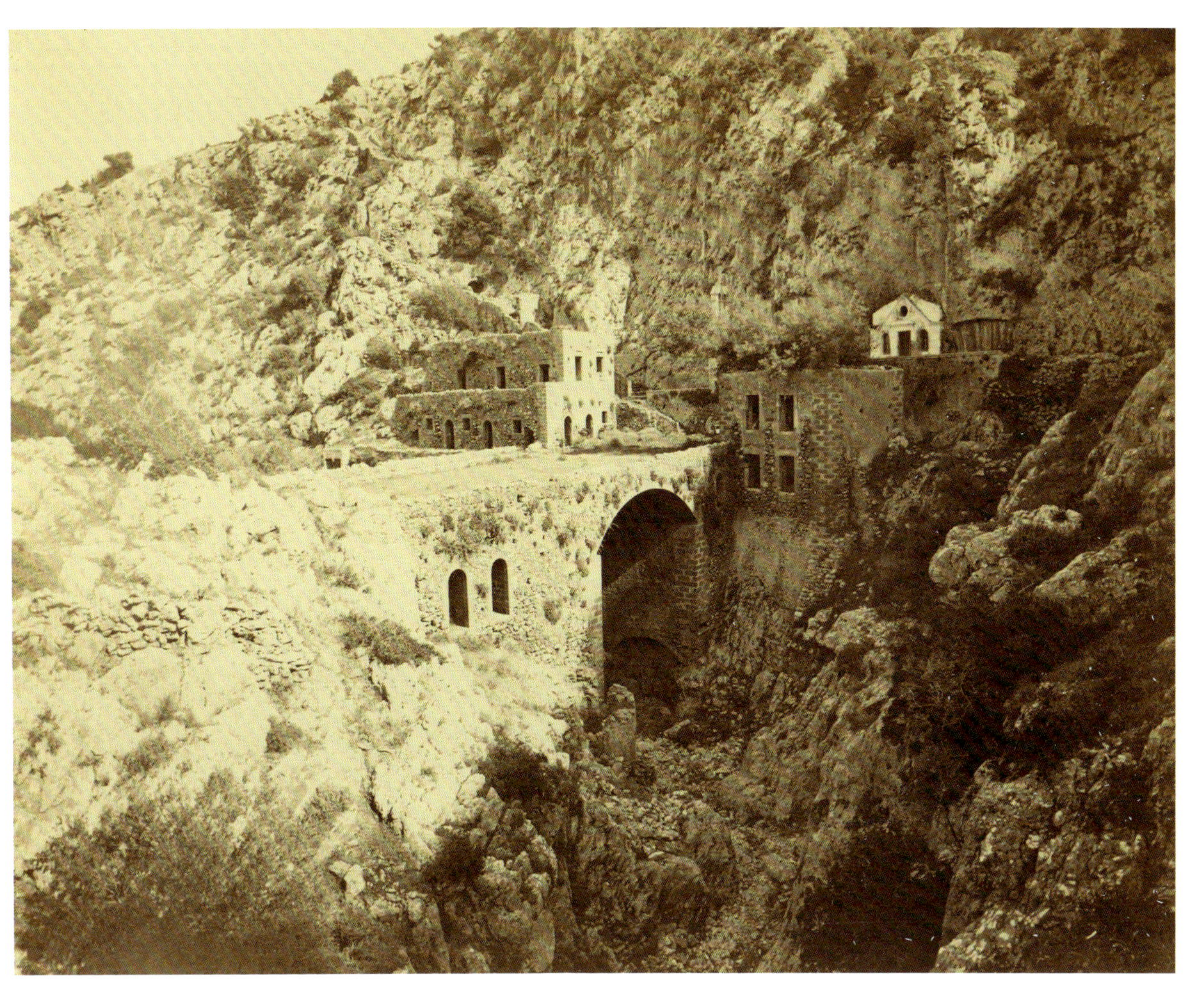

William James Stillman (1828–1901)
Hagia Triada, Crete,
ca. 1865–69
19th-century photographic print,
image size: 7 ⅛ × 9 7⁄16 inches,
historic mount: 12 ½ × 15 inches
OL.1985.889.B

William James Stillman (1828–1901)
Approach of Aghia Triadha, Crete,
ca. 1865–69
19th-century photographic print,
image size: 7 ¾ × 9 ⅝ inches,
historic mount: 13 11⁄16 × 16 3⁄16 inches
OL.1983.511

William James Stillman (1828–1901)
Convent of Catholico, Crete,
ca. 1865–69
19th-century photographic print,
image size: 7 9⁄16 × 9 9⁄16 inches,
historic mount: 13 ⅝ × 16 ⅛ inches
OL.1983.515

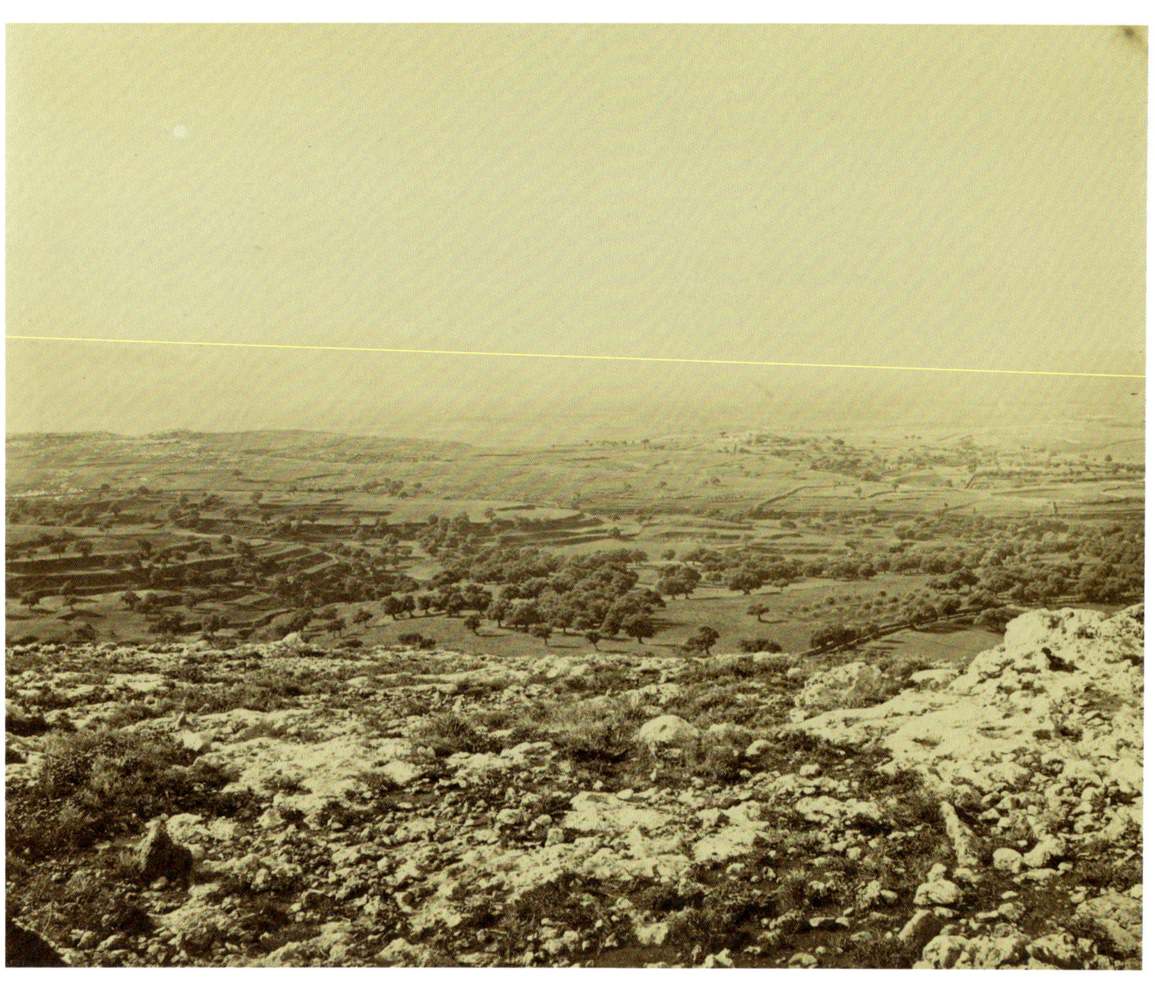

William James Stillman (1828–1901)
Convent of St. John, Crete,
ca. 1865–69
19th-century photographic print,
image size: 7 ⅞ × 9 ¹¹⁄₁₆ inches,
historic mount: 13 ⅝ × 16 ³⁄₁₆ inches
OL.1983.538

William James Stillman (1828–1901)
Plain of Canea, Crete,
ca. 1865–69
19th-century photographic print,
image size: 7 ¹¹⁄₁₆ × 9 ¹¹⁄₁₆ inches,
historic mount: 13 ⅝ × 16 ³⁄₁₆ inches
OL.1983.535

William James Stillman (1828–1901)
Wall and Moat, Kanea, Crete,
ca. 1865–69
19th-century photographic print,
image size: 7 ⅝ × 9 ⅝ inches,
historic mount: 13 ⅝ × 16 ⅛ inches
OL.1983.517

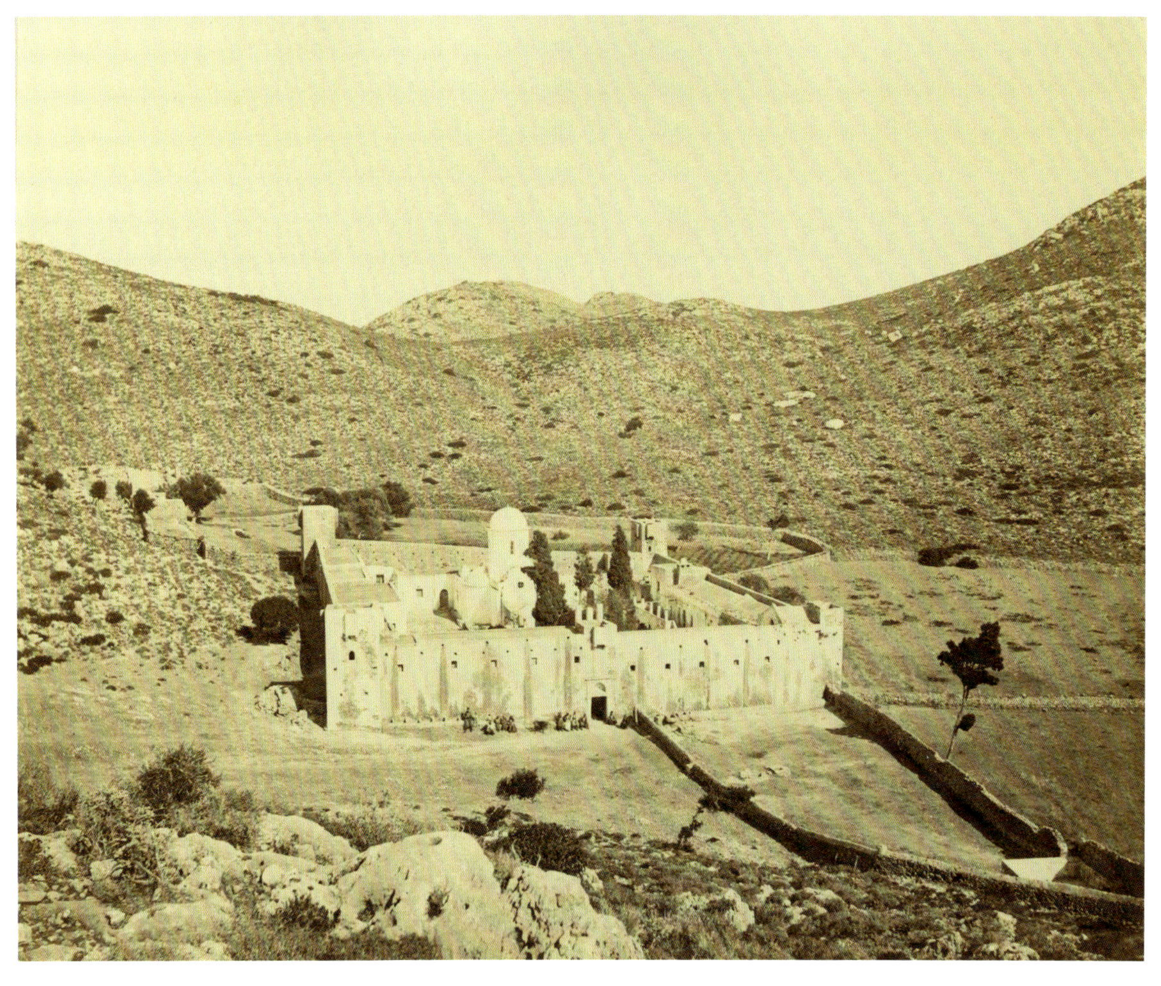

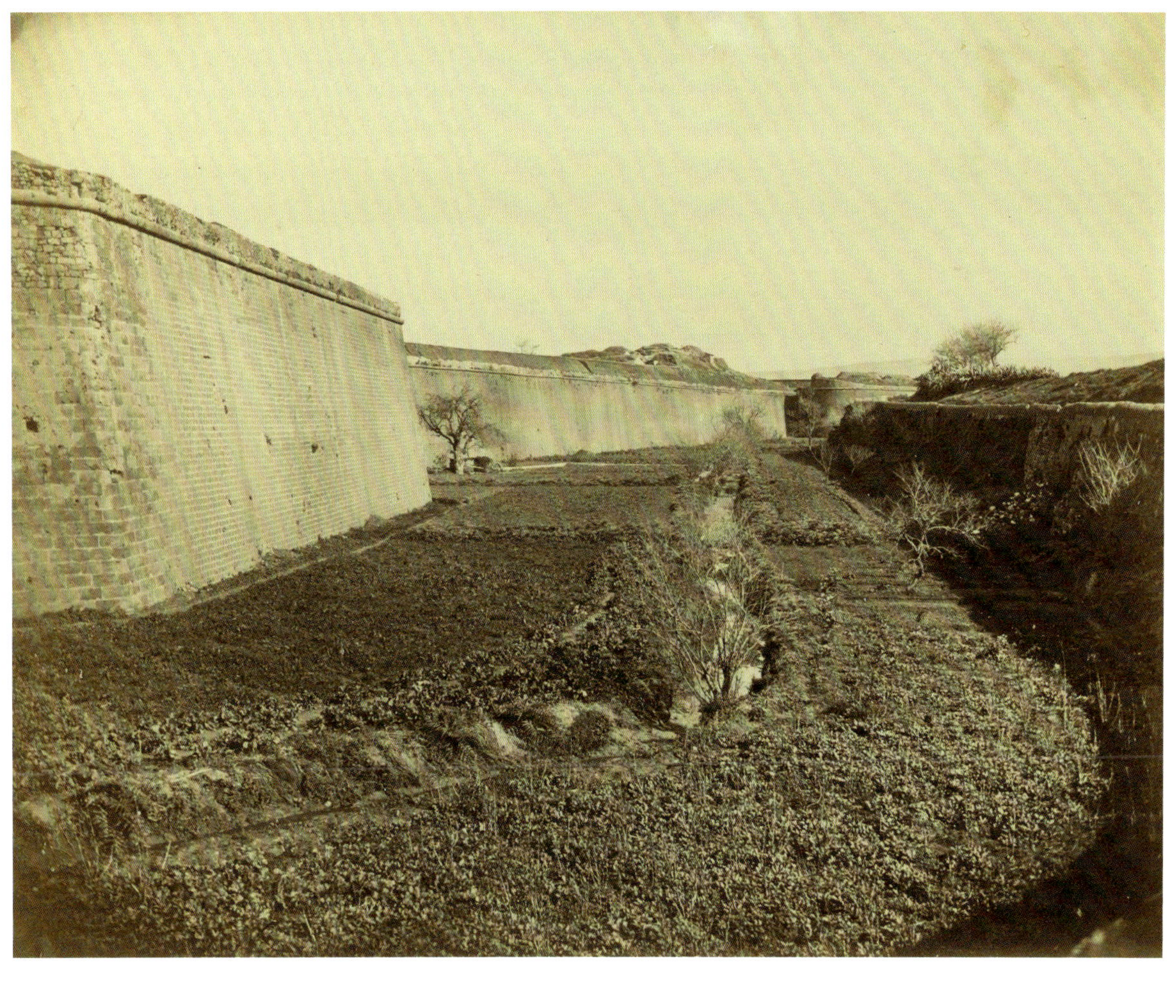

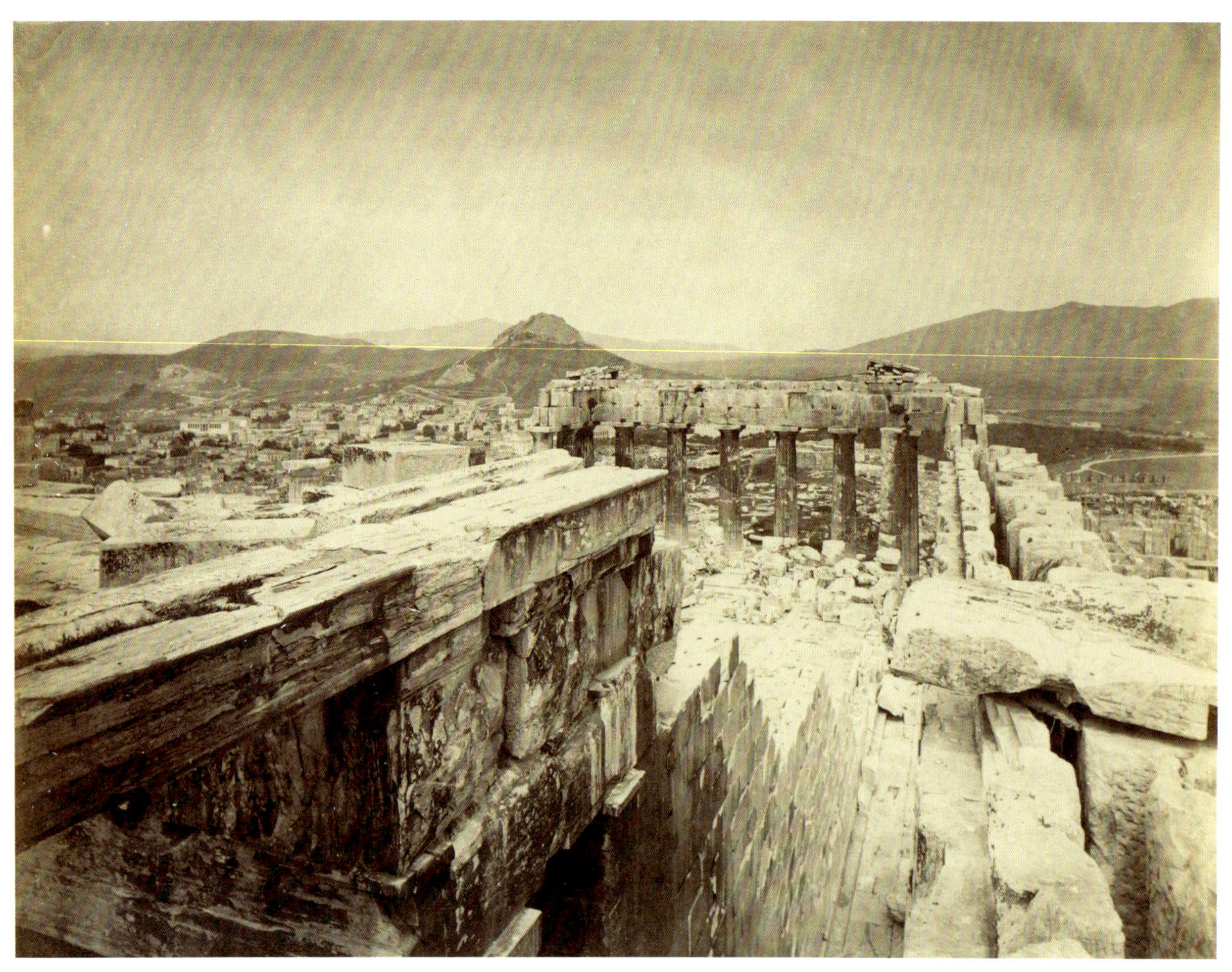

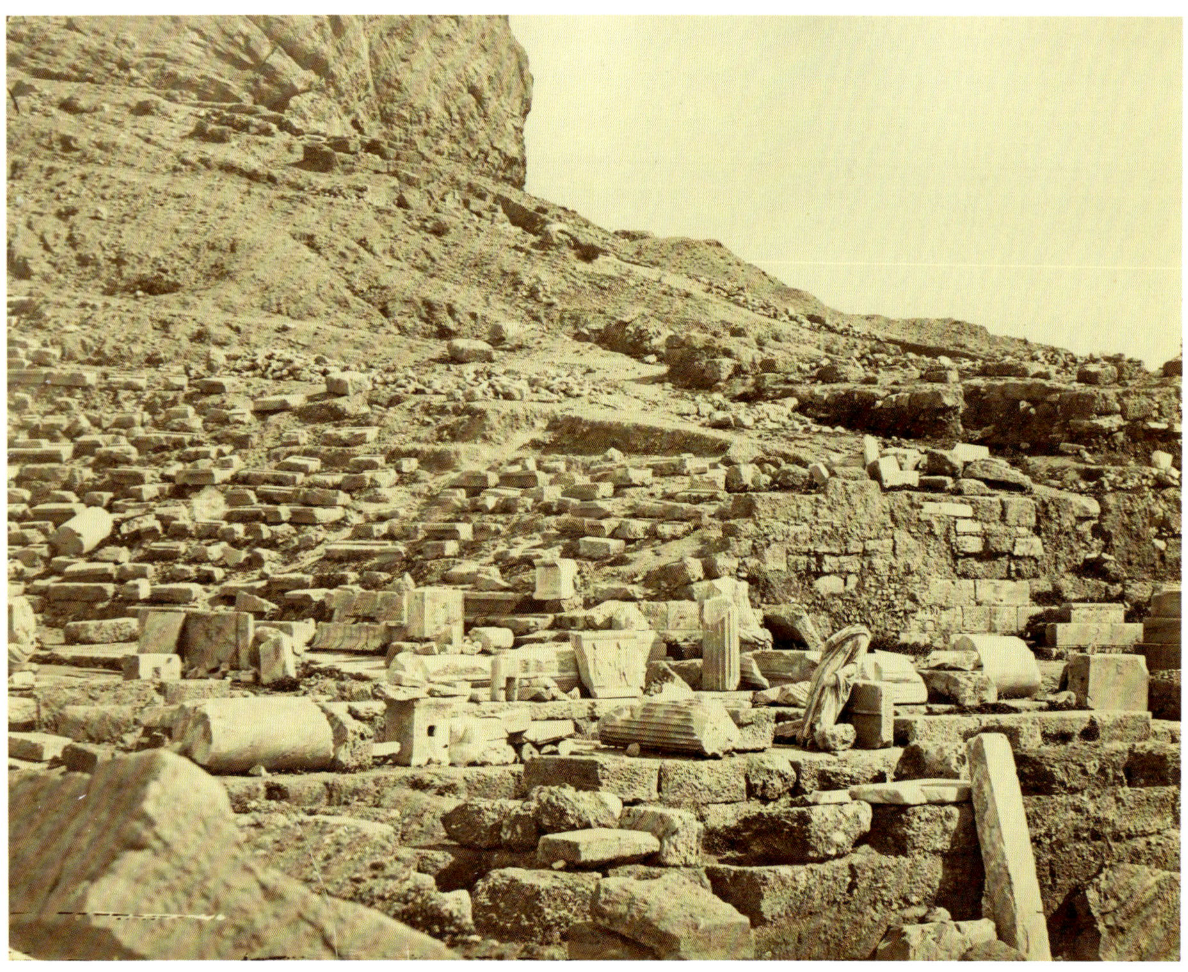

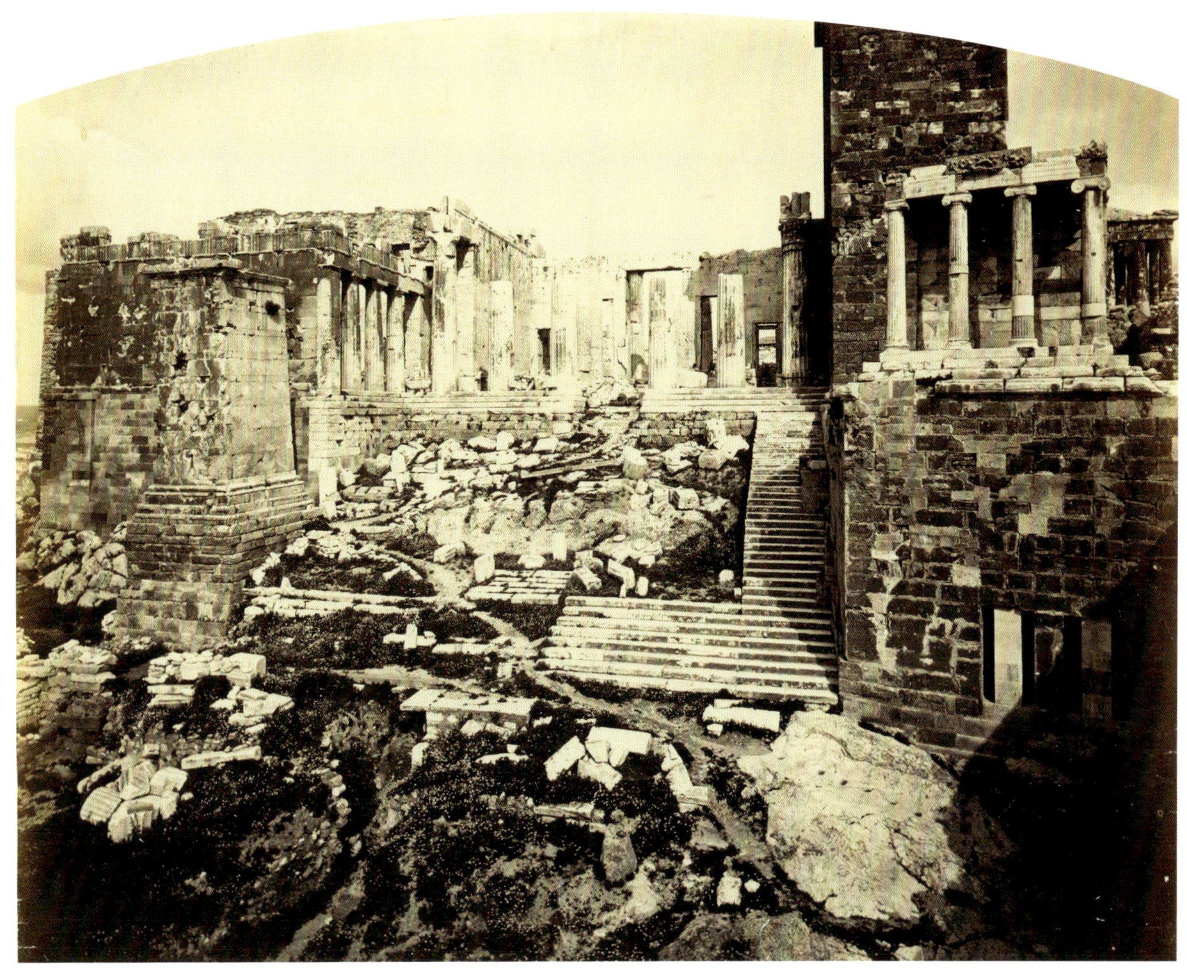

William James Stillman (1828–1901)
View from on Top of the Ruins, Acropolis,
ca. 1869
19th-century photographic print,
image size: 7 ³⁄₁₆ × 9 ½ inches
OL.1981.616.18

Photographer Unknown
Theatre of Bacchus, Athens,
late 19th century
19th-century photographic print,
image size: 9 ⅞ × 12 ¹¹⁄₁₆ inches,
historic mount: 16 ¾ × 21 ⅝ inches
OL.1985.900

William James Stillman (1828–1901)
Western Façade of Propylaea,
ca. 1869
19th-century photographic print,
image size: 7 ¾ × 9 ½ inches
OL.1981.615.3

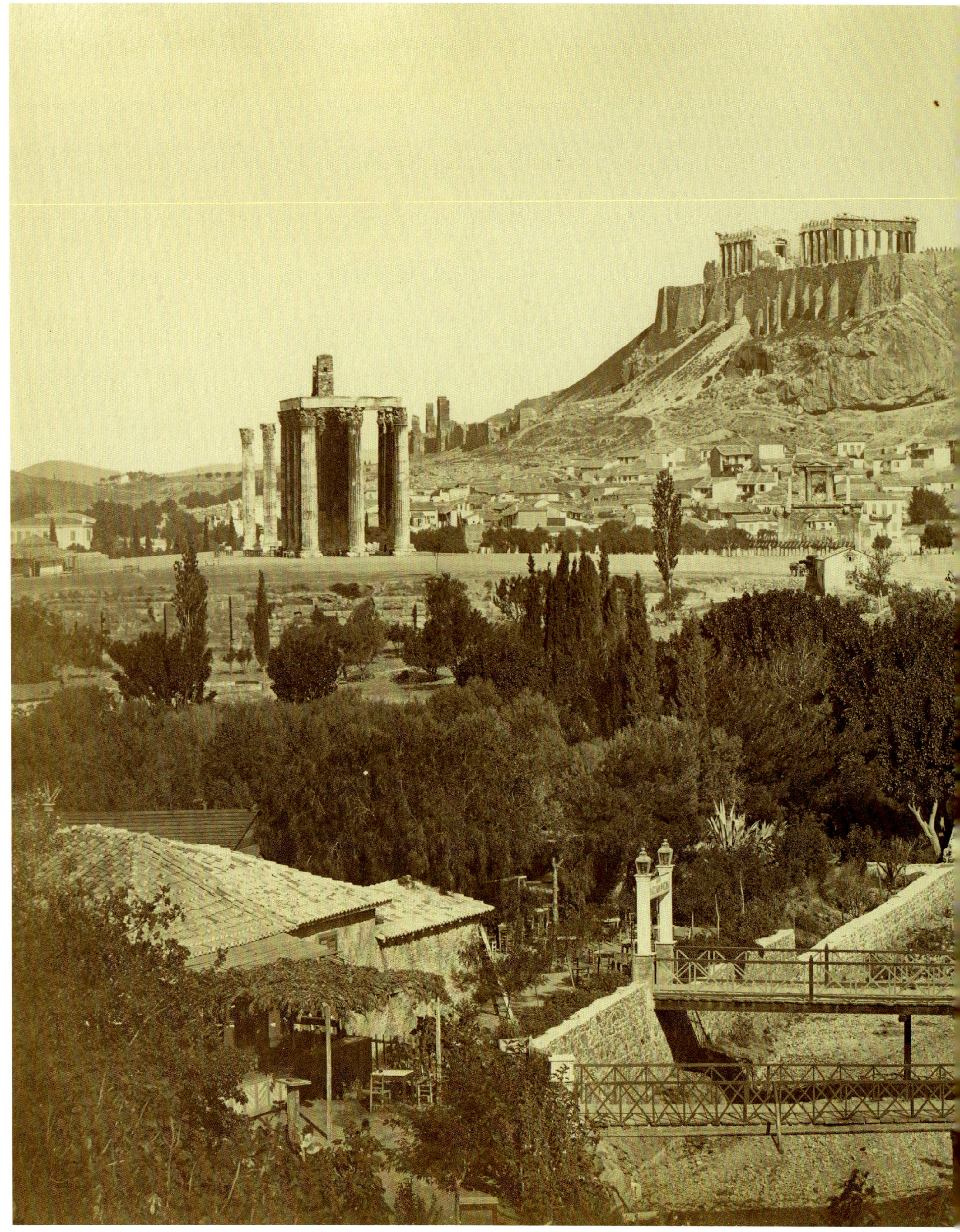

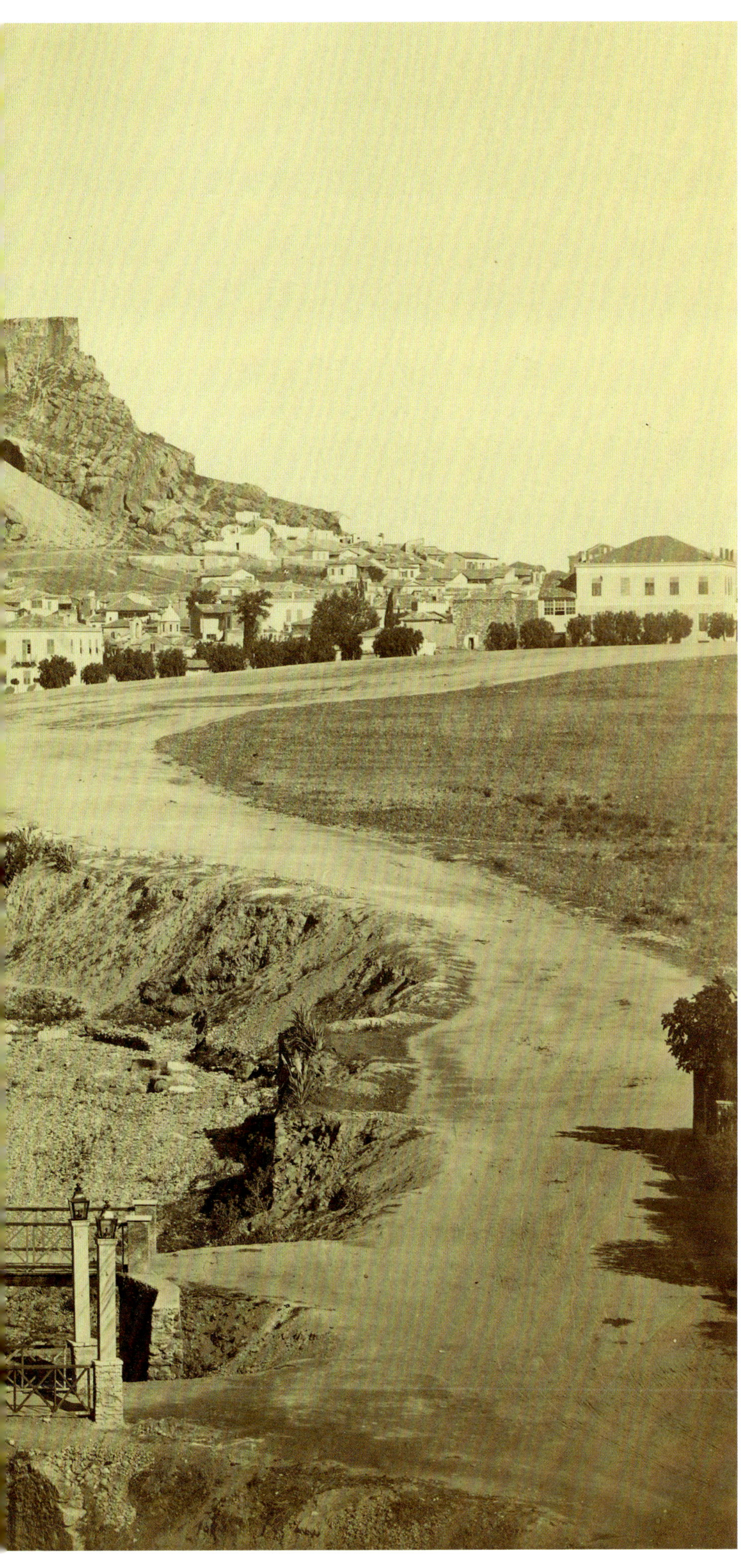

Photographer Unknown
East View of Acropolis, Athens,
late 19th century
19th-century photographic print,
image size: 11 ⅞ × 15 ⅛ inches,
historic mount: 16 ⅝ × 21 ⅝ inches
OL.1985.893

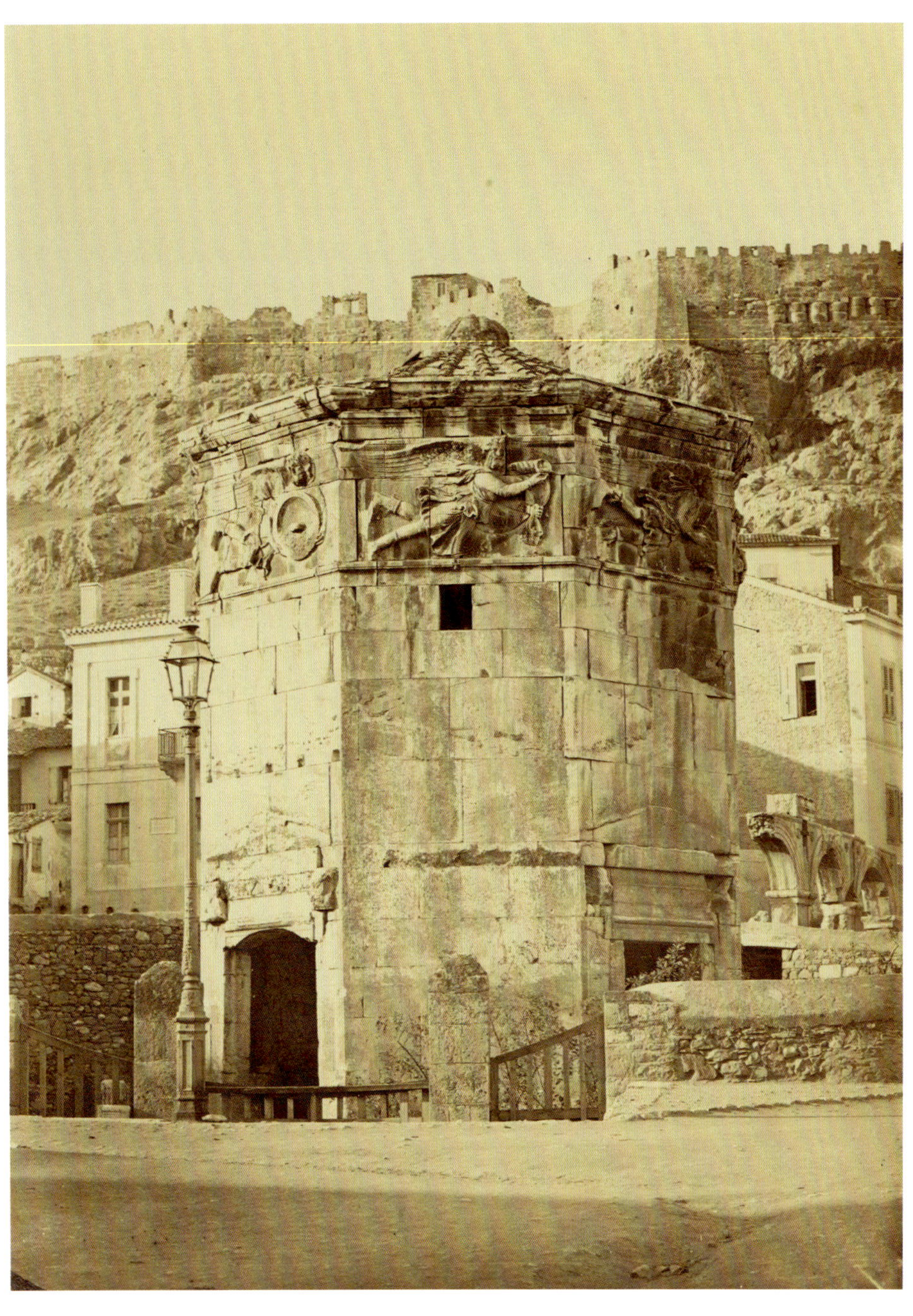

Photographer Unknown
Temple of the Winds, Athens,
late 19th century
19th-century photographic print,
image size: 15 ⅛ × 11 1/16 inches,
historic mount: 21 ⅝ × 16 11/16 inches
OL.1985.912

Photographer Unknown
Monument of Lysicrates,
late 19th century
19th-century photographic print,
image size: 15 ⅛ × 10 ¾ inches,
historic mount: 21 ⅝ × 16 11/16 inches
OL.1985.877

Photographer Unknown
Ceylinus (Silenus, Theater of Dionysus, Athens),
late 19th century
19th-century photographic print,
image size: 11 3/16 × 15 ¼ inches,
historic mount: 16 11/16 × 21 ⅝ inches
OL.1985.885

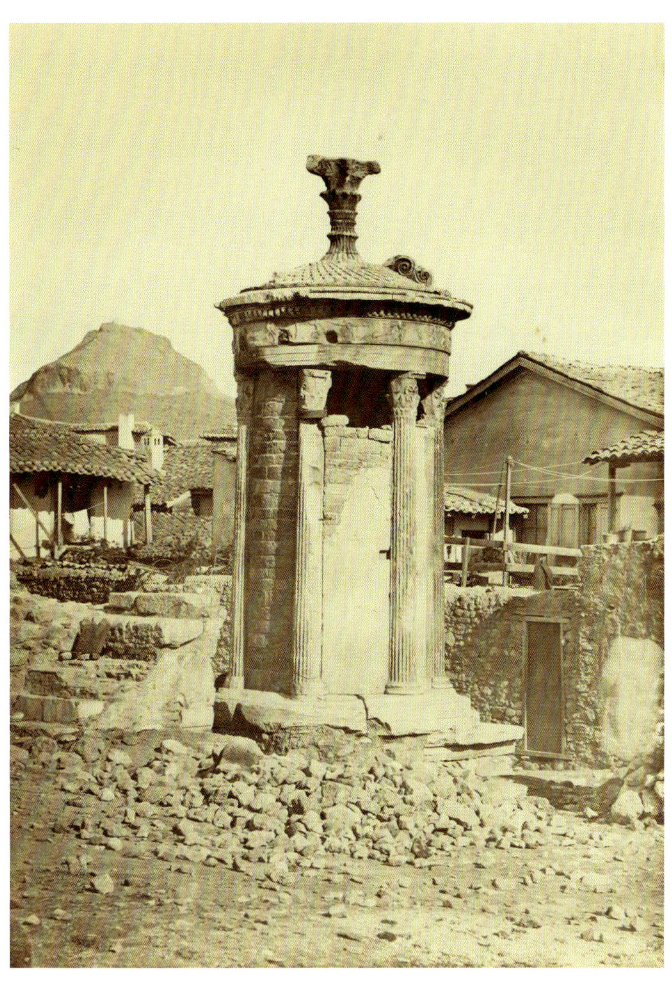

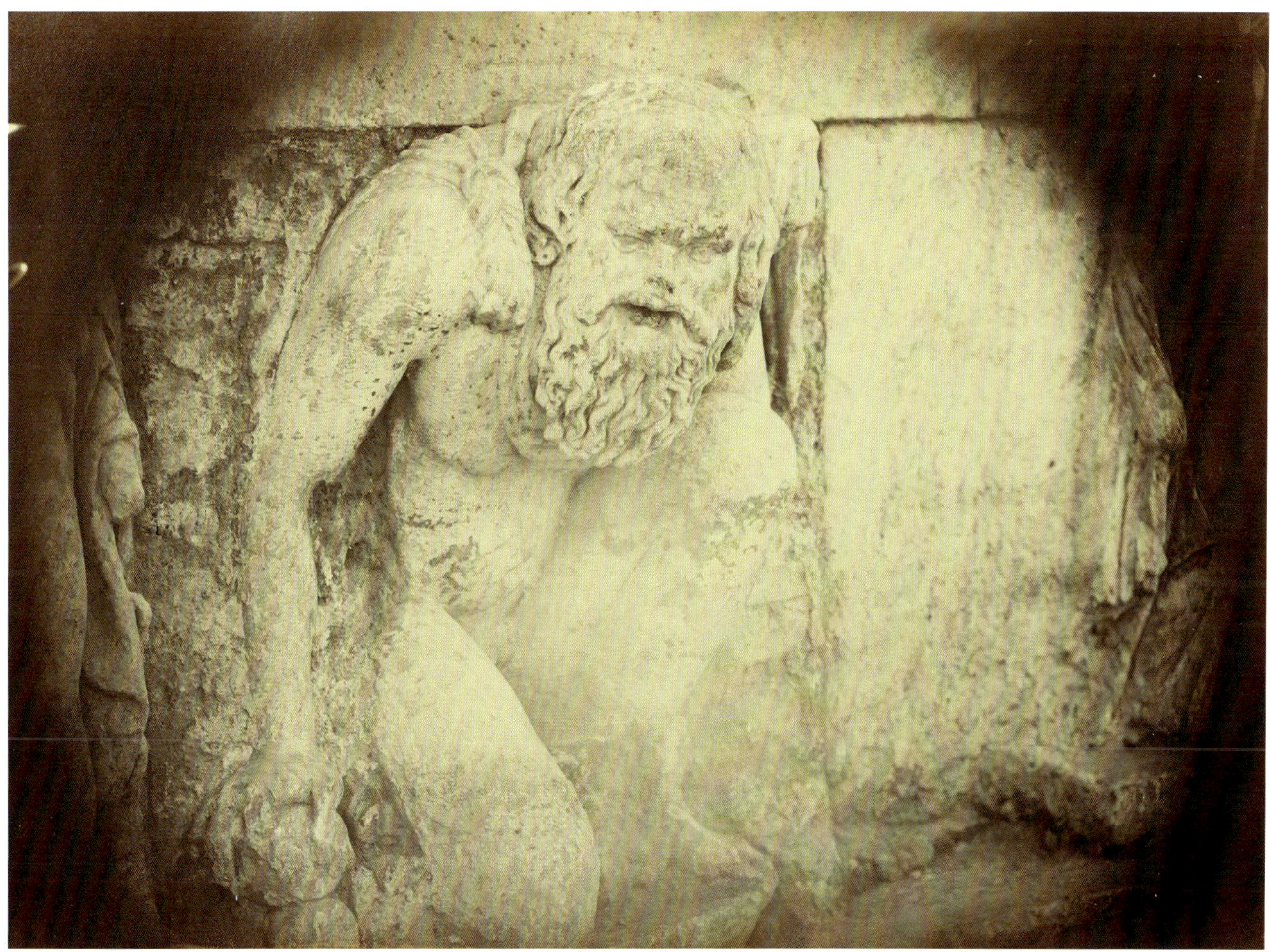

Alexandre Leroux (1836–1912)
Allée du Palmiers au Jardin d'Essai,
ca. 1876–1890
19th-century photographic print,
image size: 11 ⅝ × 9 inches
OL.1981.603.15

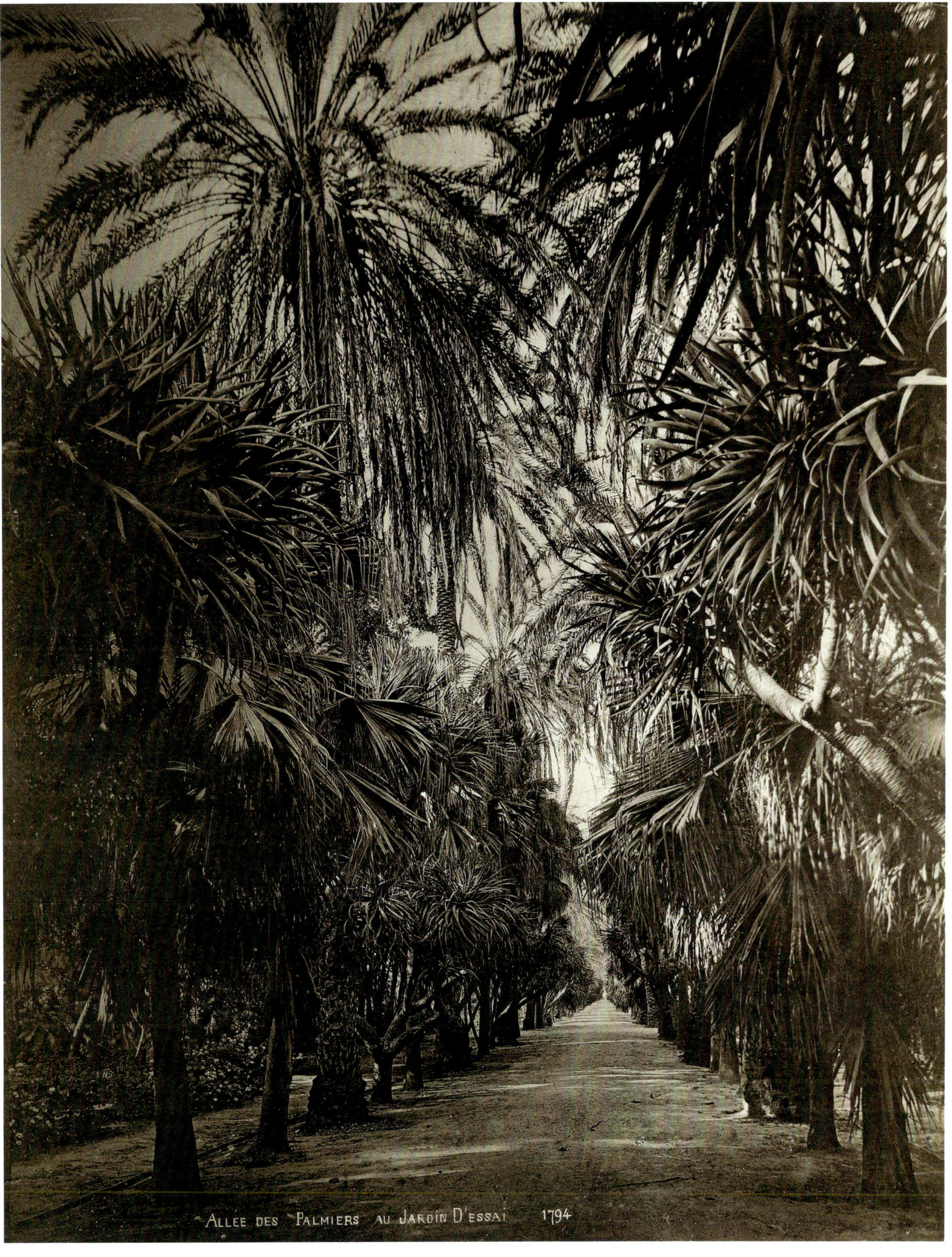
ALLEE DES PALMIERS AU JARDIN D'ESSAI 1794

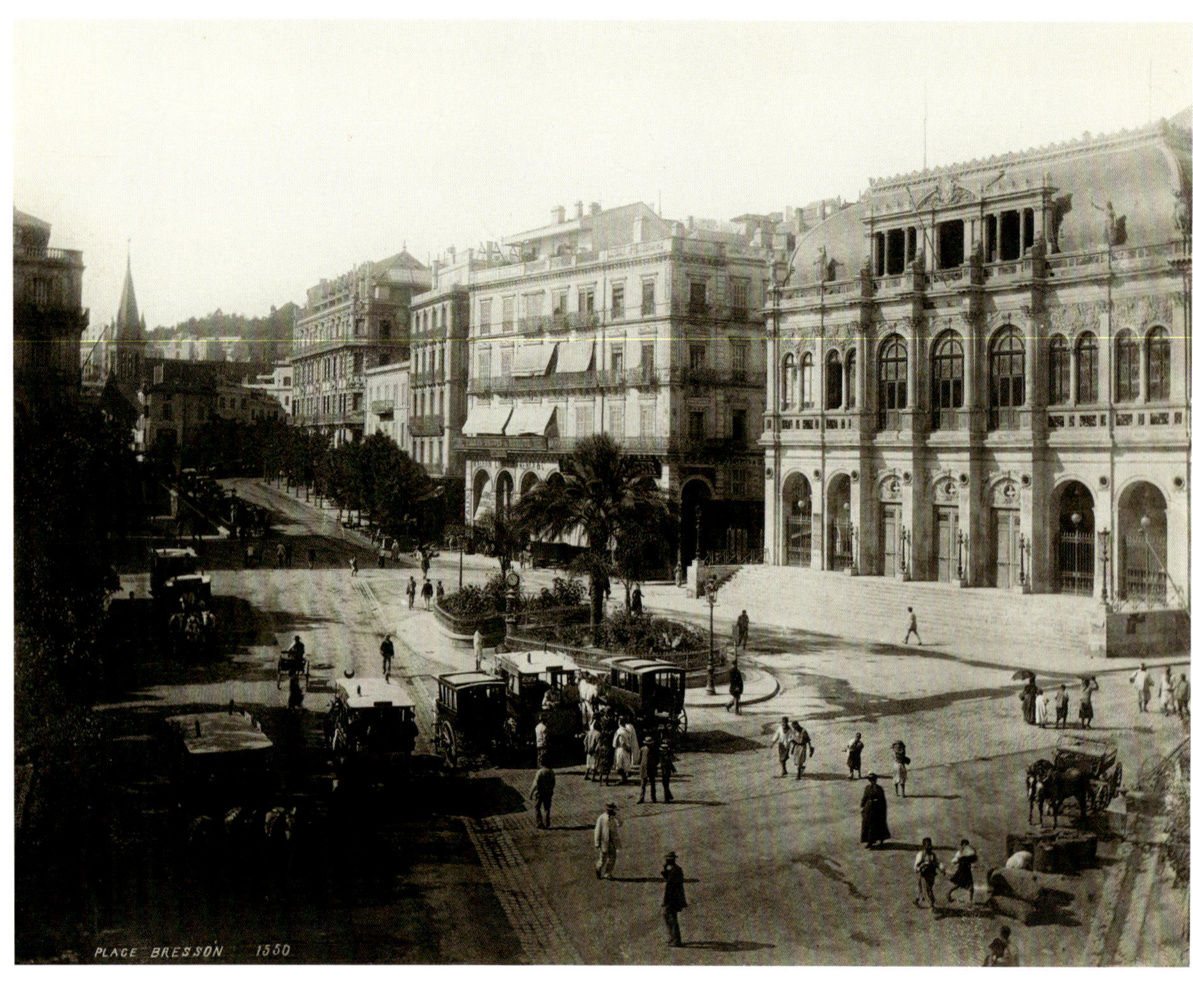

Alexandre Leroux (1836–1912)
Les Quais à Alger,
ca. 1876–1900
19th-century photographic print,
image size: 9 × 12 inches
OL.1981.603.3

Alexandre Leroux (1836–1912)
Place Bresson,
ca. 1876–1890
19th-century photographic print,
image size: 8 11⁄16 × 11 inches
OL.1981.603.7

Alexandre Leroux (1836–1912)
Alger, Vue générale à l'entrée du port,
ca. 1876–1890
19th-century photographic print,
image size: 9 × 12 inches
OL.1981.603.24

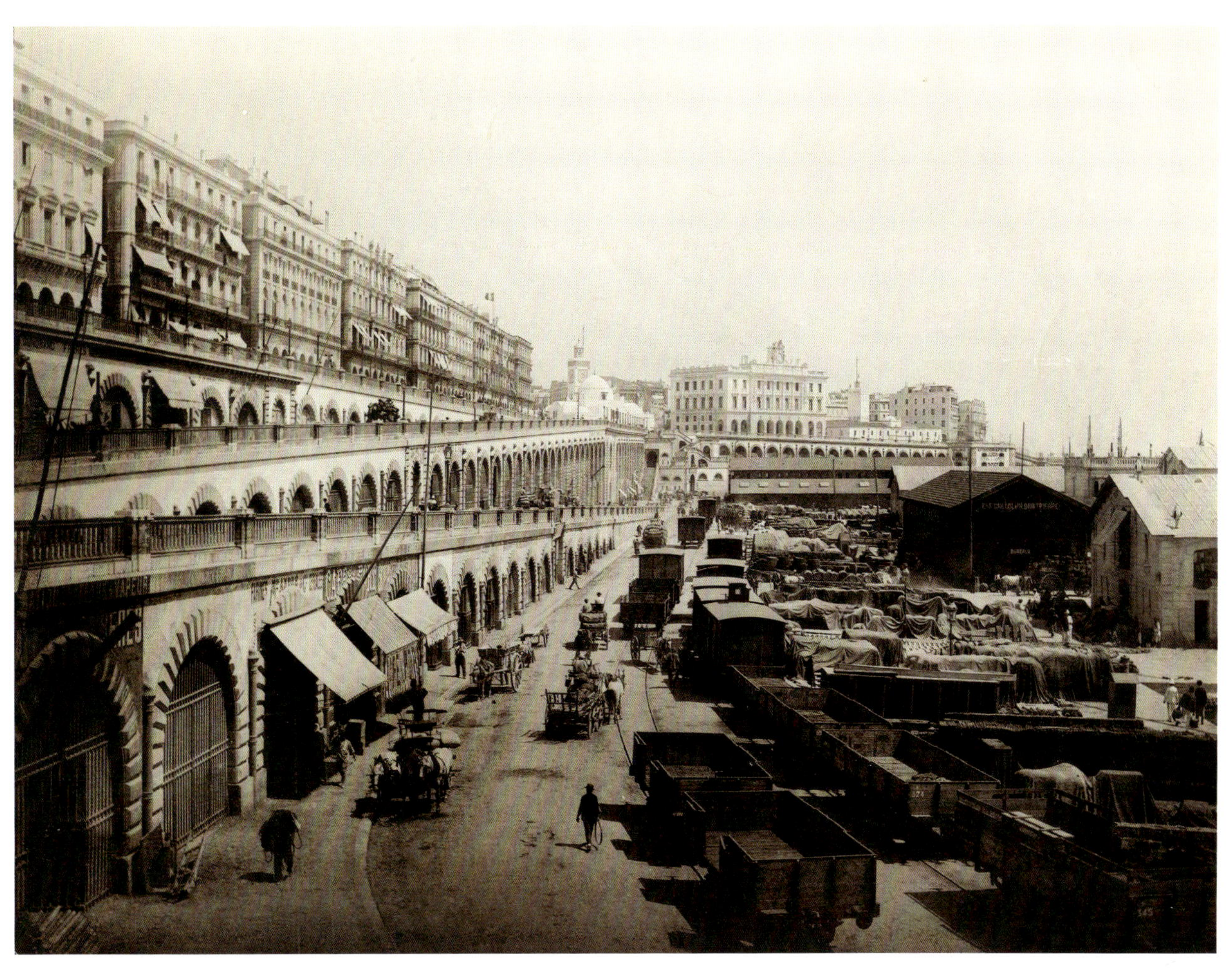

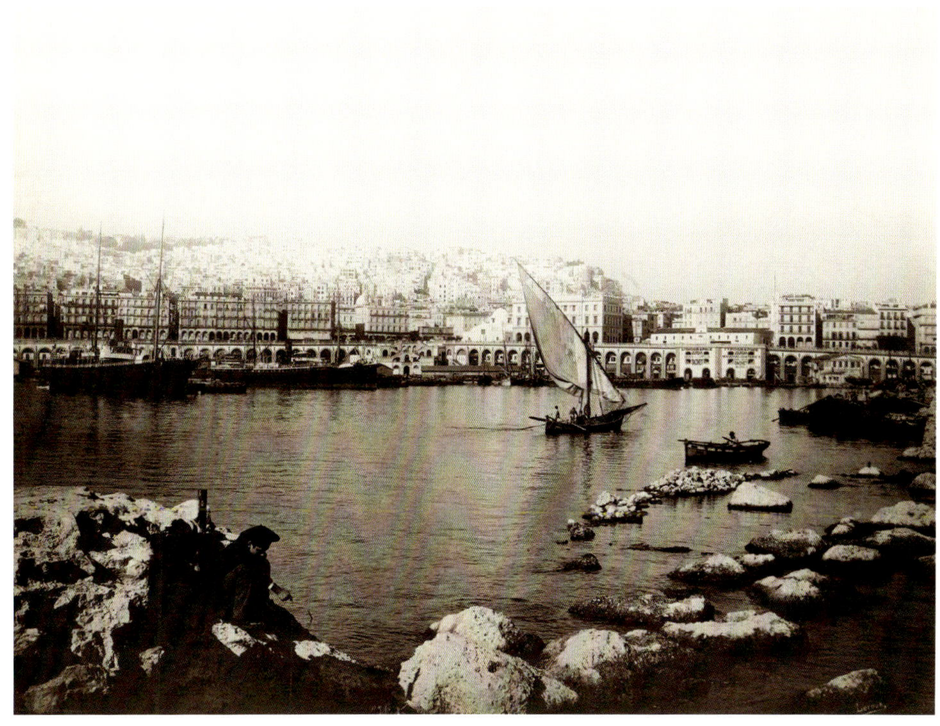

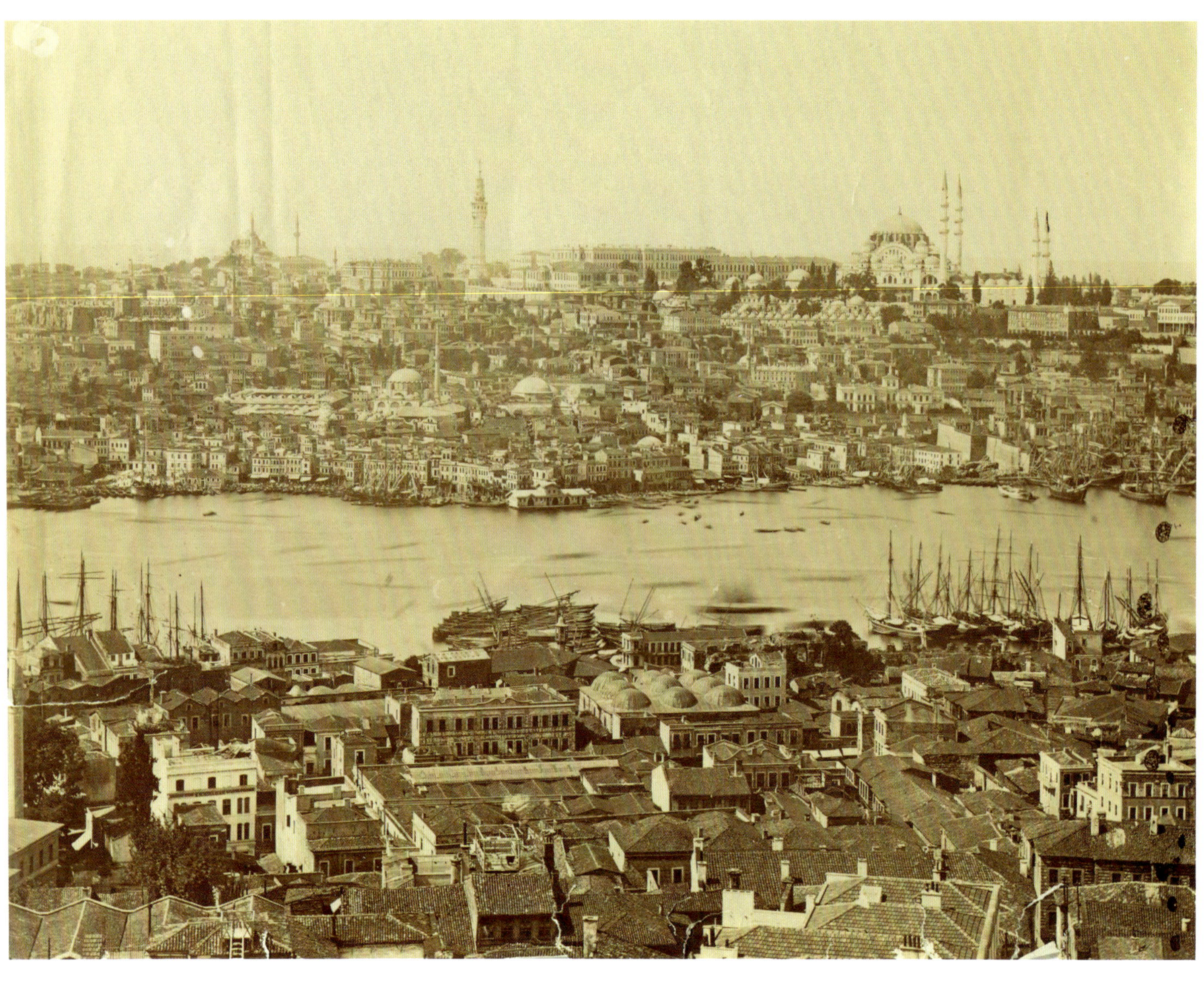

Photographer Unknown
View of Constantinople,
late 19th century
19th-century photographic print,
image size: 8 ³⁄₁₆ × 10 ⁷⁄₁₆ inches
OL.1981.621

Francis Bedford (1815–1894)
Constantinople—View from the Seraskier Tower, Showing the Golden Horn,
1862
19th-century photographic print,
image size: 8 ⅛ × 10 ½ inches,
historic mount: 15 ³⁄₁₆ × 18 ¾ inches
OL.1983.452

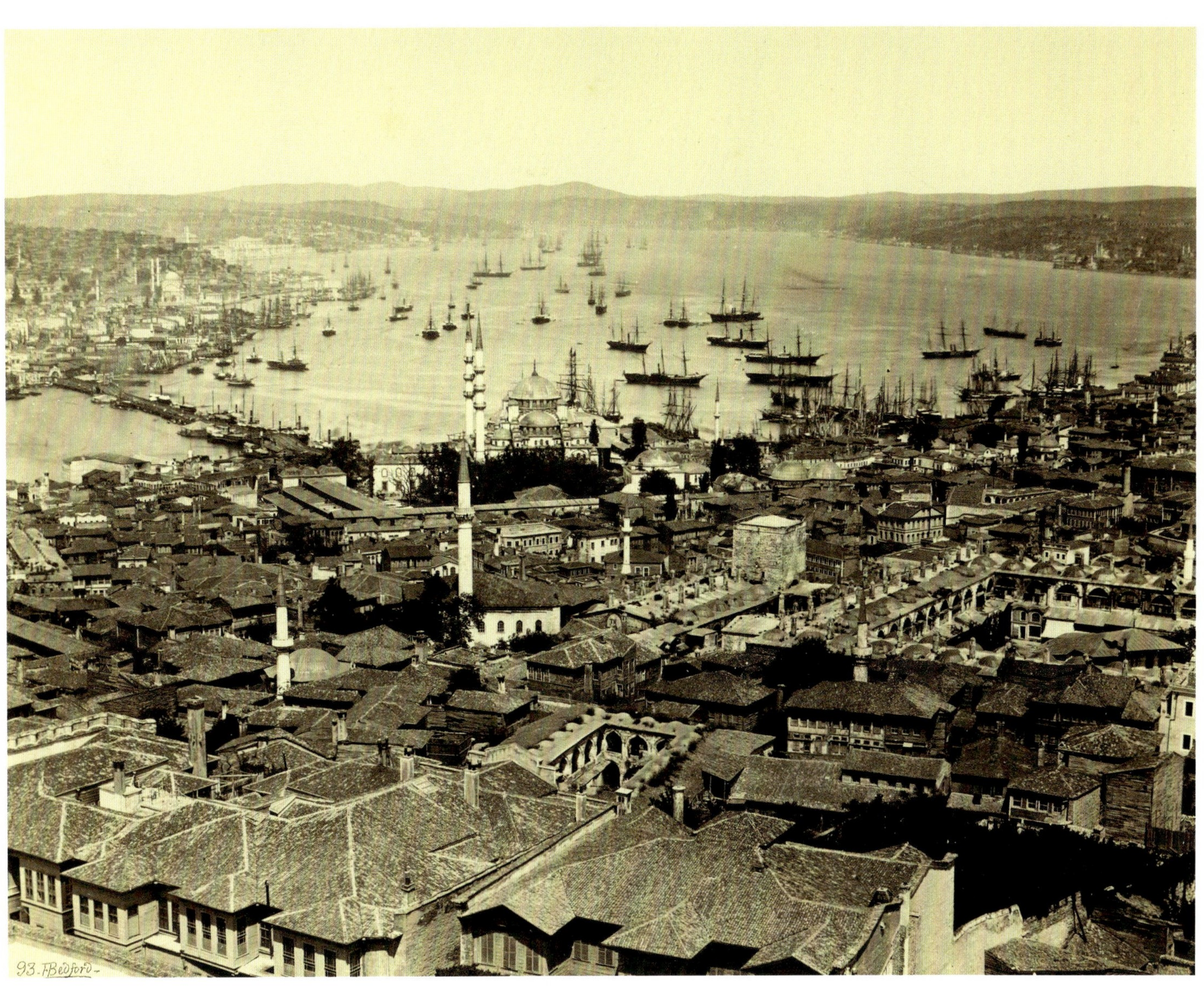
93. F.Bedford

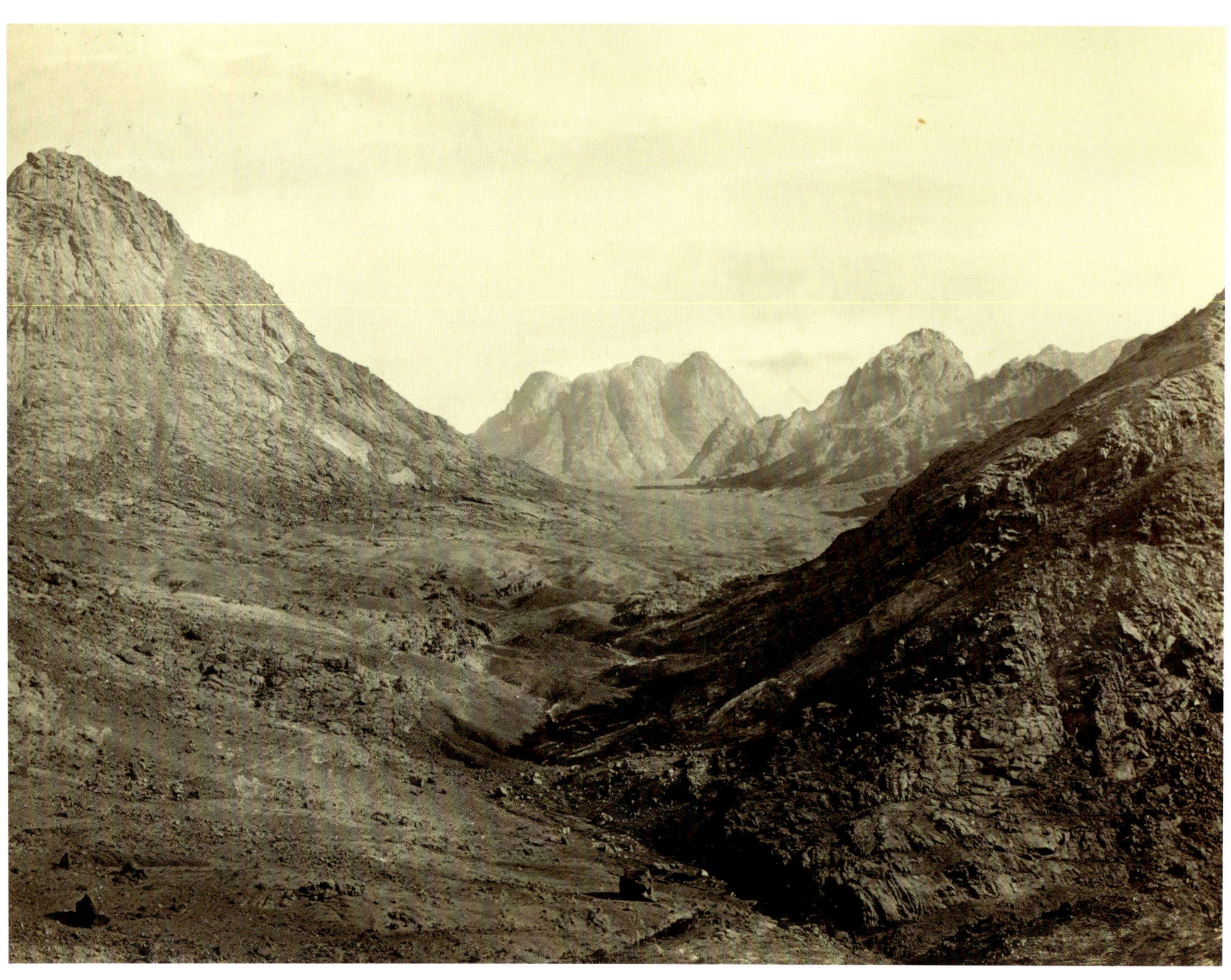

Frank Mason Good (1839–1928)
Mt. Serbal,
ca. 1860s–1870s
19th-century photographic print,
image size: 6 × 8 inches,
historic mount: 10 13⁄16 × 13 ½ inches
OL.1981.673.42

Photographer Unknown
Arch in the Ravine, Petra,
late 19th century
19th-century photographic print,
image size: 6 3⁄16 × 8 3⁄16 inches,
historic mount: 10 13⁄16 × 13 ½ inches
OL.1981.673.7

Photographer Unknown
Waterfall on the Abana River, Damascus,
late 19th century
19th-century photographic print,
image size: 5 ⅞ × 8 1⁄16 inches,
historic mount: 10 ¾ × 13 7⁄16 inches
OL.1981.673.27

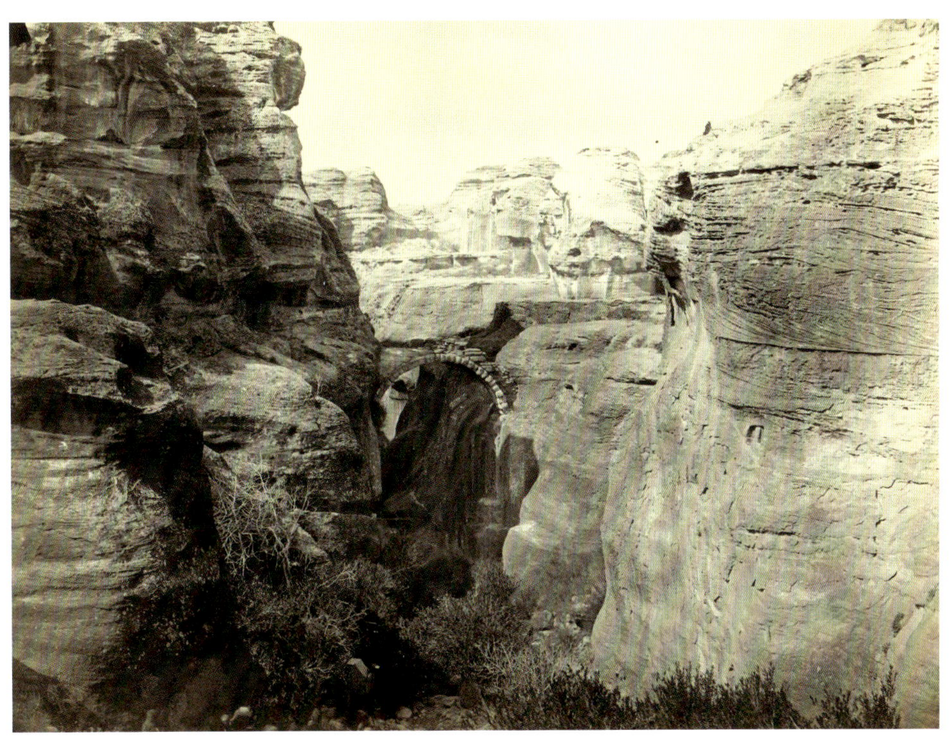

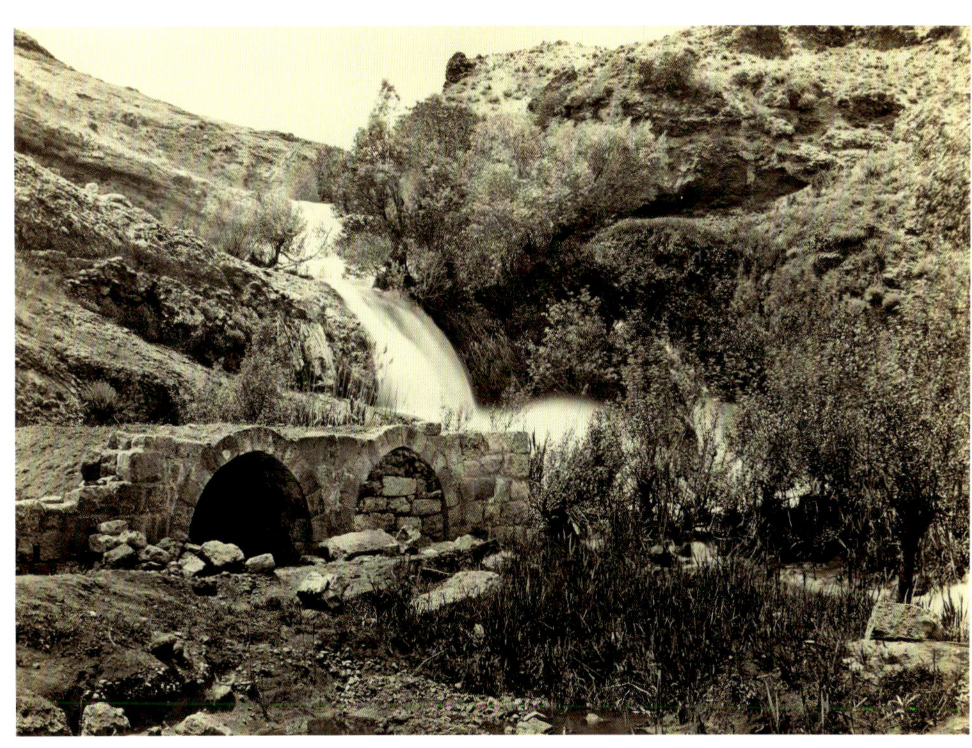

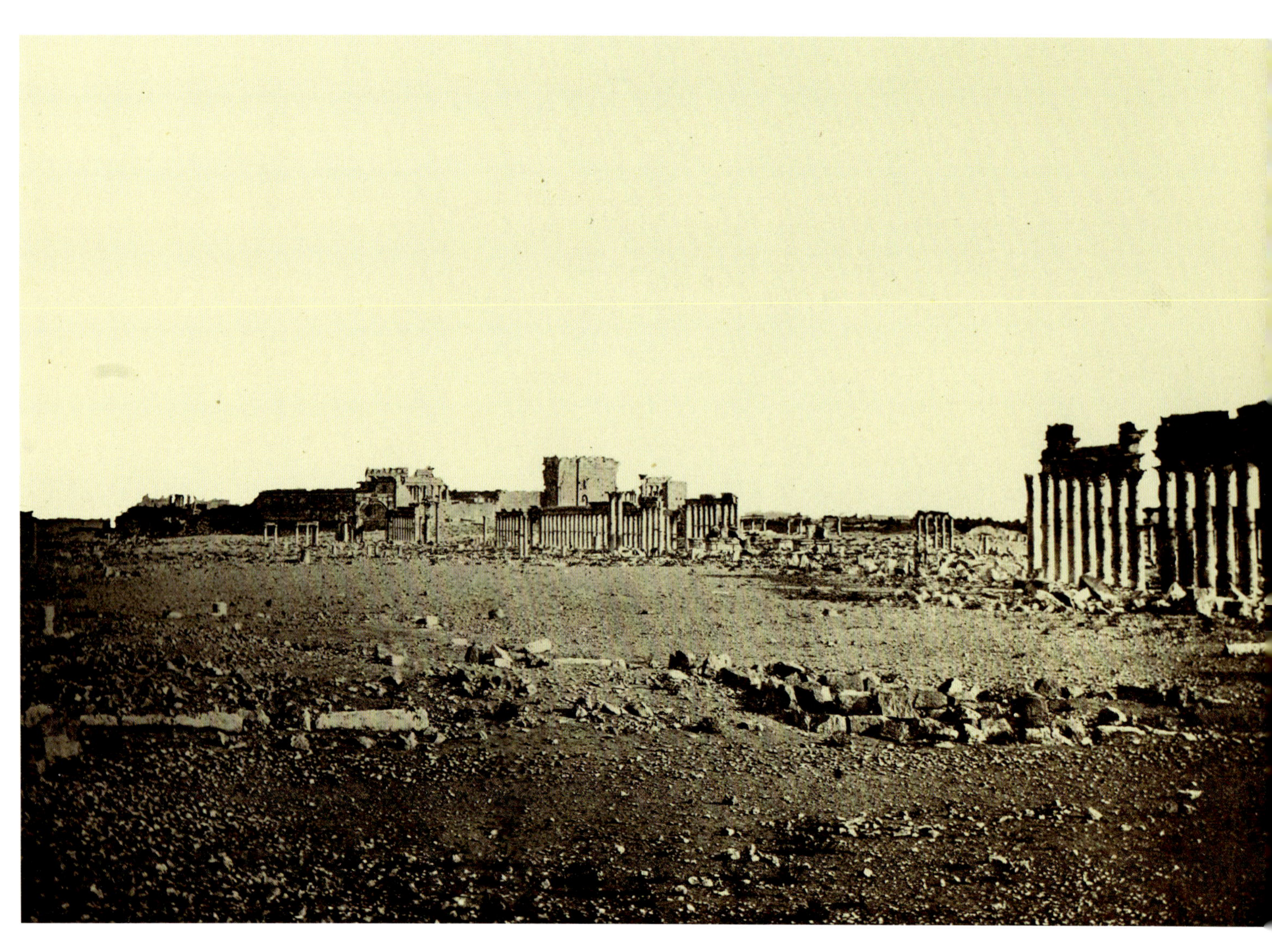

Photographer Unknown
Panoramic View of Palmyra,
late 19th century
19th-century photographic prints,
image size: 4 1⁄16 × 5 13⁄16 (L), 4 1⁄16 × 6 1⁄8 inches (R),
historic mount: 10 5⁄16 × 17 15⁄16 inches
OL.1981.625

Photographer Unknown
Jerusalem,
late 19th century
19th-century photographic print,
image size: 6 1⁄2 × 8 11⁄16 inches,
historic mount: 17 1⁄4 × 24 5⁄8 inches
OL.1985.865

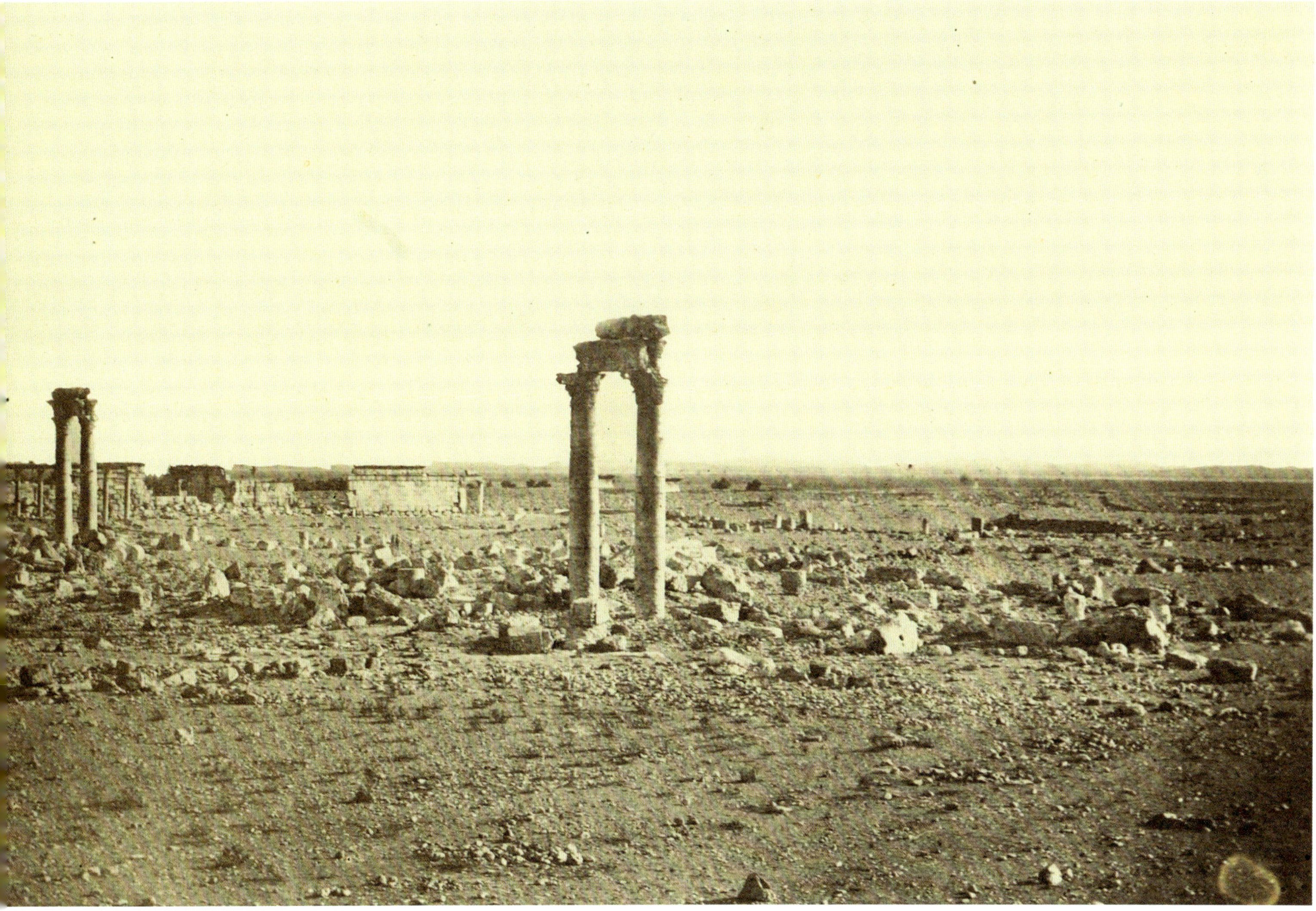

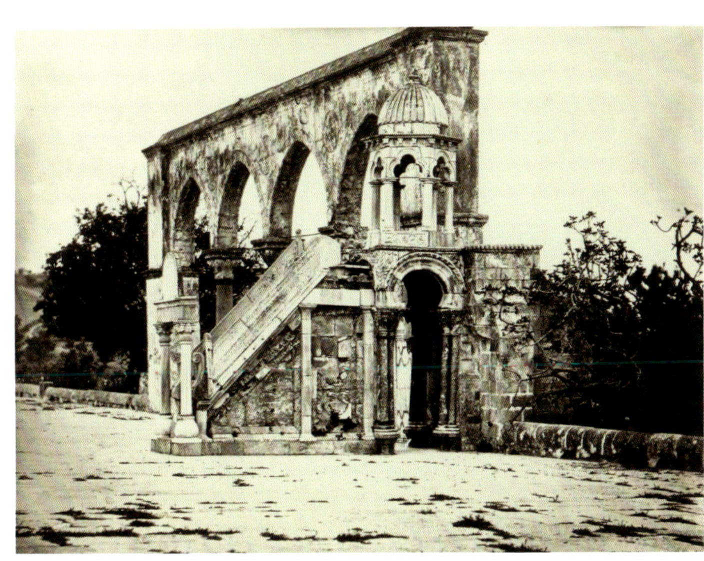

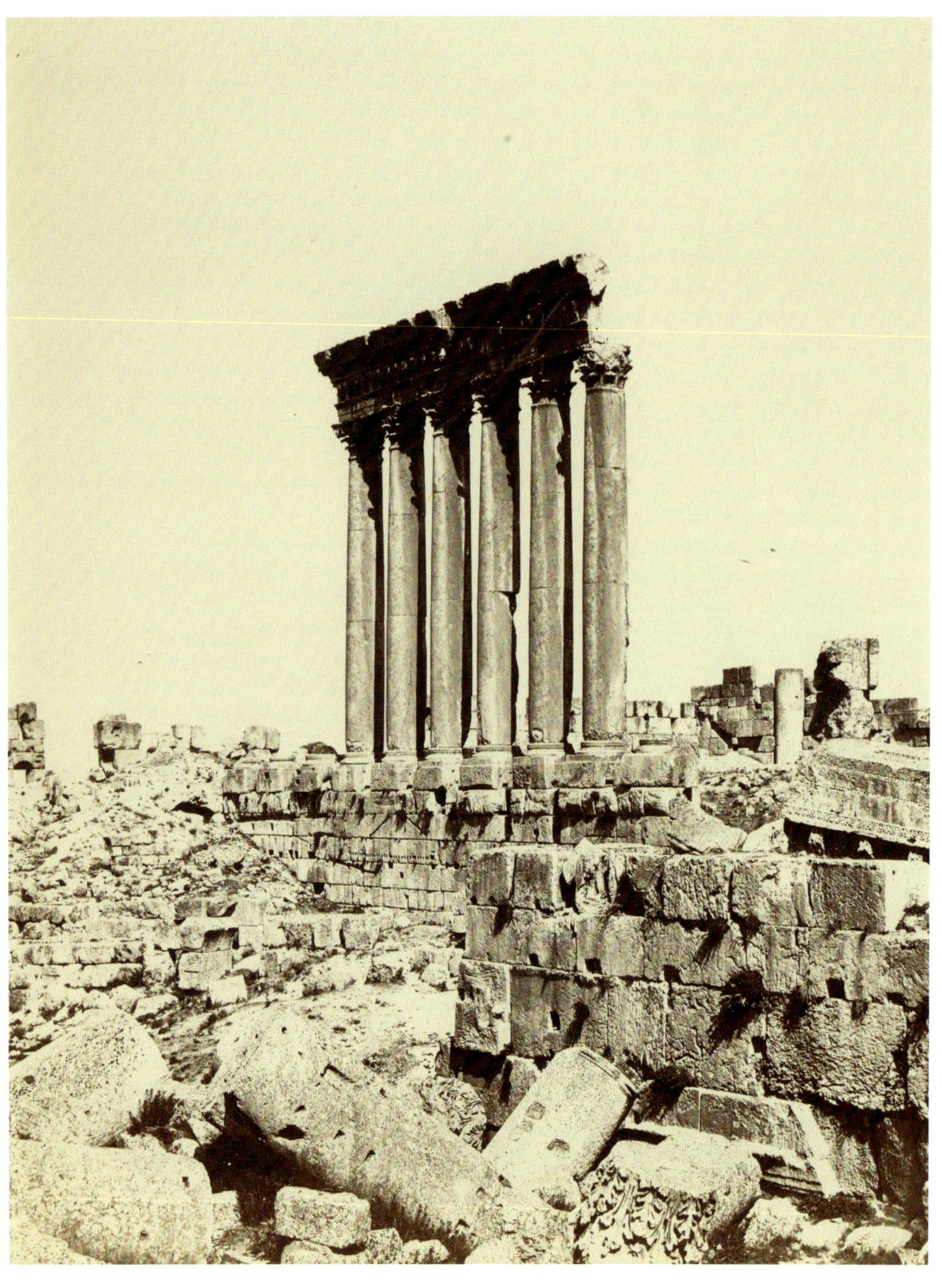

Photographer Unknown
Balbeck,
late 19th century
19th-century photographic print,
image size: 10 ¼ × 7 ¾ inches,
historic mount: 12 ½ × 9 ¼ inches
OL.1981.626.3

Photographer Unknown
Vue générale du Temple de Jupiter, Balbeck,
late 19th century
19th-century photographic print,
image size: 6 ⅛ × 9 ½ inches,
historic mount: 9 5⁄16 × 12 ¾ inches
OL.1981.626.1

Palestine Exploration Fund
Ruins of Synagogue, Meion,
late 19th century
19th-century photographic print,
image size: 6 ⅜ × 8 7⁄16 inches,
historic mount: 11 ⅜ × 14 ¾ inches
OL.1983.1341.13

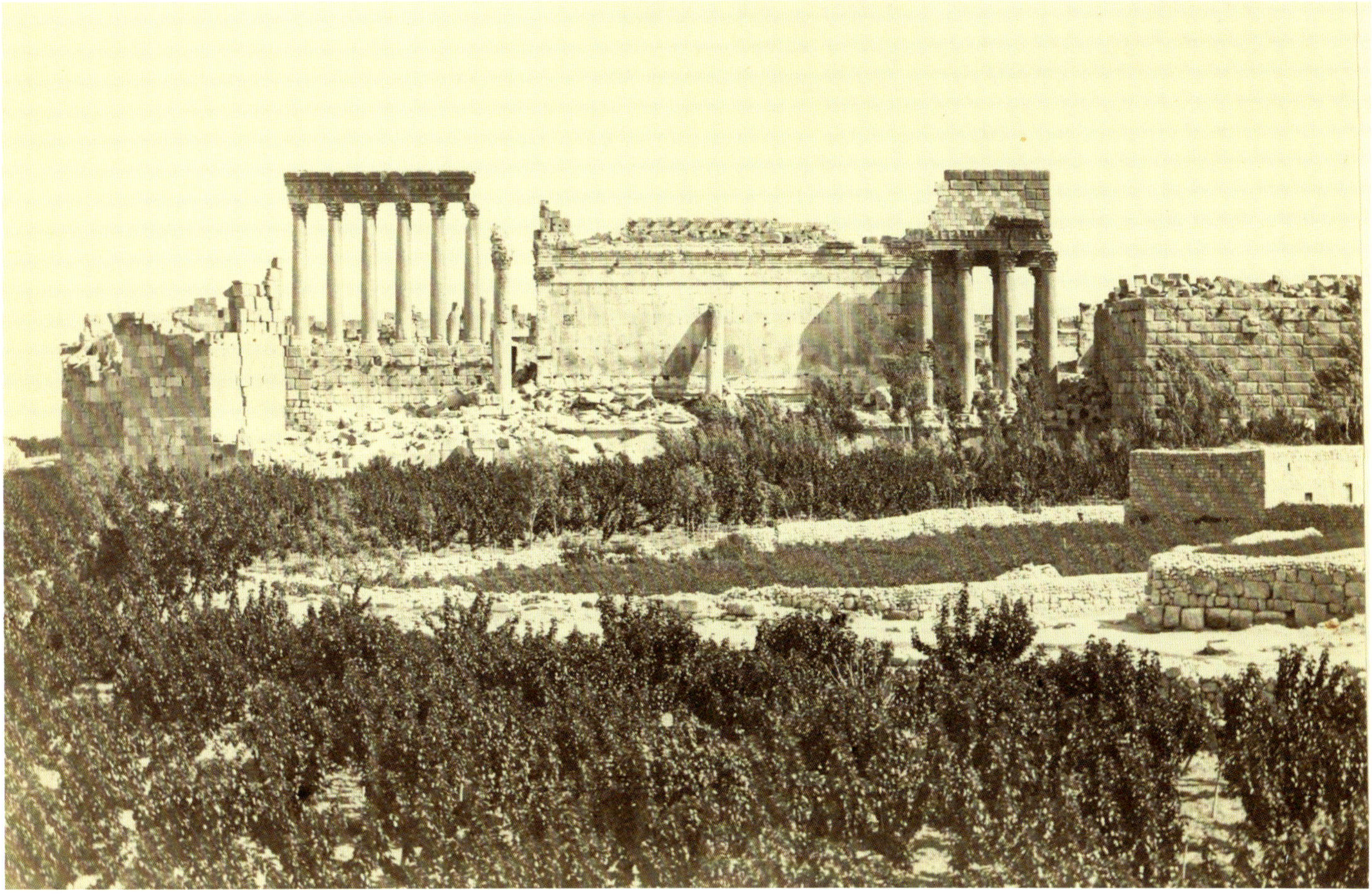

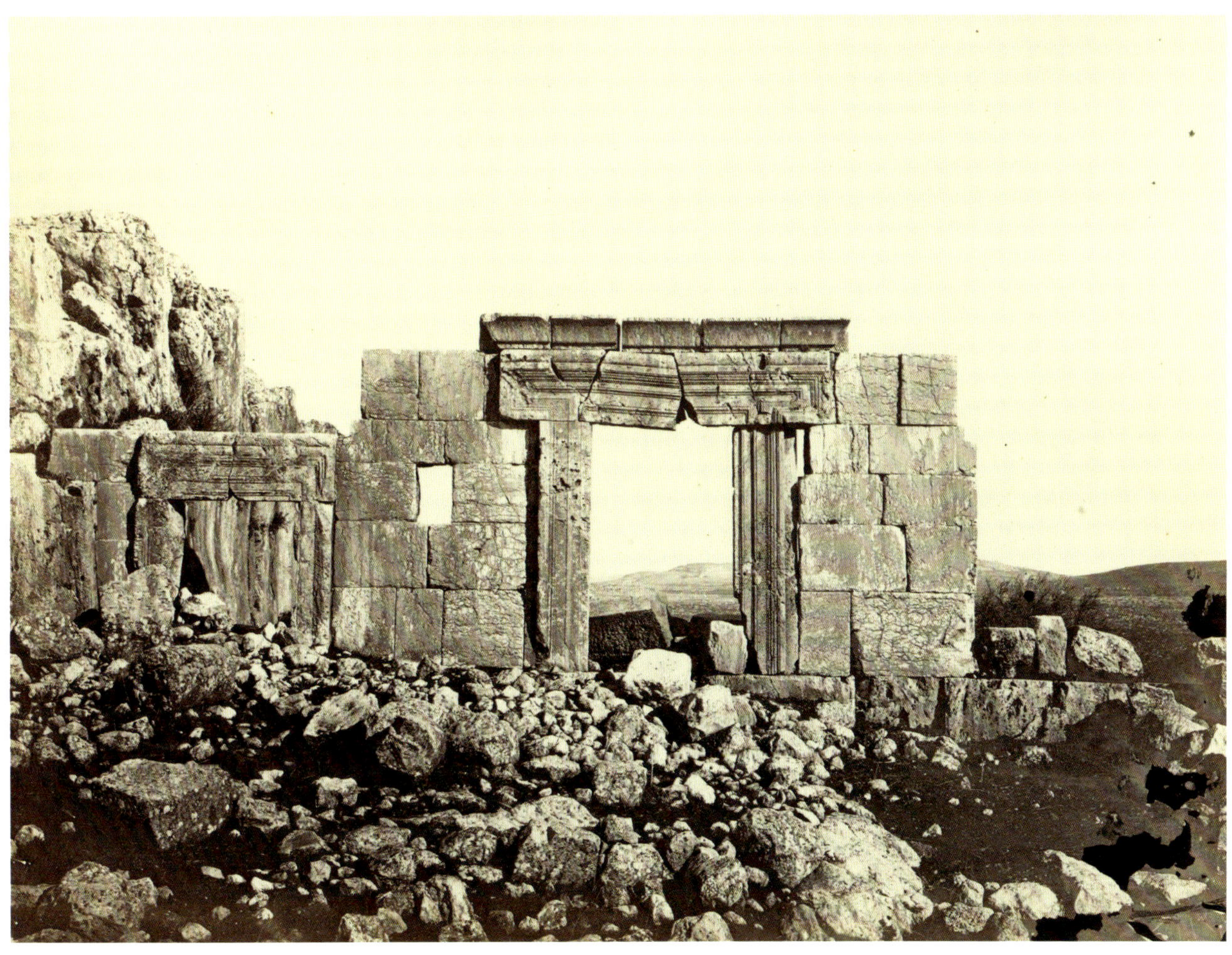

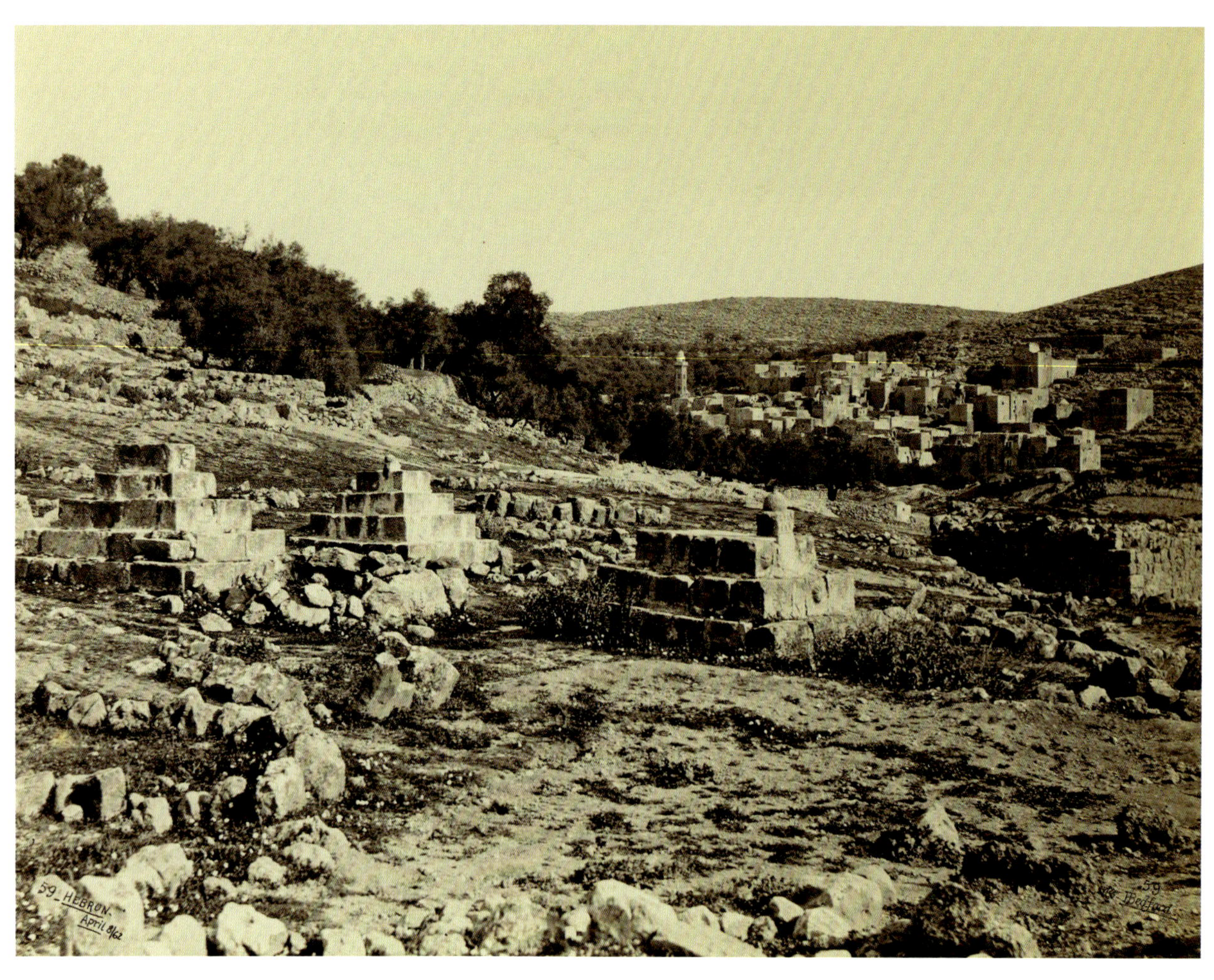
59_HEBRON.
April 8/62
59
Bedford

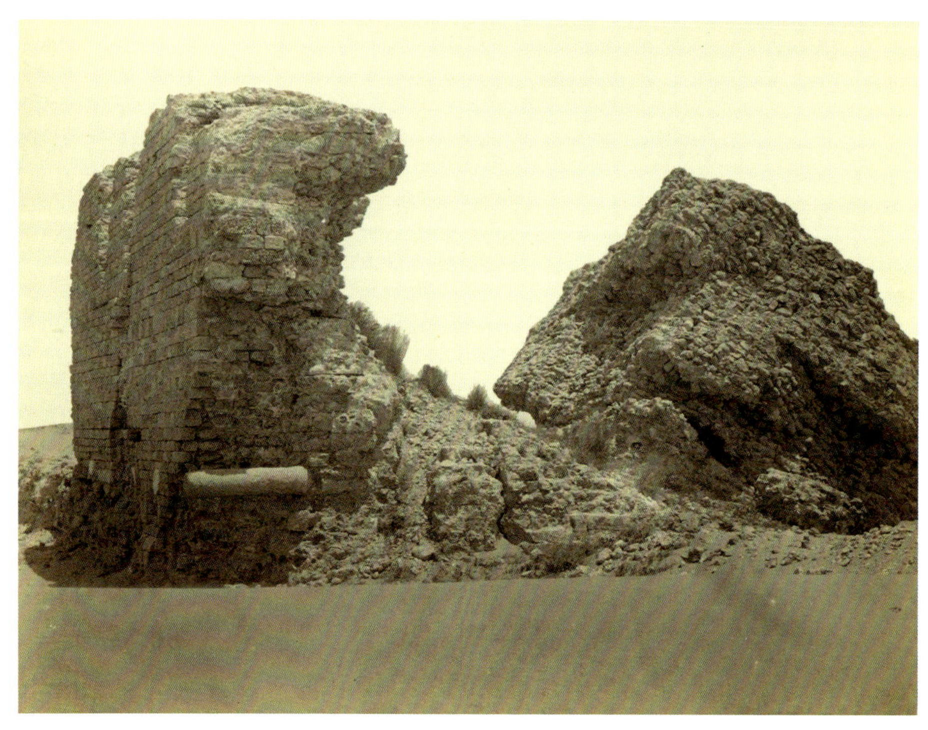

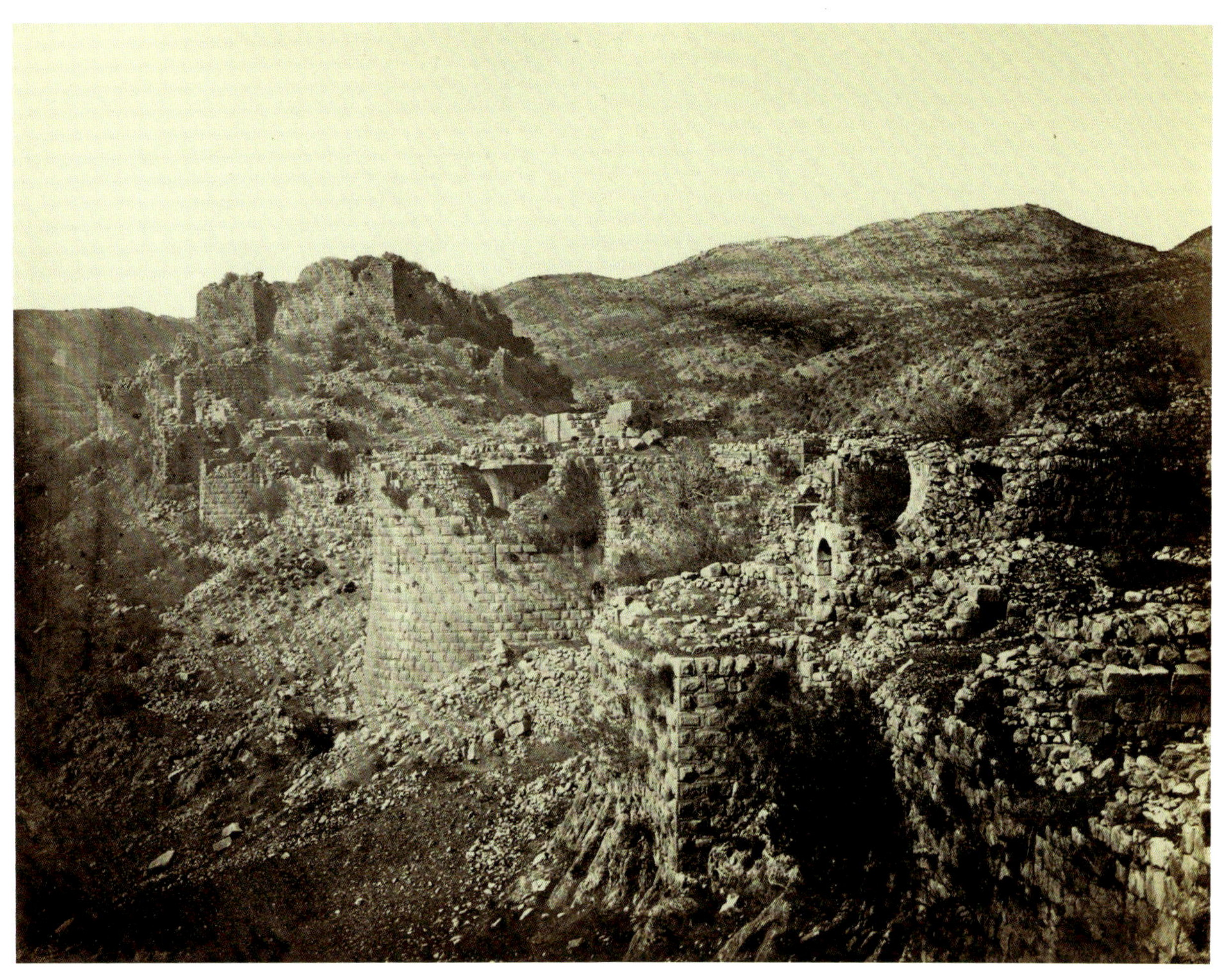

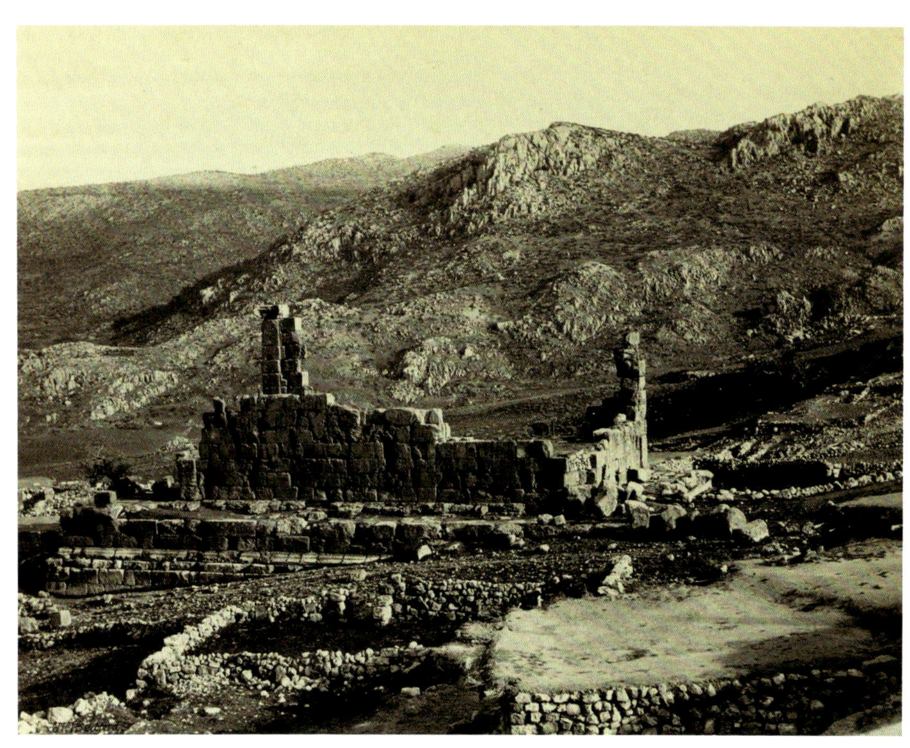

Francis Bedford (1815–1894)
Hebron,
1862
19th-century photographic print,
image size: 8 ⅛ × 10 ½ inches,
historic mount: 15 ¼ × 18 ¾ inches
OL.1983.447

Palestine Exploration Fund
Ashkelon: Ruins of an Old Wall, East Side,
late 19th century
19th-century photographic print,
image size: 6 ½ × 8 7⁄16 inches,
historic mount: 11 3⁄16 × 14 ⅞ inches
OL.1983.1341.50

Palestine Exploration Fund
Castle, Banias, From South-East Angle,
late 19th century
19th-century photographic print,
image size: 6 7⁄16 × 8 ⅜ inches,
historic mount: 11 3⁄16 × 14 ¾ inches
OL.1983.1341.3

Francis Bedford (1815–1894)
Deir-el-Ashayir (Temple Ruins, Doir al Asha-ir, Beqaa, Lebanon),
1862
19th-century photographic print,
image size: 8 × 10 ½ inches,
historic mount: 15 3⁄16 × 18 ¾ inches
OL.1983.446

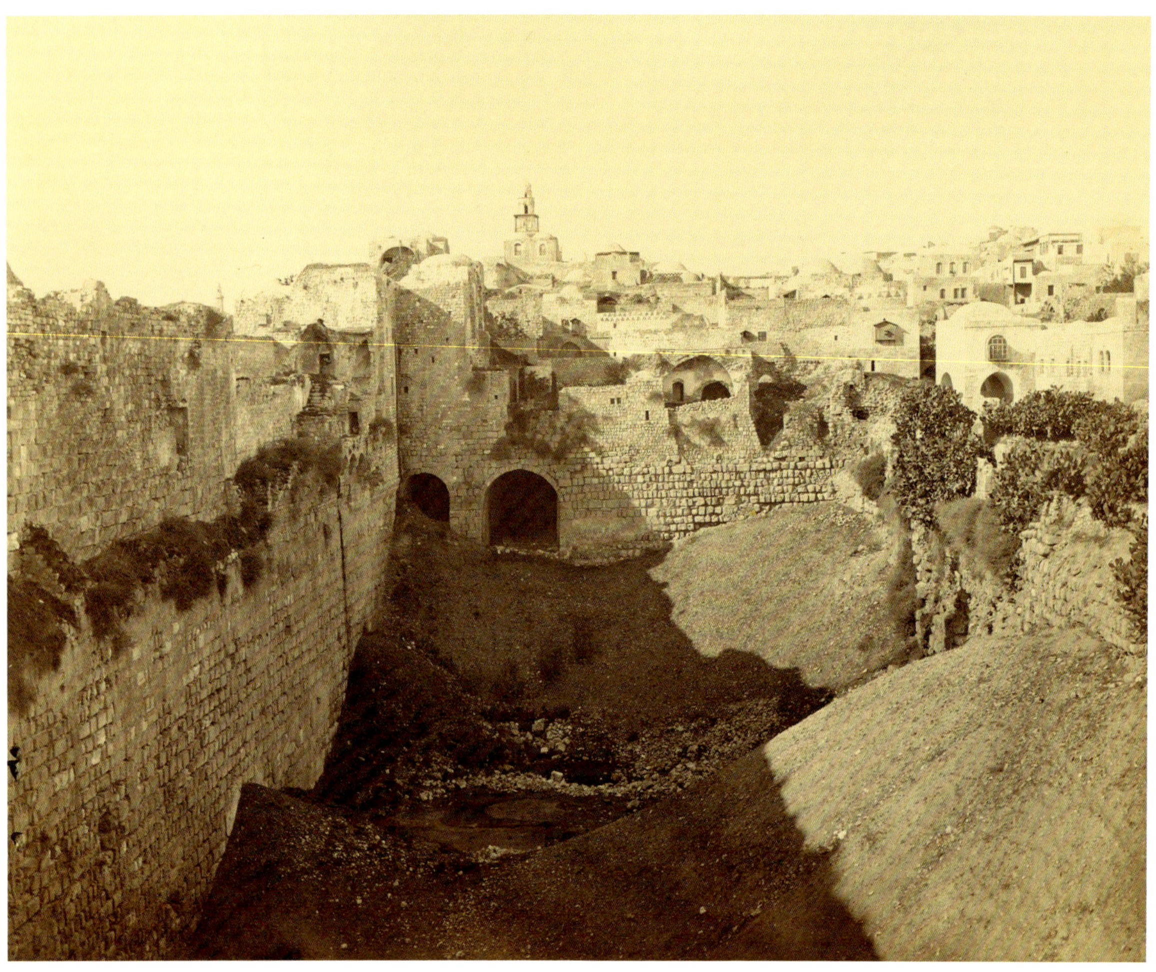

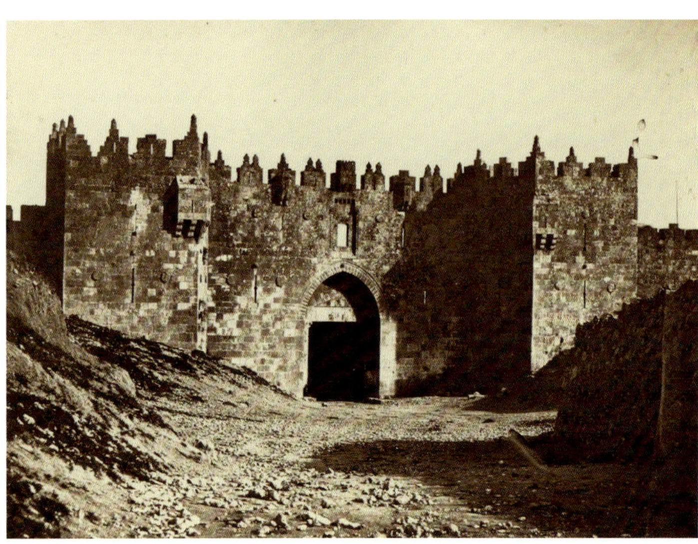

Peter Bergheim (1813–1895)
Pool of Bethesda,
ca. 1866–67
19th-century photographic print,
image size: 10 × 12 5⁄16 inches,
historic mount: 14 1⁄8 × 16 7⁄8 inches
OL.1997.41.1

Photographer Unknown
Jerusalem,
late 19th century
19th-century photographic print,
image size: 6 3⁄8 × 8 3⁄4 inches,
historic mount: 17 5⁄16 × 24 5⁄8 inches
OL.1985.867

Palestine Exploration Fund
Ruins at Mezrah,
late 19th century
19th-century photographic print,
image size: 6 3⁄8 × 8 3⁄8 inches,
historic mount: 11 1⁄4 × 14 15⁄16 inches
OL.1983.1341.23

Palestine Exploration Fund
Rock-Hewn Tomb, Tibneh,
late 19th century
19th-century photographic print,
image size: 6 1⁄8 × 8 3⁄8 inches,
historic mount: 11 3⁄16 × 14 13⁄16 inches
OL.1983.1341.22

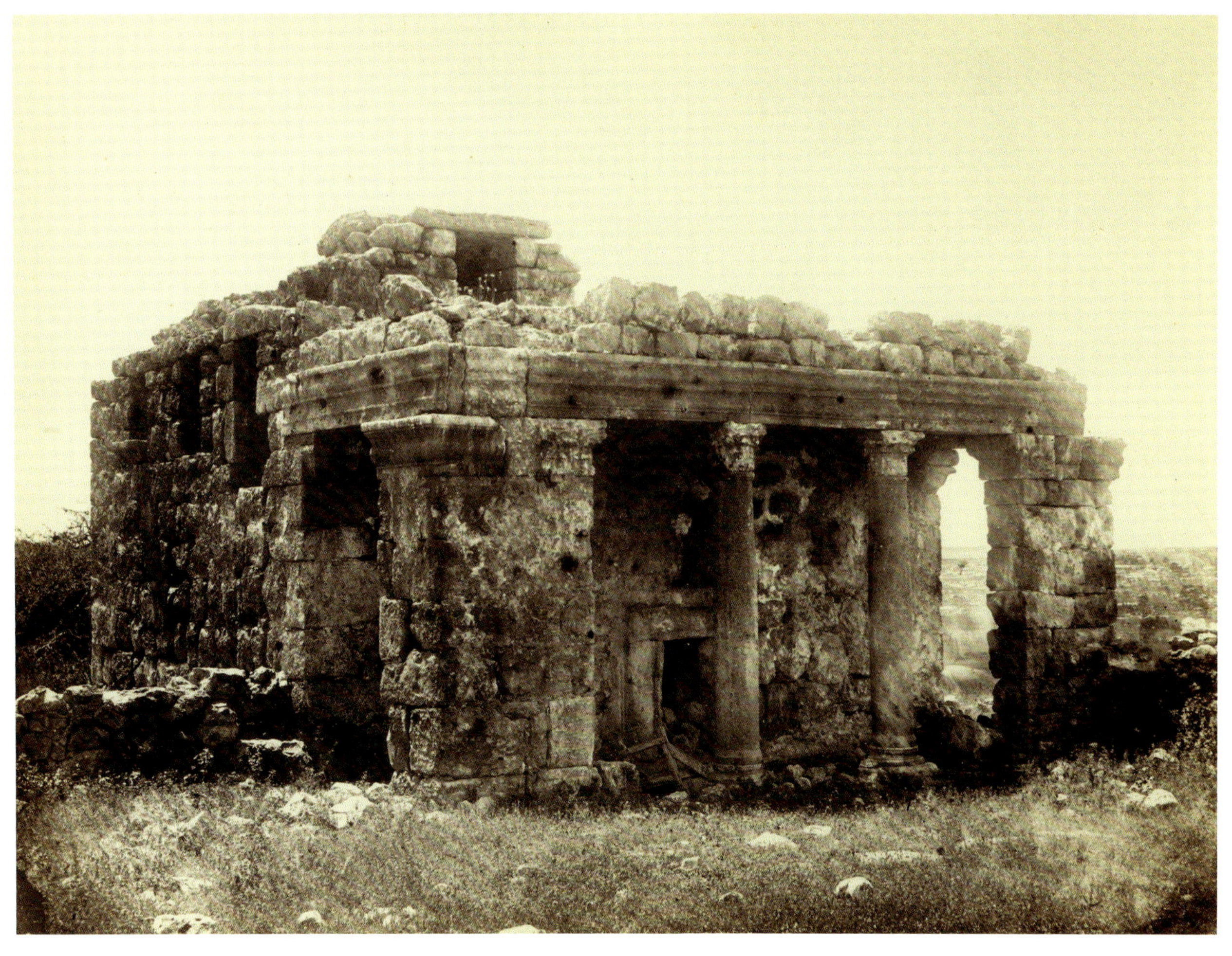

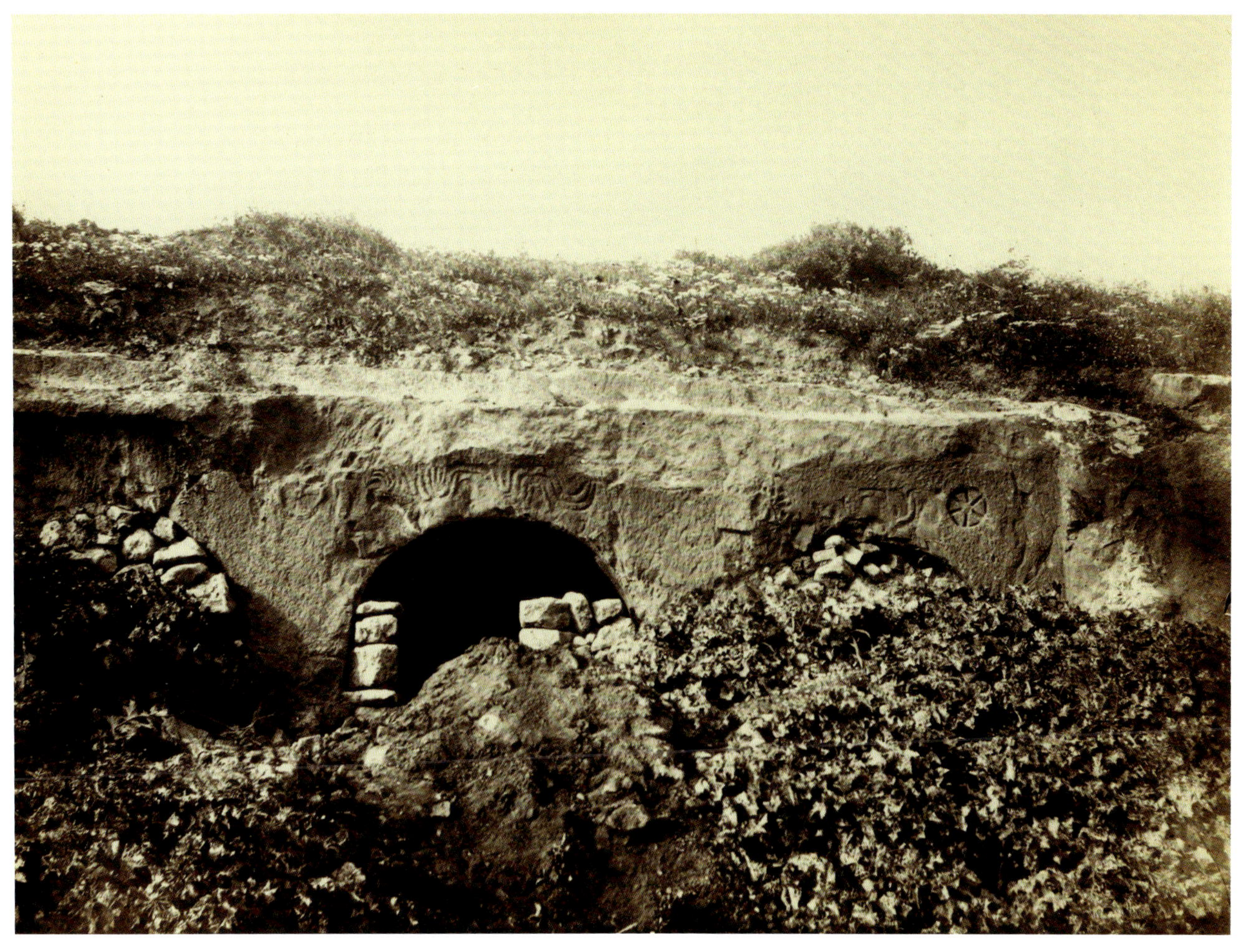

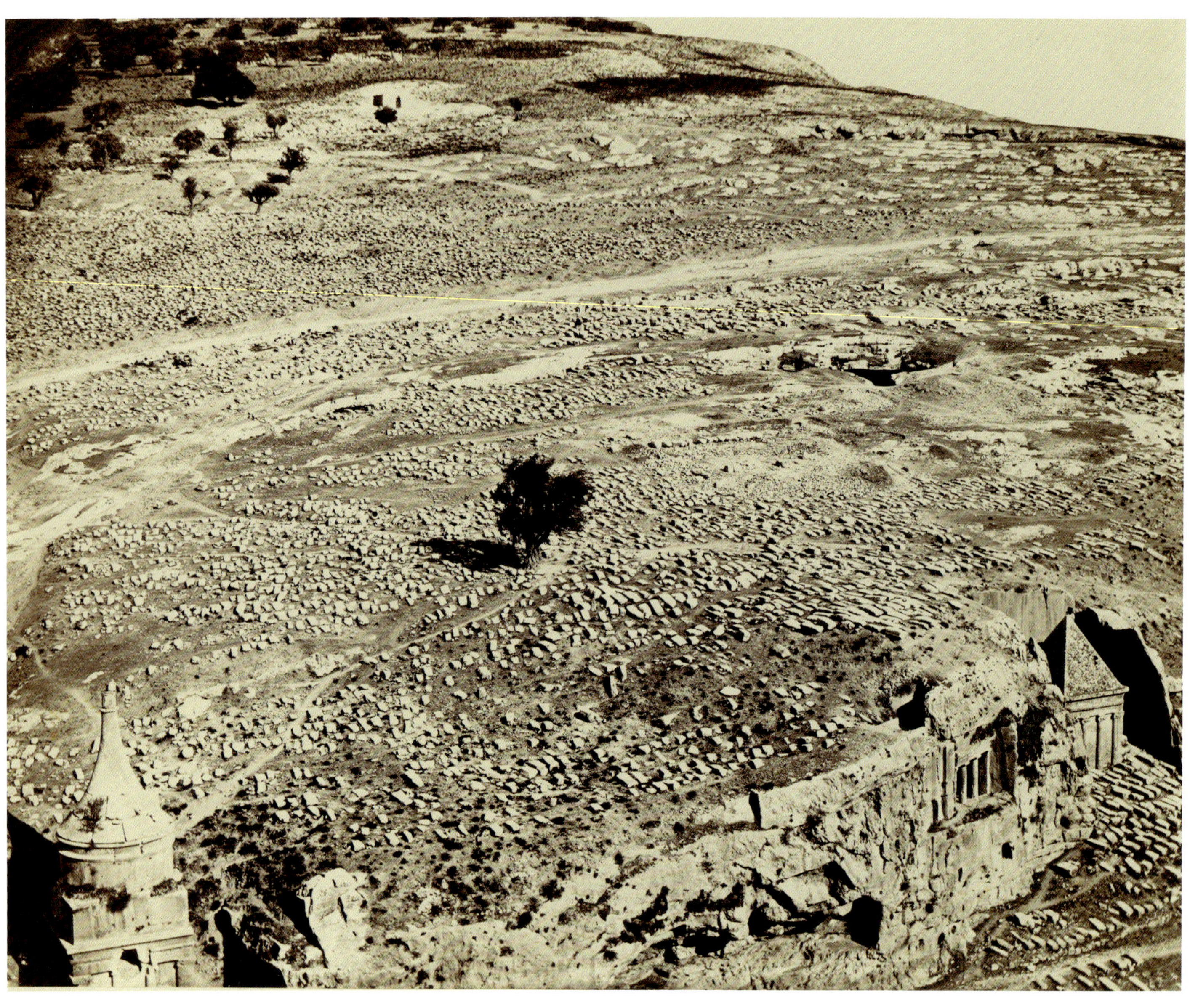

Photographer Unknown
Vallée du Gesophat, Jerusalem,
late 19th century
19th-century photographic print,
image size: 8 × 10 inches,
historic mount: 9 3⁄16 × 12 7⁄16 inches
OL.1981.538

Photographer Unknown
Valley of Josaphat,
late 19th century
19th-century photographic print,
image size: 10 × 12 ¼ inches,
historic mount: 14 ⅛ × 16 15⁄16 inches
OL.1997.41.3

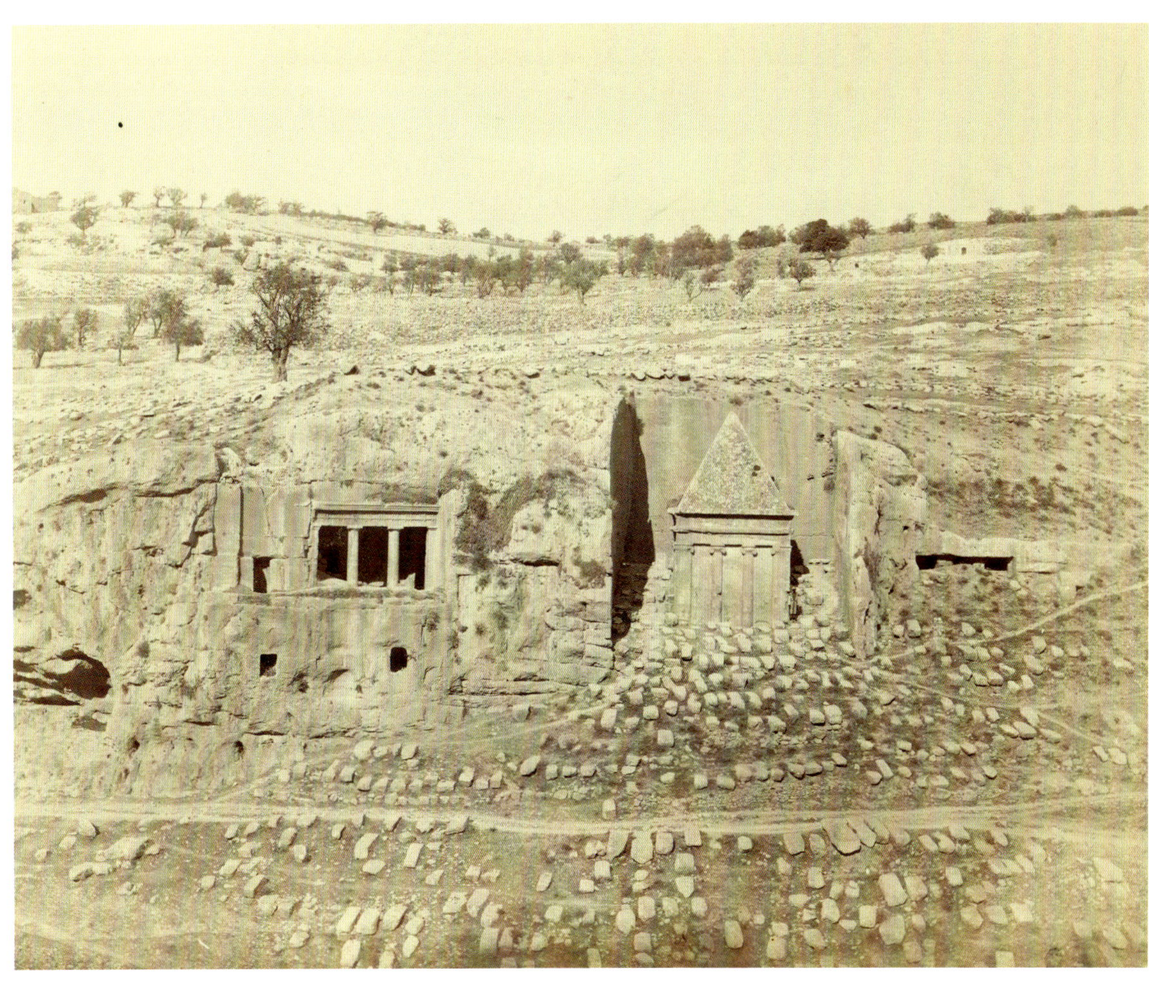

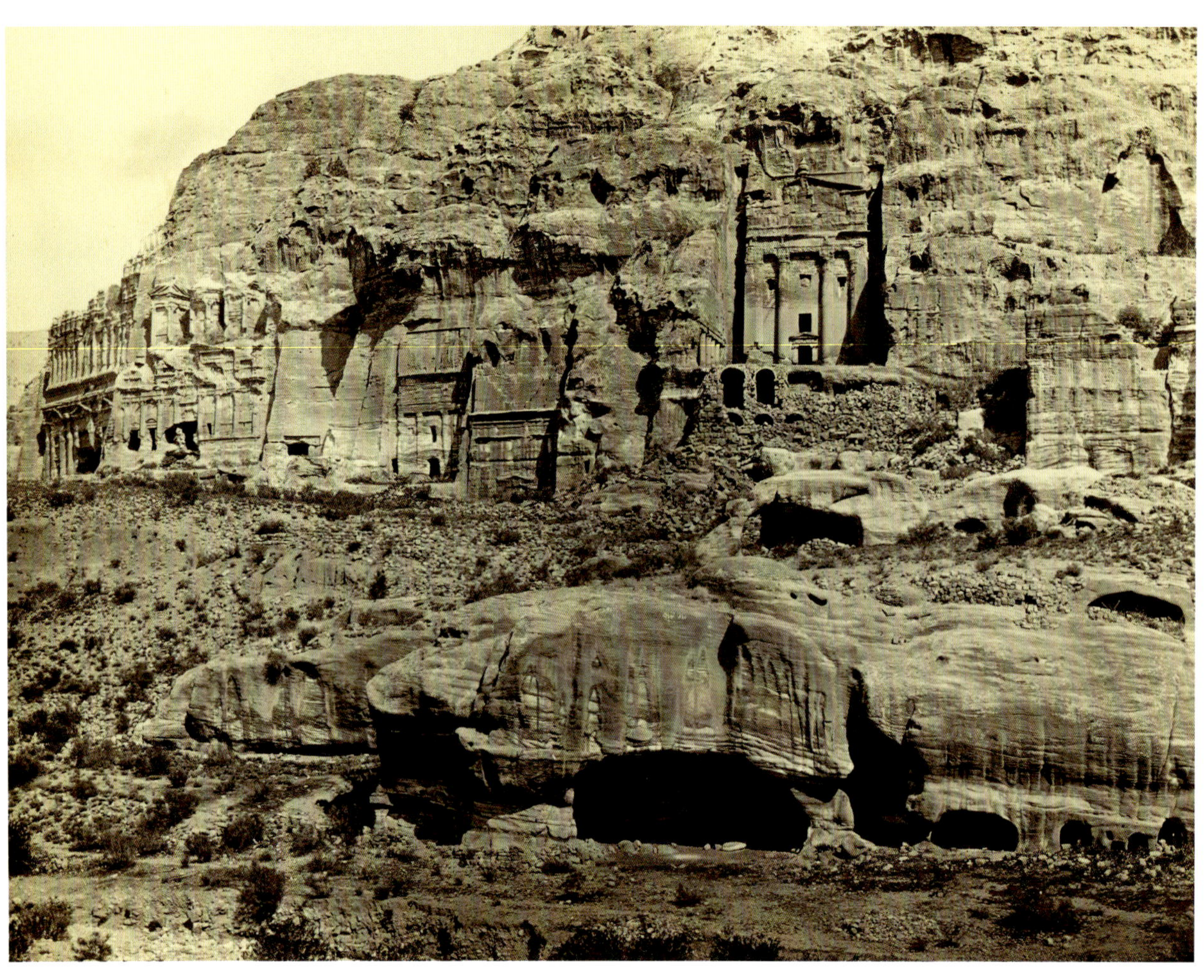

Photographer Unknown
Western Cliffs of Petra,
late 19th century
19th-century photographic print,
image size: 6 1/16 × 7 7/8 inches,
historic mount: 10 3/4 × 13 7/16 inches
OL.1981.618

Photographer Unknown
Petra,
late 19th century
19th-century photographic print,
image size: 8 5/8 × 6 7/16 inches,
historic mount: 24 5/8 × 17 1/4 inches
OL.1983.1367

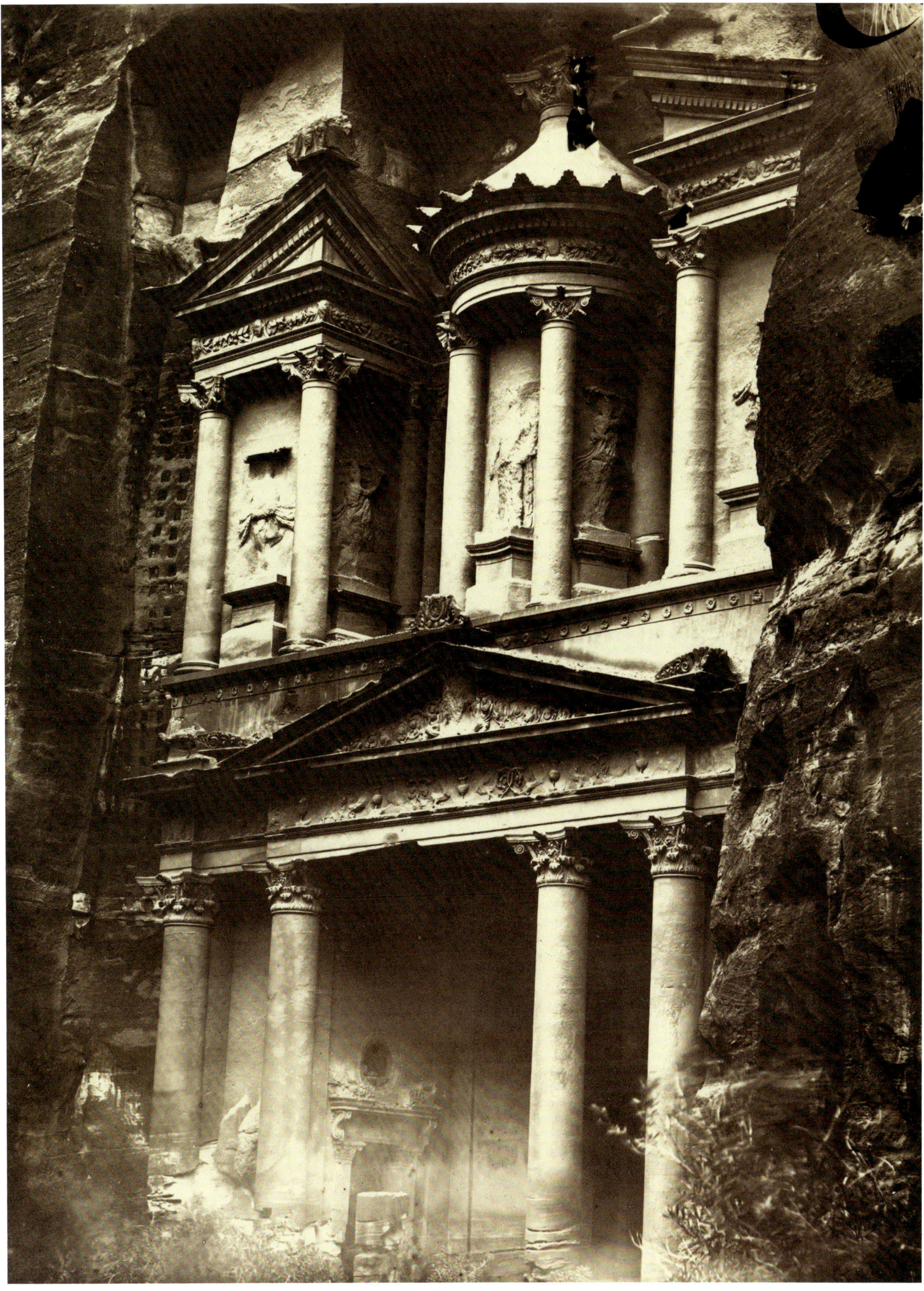

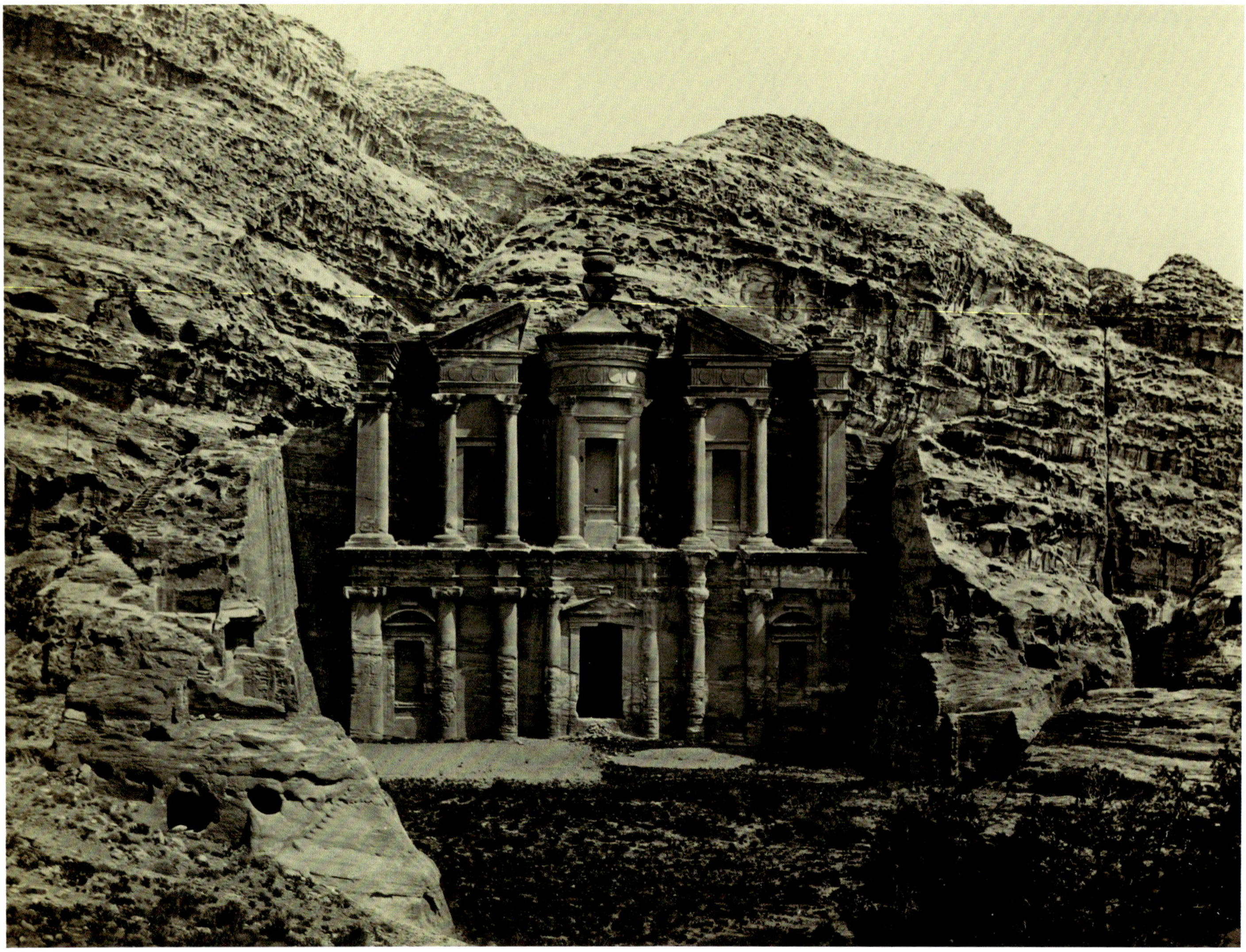

Photographer Unknown
El Deir, Petra,
late 19th century
19th-century photographic print,
image size: 6 × 8 1/16 inches,
historic mount: 10 11/16 × 13 7/16 inches
OL.1981.673.10

Photographer Unknown
Petra,
late 19th century
19th-century photographic print,
image size: 6 1/2 × 8 11/16 inches,
historic mount: 17 1/8 × 24 9/16 inches
OL.1985.842

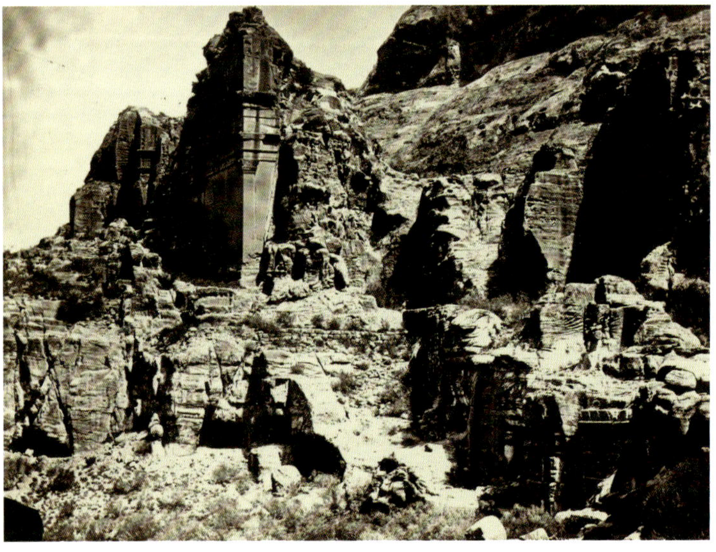

Photographer Unknown
Ruins of a Palace on South Cliff, Petra,
late 19th century
19th-century photographic print,
image size: 6 × 8 1/16 inches,
historic mount: 10 13/16 × 13 7/16 inches
OL.1981.673.9

Photographer Unknown
Petra,
late 19th century
19th-century photographic print,
image size: 6 7/16 × 8 11/16 inches,
historic mount: 17 1/8 × 24 9/16 inches
OL.1985.841

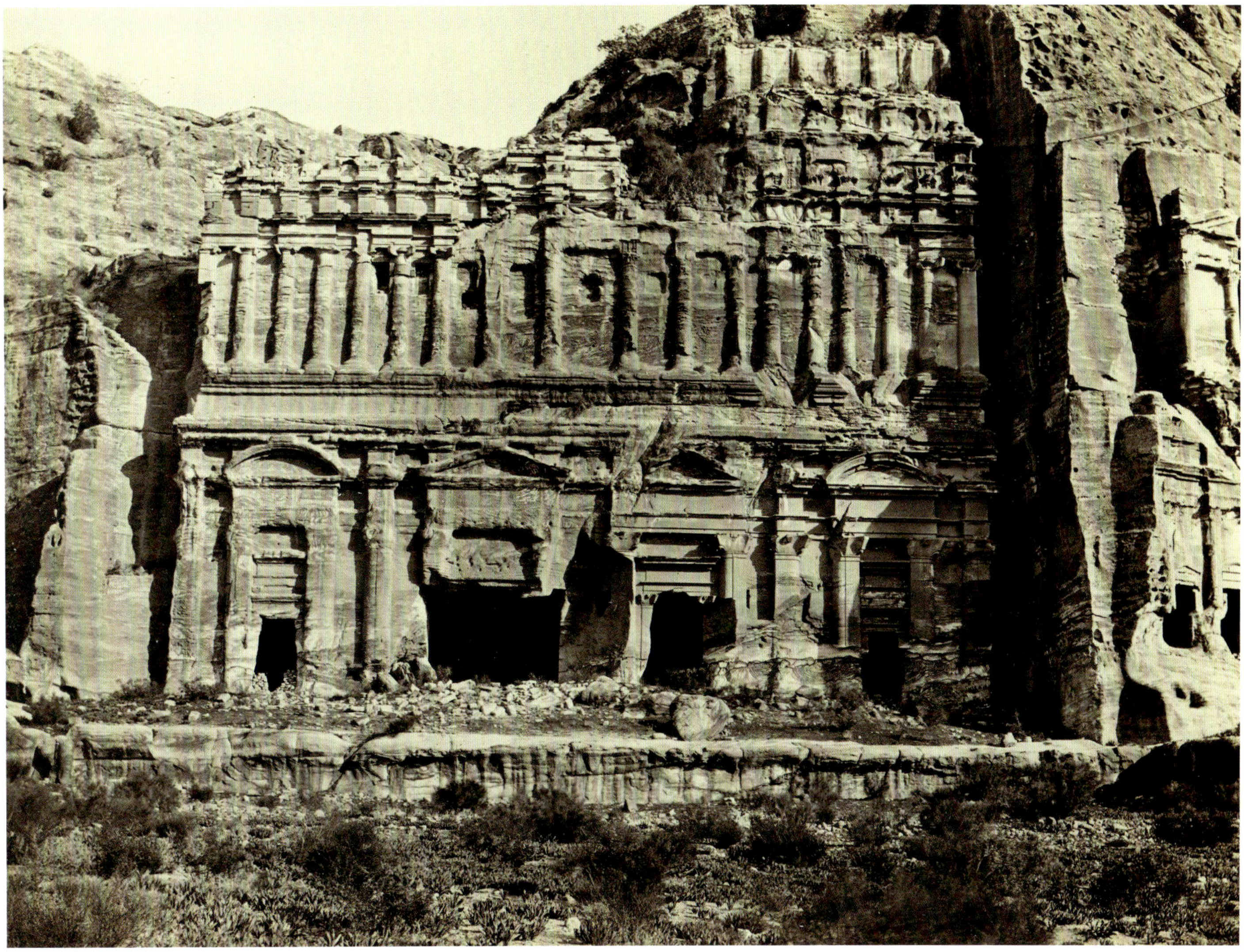

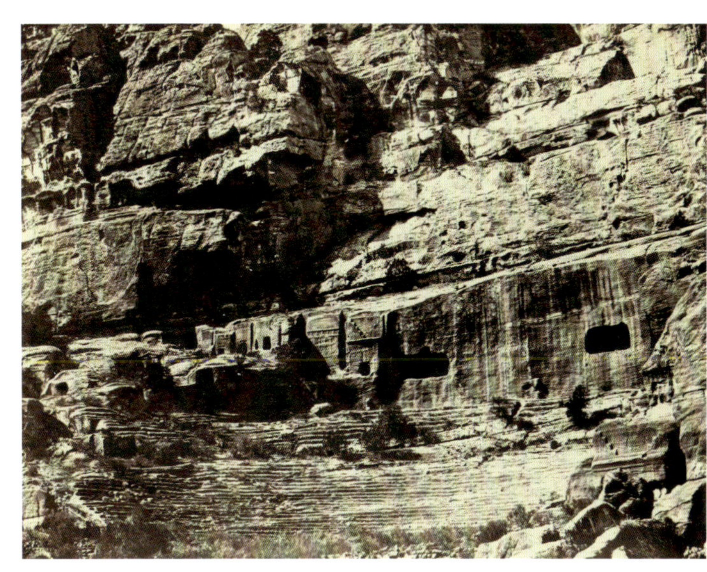

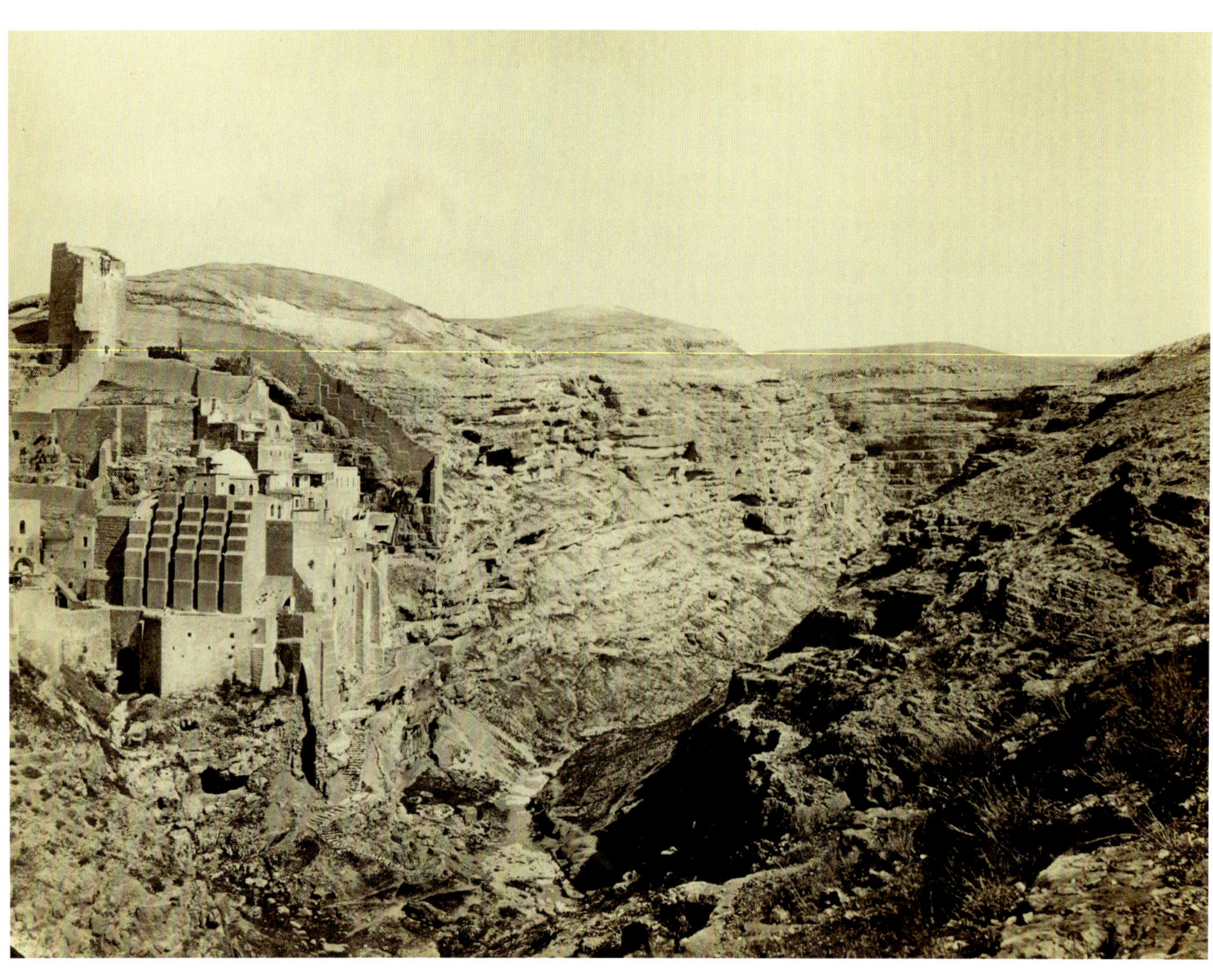

Frank Mason Good (1839–1928)
The Wilderness of Engedi
—The Convent of Mar Saba,
ca. 1866–1867
19th-century photographic print,
image size: 6 ⅛ × 8 ⅛ inches,
historic mount: 10 ¾ × 13 7⁄16 inches
OL.1981.673.60

Wilhelm Hammerschmidt (active 19th century)
Siloam, Village près de Jerusalem,
ca. 1860s–1870s
19th-century photographic print,
image size: 8 11⁄16 × 11 13⁄16 inches,
historic mount: 12 15⁄16 × 15 1⁄16 inches
OL.1997.37.1

Palestine Exploration Fund
Es-Salt: General View of Town,
late 19th century
19th-century photographic print,
image size: 6 ½ × 8 3⁄16 inches,
historic mount: 11 ¼ × 14 ⅞ inches
OL.1983.1341.65

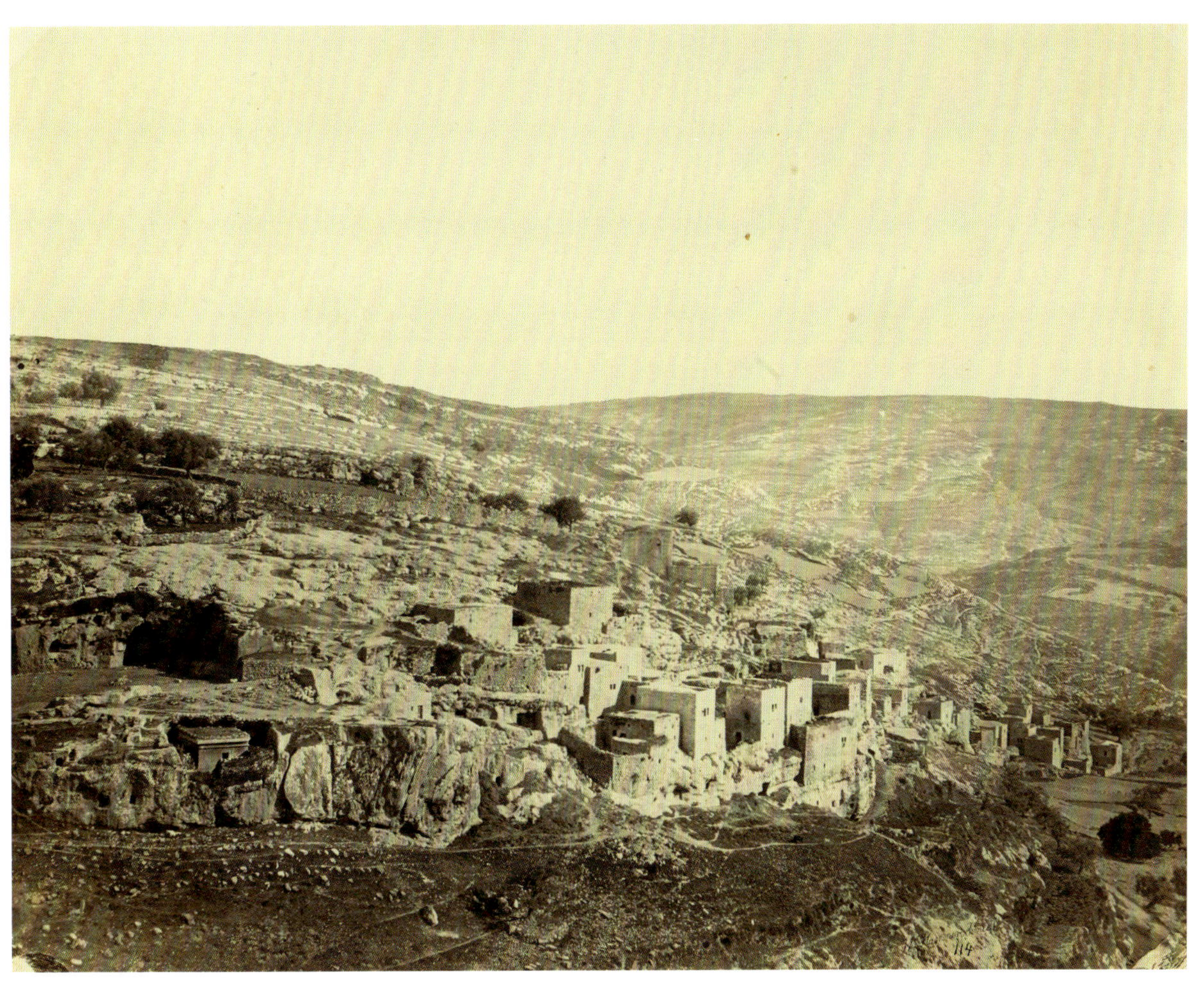

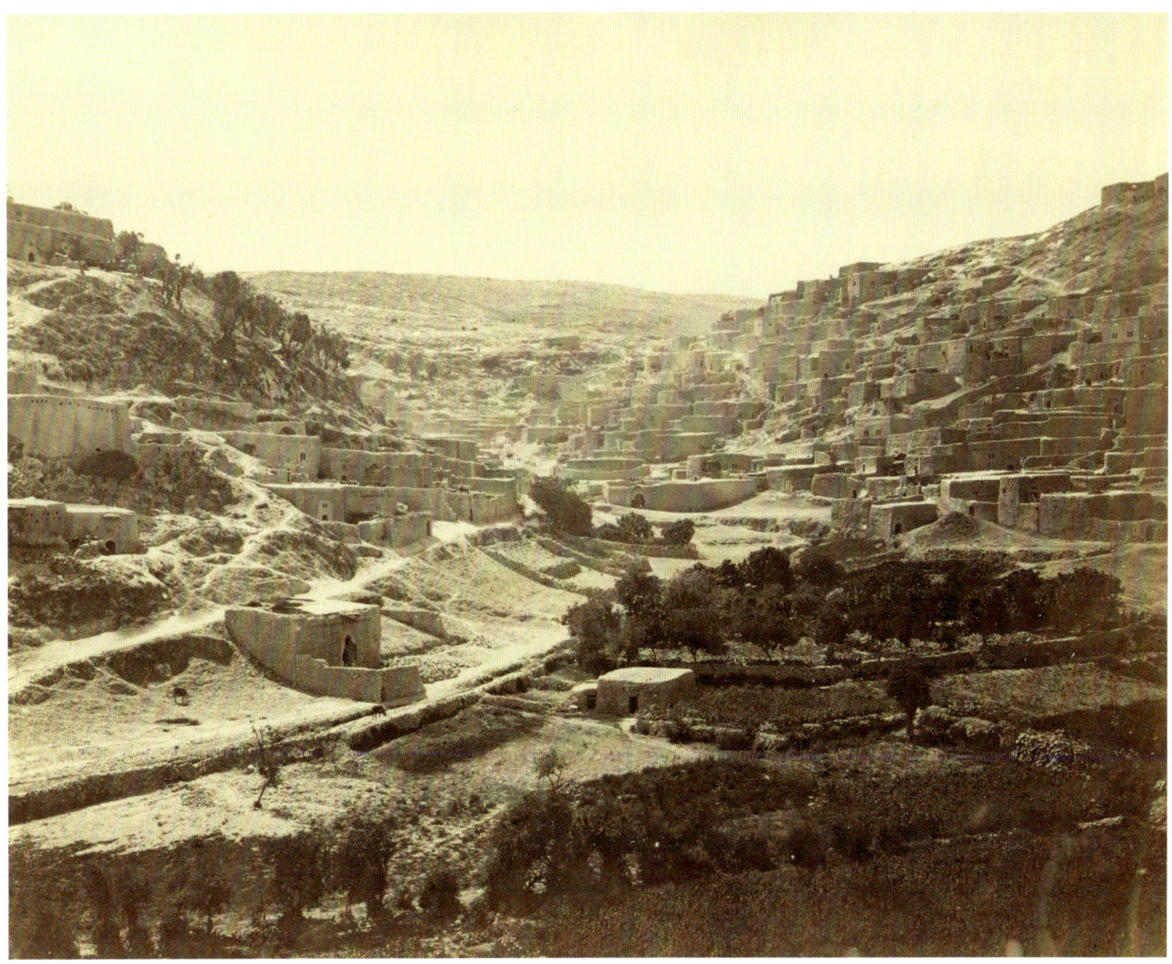

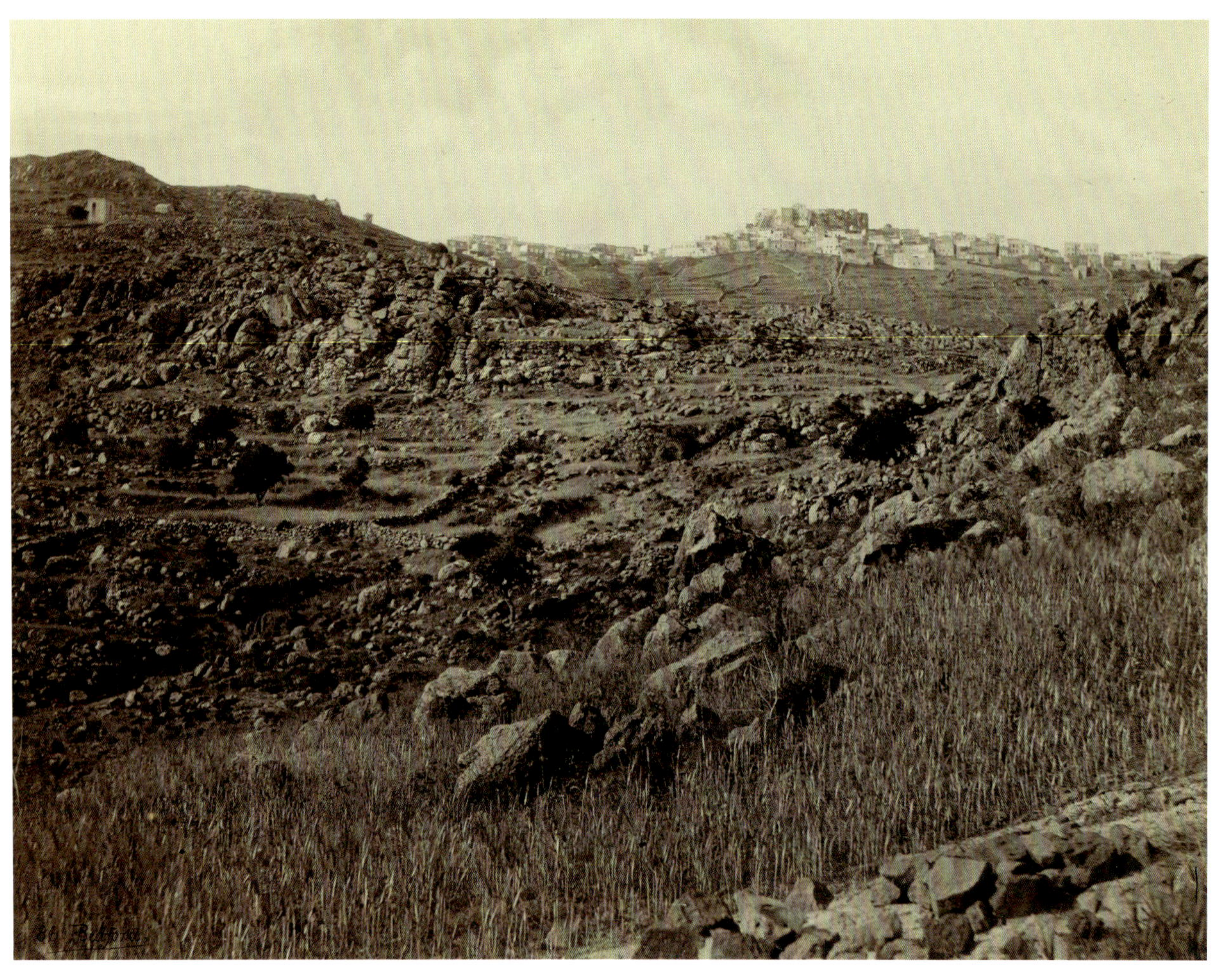

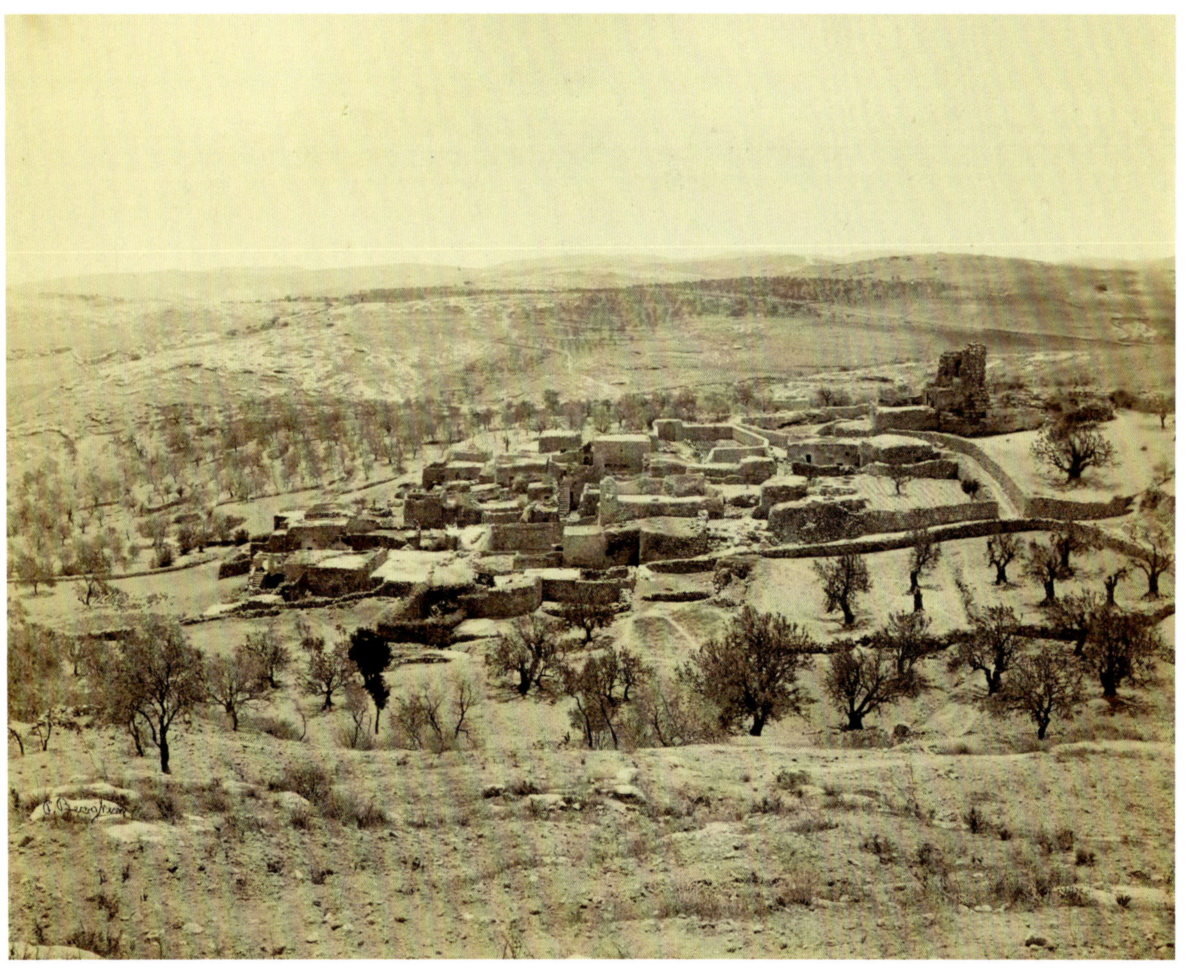

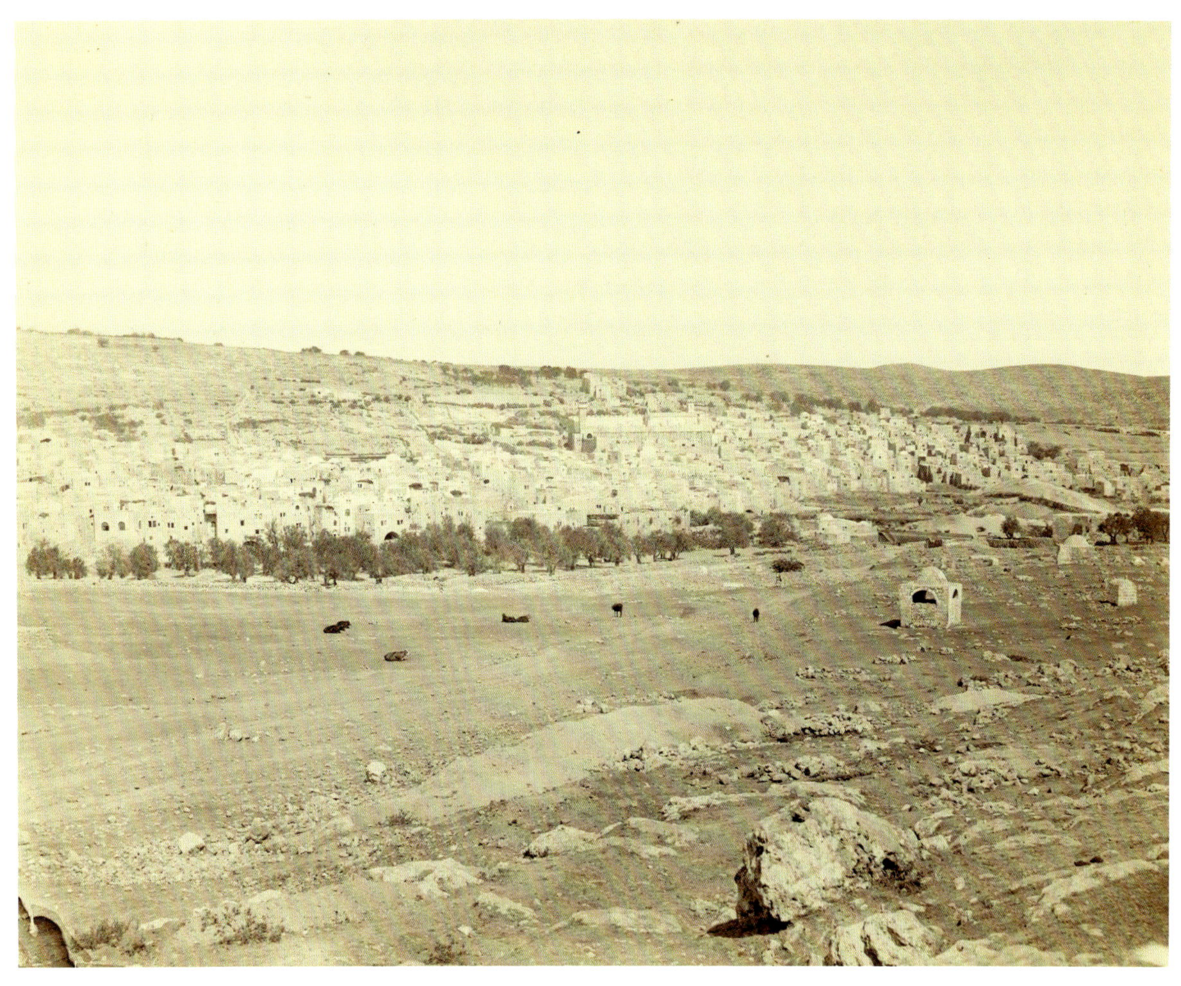

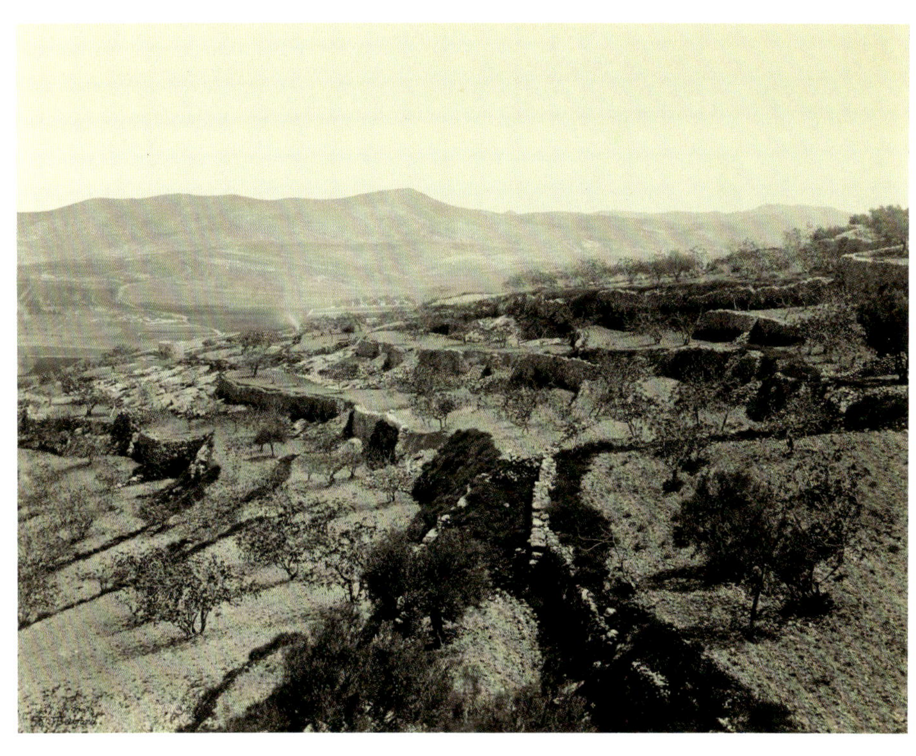

Francis Bedford (1815–1894)
Patmos—The Citadel,
1862
19th-century photographic print,
image size: 8 1⁄16 × 10 1⁄2 inches,
historic mount: 15 3⁄16 × 18 3⁄4 inches
OL.1983.457

Peter Bergheim (1813–1895)
Bethany,
ca. 1860s–1880s
19th-century photographic print,
image size: 9 7⁄8 × 12 3⁄8 inches,
historic mount: 15 × 18 3⁄4 inches
OL.1982.1378

Photographer Unknown
Hebron,
late 19th century
19th-century photographic print,
image size: 10 1⁄16 × 10 1⁄4 inches,
historic mount: 14 1⁄8 × 16 15⁄16 inches
OL.1997.41.5

Francis Bedford (1815–1894)
Bethlehem—The Shepherds' Field,
1862
19th-century photographic print,
image size: 8 1⁄16 × 10 1⁄2 inches,
historic mount: 15 1⁄16 × 18 13⁄16 inches
OL.1983.458

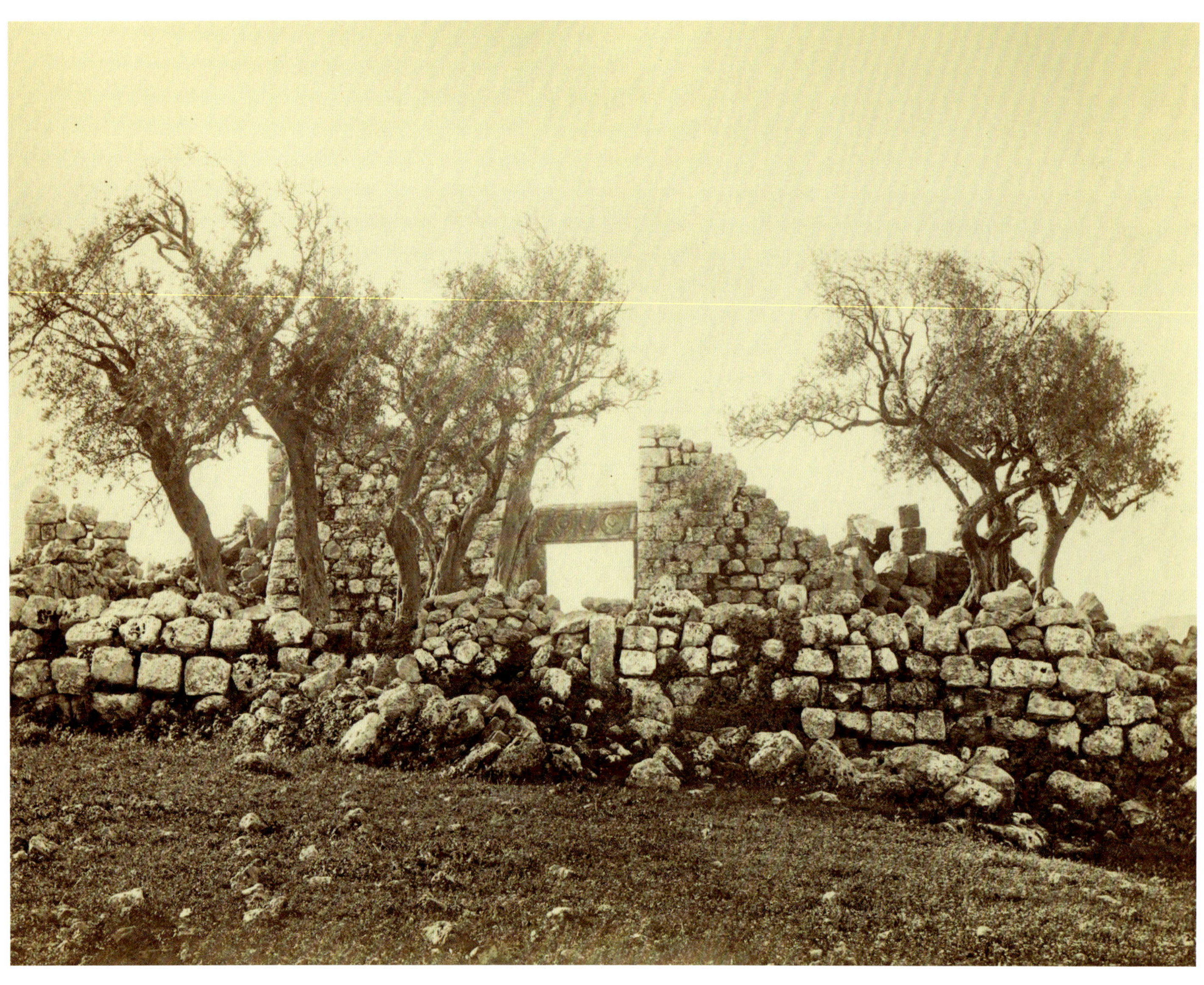

Francis Bedford (1815–1894)
Jerusalem—The Garden of Gethsemane, Looking Towards the City Walls,
1862
19th-century photographic print,
image size: 8 × 10 7⁄16 inches,
historic mount: 15 ¼ × 18 5⁄8 inches
OL.1983.459

Palestine Exploration Fund
Ruins of Mosque, Seilun (Shiloh),
late 19th century
19th-century photographic print,
image size: 6 1⁄16 × 7 7⁄8 inches,
historic mount: 11 3⁄8 × 14 13⁄16 inches
OL.1983.1341.17

Frank Mason Good (1839–1928)
Jerusalem from Mt. of Olives,
ca. 1860s–1870s
19th-century photographic print,
image size: 6 × 8 1⁄16 inches,
historic mount: 10 ¾ × 13 ½ inches
OL.1981.673.24

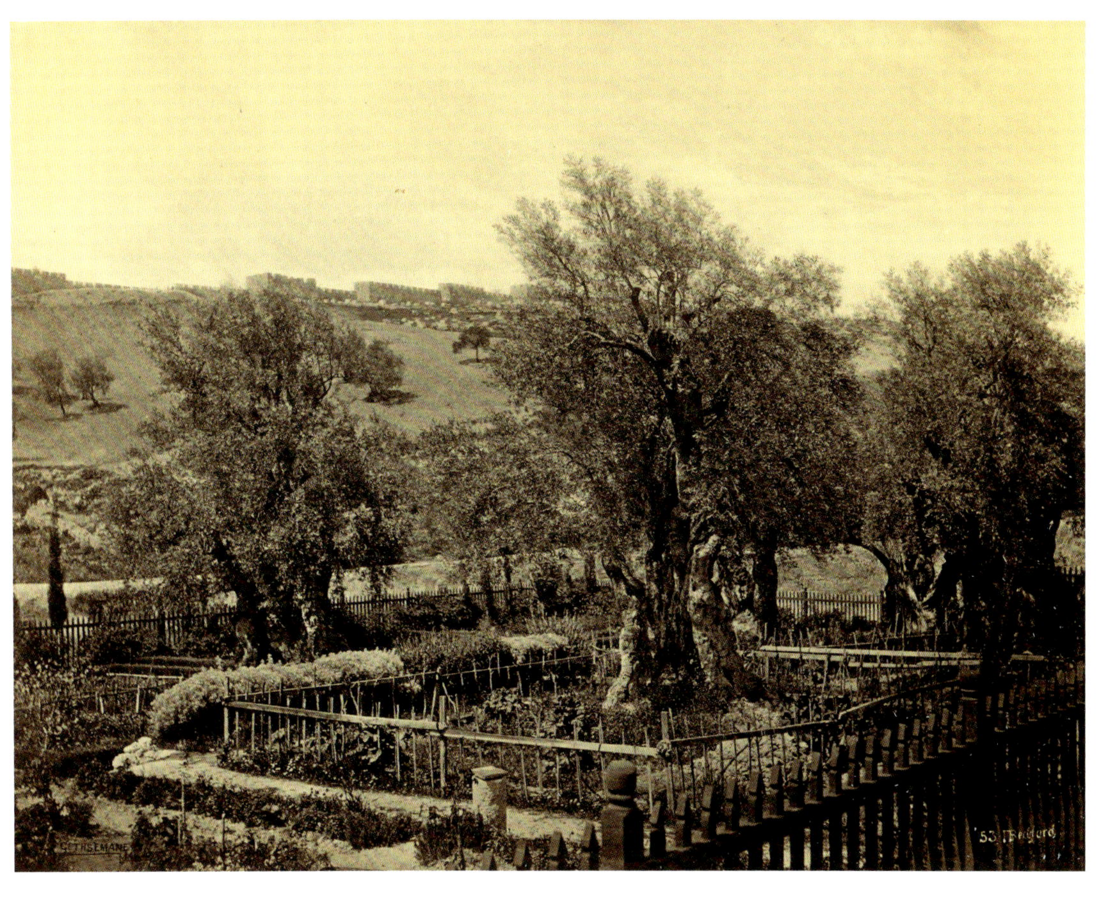
GETHSEMANE
53

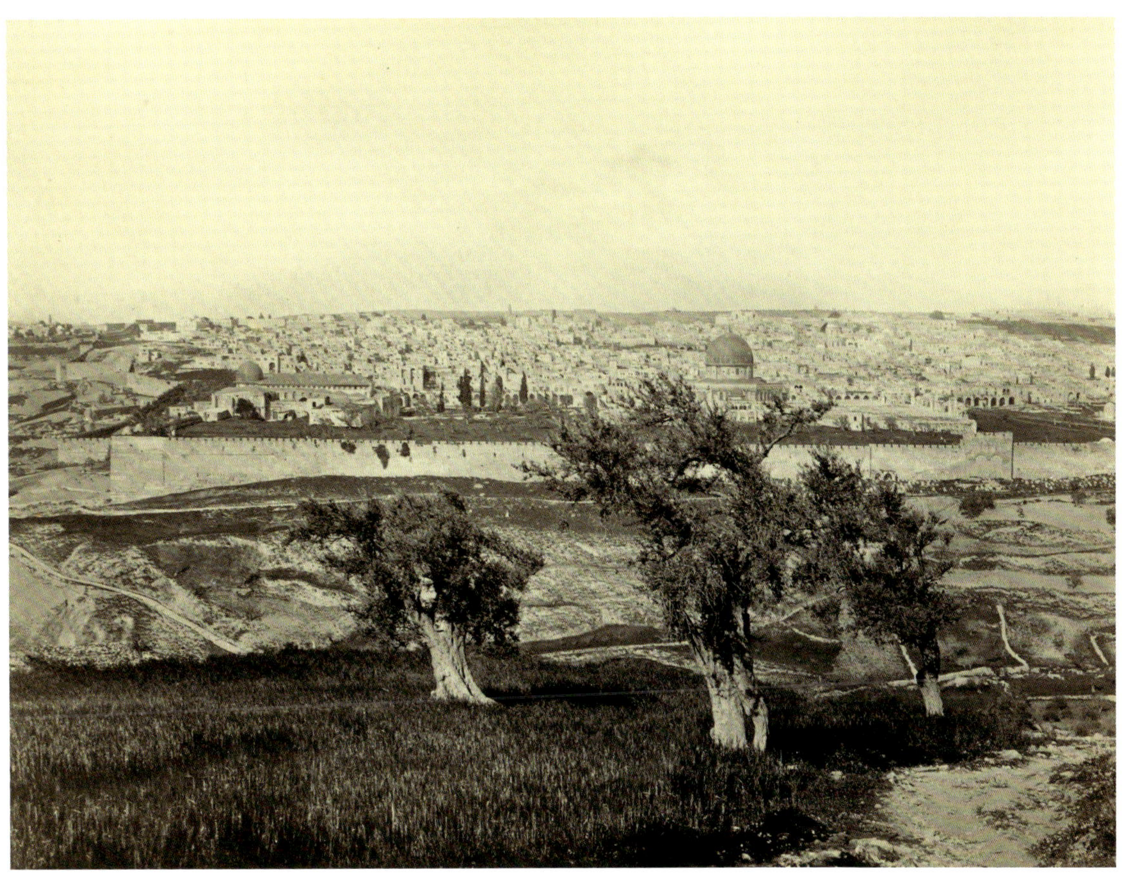

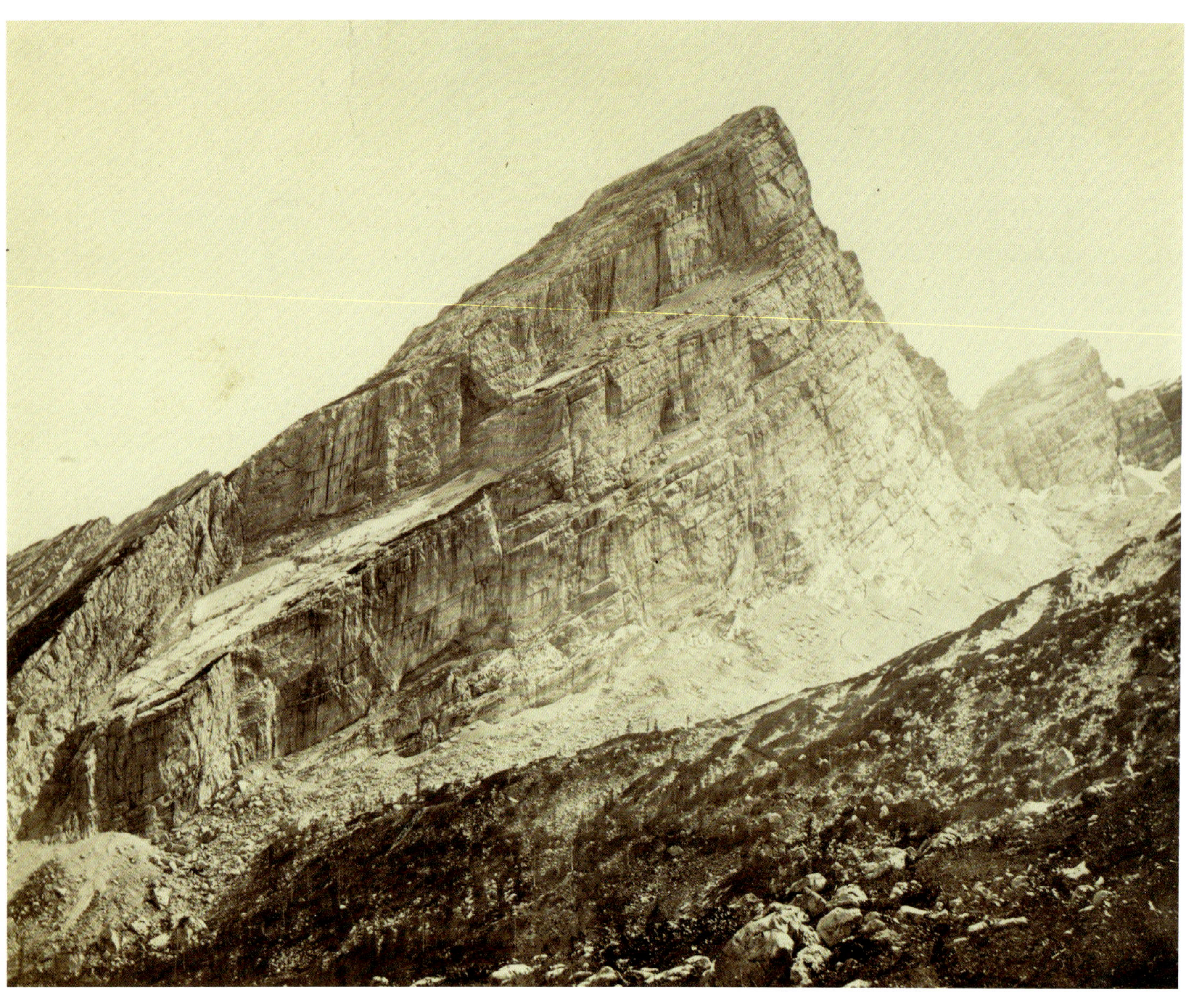

Baldi & Würthle (active 1862–1881)
Obersee bei dem Königsee,
ca. 1862–1880
19th-century photographic print,
image size: 8 ¼ × 9 ½ inches,
historic mount: 12 7⁄16 × 15 ½ inches
OL.1983.454.11

M. Walch (active 19th century)
Kleine Watzman,
late 19th century
19th-century photographic print,
image size: 6 × 7 ¾ inches,
historic mount: 9 3⁄8 × 12 11⁄16 inches
OL.1981.280.9

M. Walch (active 19th century)
Schneelawine am Hintersee bei Berchtesgaden,
1867
19th-century photographic print,
image size: 6 ¾ × 8 ¾ inches,
historic mount: 9 5⁄16 × 12 5⁄8 inches
OL.1981.280.10

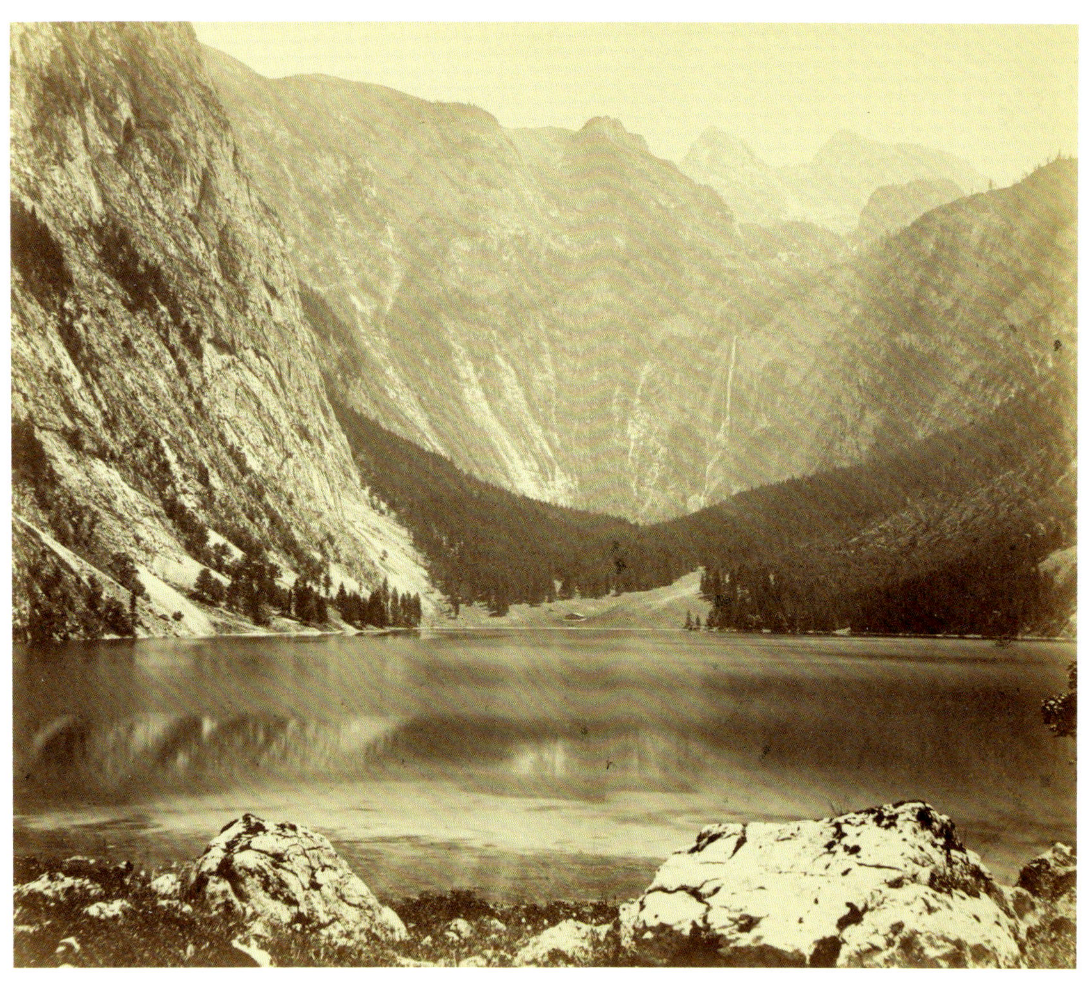

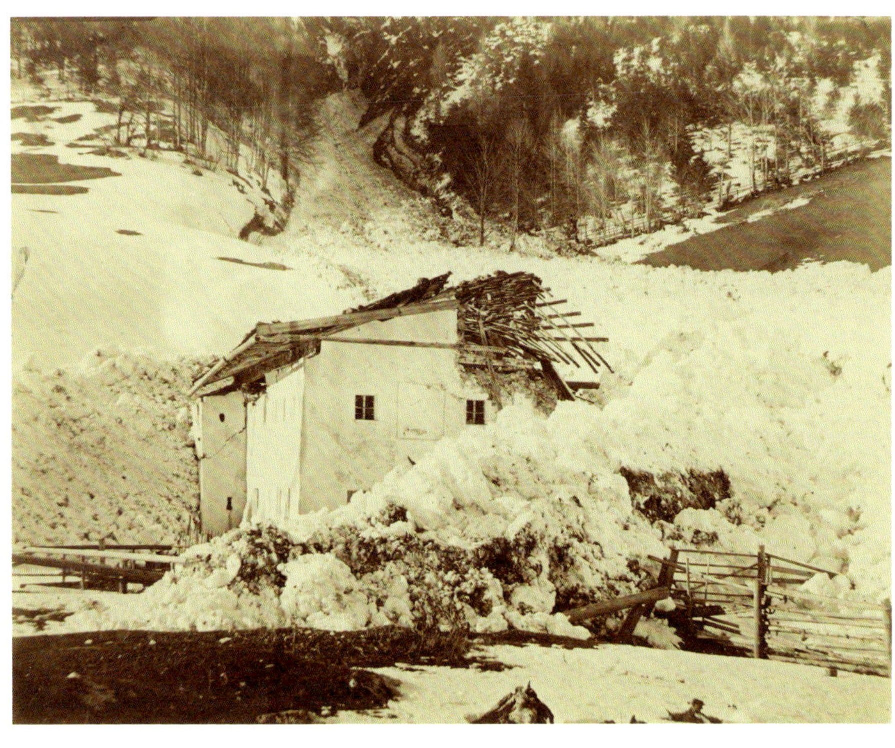

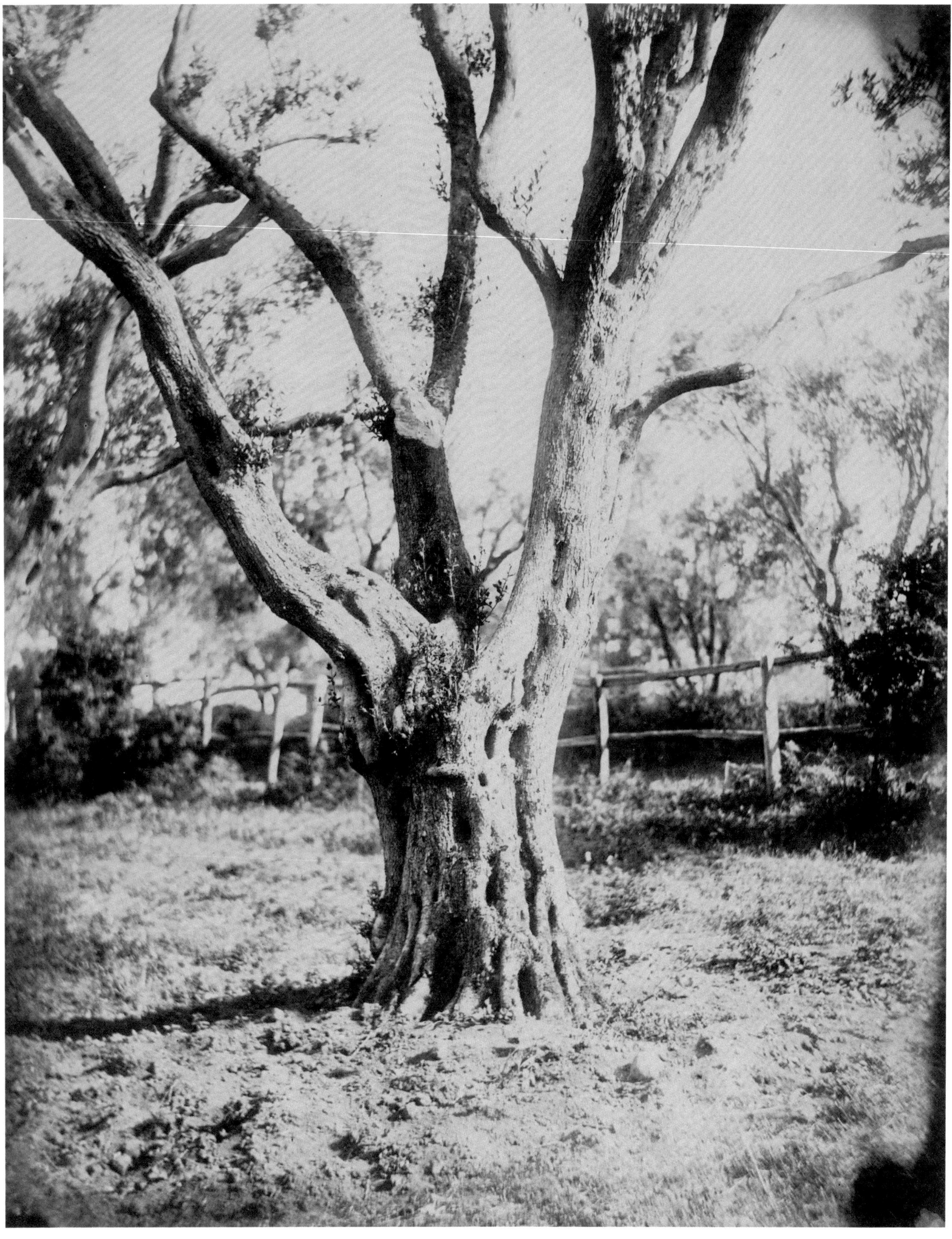

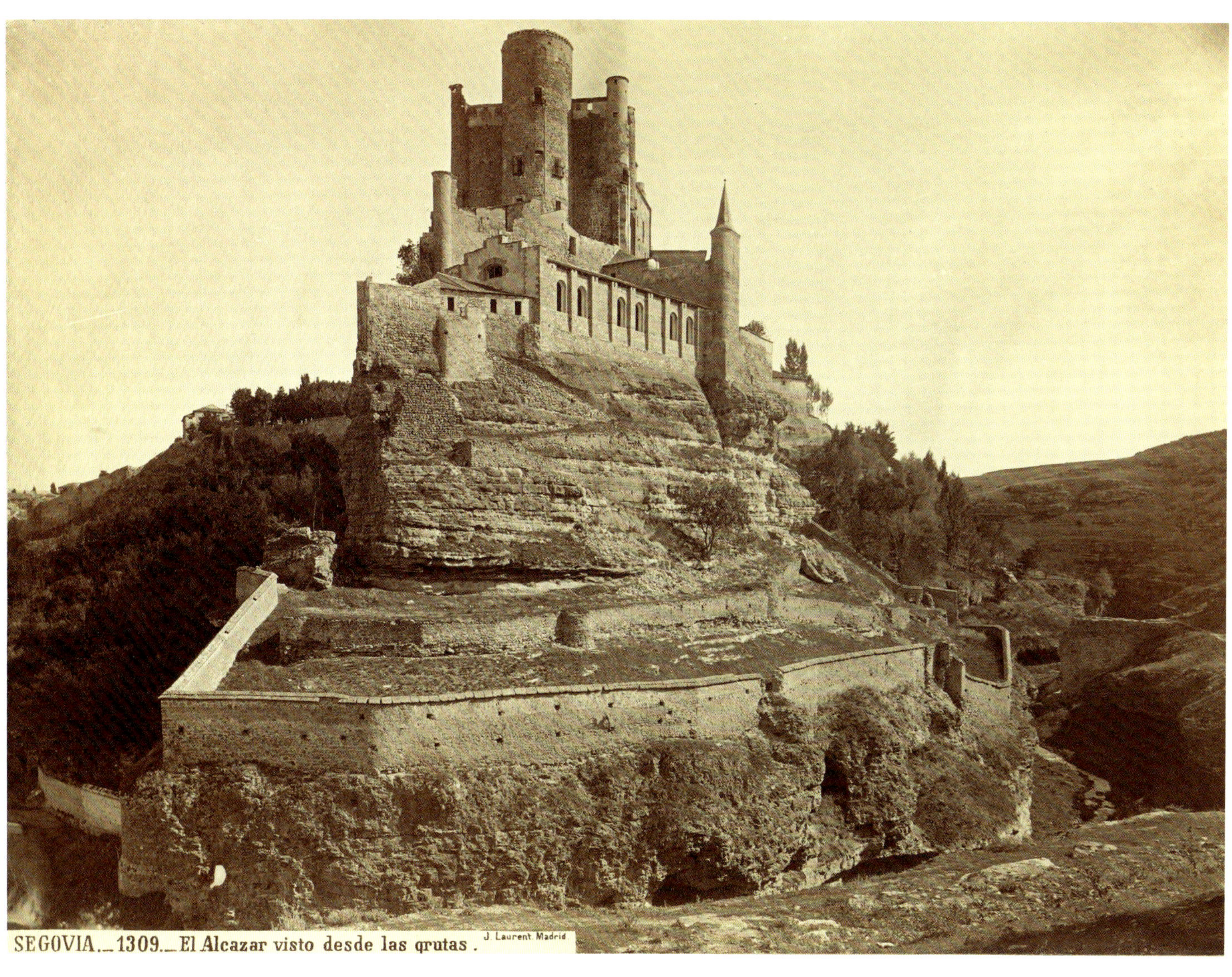

Photographer Unknown
Tree,
late 19th century
19th-century photographic print,
image size: 9 ¾ × 7 ¾ inches,
historic mount: 12 9⁄16 × 9 13⁄16 inches
OL.1981.620

Jean Laurent (1816–1886)
El Alcazar, Visto desde Las Grutas, Segovia, Spain,
ca. 1870–1880
19th-century photographic print,
image size: 10 × 13 ½ inches,
historic mount: 12 × 15 ¾ inches
OL.1983.494

Baldi & Würthle (active 1862–1881)
Wasserfall Oberhalb der Schrekbrücke, Gastein,
ca. 1862–1880
19th-century photographic print,
image size: 9 7/16 × 8 1/8 inches,
historic mount: 15 1/2 × 12 5/8 inches
OL.1983.454.10

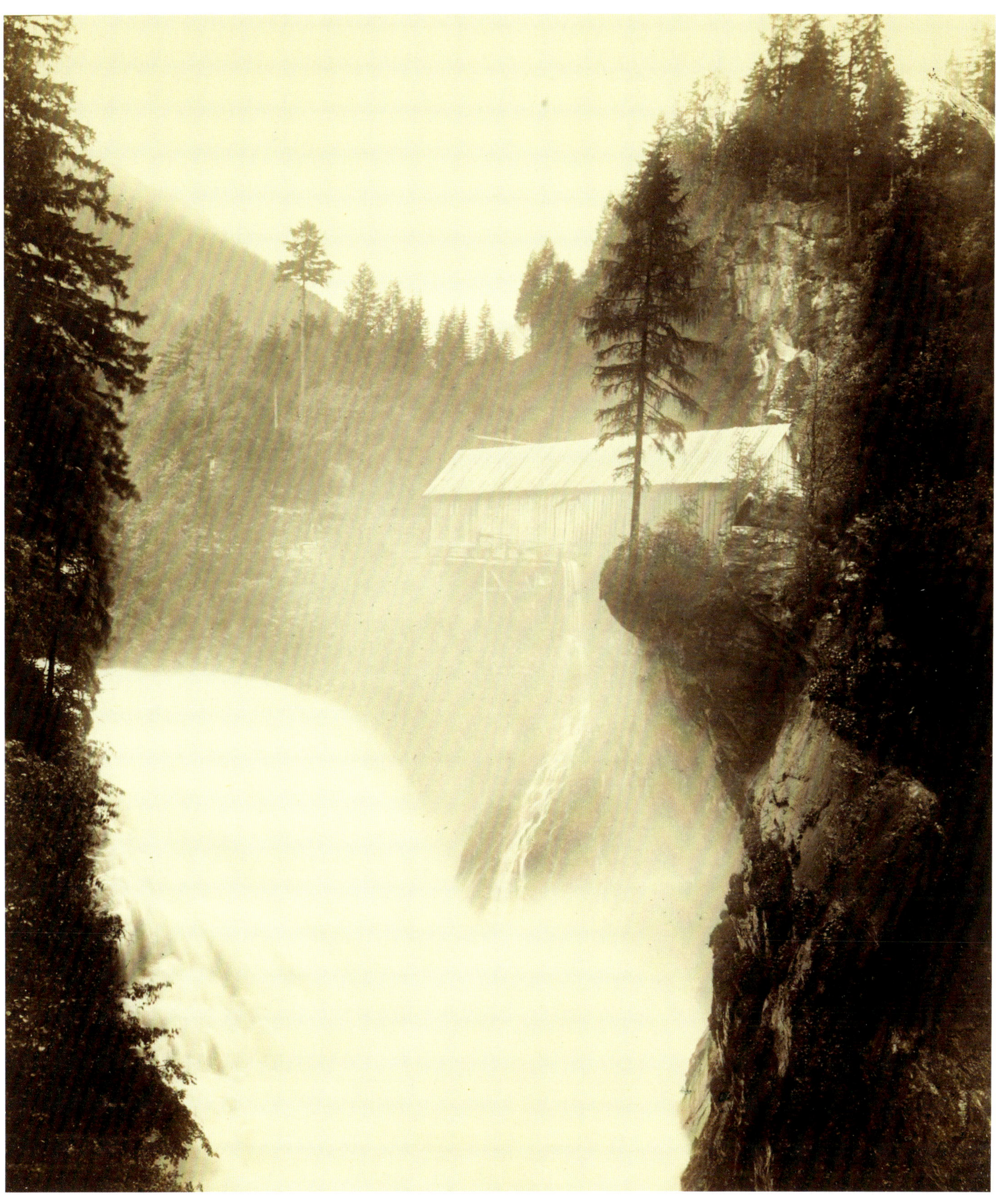

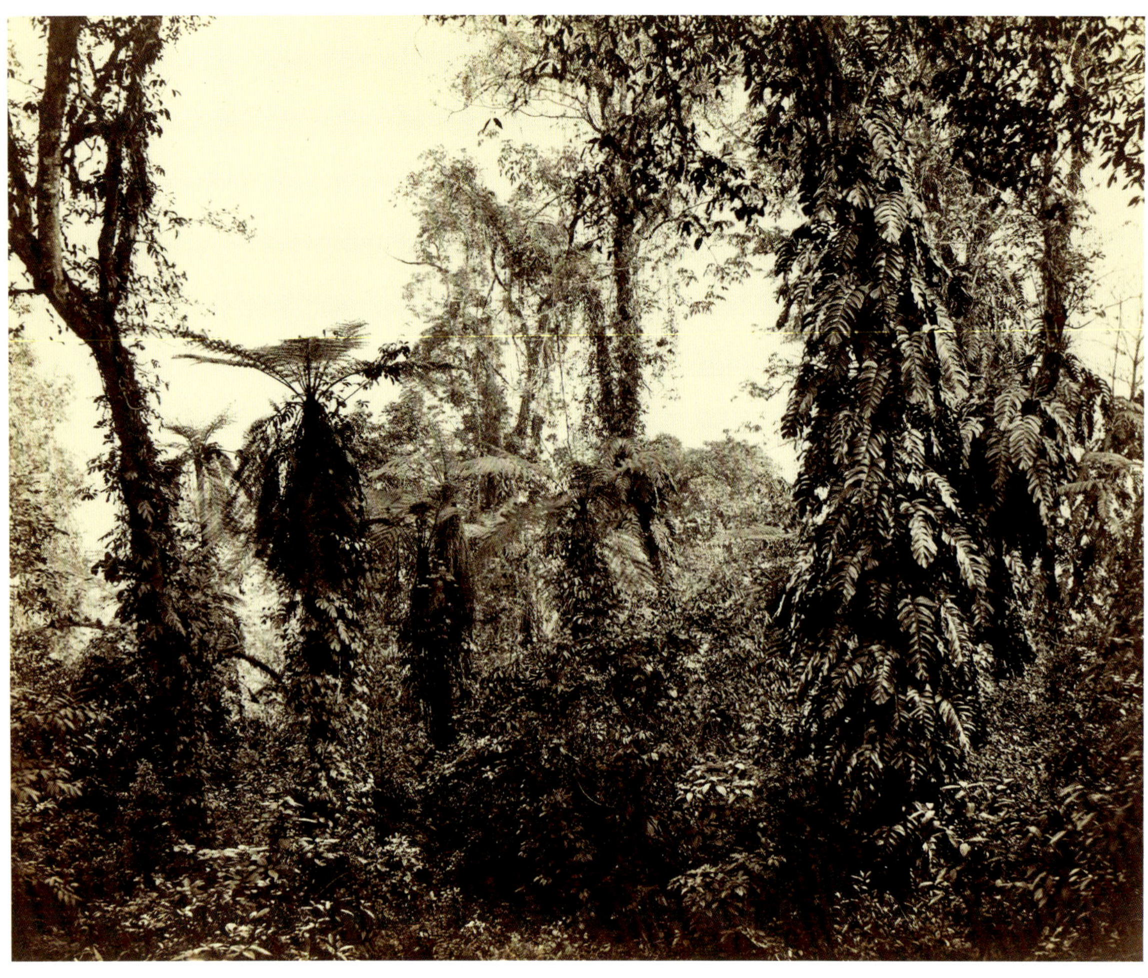

Eadweard Muybridge (1830–1904)
Central America, Clearing the Ground for a Coffee Plantation at Las Nubes,
ca. 1875
19th-century photographic print,
image size: 5 7⁄16 × 9 3⁄8 inches,
historic mount: 10 15⁄16 × 14 inches
OL.1981.398.3

Photographer Unknown
Jungle-like Vegetation,
late 19th century
19th-century photographic print,
image size: 9 9⁄16 × 11 13⁄16 inches,
historic mount: 14 × 17 inches
OL.1985.918

Photographer Unknown
Huts in the Tropics,
late 19th century
19th-century photographic print,
image size: 4 11⁄16 × 5 3⁄4 inches,
historic mount: 7 × 8 3⁄4 inches
OL.1981.483.1

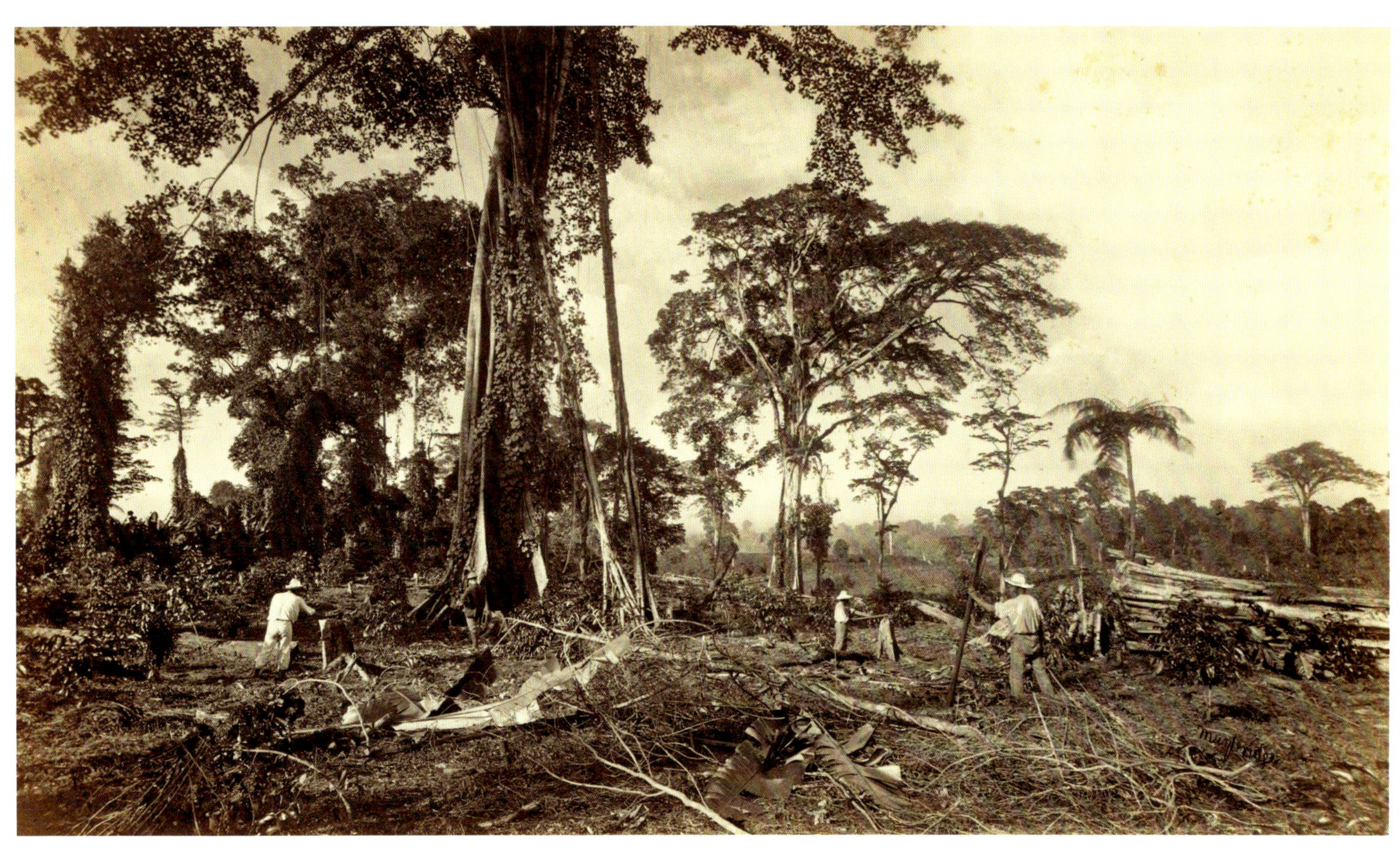

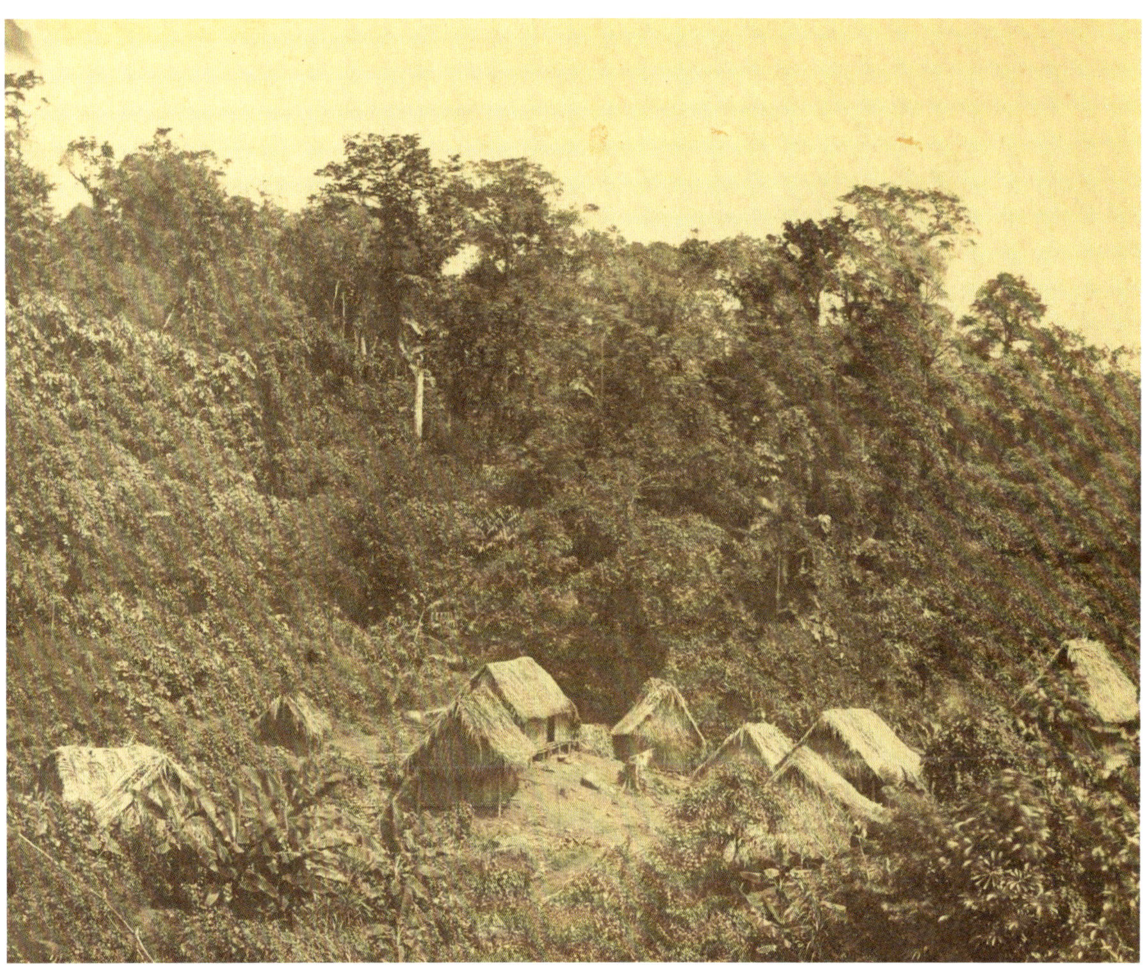

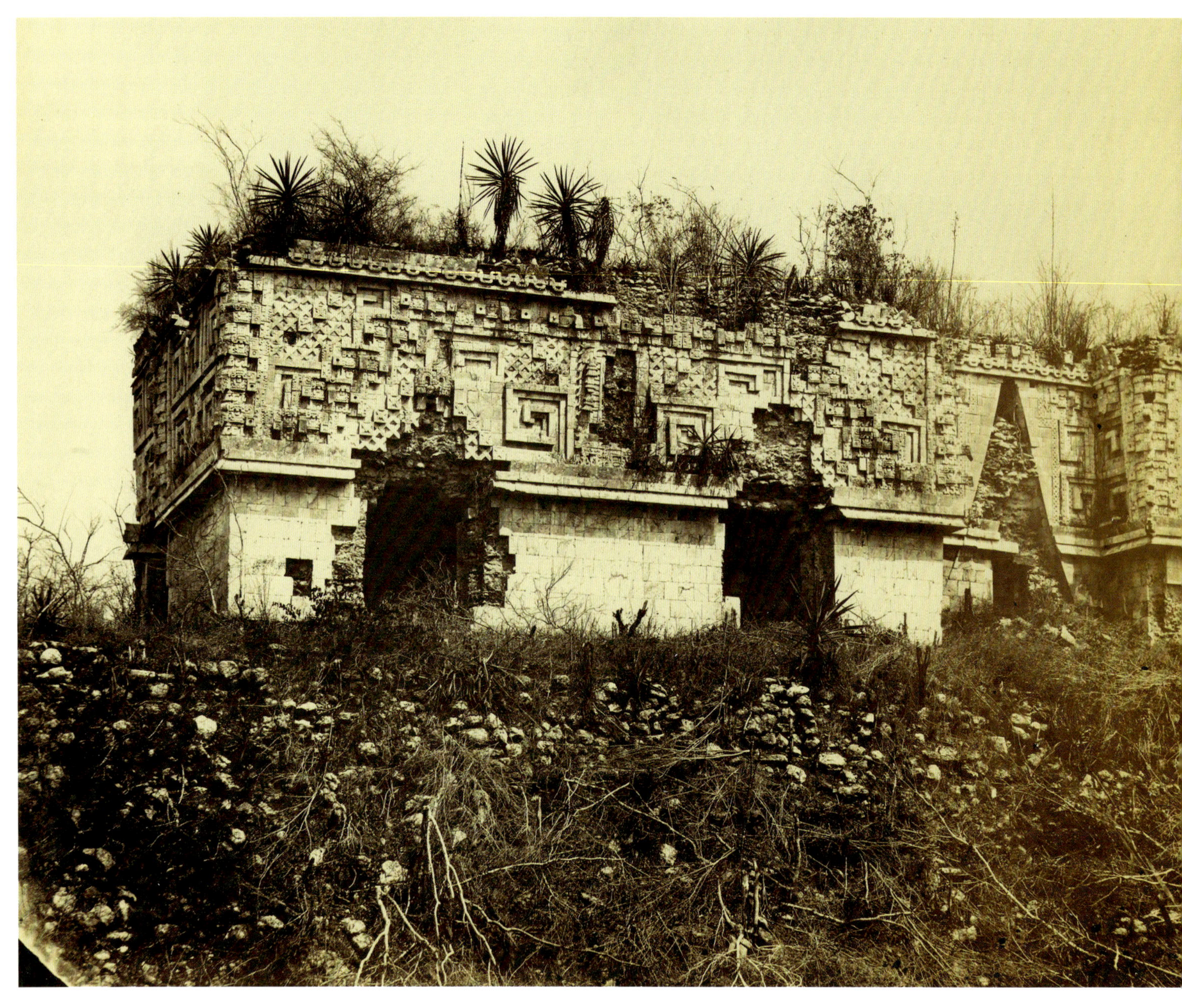

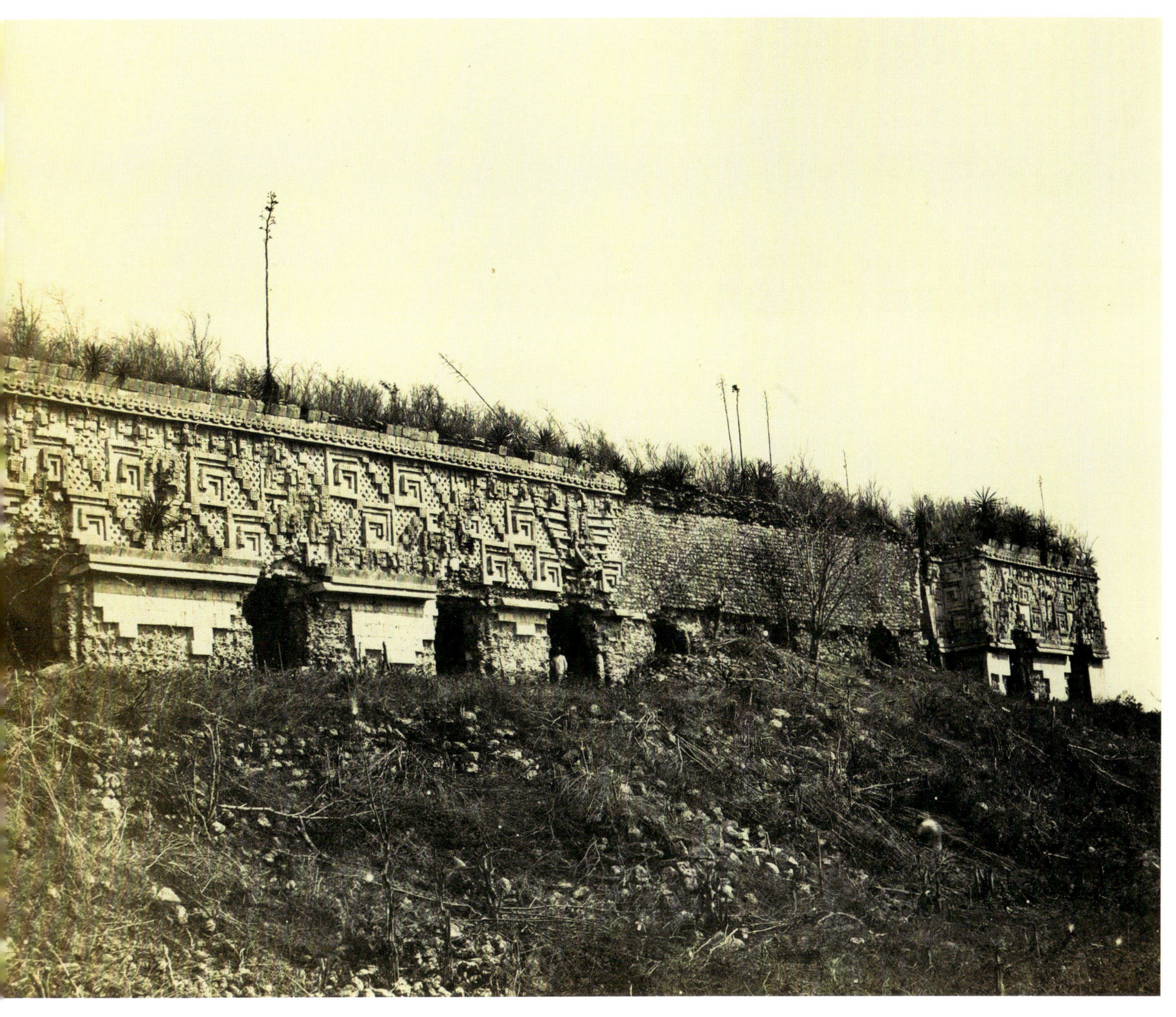

Claude-Joseph Désiré Charnay (1828–1915)
Palais du Gouverneur, à Uxmal, Façade Principale,
1860
19th-century photographic print,
image size: 13 1⁄16 × 16 ½ inches,
historic mount: 19 9⁄16 × 24 7⁄16 inches
OL.1999.94.49

Claude-Joseph Désiré Charnay (1828–1915)
Palais du Gouverneur, à Uxmal, Façade Principale,
1860
19th-century photographic print,
image size: 13 3⁄16 × 16 3⁄16 inches,
historic mount: 19 ⅝ × 24 11⁄16 inches
OL.1999.94.50

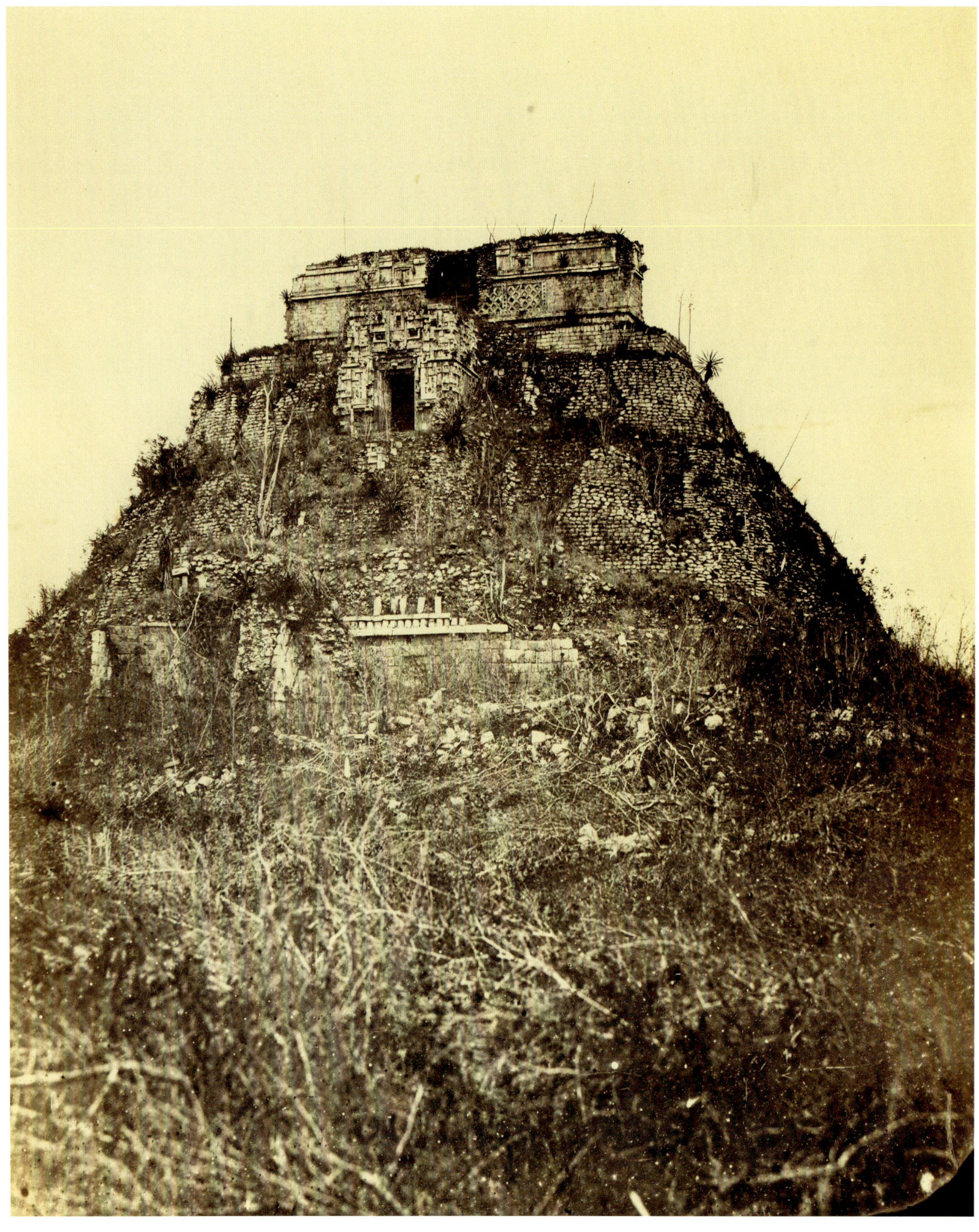

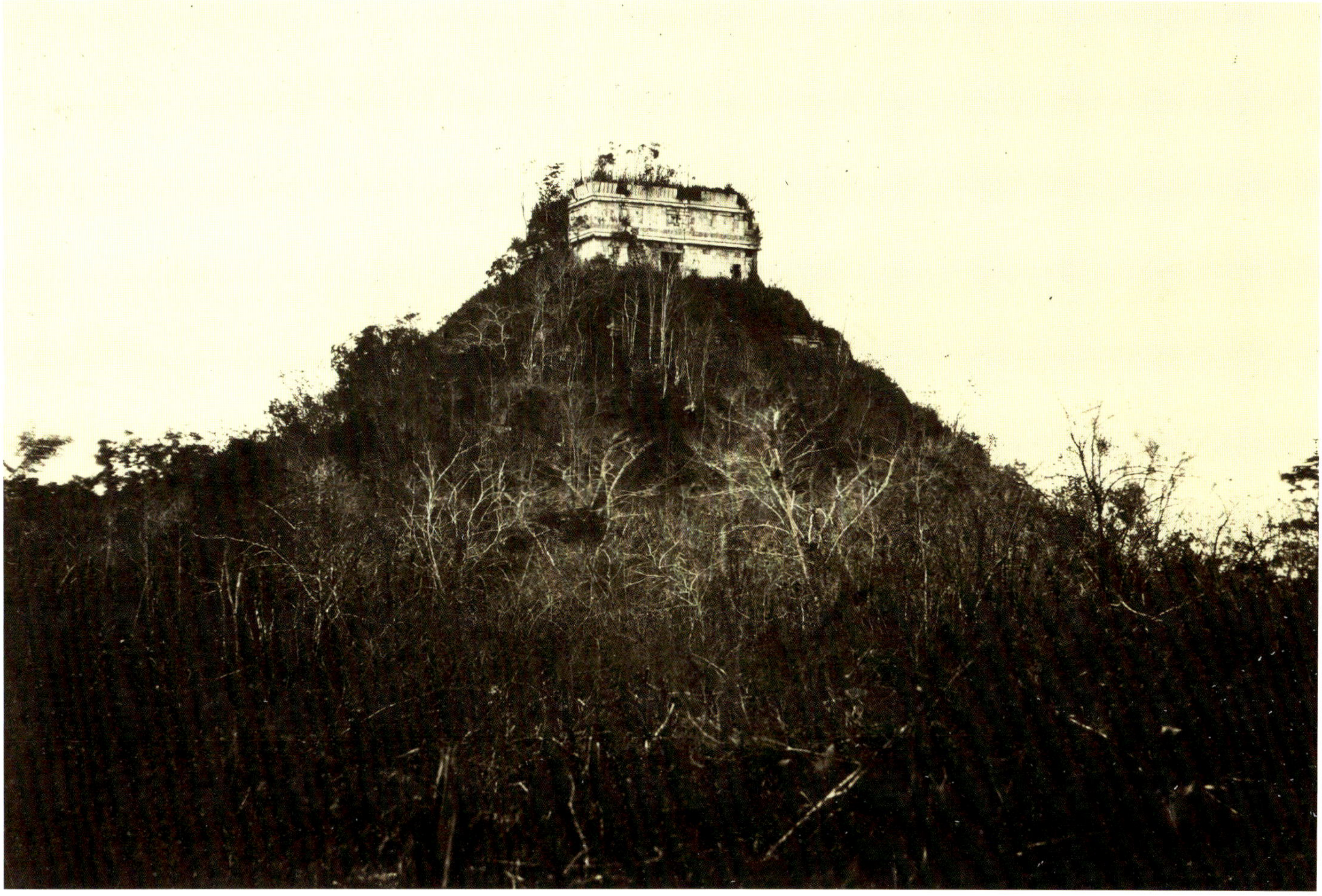

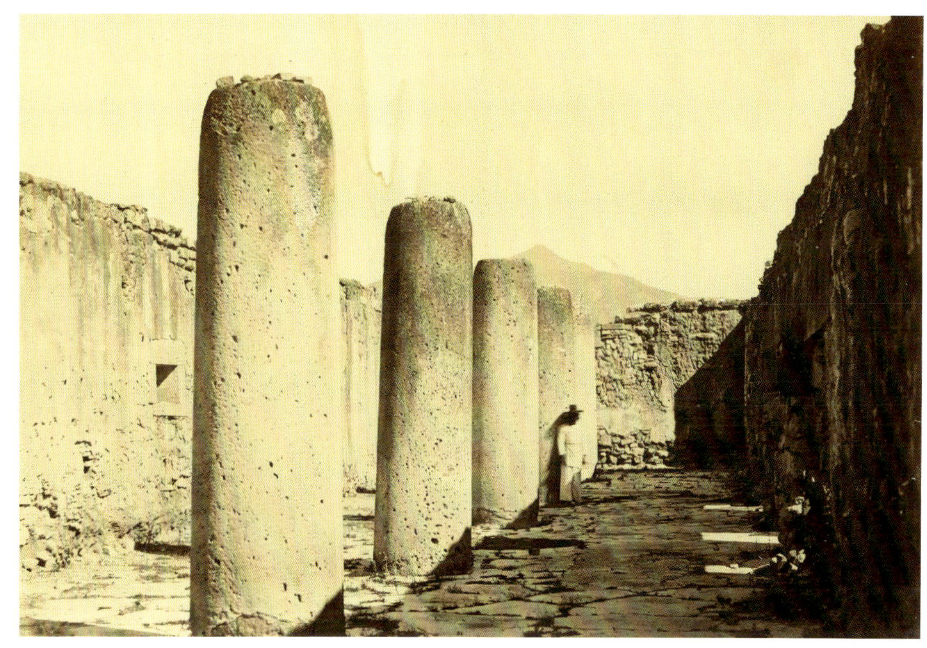

Claude–Joseph Désiré Charnay (1828–1915)
Maison du Nain, à Uxmal,
1860
19th-century photographic print,
image size: 15 ⅜ × 12 ⅝ inches,
historic mount: 24 ½ × 19 ½ inches
OL.1999.94.39

Claude–Joseph Désiré Charnay (1828–1915)
Ancien Temple, à Chichen-Itza, Appelé le Chateau,
1860
19th-century photographic print,
image size: 10 ⅜ × 15 13⁄16 inches,
historic mount: 19 ⅜ × 24 7⁄16 inches
OL.1999.94.36

Claude–Joseph Désiré Charnay (1828–1915)
Grande Palais, à Mitla, Grande Salle,
1860
19th-century photographic print,
image size: 10 11⁄16 × 16 inches,
historic mount: 19 7⁄16 × 24 ½ inches
OL.1999.94.14

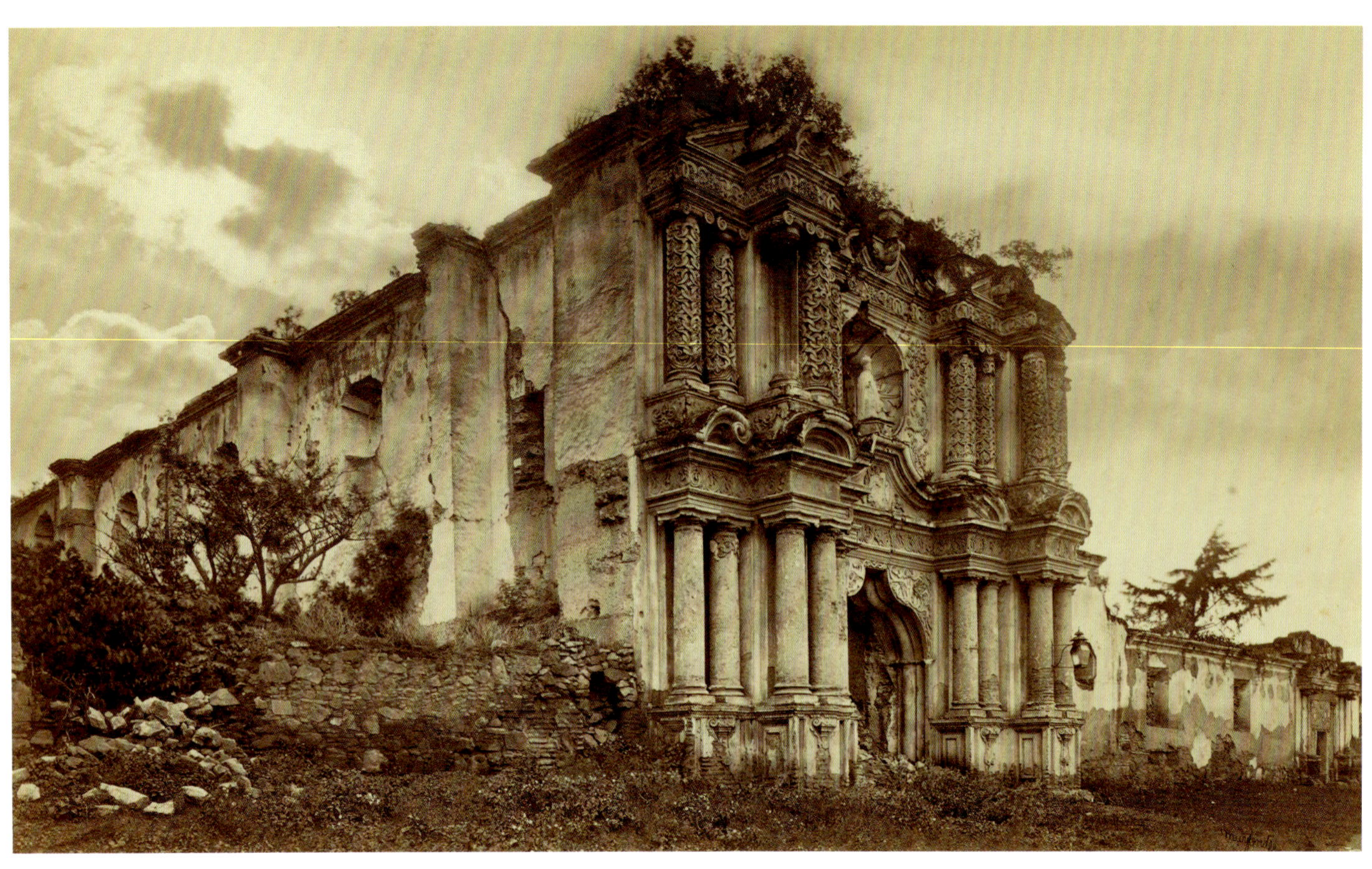

Eadweard Muybridge (1830–1904)
Antigua, Ruins of the Church of El Carmen, Destroyed by Earthquake 1774,
ca. 1875
19th-century photographic print,
image size: 5 7⁄16 × 9 5⁄16 inches,
historic mount: 10 7⁄8 × 14 inches
OL.1981.398.1

Eadweard Muybridge (1830–1904)
Ruins of the Watch Tower—Old Panama,
ca. 1875
19th-century photographic print,
image size: 5 7⁄16 × 9 3⁄8 inches,
historic mount: 10 7⁄8 × 13 15⁄16 inches
OL.1981.398.2

Otis M. Gove (1851–1931) and F.E. North (active 1870–1884)
Piramide de Cholula,
ca. 1870–1884
19th-century photographic print,
image size: 4 1⁄4 × 7 1⁄8 inches
OL.1981.451

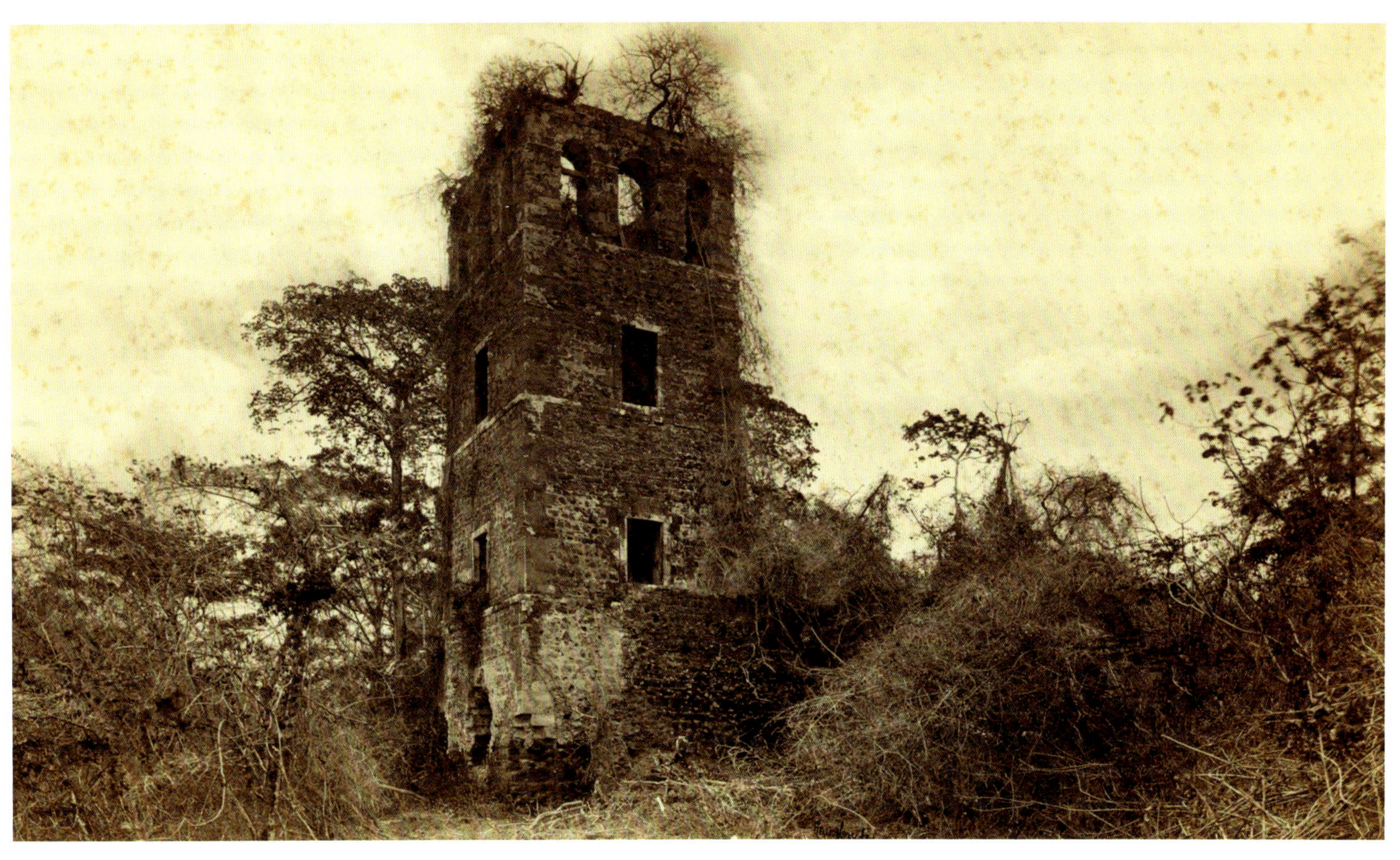

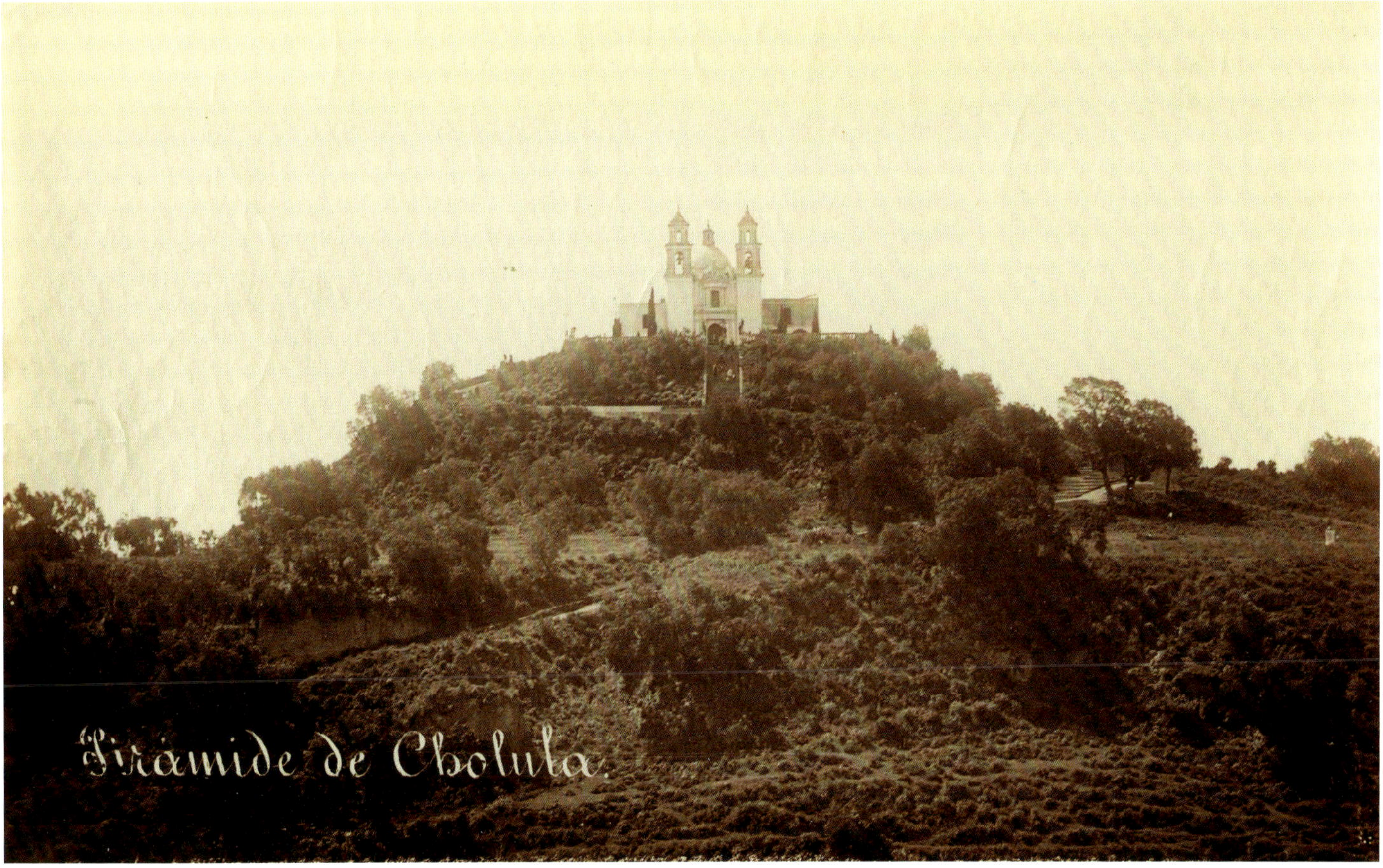

Pirámide de Cholula.

Photographer Unknown
View of Large Mound in Middle of Corn Field, with Church in Distance, Mexico,
ca. 1890–1910
19th-century photographic print,
image size: 4 15⁄16 × 8 1⁄16 inches,
historic album: 9 3⁄8 × 12 1⁄2 × 1 3⁄4 inches
OL.1992.3.59

John L. Dunmore (flourished 1875–1899) and George P. Critcherson (1823–1892), commissioned by William Bradford (1823–1892)
Ruins of the Ancient Norse Church at Krakotok, Near Julianehab, South Greenland,
1869
19th-century photographic print,
image size: 10 15⁄16 × 15 1⁄4 inches,
historic mount: 16 7⁄8 × 21 inches
OL.2004.148

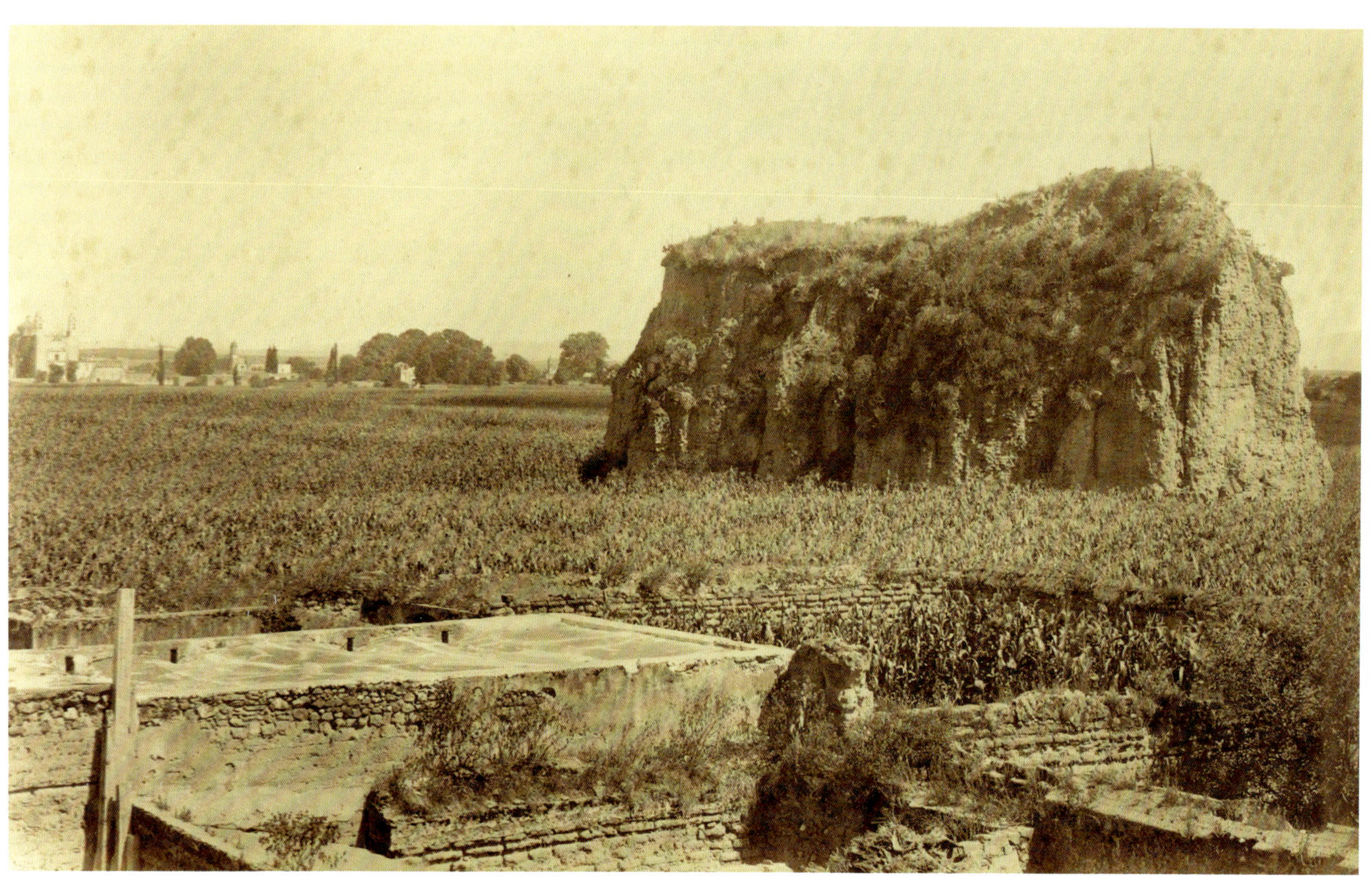

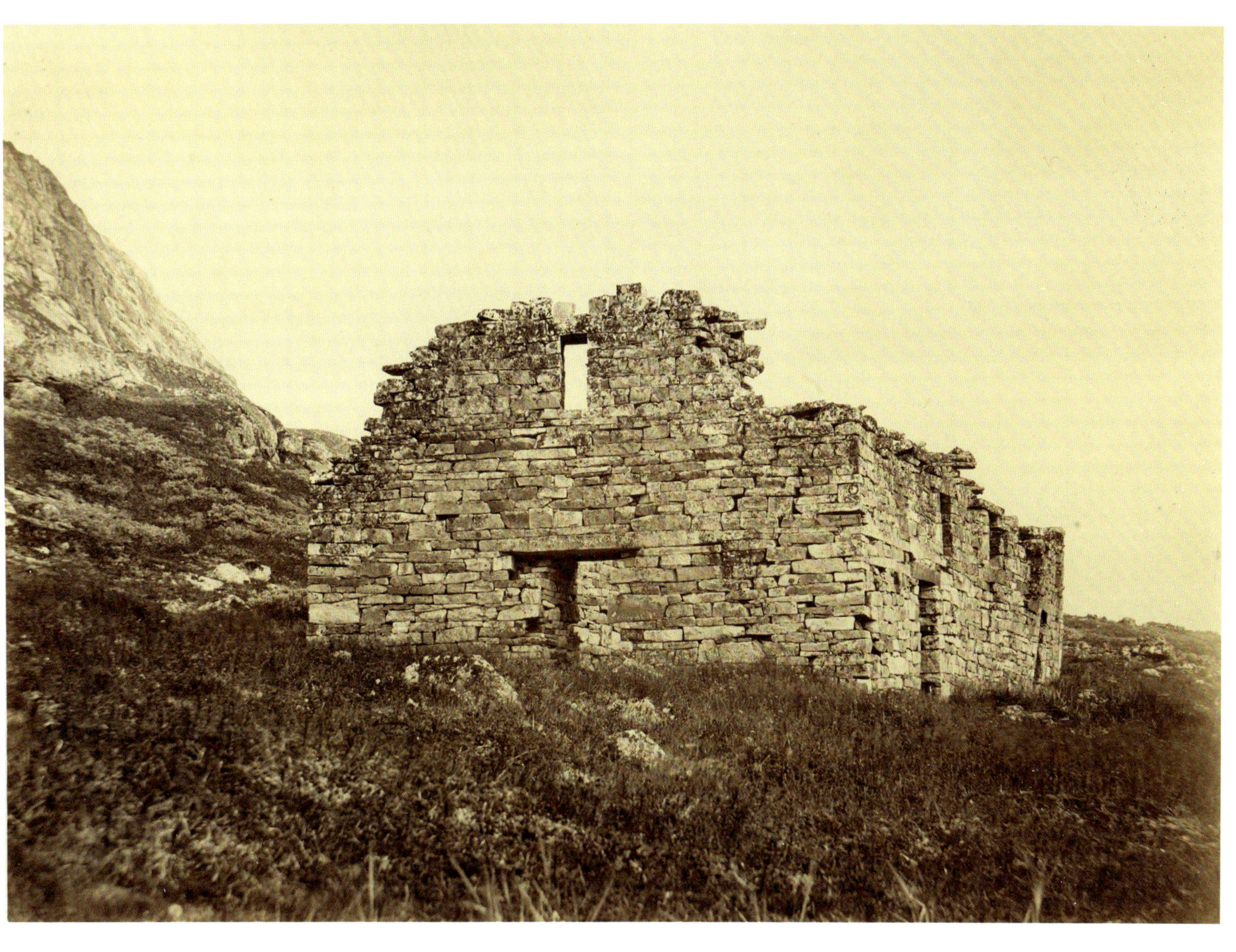

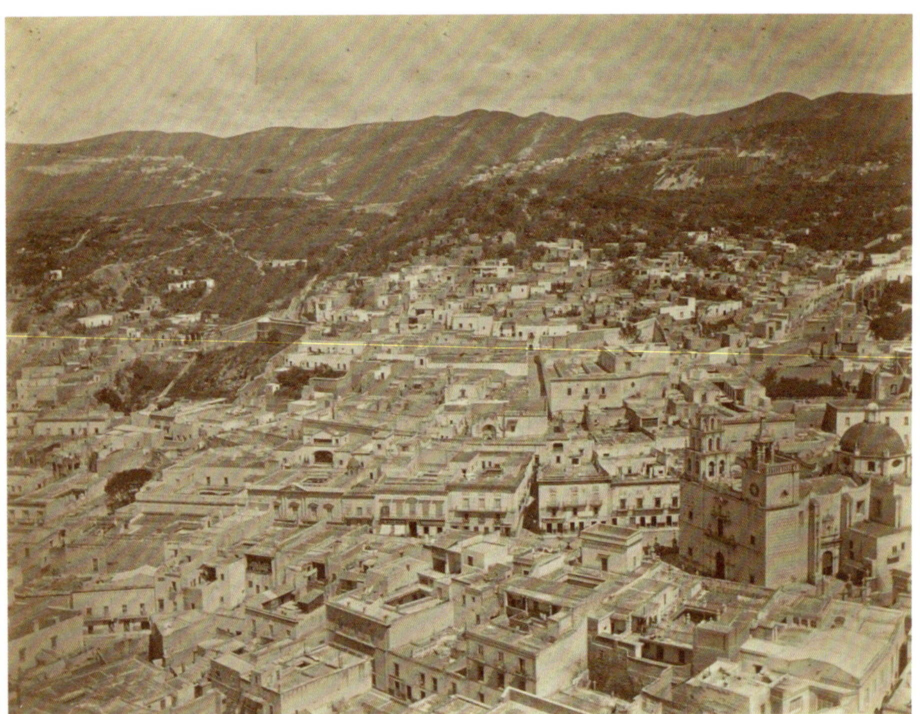

V. Contreras (active 19th century)
Guanajuato,
late 19th century
19th-century photographic print,
image size: 6 9/16 × 8 ¾ inches,
historic mount: 9 7/16 × 12 ⅜ inches
OL.1981.402.3

Photographer Unknown
View of Park-like Area, With Beach at Low Tide, Mexico,
ca. 1890–1910
19th-century photographic print,
image size: 4 ⅞ × 8 1/16 inches,
historic album: 9 ⅜ × 12 ½ × 1 ¾ inches
OL.1992.3.48

Photographer Unknown
View of Puebla,
ca. 1890–1910
19th-century photographic print,
image size: 4 ⅞ × 8 inches,
historic album: 9 ⅜ × 12 ½ × 1 ¾ inches
OL.1992.3.58

Photographer Unknown
Que Passéo de Cacon, Havana,
late 19th century
19th-century photographic print,
image size: 10 ½ × 13 ½ inches,
historic mount: 13 9/16 × 19 ¼ inches
OL.1982.1257

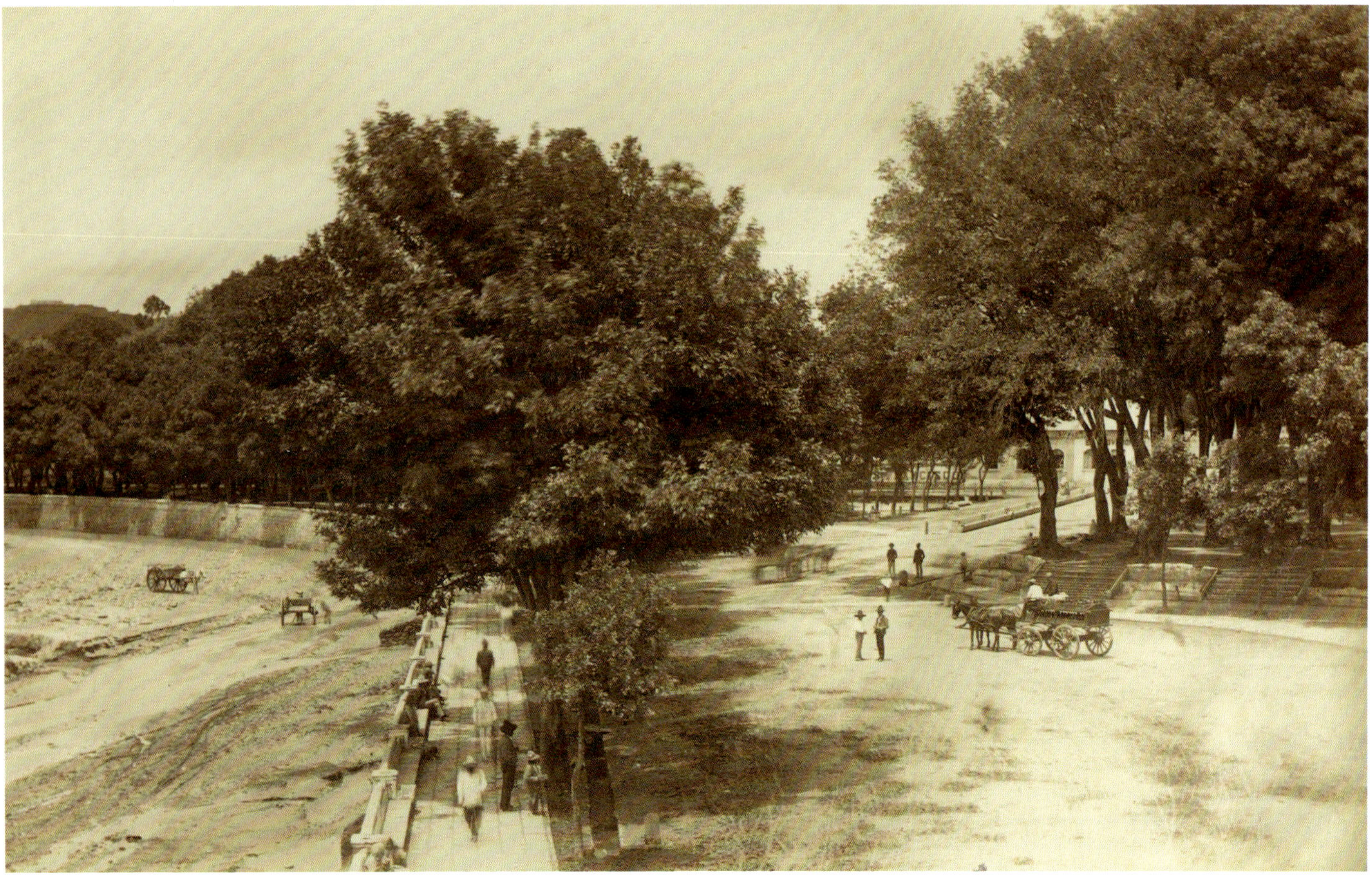

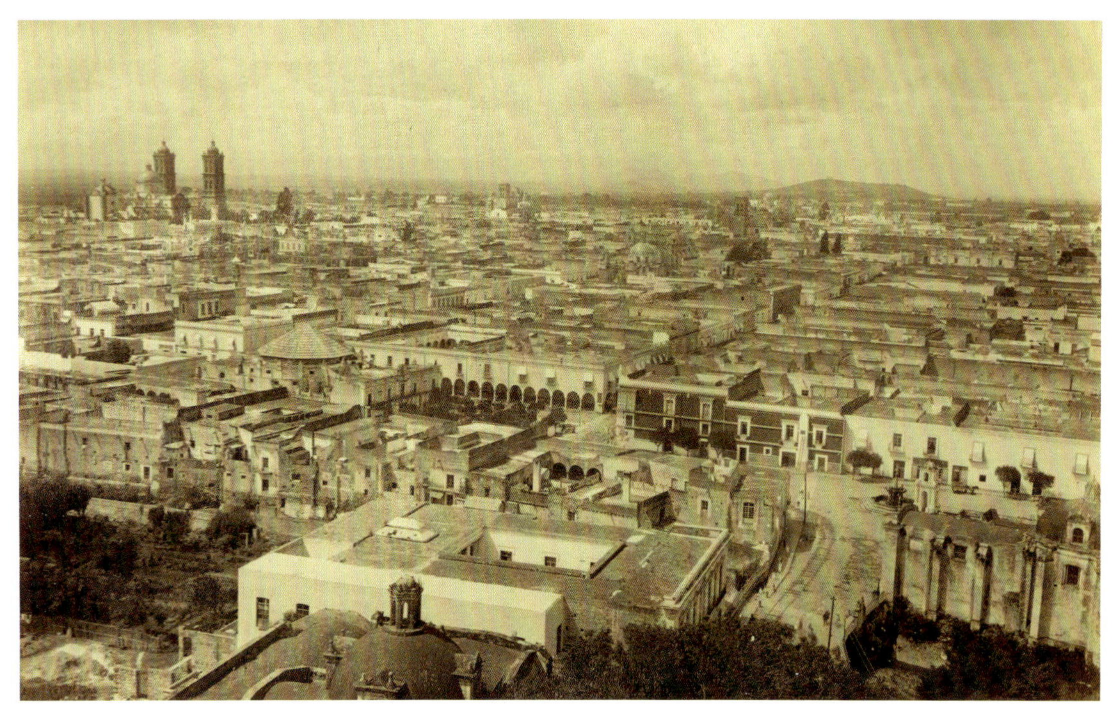

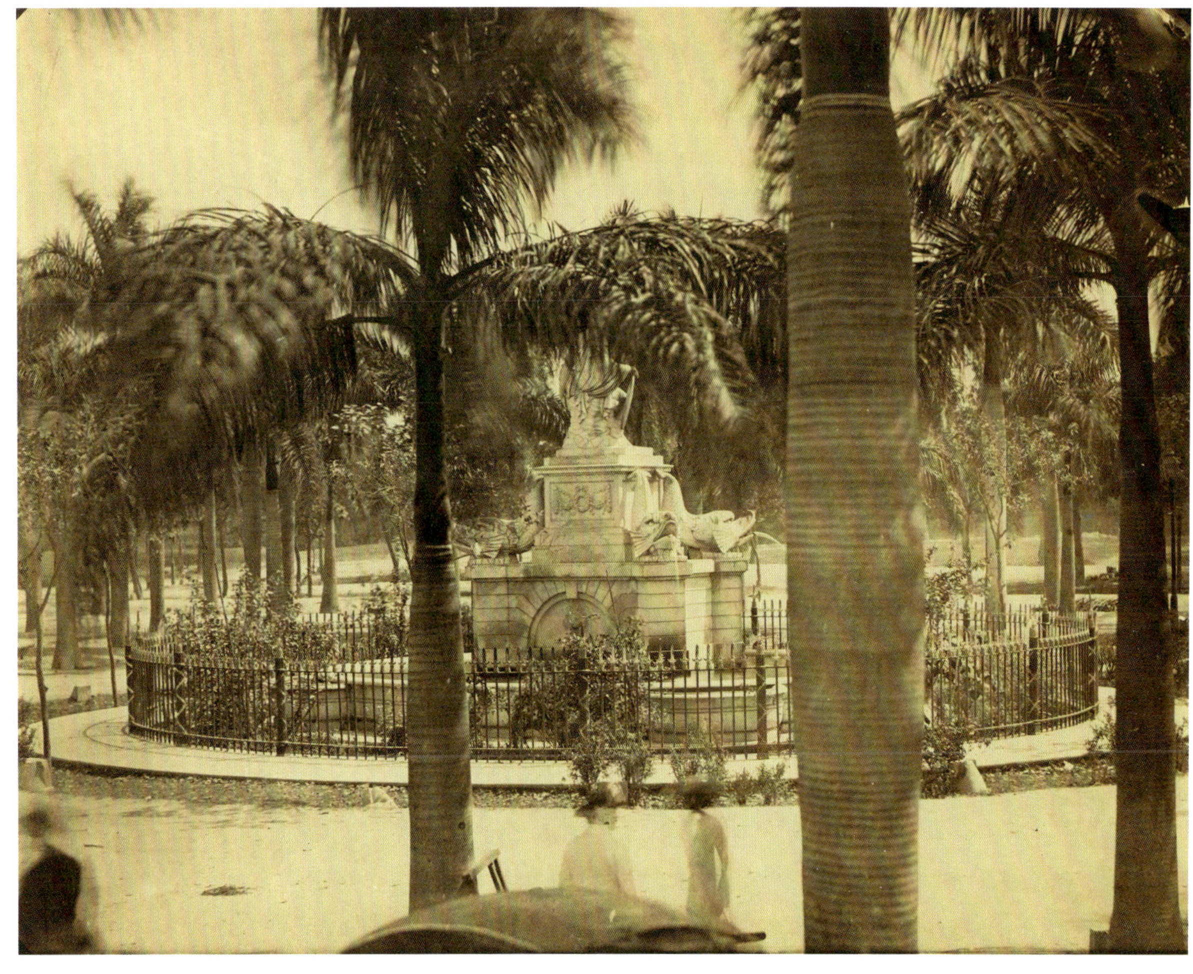

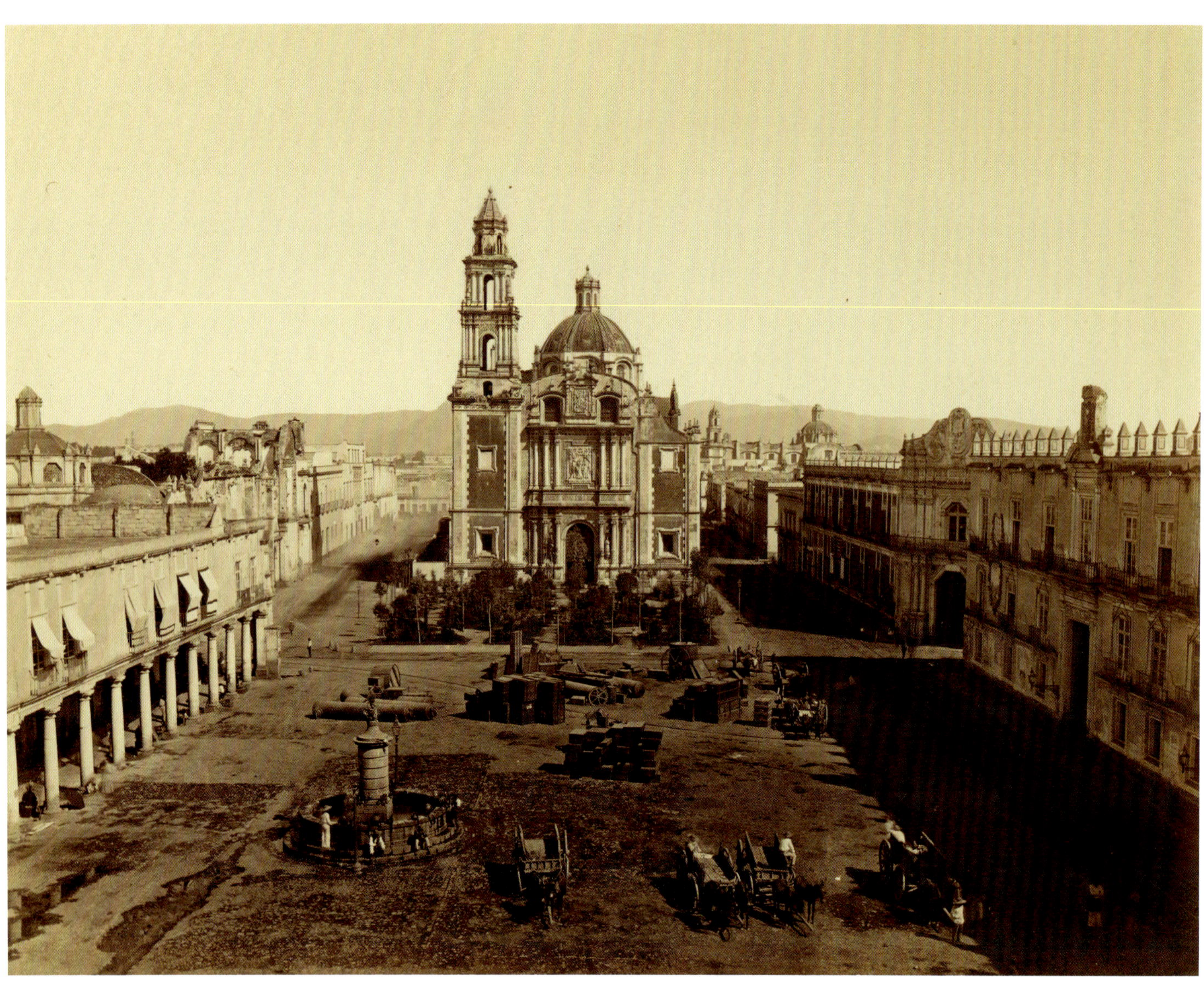

Abel Briquet (1833–1926)
Plaza Sta. Dominga, Mexico,
ca. 1870s
19th-century photographic print,
image size: 7 ⅜ × 9 ¹¹⁄₁₆ inches,
historic mount: 12 ⅜ × 19 ⅛ inches
OL.1982.1325.3

Otis M. Gove (1851–1931)
and F.E. North (active 1870–1884)
Iglesia y Plazuela de Santo Domingo,
ca. 1870–1884
19th-century photographic print,
image size: 8 ³⁄₁₆ × 10 ⁹⁄₁₆ inches,
historic album: 9 ⅜ × 12 ½ × 1 ¾ inches
OL.1992.3.95

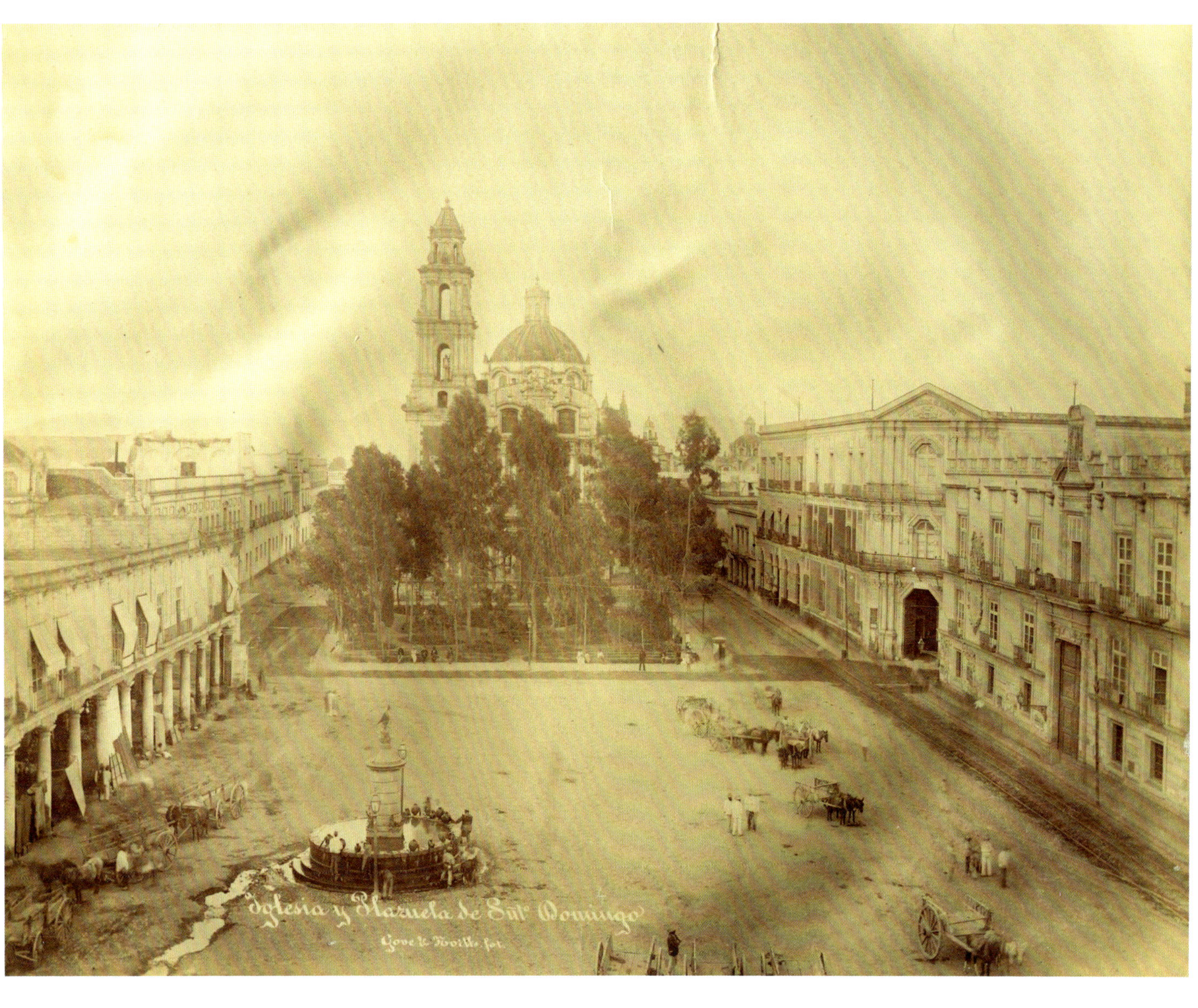
Iglesia y Plazuela de Sto Domingo
Gove & North. fot.

Photographer Unknown
Tree with Small Pond and Stone Bridge,
late 19th century
19th-century photographic print,
image size: 13 ⅜ × 16 ½ inches,
historic mount: 21 × 26 ¹¹⁄₁₆ inches
OL.1999.106

Torres Bros. (active 19th century)
Acueducto de S. Pedro, Morelia,
late 19th century
19th-century photographic print,
image size: 7 ½ × 5 ¾ inches
OL.1981.443.4

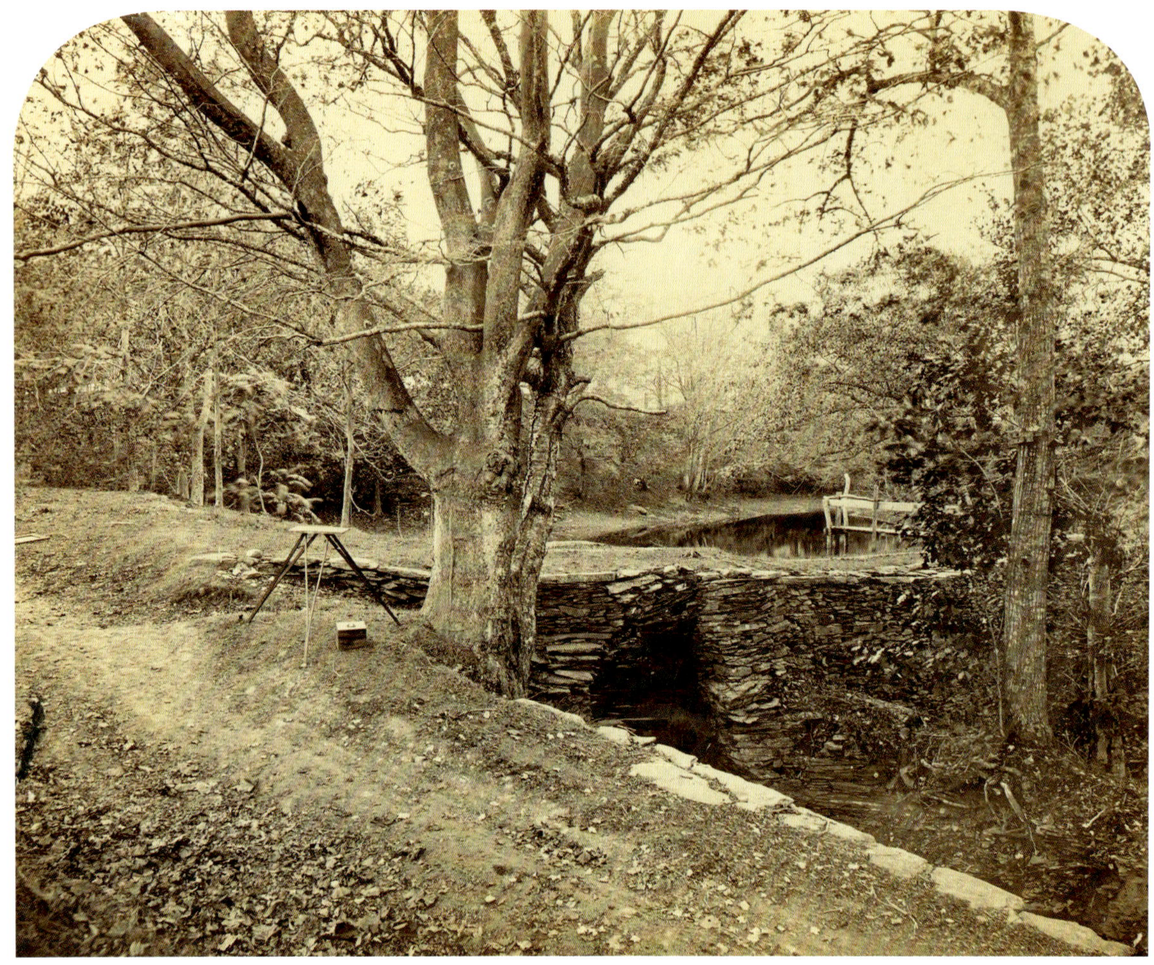

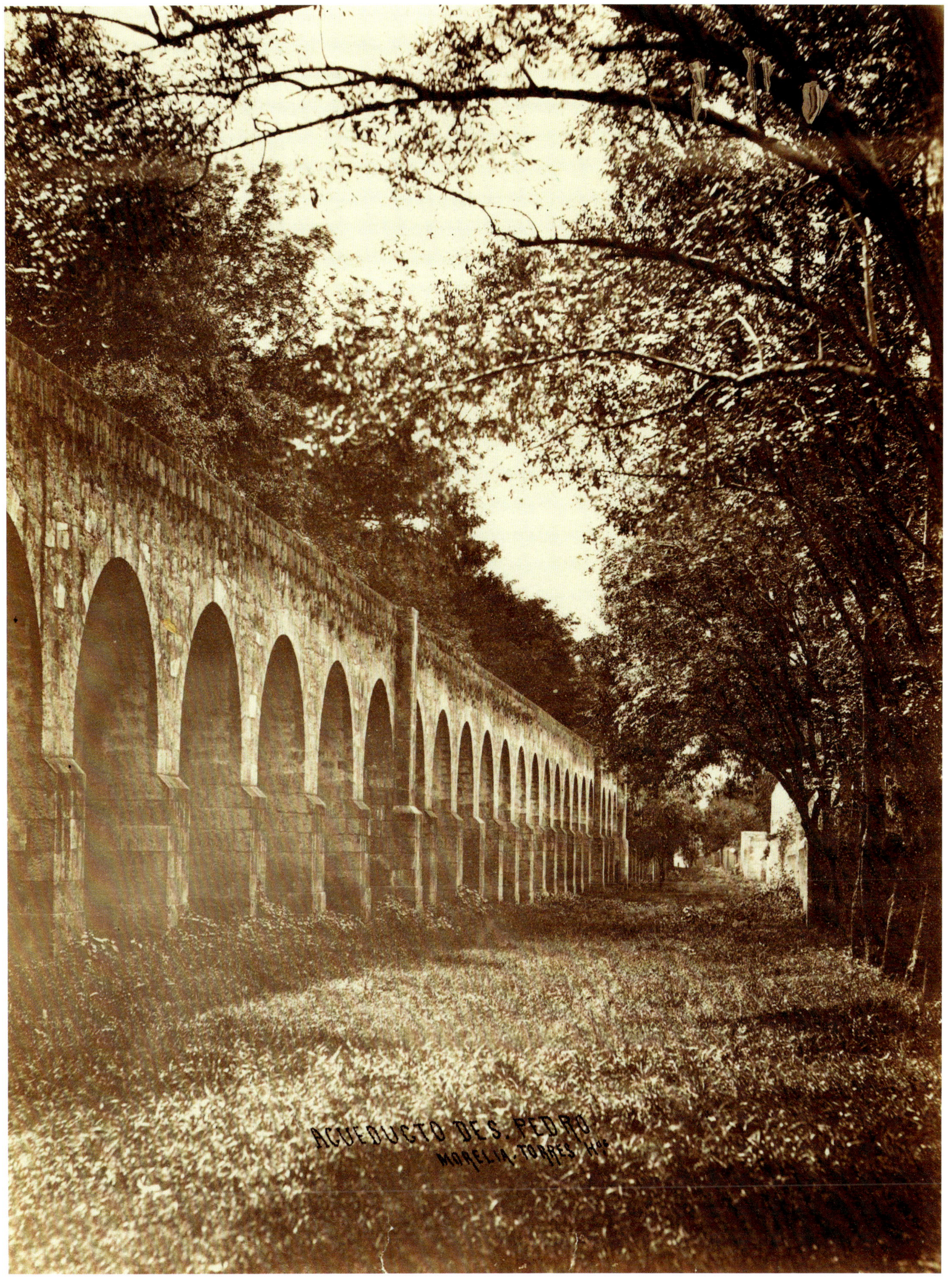
ACUEDUCTO DE S. PEDRO
MORELIA. TORRES Hno.

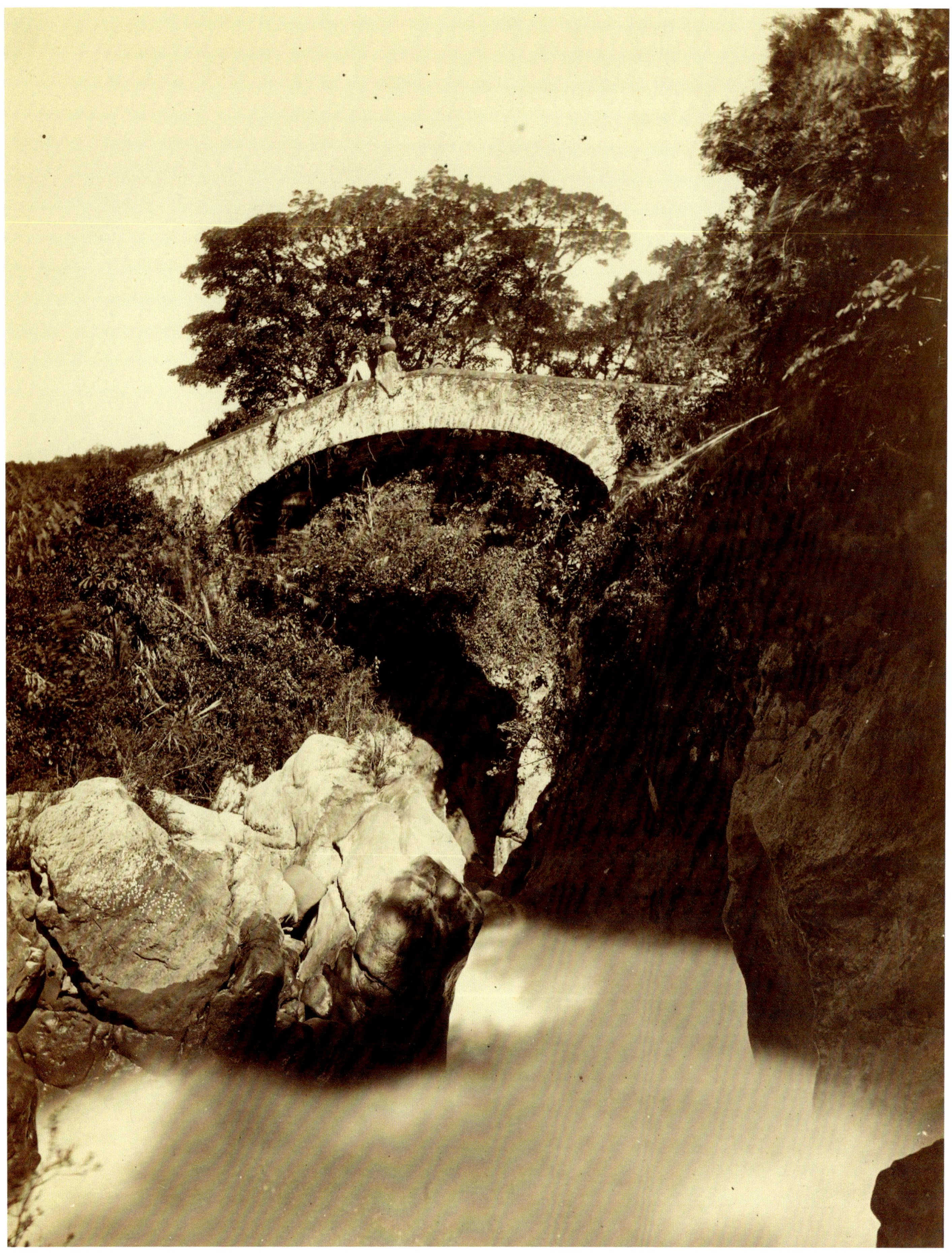

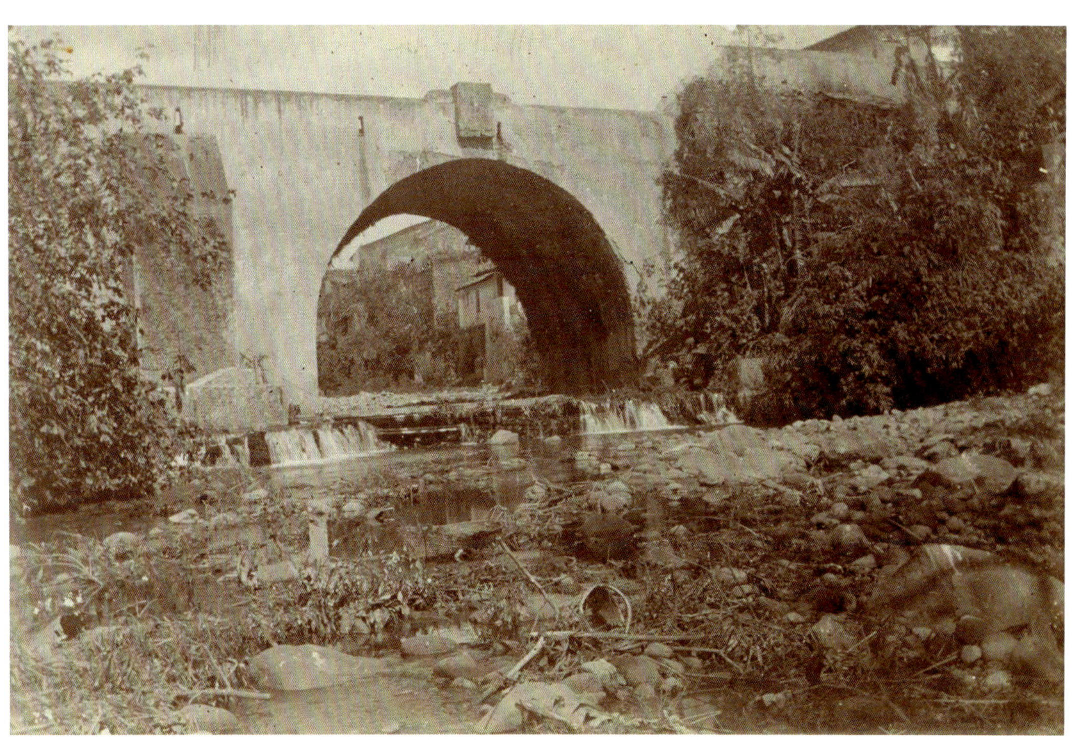

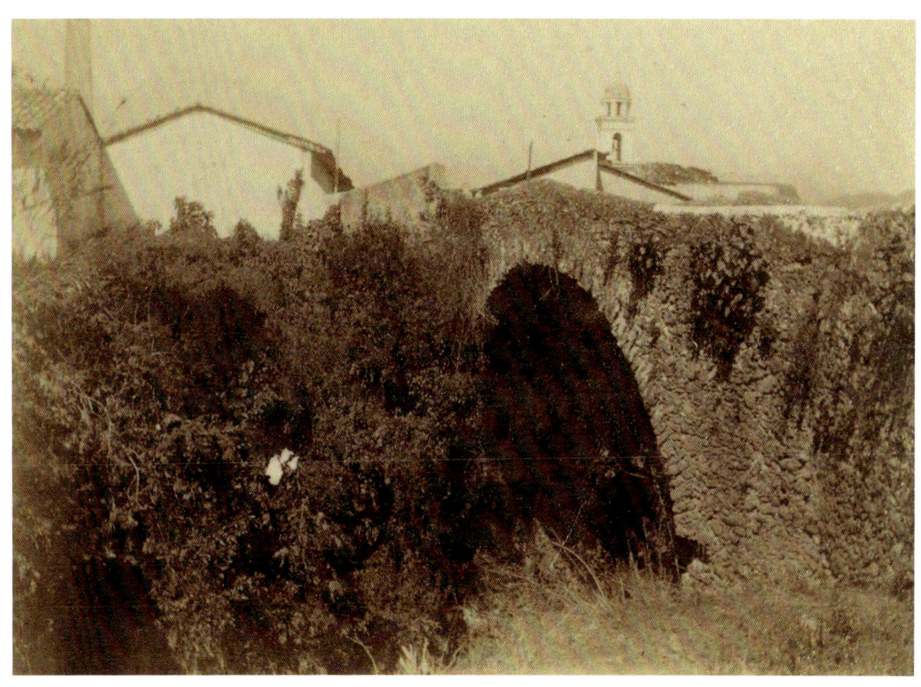

Abel Briquet (1833–1926)
Puenta de Mica, Estado de Vera Cruz,
ca. 1870s
19th-century photographic print,
image size: 10 3⁄8 × 8 3⁄16 inches,
historic mount: 18 11⁄16 × 12 3⁄8 inches
OL.1982.1325.2

Walter Launt Palmer (1854–1932)
Orizaba
1895
19th-century photographic print,
image size: 2 3⁄16 × 3 5⁄16 inches,
historic mount: 2 1⁄8 × 3 3⁄8 inches,
historic album: 6 1⁄4 × 8 1⁄2 × 1 7⁄8 inches
OL.1992.52.33

Walter Launt Palmer (1854–1932)
Near Orizaba,
1895
19th-century photographic print,
image size: 2 5⁄16 × 3 1⁄4 inches,
historic mount: 2 1⁄8 × 3 3⁄8 inches,
historic album: 6 1⁄4 × 8 1⁄2 × 1 7⁄8 inches
OL.1992.52.32

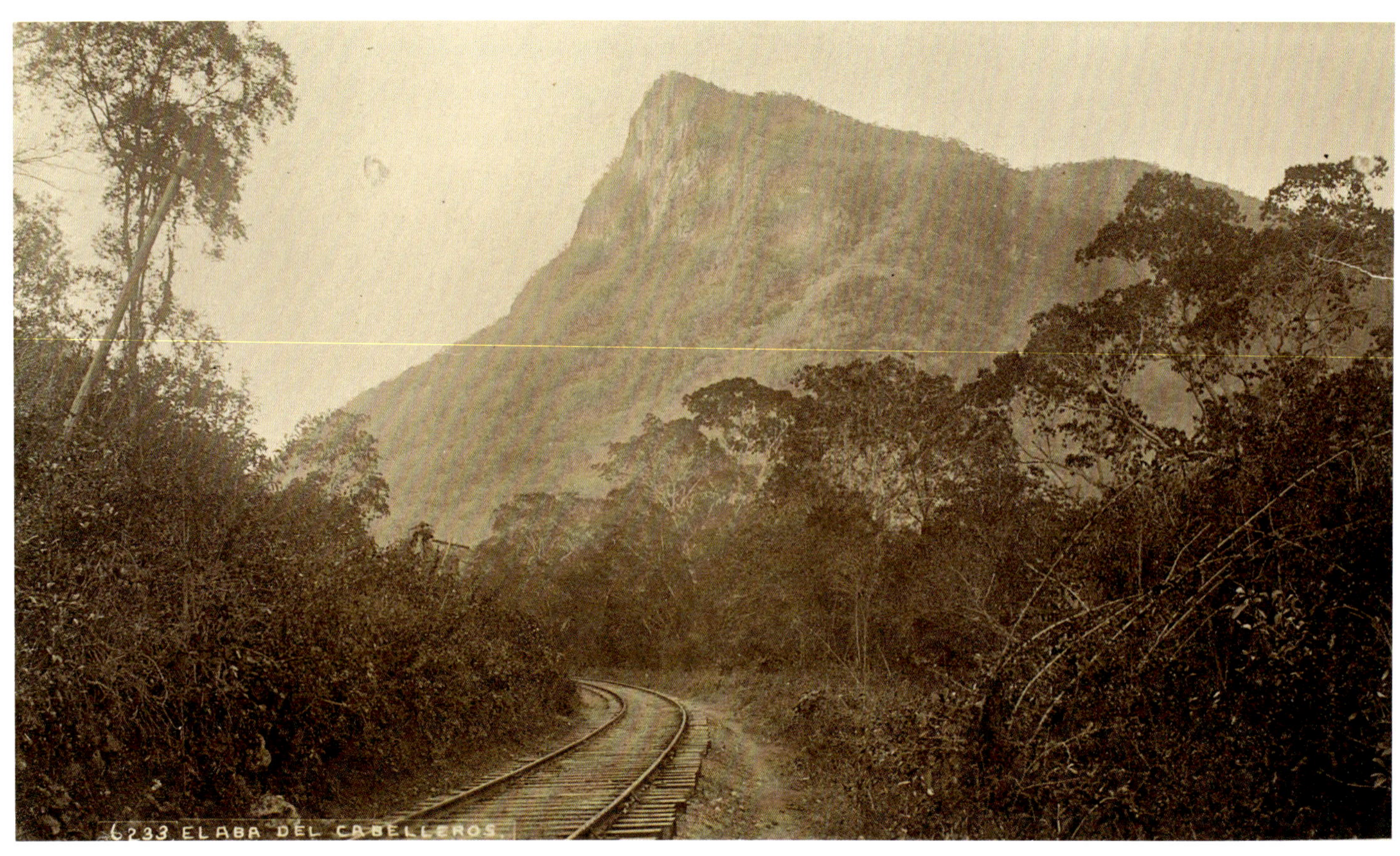

Photographer Unknown
El Aba del Cabelleros,
ca. 1890–1910
19th-century photographic print,
image size: 4 ¼ × 7 5⁄16 inches,
historic album: 9 ⅜ × 12 ½ × 1 ¾ inches
OL.1992.3.61

William Henry Jackson (1843–1942)
In the Canon of the Rio Las Animas Near Rockwood, Colorado,
ca. 1880–1886
19th-century photographic print,
image size: 10 ⅛ × 13 7⁄16 inches,
historic mount: 16 × 20 ⅛ inches
OL.1997.47

Photographer Unknown
Puente del Atoyac Tomada del Rio,
ca. 1890–1910
19th-century photographic print,
image size: 7 ¾ × 9 ⅞ inches,
historic album: 9 ⅜ × 12 ½ × 1 ¾ inches
OL.1992.3.96

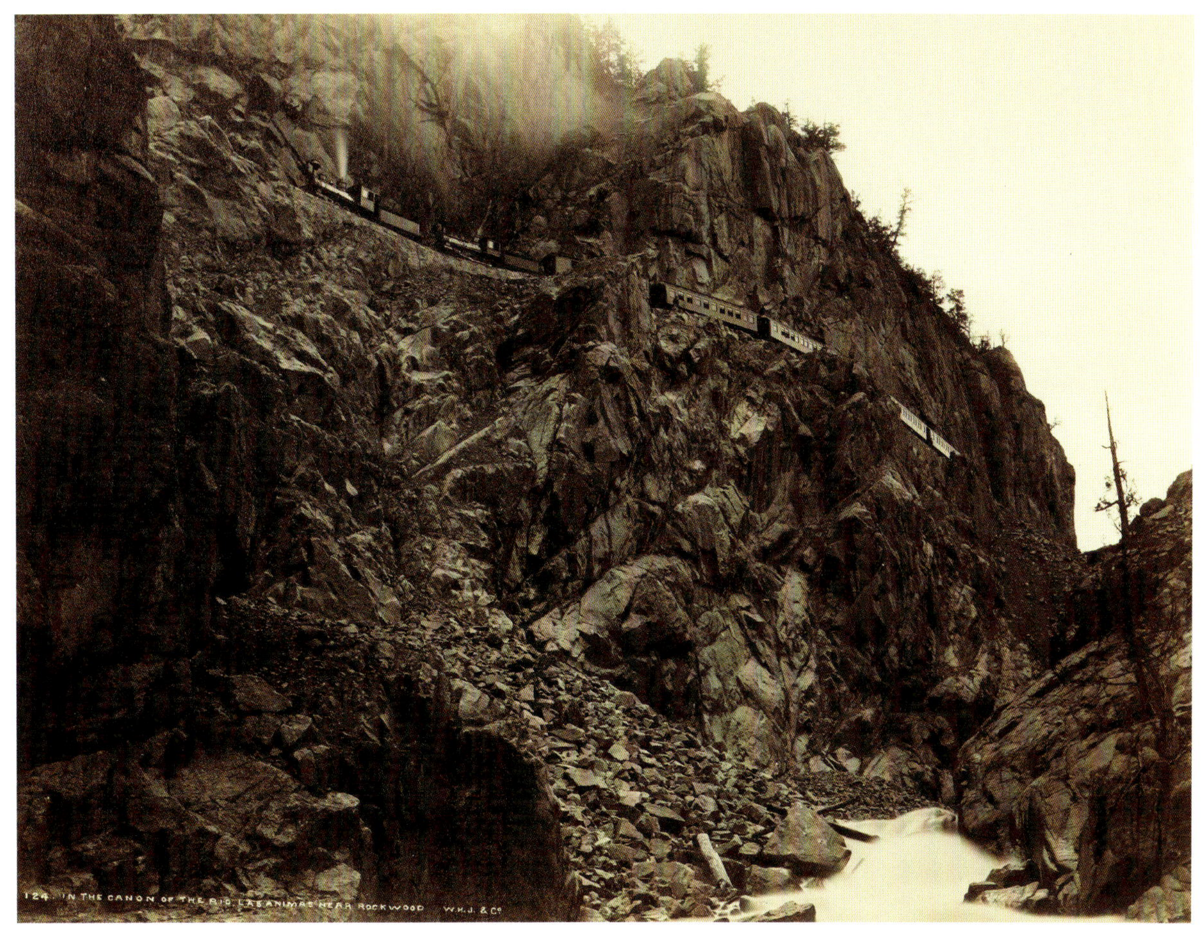
124. IN THE CANON OF THE RIO LAS ANIMAS NEAR ROCKWOOD W.H.J. & Co

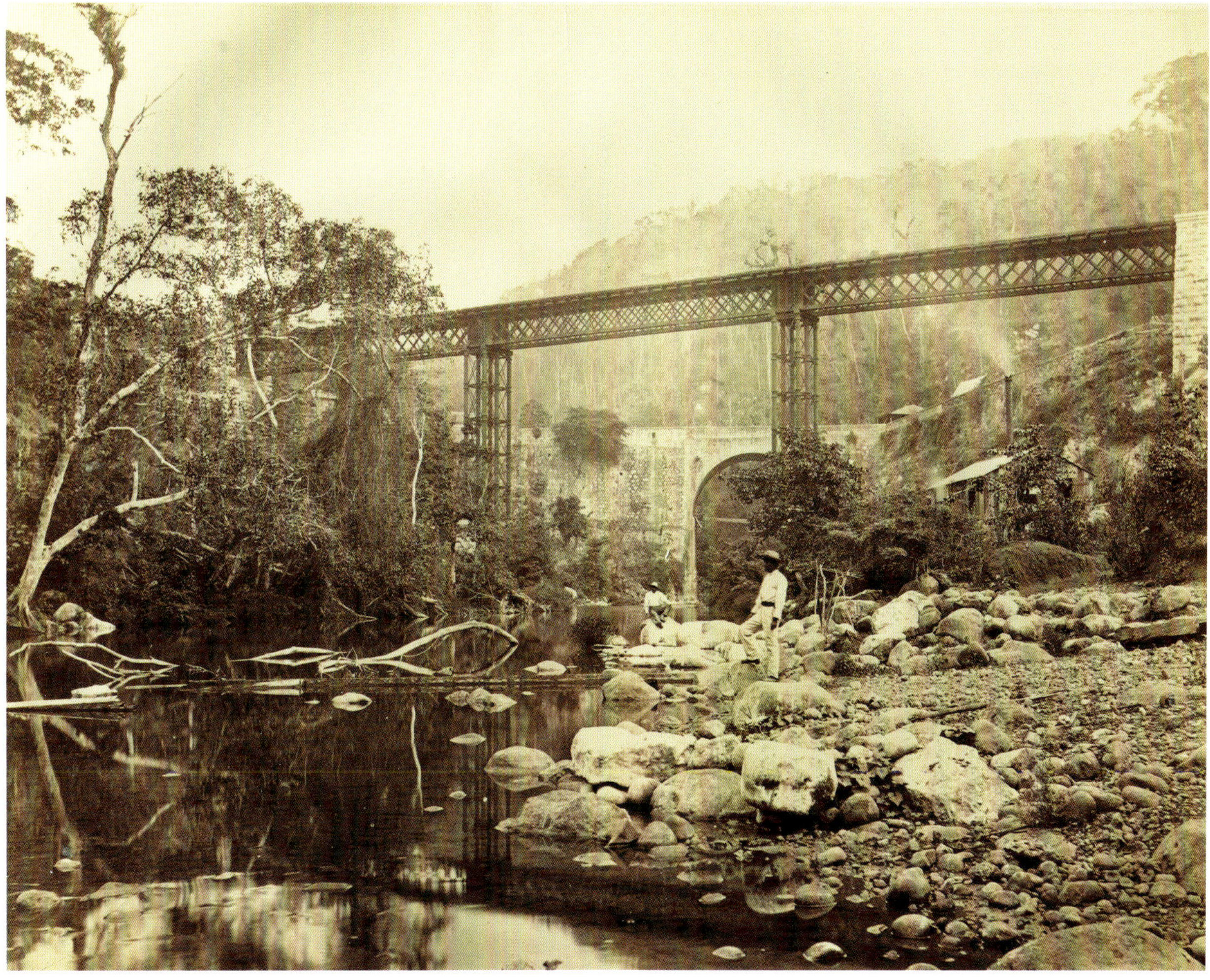

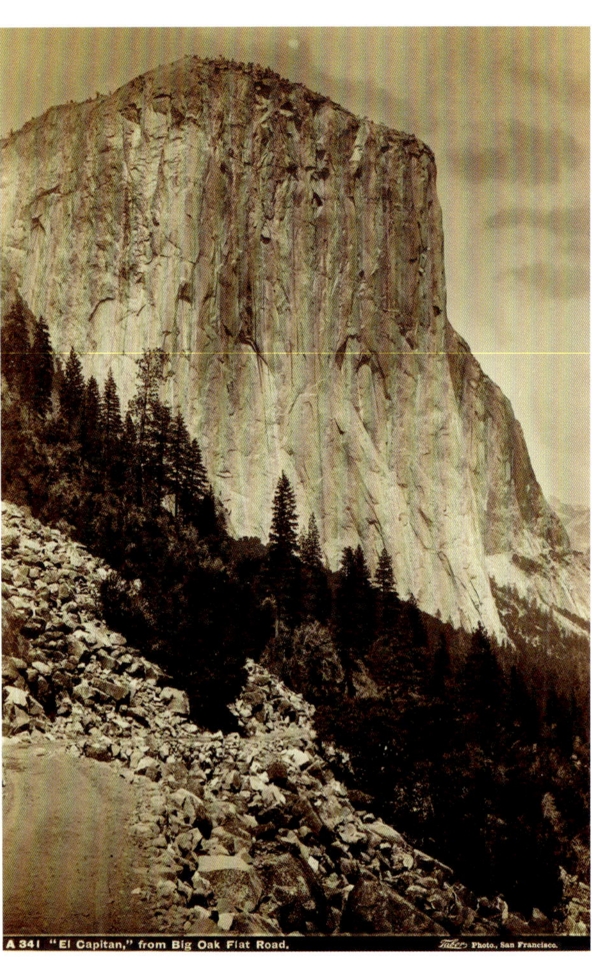

Isaiah West Taber (1830–1912)
"El Capitan," from Big Oak Flat Road,
late 19th century
19th-century photographic print,
image size: 12 5/16 × 8 3/16 inches,
historic mount: 20 1/8 × 16 1/16 inches
OL.1997.46.7

John L. Dunmore (flourished 1875–1899)
and George P. Critcherson (1823–1892),
commissioned by William Bradford (1823–1892)
Part of the Side of a Glacier,
1869
19th-century photographic print,
image size: 16 1/2 × 13 1/4 inches,
historic mount: 20 15/16 × 16 7/8 inches
OL.2004.146

Samuel Bourne (1834–1912)
Snowy Peaks near the Gangootri Glacier,
ca. 1866
19th-century photographic print,
image size: 9 5/8 × 11 3/16 inches,
historic mount: 15 3/16 × 18 3/4 inches
OL.1982.1402

Carleton E. Watkins (1829–1916),
published by Isaiah West Taber (1830–1912)
The Half Dome and Mirror Lake, from Glacier Point, Yosemite, California,
ca. 1870–1890
19th-century photographic print,
image size: 15 15/16 × 20 1/8 inches,
historic mount: 22 × 28 inches
OL.1982.1279.2

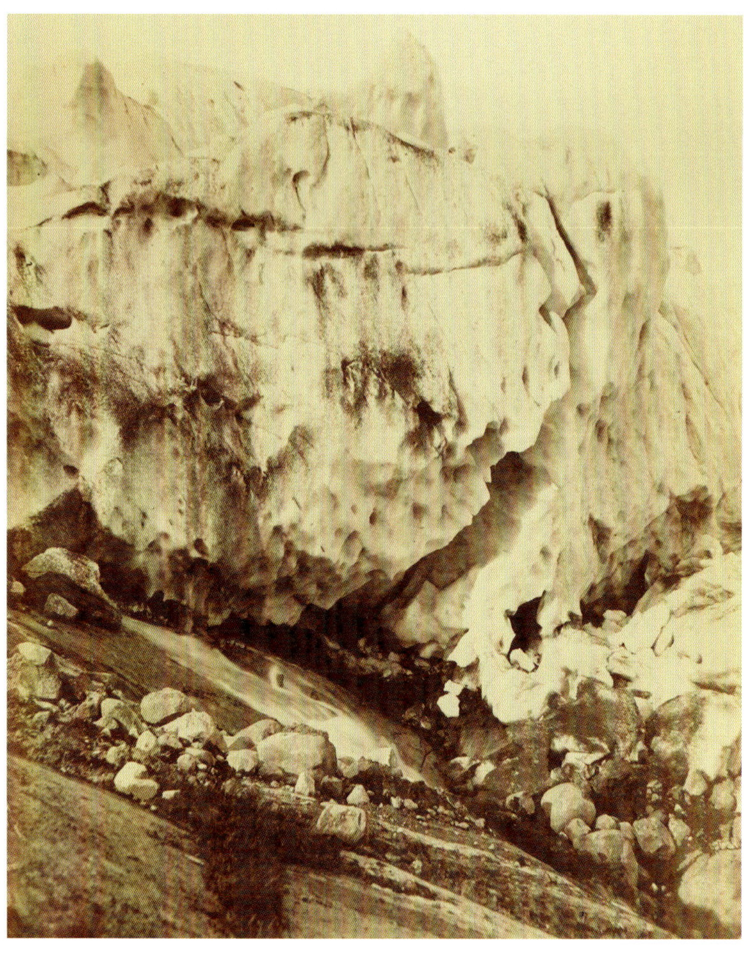

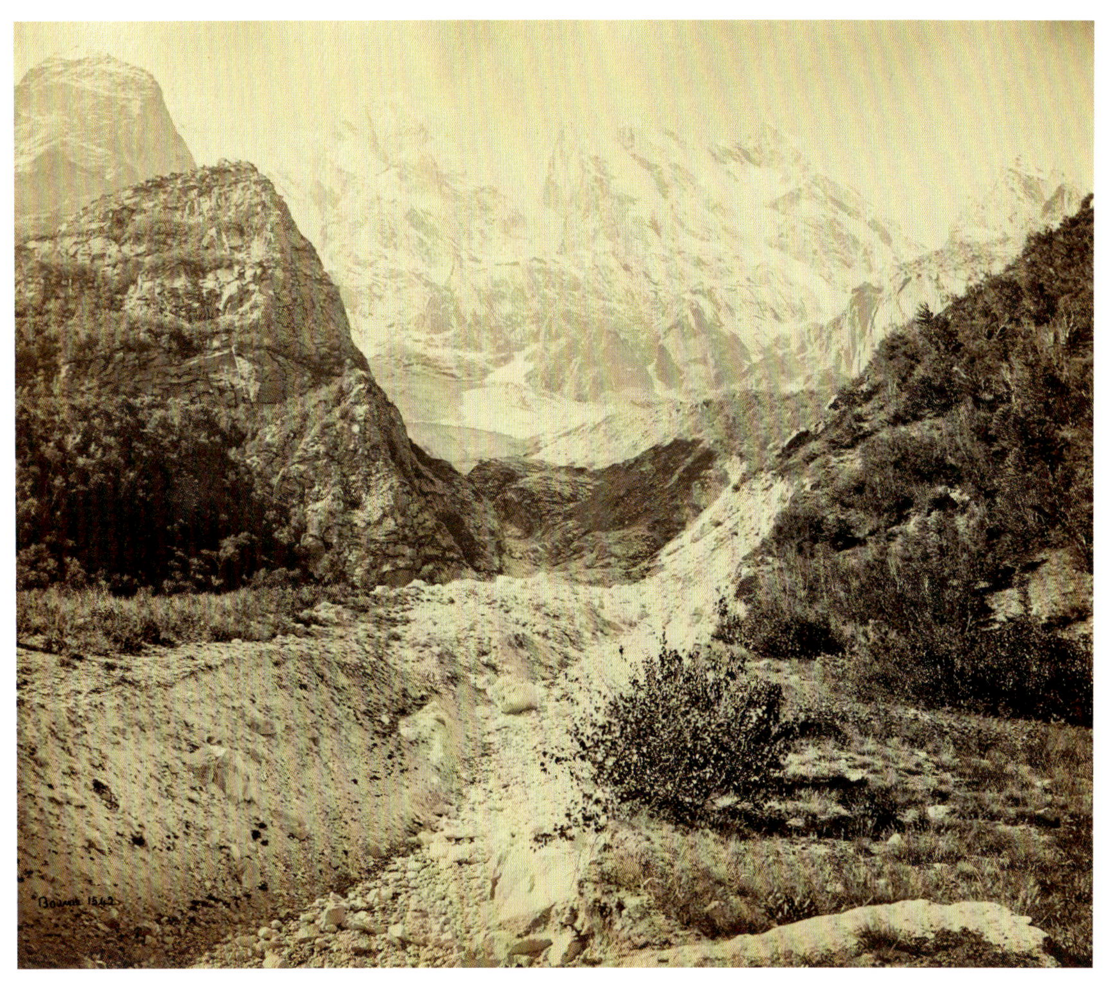
Bourne 1542

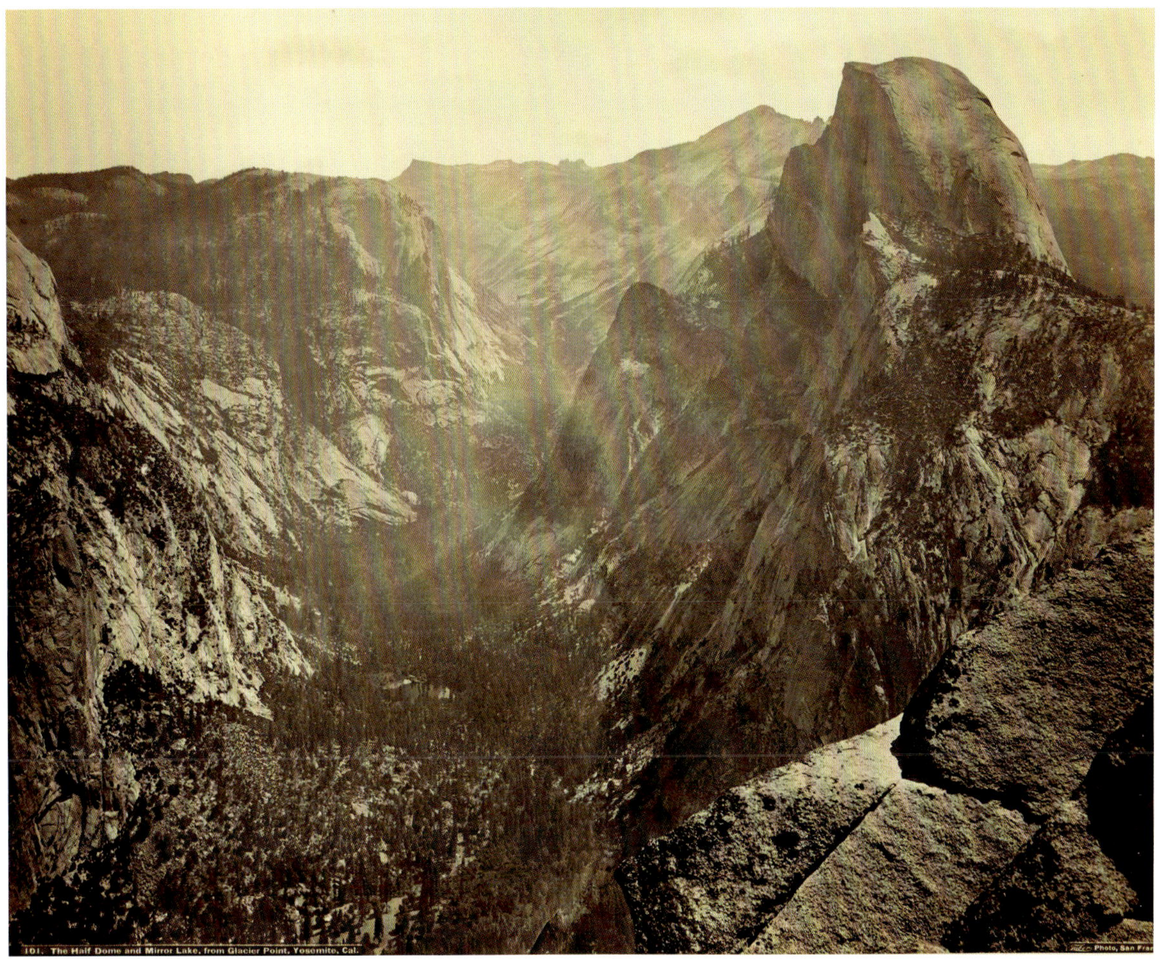
101. The Half Dome and Mirror Lake, from Glacier Point, Yosemite, Cal.

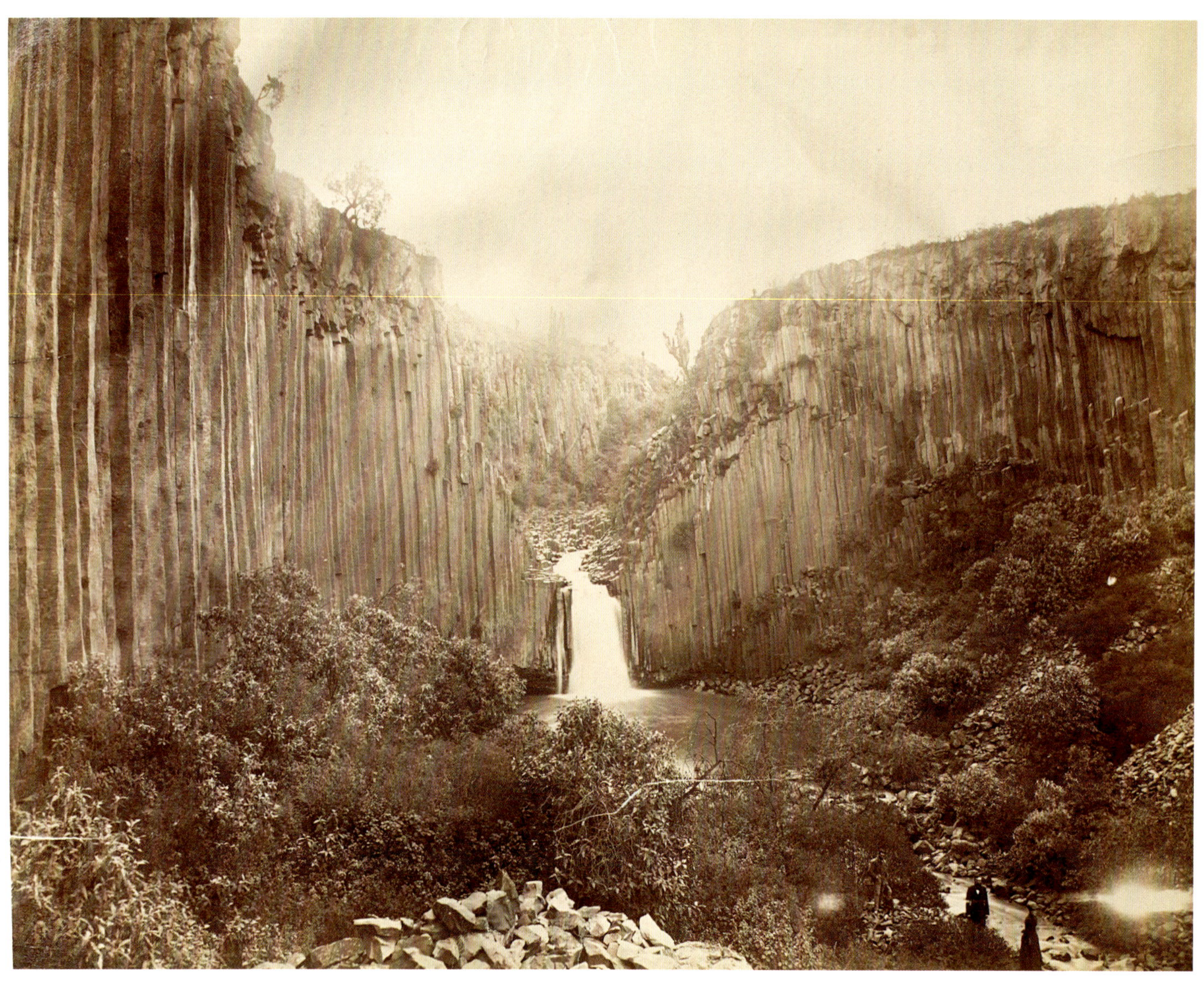

Photographer Unknown
Basaltic Prisms of Santa María Regla,
ca. 1890–1910
19th-century photographic print,
image size: 8 ¼ × 10 ½ inches,
historic album: 9 ⅜ × 12 ½ × 1 ¾ inches
OL.1992.3.94

Frank Jay Haynes (1853–1921)
Jupiter's Terrace,
ca. 1881–1889
19th-century photographic print,
image size: 6 ⅝ × 8 ⅝ inches,
historic mount: 10 × 12 inches
OL.1981.365.7

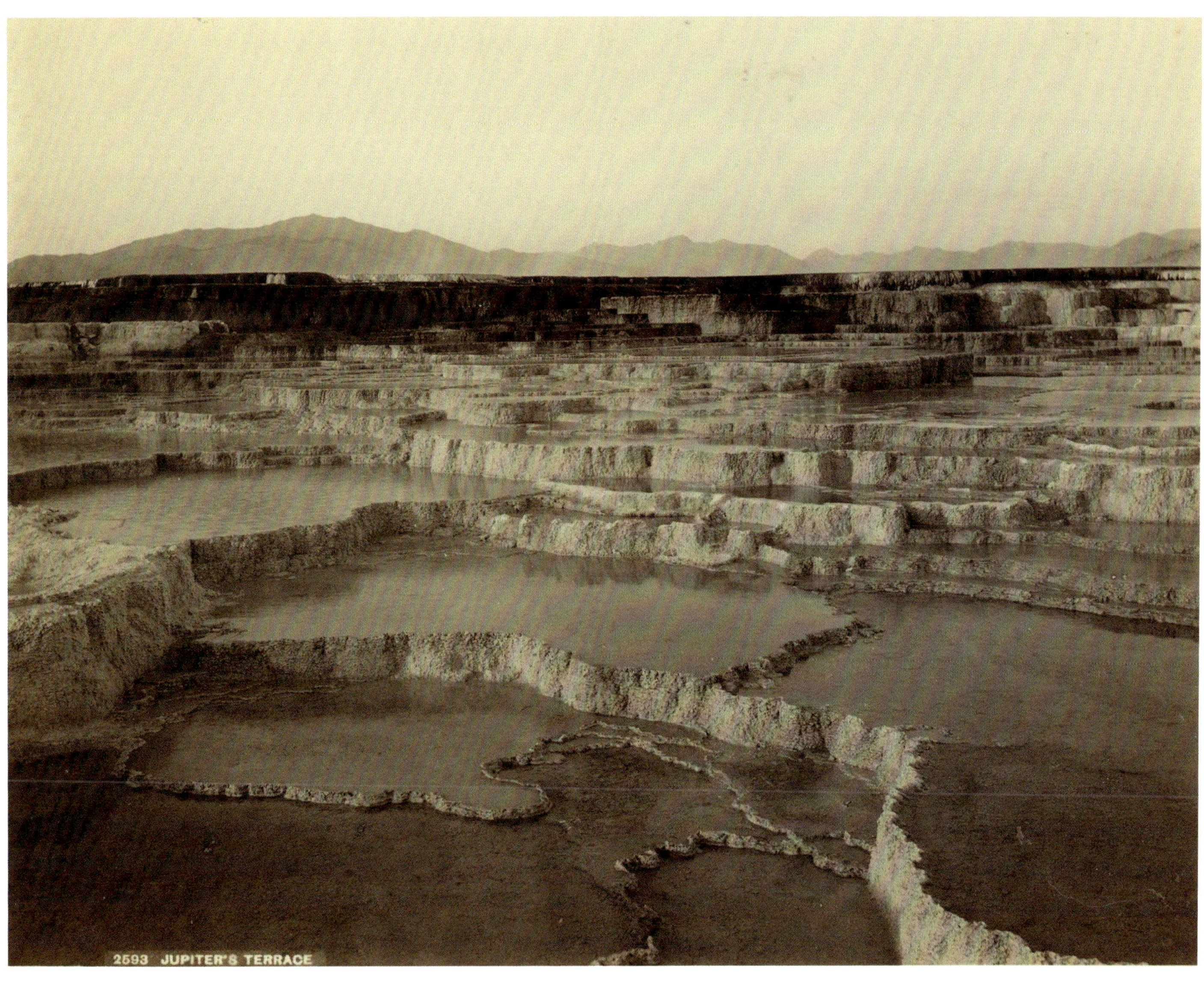

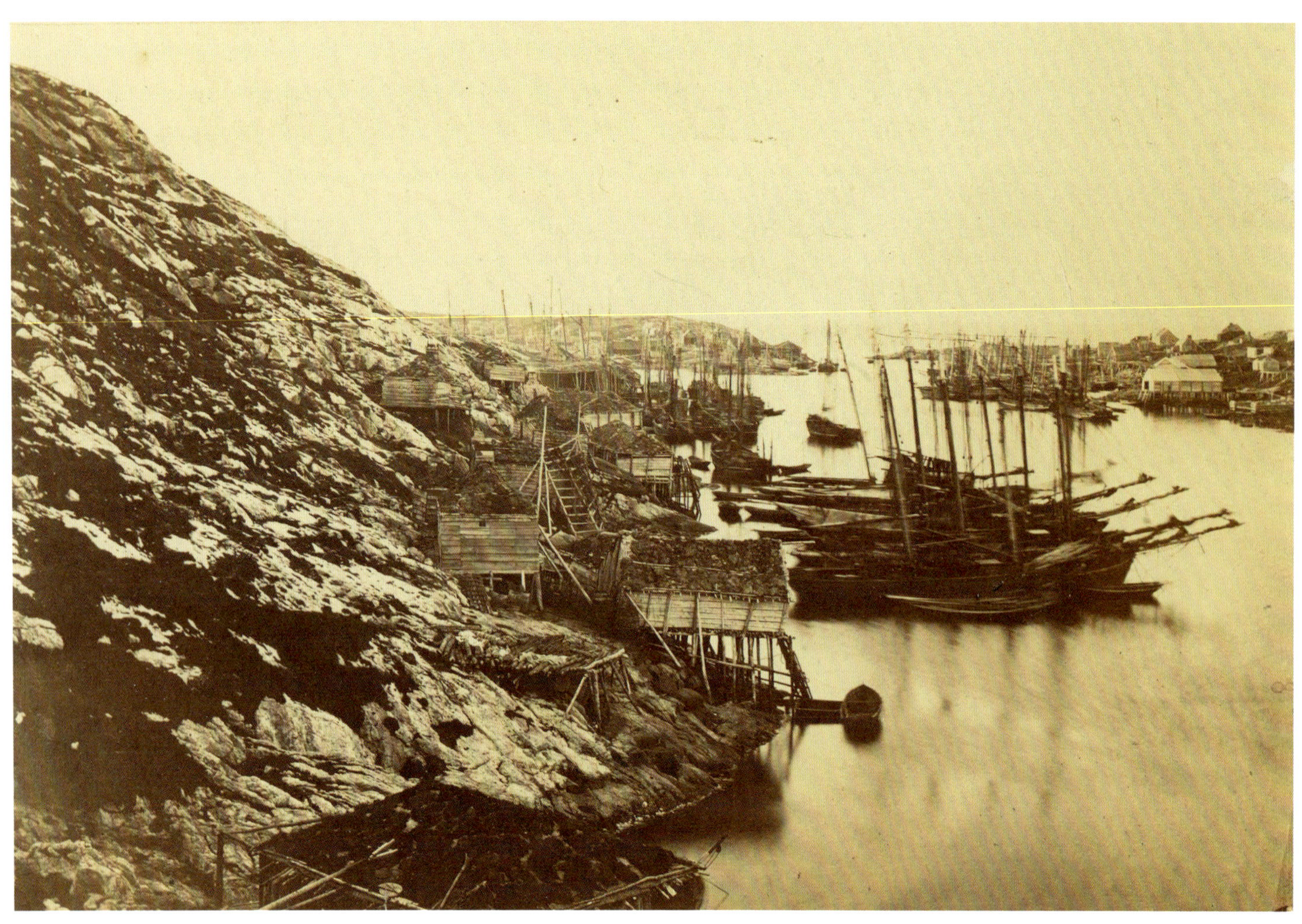

Photographer Unknown
Battle Harbor, Labrador,
ca. 1860
19th-century photographic print,
image size: 5 ¾ × 8 ½ inches,
historic mount: 10 ⅝ × 13 ⅝ inches
OL.1981.331.2

Platt D. Babbitt (1823–1879)
Niagara Falls from the Canadian Side,
ca. 1850–1855
Daguerreotype,
image size: 8 ⁹⁄₁₆ × 6 ⅞ inches
OL.1981.604

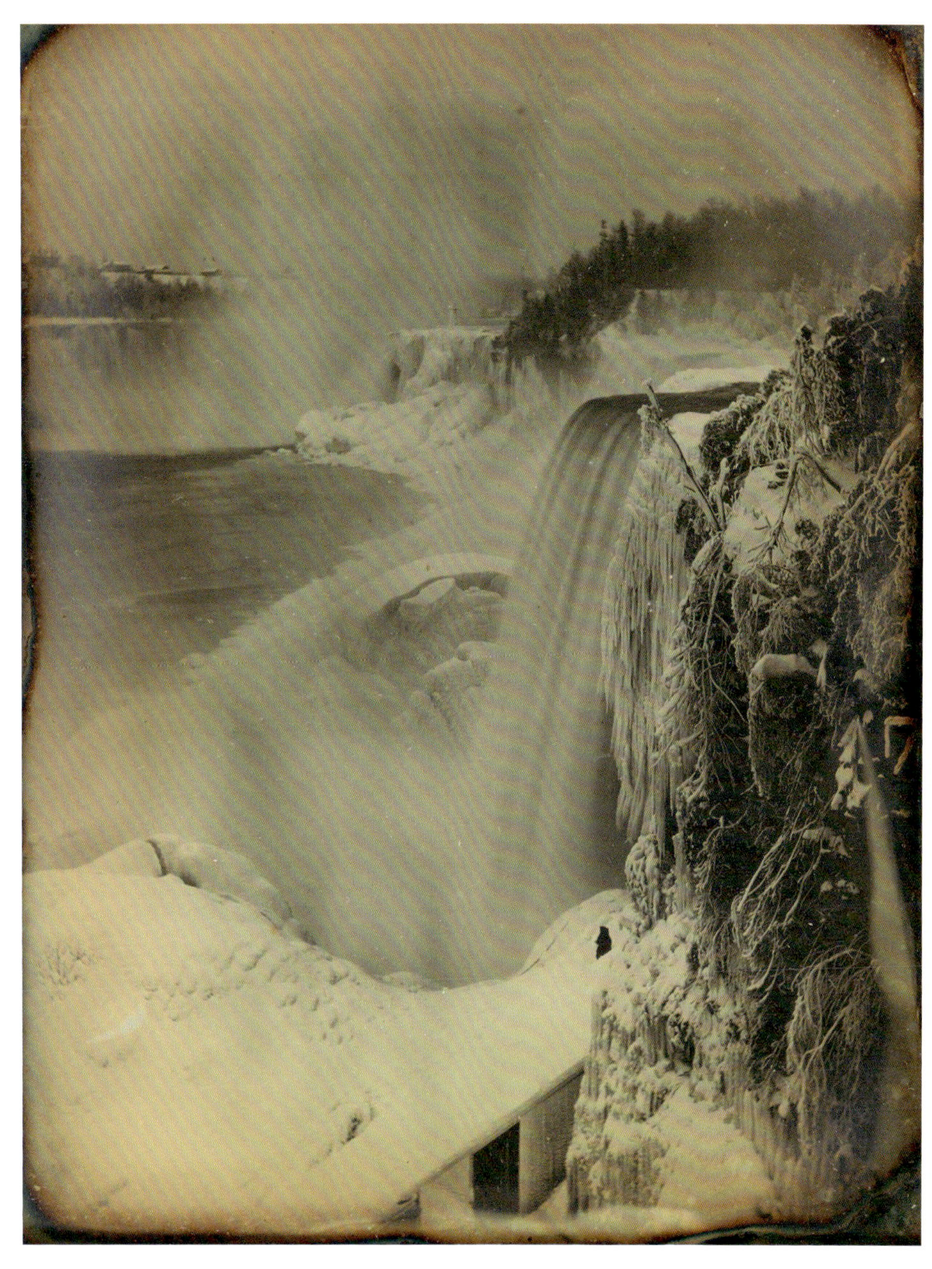

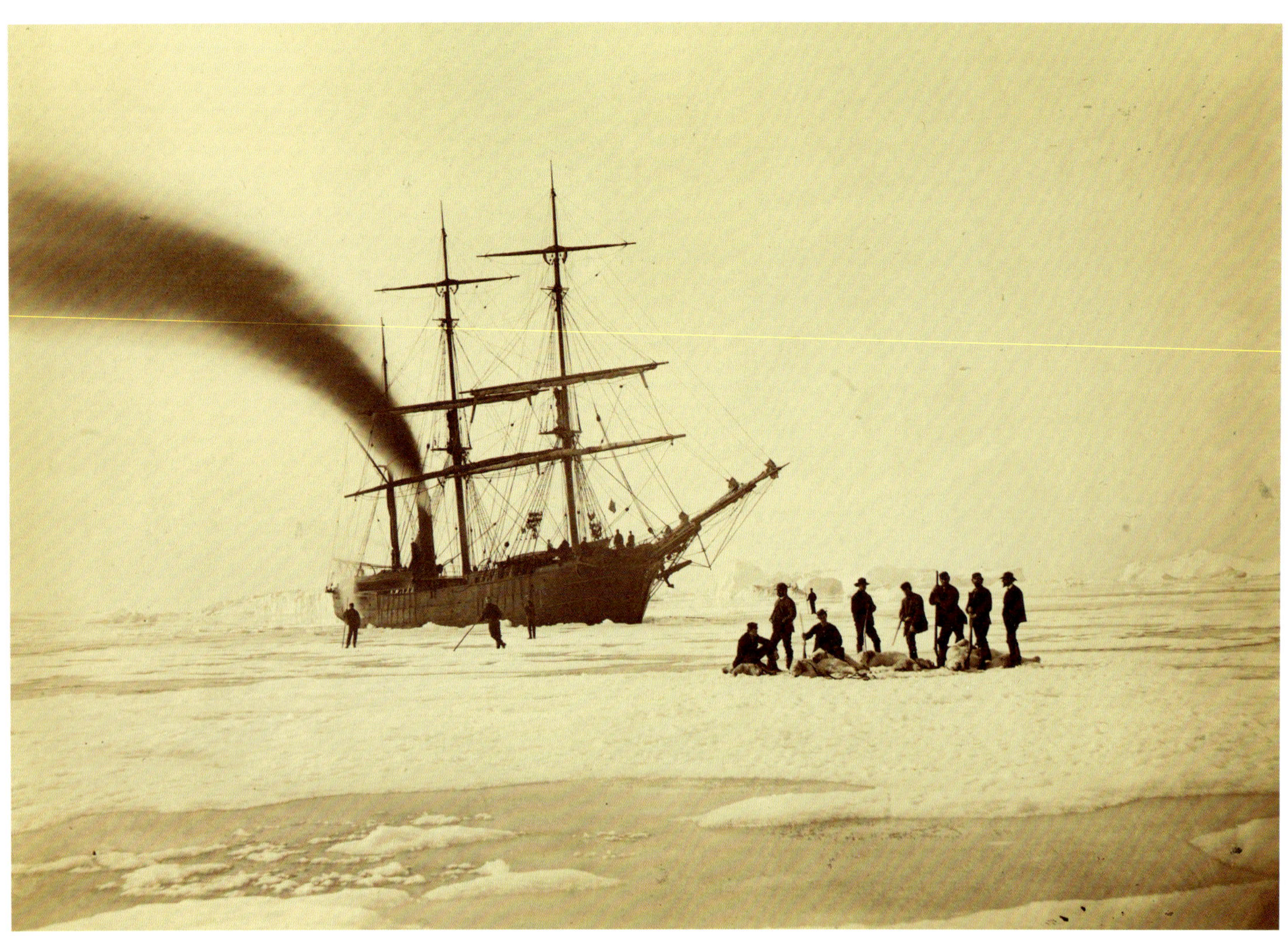

John L. Dunmore (flourished 1875–1899) and George P. Critcherson (1823–1892), commissioned by William Bradford (1823–1892)
Among the Field Ice in Melville Bay (A Hunting Party with Five Captured Bears in the Foreground),
1869
19th-century photographic print,
image size: 11 9/16 × 16 5/8 inches,
historic mount: 16 7/8 × 21 inches
OL.2004.149

John L. Dunmore (flourished 1875–1899) and George P. Critcherson (1823–1892), commissioned by William Bradford (1823–1892)
July in Melville Bay,
1869
19th-century photographic print,
image size: 11 5/8 × 16 7/16 inches,
historic mount: 16 7/8 × 21 inches
OL.2001.41

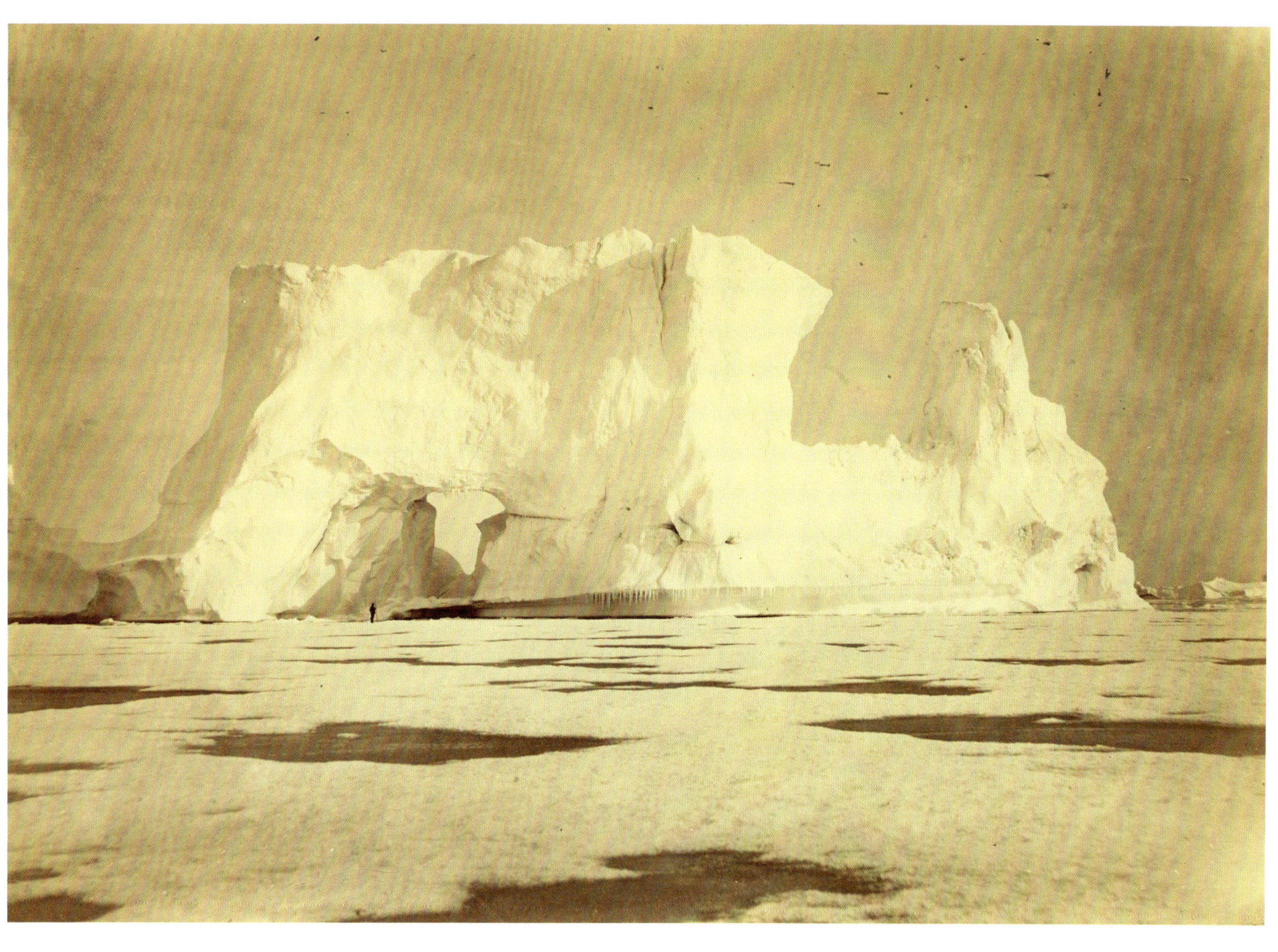

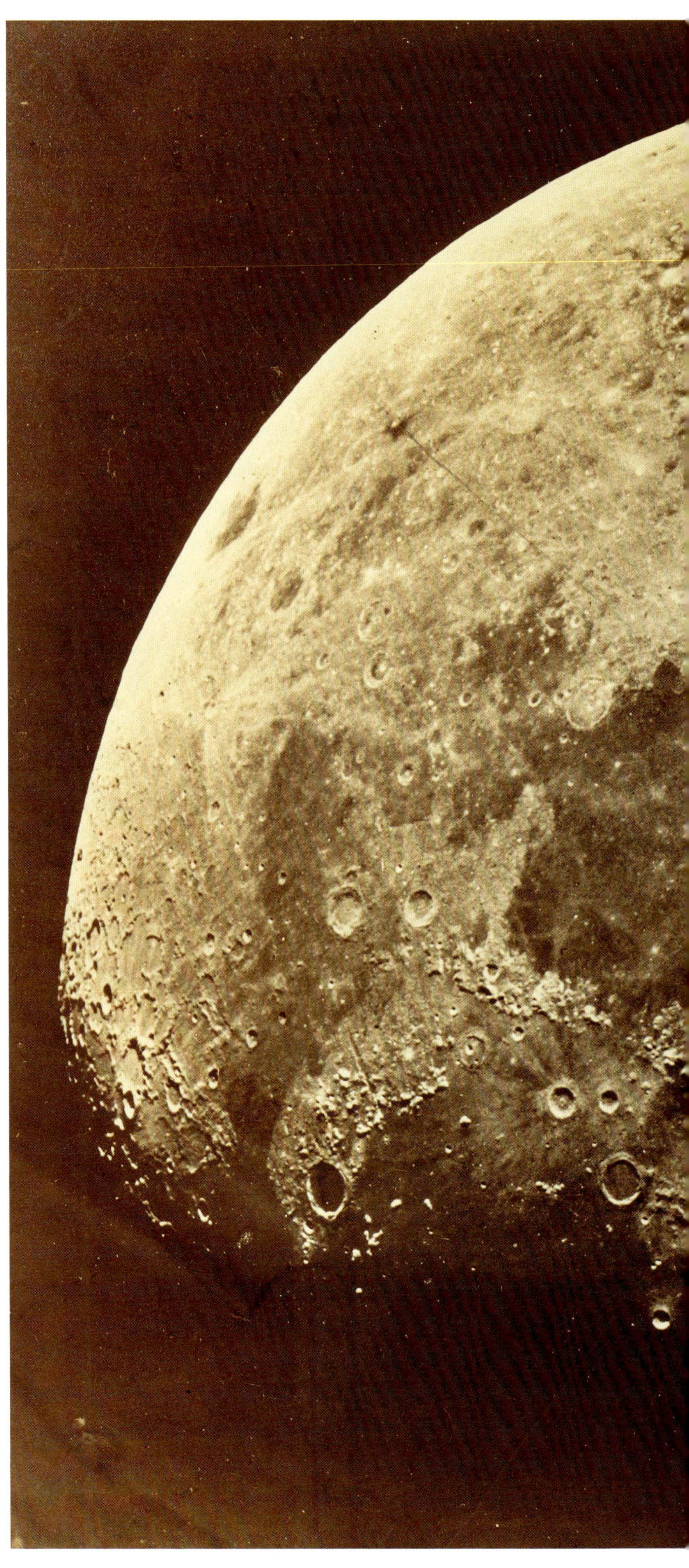

Lewis M. Rutherfurd (1816–1892)
The Moon, New York,
1865
19th-century photographic print,
image size: 17 × 22 ½ inches,
historic mount: 21 × 26 ⅞ inches
OL.1982.1277

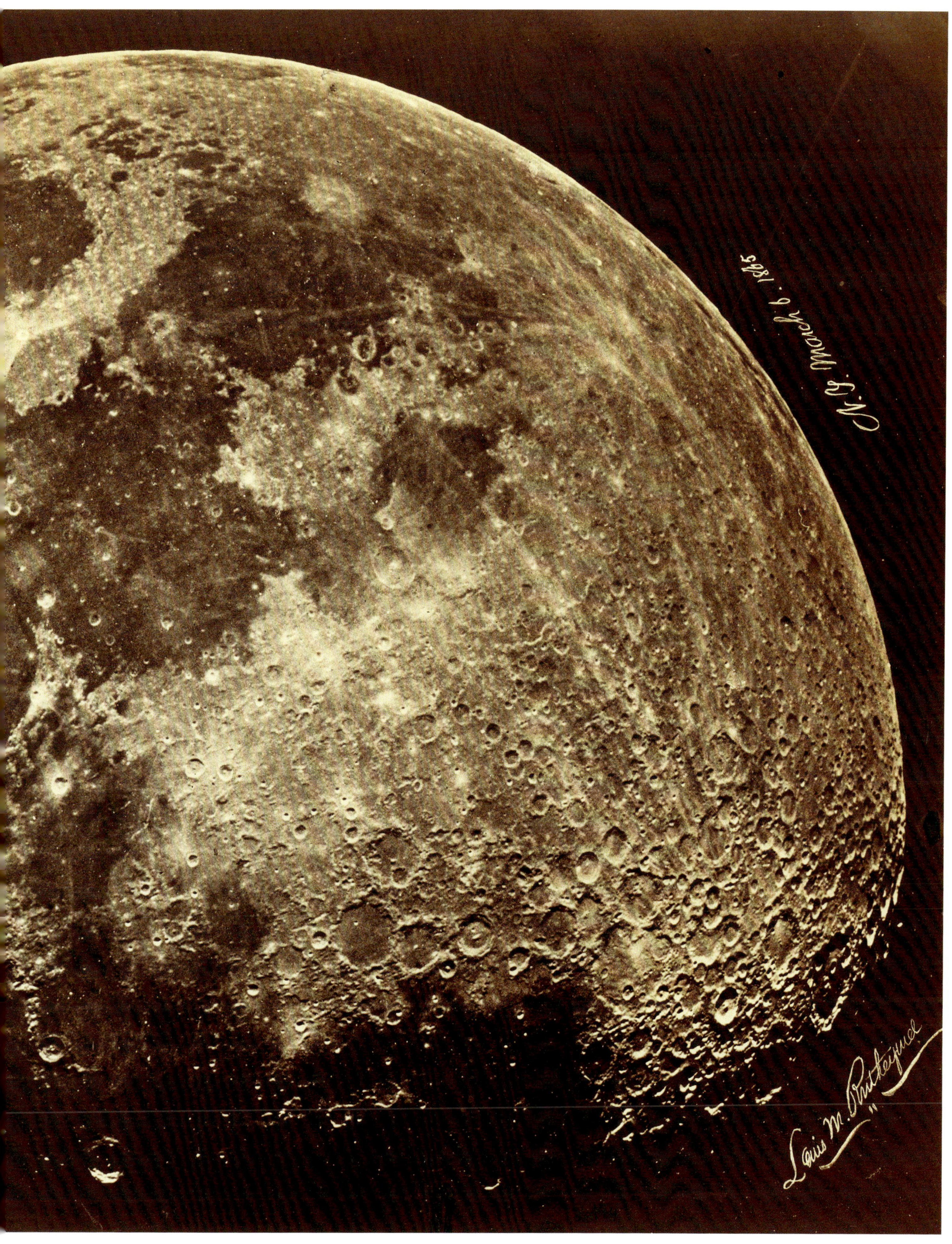
N.Y. March 6. 1865
Lewis M. Rutherfurd

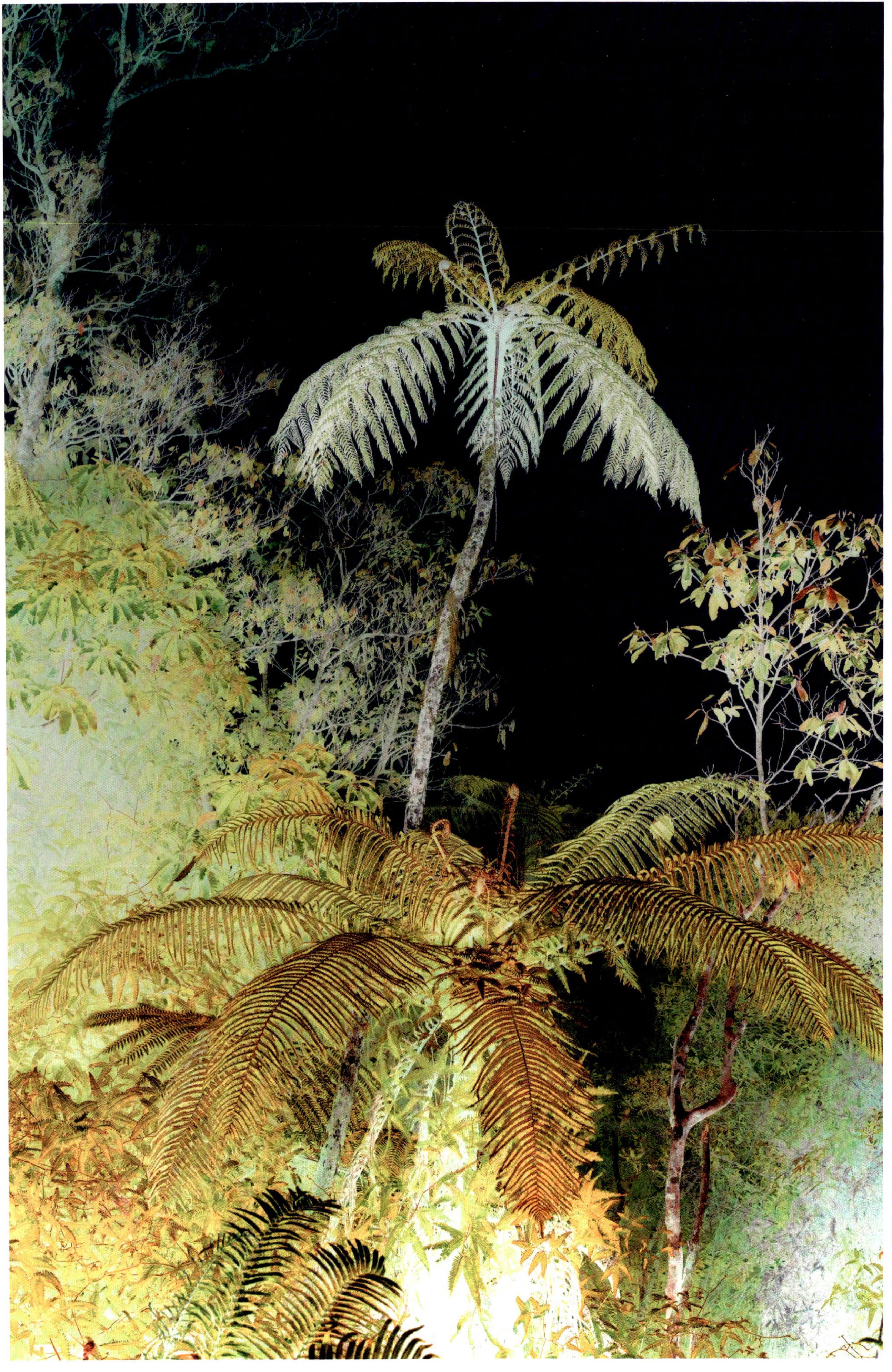

David Hartt
Source image for:
The Histories (after Church), Version with xenoformed atmosphere/ Rayleigh scattering spectrum shift,
2023
Tapestry,
90 × 60 inches

TERRAFORMING/XENOFORMING

David Hartt

The landscape is always moving, a thin crust of earth and rock that drifts along the earth's mantle. Water carves the landscape, as glacier, and ocean, and river, and as rain. Plants are organic beings that have, over a period of eons, fully colonized the land and water; they represent the majority of living matter on the planet, and through their ubiquity, act as temporal and physical intermediaries between us and the landscape. Plants are autotrophs, primary producers that convert light from the sun and inorganic chemicals from the earth into energy and atmosphere. Humanity and other heterotrophs consume the body and breath of plants, our biological form has evolved and is contingent on their benevolence. We inhabit the atmosphere,[1] an impossibly narrow space conceived and established by plants between the land and sky.

Near the town of Gilboa, in Schoharie County to the west of the Hudson River, the fossilized remnants of trees from the Devonian period (380–360 million years old) were discovered, evidence perhaps of Earth's oldest forest. While stump samples of the *Eospermatopteris* were excavated from a local quarry in the 1870s, it wasn't until 2006 when nearby, an intact crown belonging to Cladoxylopsid *Wattieza* (Pseudosporochnales) was found attached to an *Eospermatopteris* trunk and base. The ancient tree-fern-like plant is estimated to have stood at least eight meters tall, and forests of them would have slowly shaped the atmosphere, while their cast-off fronds provided a thick humus of nourishment to early arthropods.[2]

The landscape of the Hudson River Estuary has been tectonically stable for the last 300 million years.[3] Besides the slow constant drift of continents, the last major geologic force effecting the region and its topography was twenty thousand years ago, with the advance and retreat of the Laurentide ice sheet which established the features of the landscape we recognize today. Wedged between the Catskill Mountains to the west and the Taconic Mountains to the east, the Hudson Lowlands are a fertile territory whose bedrock consists of sandstone, siltstone, shale, limestone, and carbonate blocks in Taconic Mélange.[4] Retreating glaciers left surficial deposits of lacustrine silt and clay, fluvial gravel, kame moraines and undifferentiated drift complex to enrich the soil.[5]

The American geographer and anthropologist Carl Ortwin Sauer gives us a useful description in his essay *The Morphology of Landscape* that expands our understanding of the terrain beyond its geologic and botanical features:

> The term "landscape" is proposed to denote the unit concept of geography, to characterize the peculiarly geographic association of facts. Equivalent terms in a sense are "area" and "region." Area is of course a general term, not distinctively geographic. Region has come to imply, to some geographers at least, an order of magnitude. Landscape is the English equivalent of the term German geographers are using largely, and strictly has the same meaning: a land shape, in which the process of shaping is by no means thought of as simply physical. It may be defined, therefore, as an area made up of a distinct association of forms, both physical and cultural.[6]

The landscape has existed long before humankind began to modify or describe it. We can, however, begin to follow the history of a place by tracing the names it might have had given to it by different communities. An ancient river, variously called Ka'nón:no, Mahicannittuk, Rio San Antonio, and Groote Rivier, is now named the Hudson and has continued to flow from its mountain

1 Emanuele Coccia, *The Life of Plants: A Metaphysics of Mixture* (Cambridge, UK; Medford, MA: Polity, 2019): 8-11.

2 William H. Stein et al., "Giant Cladoxylopsid Trees Resolve the Enigma of the Earth's Earliest Forest Stumps at Gilboa," *Nature* 446, no. 7138 (April 1, 2007): 904–7, https://doi.org/10.1038/nature05705.

3 Roy T. Budnik, Jeffery R. Walker, and Kirsten Menking, *Geology and Topography of Dutchess County NY*, revision of the Natural Resource Inventory of Dutchess County (May 2010), https://www.dutchessny.gov/Departments/Planning/Docs/nrichapthree.pdf

4 Rickard Fisher, *Geologic Map of New York; Hudson-Mohawk Sheet, 1:250,000*, map (The University of the State of New York, 1971), http://www.nysm.nysed.gov/research-collections/geology/gis.

5 Dineen Caldwell, *Surficial Geologic Map of New York, Hudson–Mohawk Sheet*, map (The University of the State of New York, 1987), http://www.nysm.nysed.gov/research-collections/geology/gis.

6 Carl Ortwin Sauer, *Land and Life: A Selection from the Writings of Carl Ortwin Sauer* (Berkeley: University of California Press, 1963): 321.

sources in the north to eventually deposit water and sediment into an ocean now known as the Atlantic. Each name for the river is a marker of those who would eventually establish settlements along its shore. Water and climate erode the riverbank just as the forces of migration, disease and conflict erase subsequent layers of human habitation. Sauer continues: "Under the influence of a given culture, itself changing through time, the landscape undergoes development, passing through phases, and probably reaching ultimately the end of its cycle of development. With the introduction of a different—that is, an alien—culture, a rejuvenation of the cultural landscape sets in, or a new landscape is superimposed on remnants of an older one."[7]

The river would eventually give its name to a group of artists living and working in its vicinity during the nineteenth century. Established by English émigré artist Thomas Cole, the Hudson River School consisted of several individuals including Asher Brown Durand, Sanford Robinson Gifford, John Frederick Kensett, Susie M. Barstow, and Frederic Edwin Church. They would hike to make *plein air* sketches of the Hudson River Estuary and its surrounding region, which became references for the landscape paintings later composed in their studios. Considered remote from the metropolises of New York, Hartford, and Boston, the area was largely unspoiled by industry. The work and renown of these artists influenced others active in the genre of landscape painting, such as Robert Seldon Duncanson and William Louis Sonntag who worked in Cincinnati or Martin Johnson Heade, from Pennsylvania, who initially made serene studies of coastal New England. While the estuary forged the style of the Hudson River School painters, their subject matter followed the expansionist ambitions of America both to the West of the Hudson and much further abroad. Frederic Church, for instance, would venture from the heart of the Andes, and the fern laden hills of Jamaica, to the ancient ruins of Petra in the Ottoman territory of Jordan. Church would eventually settle and make his home on a promontory overlooking the Hudson, across the river from his teacher, Thomas Cole, and it is there that he would begin to shape the land as a place that best expressed all that he saw as good and special in the region, but also a place inflected by the diversity of his travels.

The original site of what would become Olana was a 126-acre farm purchased by Church in 1860; he would eventually expand this through the acquisition of adjacent properties to form an estate of 250 acres. Church worked with architect Calvert Vaux on the Persian-inspired house that was to crown the highest elevation on his land. This vantage point allowed him to observe not only his extensive grounds but also provided magnificent views of the river to the south and to the west where the peaks of the Catskills marked the horizon. Surrounding the house Church designed a landscape that included fields for the working farm, gardens, forests, and a man-made lake. He laid roads of red shale, quarried on the site, that served more than facilitating transit; it wound around the lake, through grazing fields and the newly planted stands of native trees like maples, birches, hickories, hemlocks, chestnuts, pines and oaks; a meandering journey that took the visitor through a carefully calibrated sequence of picturesque scenes. The land was graded and retaining walls were established near and around the house to frame and secure its position. In many ways the work on the landscape was an extension of Church's work as an artist as is evidenced in a letter he wrote to his friend and fellow artist Erastus Dow Palmer: "I have made about one and three-quarters miles of roads this season, opening entirely new and beautiful views—I can make more and better landscapes in this way than by tampering with canvas and paint in the Studio."[8]

In 1865, Church and his wife Isabel Carnes Church traveled to Jamaica. The Civil War was still being fought in a divided America and President Abraham Lincoln had just been assassinated. The Churches however were perhaps seeking solace after the tragic death of their two young children. After

7 Ibid, 343.

8 Robert E. Henshaw, *Environmental History of the Hudson River: Human Uses That Changed the Ecology, Ecology That Changed Human Uses* (Albany: State University of New York Press, 2011): 303.

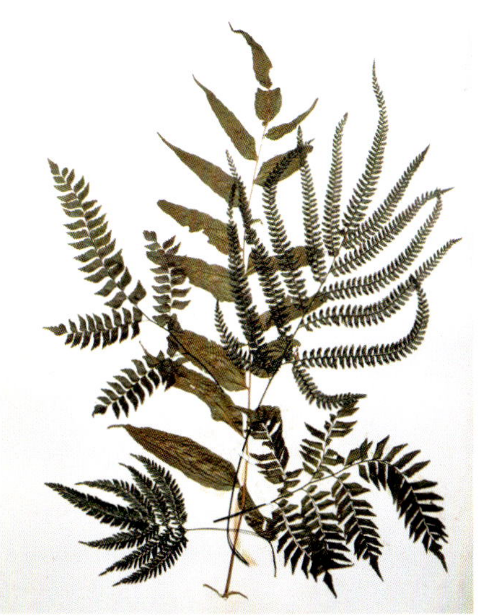

Isabel Carnes Church (1836-1899)
Pressed Ferns in an Herbarium,
1865
Plant mounted on cardboard,
27 x 21 inches
OL.2001.366.3

settling in Jamaica, Frederic quickly got to work losing himself in making detailed *plein air* studies of the island's topography, plant life and weather. Isabel developed a fascination for the flora of the island too, specifically the native ferns. She collected specimens of these, pressing them into herbarium albums. Some years later at Olana, Isabel established a fern garden below the home's northern retaining wall.[9]

Isabel's desire to transplant specimens of exotic flora into the family garden was not an isolated example. In the nineteenth century, writer and landscape gardener Alexander Jackson Downing advocated for the aesthetic value of introducing exotic ornamental plants into American gardens through his book *A Treatise on the Theory and Practice of Landscape Gardening, Adapted to North America; With a View to the Improvement of Country Residences,* published in 1849. Country estates and smaller plots owned by amateur gardeners followed Downing's advice, which had a dramatic effect on reshaping the ecosystem of the Hudson Valley. Some of the foreign varieties Downing suggested included: European sycamore maple, Japanese princess tree, Chinese White mulberry, the Eurasian Norway maple, and the Chinese tree of heaven. As their seeds spread through natural forces or simply untended gardens, many of these species began to displace native flora due to factors such as faster growth rates and leaves that were unpalatable to grazers. The planting affected more that the diversity of forests in the area but also resulted in changes to both the soil chemistry and the microbiology of the landscape.[10]

One index of successful European colonial expansion into foreign lands was the establishment of infrastructure in the colonies. An historical precedent would be to trace the network of roads and aqueducts that interconnected the various provinces of the Roman Empire. In this way, a peripheral territory began to resemble its distant metropolitan center, regardless of differences in climate or topography. It also facilitated the exploitation of resources from the area's land and fields. The effects on the European and colonial landscapes were reciprocal but wildly asymmetrical. For instance, the forests of Jamaica were transformed into vast plantations through the introduction of monocultural crops like sugarcane, which originated in the East Indies (Java). The products of the harvest were shipped back to Europe to became table sugar and rum.[11] Exotic indigenous specimens from the Caribbean also made their way to Europe, prized for their ornamental and medicinal properties, appearing in the formal gardens and pharmacies of the metropolis. The effects of this exchange were contained and structured on the European continent while in the periphery the change was a catastrophic and violent form of erasure.

In his two-volume memoir *Plant Hunting* Ernest H. Wilson describes his work obtaining botanical specimens in Africa for purposes of both study and commercialization. After a journey by train to the Victoria Falls, he muses on what the Scottish missionary David Livingstone, who is credited with naming the Falls, might have thought if he were by his side that day:

> The iron horse has brought the comforts and amenities of western civilization to the heart of Africa; life and property are safe and dainty ladies from America and Europe visit and take pleasant walks where twenty-five years ago only hunters ventured among the warring savages that disputed with the lordly game for the possession of the region. Except that the game has mostly departed, the region has not changed neither have its beauties been diminished. The railway does not wantonly obtrude neither does the low well-built hotel, which from a distance suggests a large country mansion set in its own park land. The bridge alone stands conspicuous but no one can quarrel with the outlines of this masterpiece of engineering. Did the spirit of its discoverer return one thinks he would be satisfied with what has

9 Frederic Edwin Church, Elizabeth Mankin Kornhauser, and Katherine Manthorne, *Fern Hunting Among These Picturesque Mountains: Frederic Edwin Church in Jamaica: The Olana Collection* (Ithaca: Cornell University Press, 2010): 15-27.

10 Henshaw, *Environmental History,* 186.

11 Jill H. Casid, *Sowing Empire: Landscape and Colonization* (Minneapolis: University of Minnesota Press, 2005): 11.

happened since the white man took over dominion.[12]

Concepts of progress and civilization do little to anesthetize the violent ordering of the land or the equally brutal hierarchical ordering of culture and race. Infrastructure and names are two methods of inscription that indelibly mark a landscape as a territory.

The Heliographic Mission

In this era of asymmetrical exchange, where vast quantities of plant matter traverse the globe in the service of empire, we see a new technology emerge, one that is capable of describing the world with exacting detail. Photography is an analytical tool, from its inception in 1839, it found purpose in the service of archeology, philology, anthropology and cartography. It documented site evidence and cultural environments, it reproduced details of nature and of objects, it was used to survey the land and to provide topographic perspective. All of which is to say that photography's invention and early use were deeply connected to the colonial.

Photography had not yet been invented when excavations began that provided artifacts for a series of publications called *Description de l'Égypte, ou Recueil des observations et des recherches qui ont été faites en Égypte pendant l'expédition de l'armée française, publié par les orders de Sa Majesté l'Empereur Napoléon le Grand (Description of Egypt, or the collection of observations and researches which were made in Egypt during the expedition of the French Army, published by the order of His Majesty the Emperor, Napoleon the Great*). Shortly after the French invasion of Egypt in 1798, Napoleon Bonaparte directed his surplus workforce of scientists and engineers, who were originally tasked with providing military support, hydrological research and land surveying, to turn their attention to the creation of a detailed record and inventory of the ruins and artifacts of ancient Egypt. Both as subject and site, Egypt became ground zero for the practice and codification of archeological fieldwork. This also began the process of widescale cultural appropriation of ancient Egyptian culture into the broader network of French patrimony. Massive stone remnants of Egyptian history were excavated and brought once more to the surface, a deliberate reverse engineering of the landscape. What was lost to time had now been made visible again, not as a sign of the rebirth of a buried civilization but rather as a marker of the enlightenment of another ascendant one.

In 1851, the French government commissioned the Heliographic Mission, a detailed photographic inventory of important historic structures and sites, related to French history and pre-history, and in need of preservation and restoration. The images made by the photographers, Édouard Baldus, Hippolyte Bayard, Gustave Le Gray, Henri Le Secq, and Auguste Mestral, showed sites of both deterioration and adaptive reuse. While primarily examples of medieval architecture, pre-historic and Roman sites were also included in this concept of French heritage. Stephen Monteiro writes that:

> [with] the rise of nationalism surrounding Napoleon III, the task of promoting the cultural value of such buildings at a national level became a problem of eliding space and time. It entailed converting ancient sites from landmarks of particular regional significance into durable symbols of a unified country via renovations that could signify both a new and an ancient France, thereby confounding the passage of time. Intersecting national and local, ancient and new, within a single site could satisfy local pride while also promoting empire as the descendant of a gloried past of autocratic rule.[13]

This conflation of two projects separated by time, discipline and geography is deliberate in both their allusion to a narrative of unbroken dynastic empire, and

12 Ernest Wilson, *Plant Hunting*, Vol. 1 (Boston, MA: The Stratford Company, 1927): 92.

13 Stephen Monteiro, "'Nothing is So Dangerous as Hypothesis': The *Mission Héliographique*, Photography, and the Spectacle of History," *Photography and Culture*, vol. 3, no. 3 (November 1, 2010) https://doi.org/10.2752/175145109x12804957025598: 303.

to the development of tools and documents used to both unravel and rewrite the narrative of history inscribed on the land.

The French archeologist Claude-Joseph Désiré Charnay made some of the first photographs of Mayan ruins near Mérida in the Yucatán during the 1860s, traveling with pack mules, two local guides and a retinue of forty indigenous laborers who worked for three days at one site clearing the brush and debris that hid the facades of the magnificent structures. Once revealed the sites were documented, and most of the photographs show a pronounced crown of flora that almost decoratively surrounds the ruins.[14] We can interpret these images as evidence of the constant negotiation or struggle for power written into the landscape. We see evidence of plant life accelerated by tropical conditions, waiting for a moment of human neglect that would allow it to reclaim the carefully constructed structures of carved stone and reintegrate them into the landscape. This is just one aspect of an unending cycle of conditions that manifest changes to the landscape. Other forces are more discreetly human in nature, such as conflict, cultivation, extraction, and development. The concept of landscape is continuously being authored by the hegemony of one position, slowly erasing and replacing another.

The meaning of the word 'landscape' loses something in translation across cultures. While the English term refers to the appearance of the land as we perceive it, lending it a pronounced aesthetic dimension, the German term *Landschaft,* for example, has a double meaning that additionally addresses a territory as being restricted, giving legal qualities to its description.[15] When art historian Charmaine Nelson writes about nineteenth-century marine landscapes, she effectively describes the intersecting capacities of these aesthetic and restrictive dimensions that further the agenda of empire's expansion and reification: "To analyze these images not solely in terms of an emptied-out depoliticized aesthetics or formal methodology, but rather within their colonial contexts, addressing their implications for processes and practices of empire, is, I believe, what (Edward) Said meant when he argued for an analysis capable of reconnecting cultural forms to "their actuality.""[16]

Terraforming

Today, our understanding of landscape represents the entanglement of human activity with all other environmental actors in a described territory. From wilderness through to the legislated protection of a zone such as a state park, the status of landscapes are dependent on the contingent presence of humankind. Environmental philosopher Steven Vogel insists on defining this broad concept of the landscape as the built environment, or the totality of life on earth, and by this more fully implicating us in its manifestation: "Our environment is not something we passively confront or experience or perceive or know; rather, it is the object of our practices. And since nothing is a practice unless it changes the world (because all practices are transformative), it follows that the environment is the product of our practices as well. In this sense we construct the environment, and do so socially."[17]

Terraforming is the hypothetical process of reshaping the terrain and atmosphere of an alien planet so that it may sustain human life. It is part of the colonial enterprise, and its effects so alter the existing context as to make it uninhabitable to native flora and fauna. Metaphorically, it can be seen as the rapacious tool of empire that only recognizes the commodifiable values of an environment. It represents a process by which those species and cultures not hardy enough to provide for empire's distant metropolitan markets or who are in direct competition with them are gradually erased or marginalized.

Terraforming is the result of cascading changes to the environment brought on by a multitude of human cultural, political, and economic factors. It is a process of constant encroachment, the slow metabolic shift from one reality to

14 Keith F. Davis, *Désiré Charnay, Expeditionary Photographer* (Albuquerque: University of New Mexico Press, 1981): 13-17.

15 Kenneth R. Olwig, "Recovering the Substantive Nature of Landscape," *Annals of the Association of American Geographers* 86, no. 4 (December 1, 1996): 630–53, https://doi.org/10.1111/j.1467-8306.1996.tb01770.x.: 630.

16 Charmaine A. Nelson, *Slavery, Geography and Empire in Nineteenth-Century Marine Landscapes of Montréal and Jamaica* (London; New York: Routledge, 2017): 50.

17 Steven Vogel, *Thinking like a Mall: Environmental Philosophy after the End of Nature* (Cambridge, MA: MIT Press, 2016): 65.

another. The European colonizers of the Caribbean and the Americas did not necessarily understand the dramatic changes they were making to the native ecosystem. They shaped the landscape into one that was better suited to fulfill the needs of their European economies. For example, colonists brought pigs, cows, sheep and horses to the northeast of America. Their grazing needs explain the presence of certain plant species present on the continent today. Environmental historian William Cronon shares his analysis of a description of New England in the seventeenth century by William Wood, a visiting Englishman:

> "In such places where the cattle use to graze," wrote Wood, "the ground is much improved in the woods, growing more grassy and less weedy." What in fact was happening was that a number of native grasses and field plants were slowly being destroyed and replaced by European species. Annual grasses were quickly killed off if grazed too closely, and the delicate crowns of some perennials fared little better. Not having evolved in a pastoral setting, they were ill prepared for their new use. That was why European grasses, which had adapted themselves to the harsh requirements of pastoralism, began to take over wherever cattle grazed. 'English grasses,' such as bluegrass and white clover, spread rapidly in newly settled areas. Initially carried to the New World in shipboard fodder, and in the dung of the animals which ate them, these European species were soon being systematically cultivated by colonists. By the 1640s, a regular market in grass seed existed in the Narragansett country, and within one or two generations, the plants had become so common that they were regarded as native.[18]

How might a contemporary visitor to the Hudson River Estuary or Olana begin to describe the landscape visible today? One might make the argument that landscape is a product of zoning as photographer Lewis Baltz does in his *Notes on Recent Industrial Developments in Southern California.* His description anticipates the bland reality of the structures he photographs and that conform to these regulations:

> One developer plans the entire industrial area, usually in conformity with a county or regional master plan. The site is divided into a simple grid of streets and blocks. The grid pattern is broken only at the perimeter of the development, where an encircling frontage road may channel traffic to freeway access or to previously existing surface streets. Broad interior streets are designed to accommodate large numbers of heavy vehicles. Lot sizes, setbacks, and other zoning determinations are incorporated into the master plan and maintained uniformly throughout the development.[19]

Zoning regulations, master plans and environmental law have all produced the landscape visible from Olana today. Views of the Hudson River are vigorously protected and have been the subject of several legal battles that determine the kind of development that might happen in the region. In one landmark case concerning the viewshed (visible territory) surrounding Olana, the work of Church was brought forth as legal evidence of the region's cultural significance. The outcome was that the U.S. Nuclear Regulatory Commission (NRC) denied permission for a power plant to be built at Cementon on the western bank of the Hudson, six miles downriver from Olana. "The NRC analysis cited the importance of Church's paintings in their decision: "A 10-mile radius around the proposed power plant would take in literally dozens of the scenic views and picturesque areas that were eventually transferred to canvases now hanging in the country's major museums and art galleries" (U.S. Nuclear Regulatory Commission 1979, 5–68). For the NRC, it was specifically the southwesterly view from Olana, "painted by Church at least 35 times," that was a crucial determinant in the final negative assessment (1979, 5-71)."[20]

18 William Cronon, *Changes in the Land: Indians, Colonists, and the Ecology of New England,* rev. ed. (New York: Hill and Wang, 2003): 142.

19 Lewis Baltz, *Lewis Baltz: Texts* (Göttingen: Steidl, 2012): 13.

20 Henshaw, *Environmental History,* 304.

Despite the protections to the viewshed in place, the landscape that surrounds Olana has been massively transformed in the past 150 years. Some of the changes were already well underway in the nineteenth century: There has been continuous grading and quarrying of the land, the river is occasionally dredged to maintain the waterways, new paths and roads are built that lead to interstate highways and complement the railroad that follows the river's shoreline, the Rip Van Winkle bridge has spanned the river since 1935, new factories, schools, and office parks have been built with their attendant parking lots, culverts, and retention basins, while a new species of mega structure in the form of regional distribution centers hides on the periphery. And there below the northern retaining wall is a ramshackle bed of self-seeded native ferns.

Xenoforming

The forest floor is lit from the bioluminescent glow of the creeper vines that cling to the ghost white and red velvet patched trunks of the enormous tree ferns. The copper leaves of the ferns reminiscent of ancient circuit board filigrees; their new growth fiddleheads arch towards the deep Prussian blue sky. But velvet, circuit boards and Prussians no longer exist on this world, perhaps ghosts still do. When the ferns arrived, they slowly reconstituted the atmosphere of our planet. No one knows where they first landed on Earth nor how they spread so quickly undetected. It was said that they settled first in the neglected and overlooked regions of the global south, long since abandoned due to sea level rise and the forced migrations north. They thrived at first in the empty wetland cities of Lagos and Dhaka. Their spores dispersed in the air following jet streams to eventually blanket all the remaining land masses. The vastly increased aerosol activity changed the Rayleigh scattering index and shifted the sky's color spectrum. We discovered that only plants managed to adapt to the new atmospheric conditions, and then we retreated to the water leaving all other land-based fauna to fend for itself. We survived for a period living off fish and kelp but soon the fish were gone too, and the water borne plants became unpalatable, and finally you could no longer define the liquid we inhabited as water. Perhaps something remains of us on the land, our cities in ruin, entangled in the root structures of the ferns, buried rooms illuminated by the radiance of the vines.

Landscape, as a genre, has the potential to address something larger than the human condition. By that I don't mean that it should represent the environment as it is constituted exclusively by non-human actors but rather how it might represent our full immersion into it as context. We need to redress the dialectic that sees our economic, political, and social energies as oppositional to those embodied in the ontological otherness of nature. We need contextual measures to understand the value different actors contribute to the health of this expanded concept of society. The new civic landscape is an idea that recognizes the participation and agency of not only different cultural positions, both hegemonic and marginal, but also the collective of non-human agents that contribute towards the full realization of our shared environment.

David Hartt
The Histories (after Church),
Version with xenoformed atmosphere/
Rayleigh scattering spectrum shift,
2023
Tapestry,
89 ½ x 60 ½ inches
Installed in the central Stair Hall of
Olana's Main House.

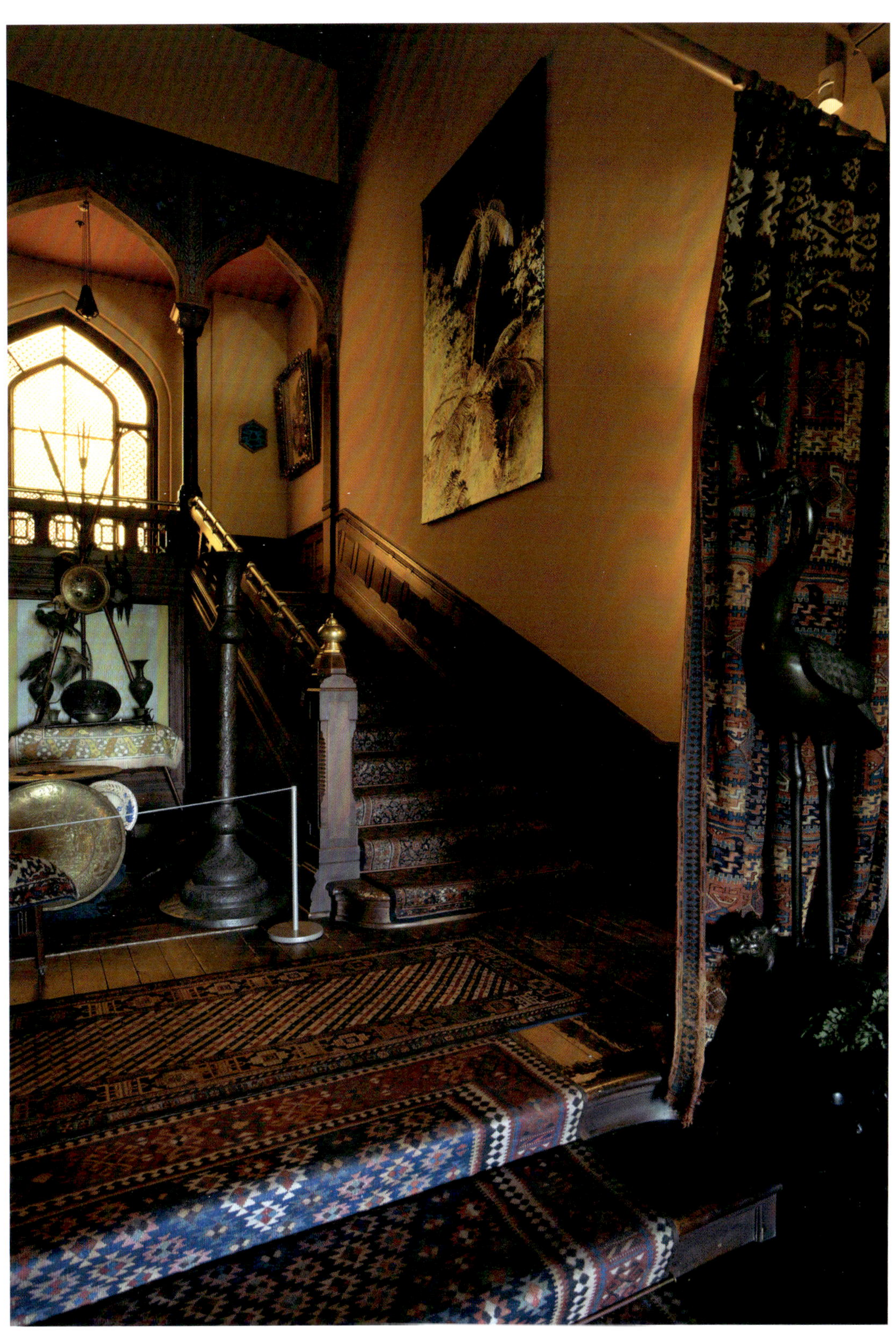

David Hartt
Specimen,
2023
Bronze,
Two elements: 52 x 19 x 8 inches and
37 ½ x 12 x 7 ½ inches
Installed below the northern retaining wall of Olana's Main House environs in the former fern garden.

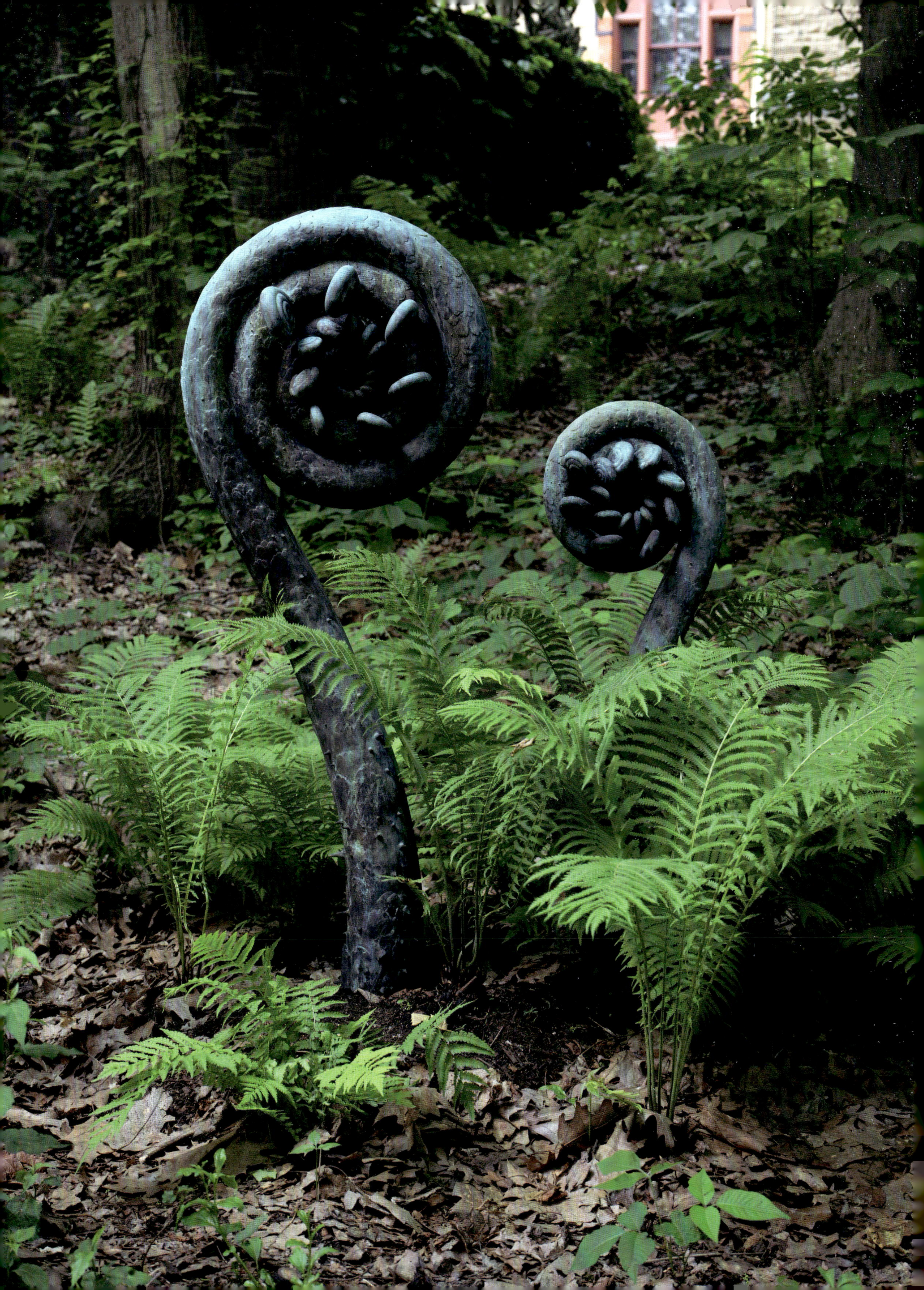

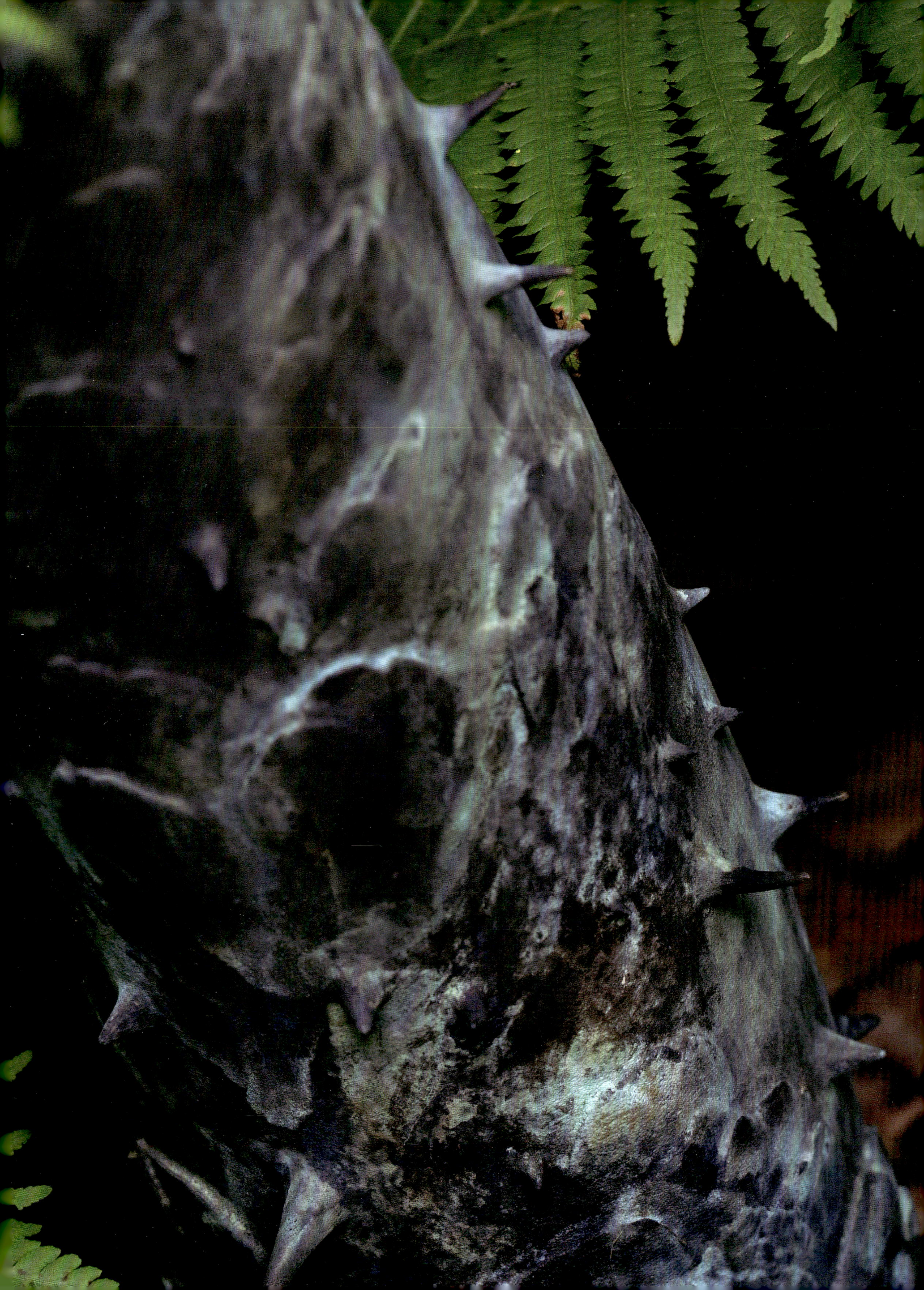

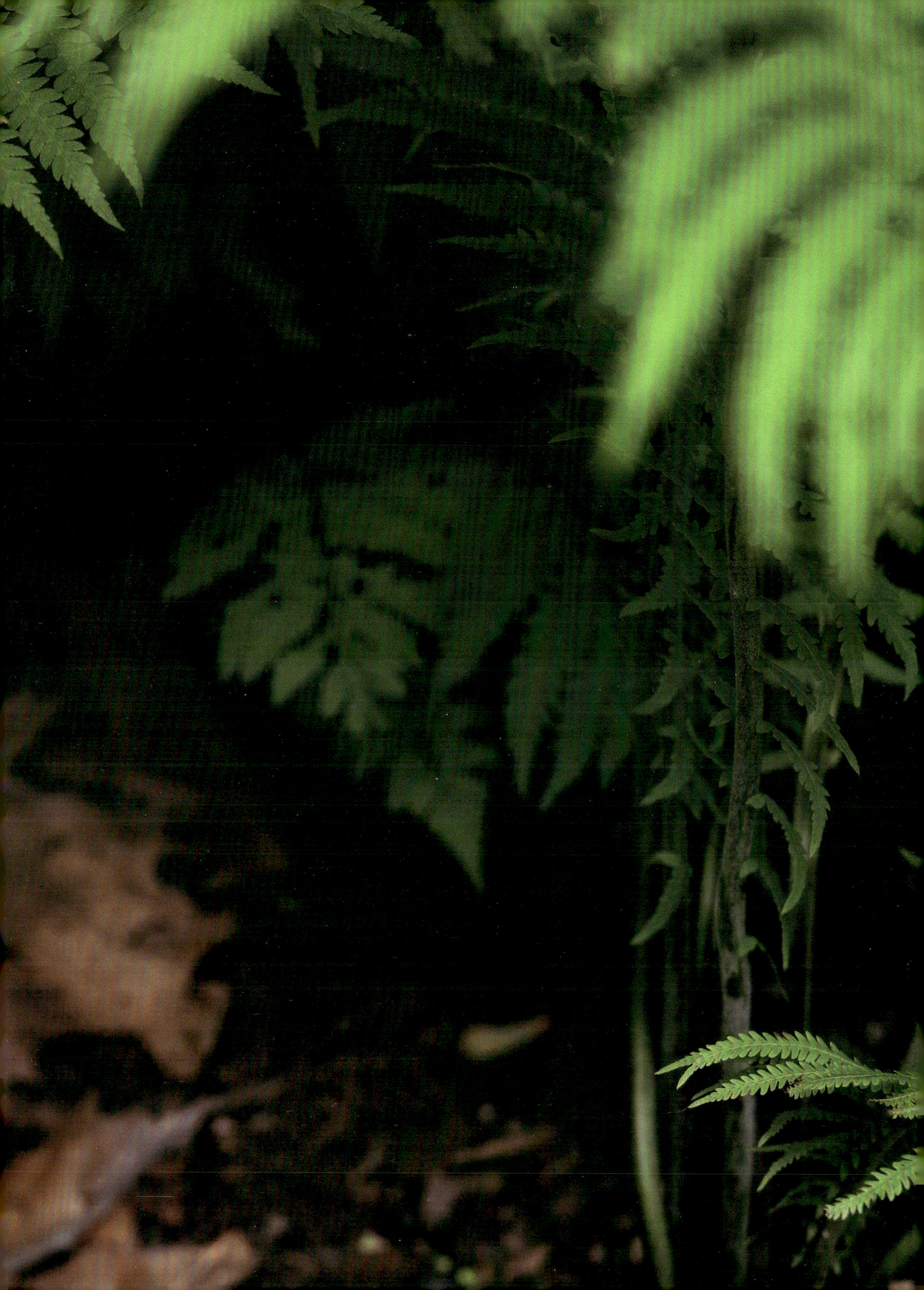

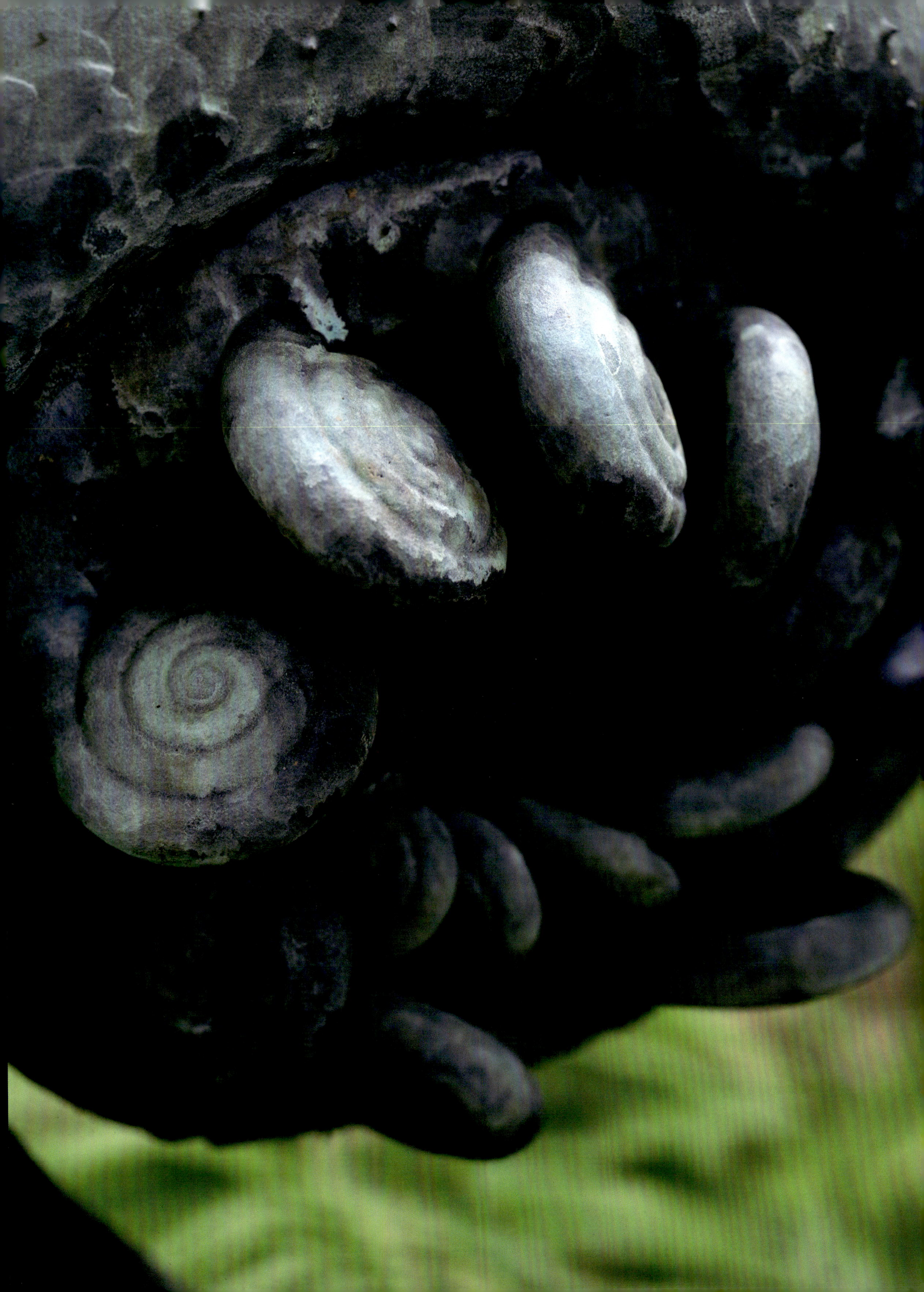

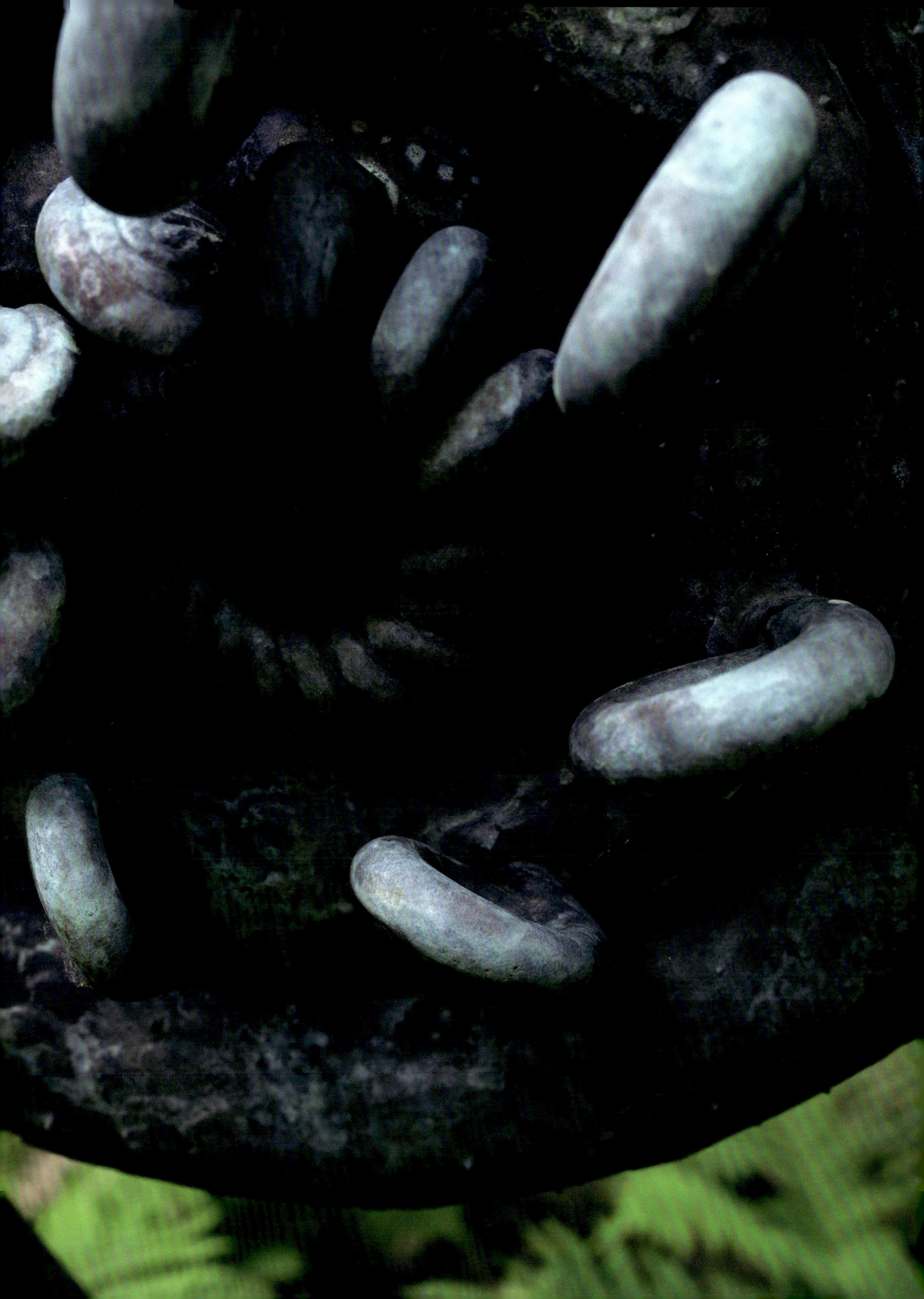

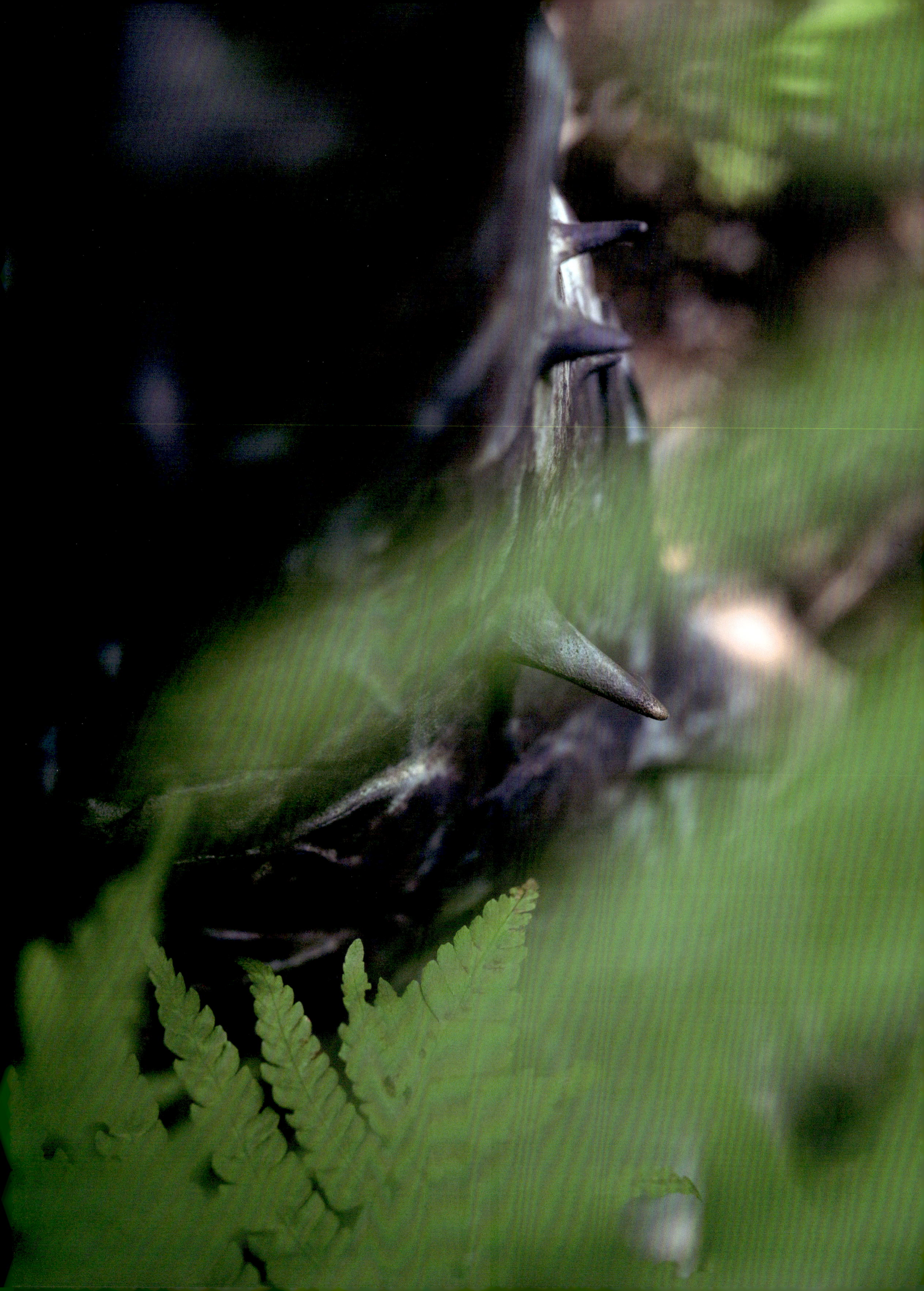

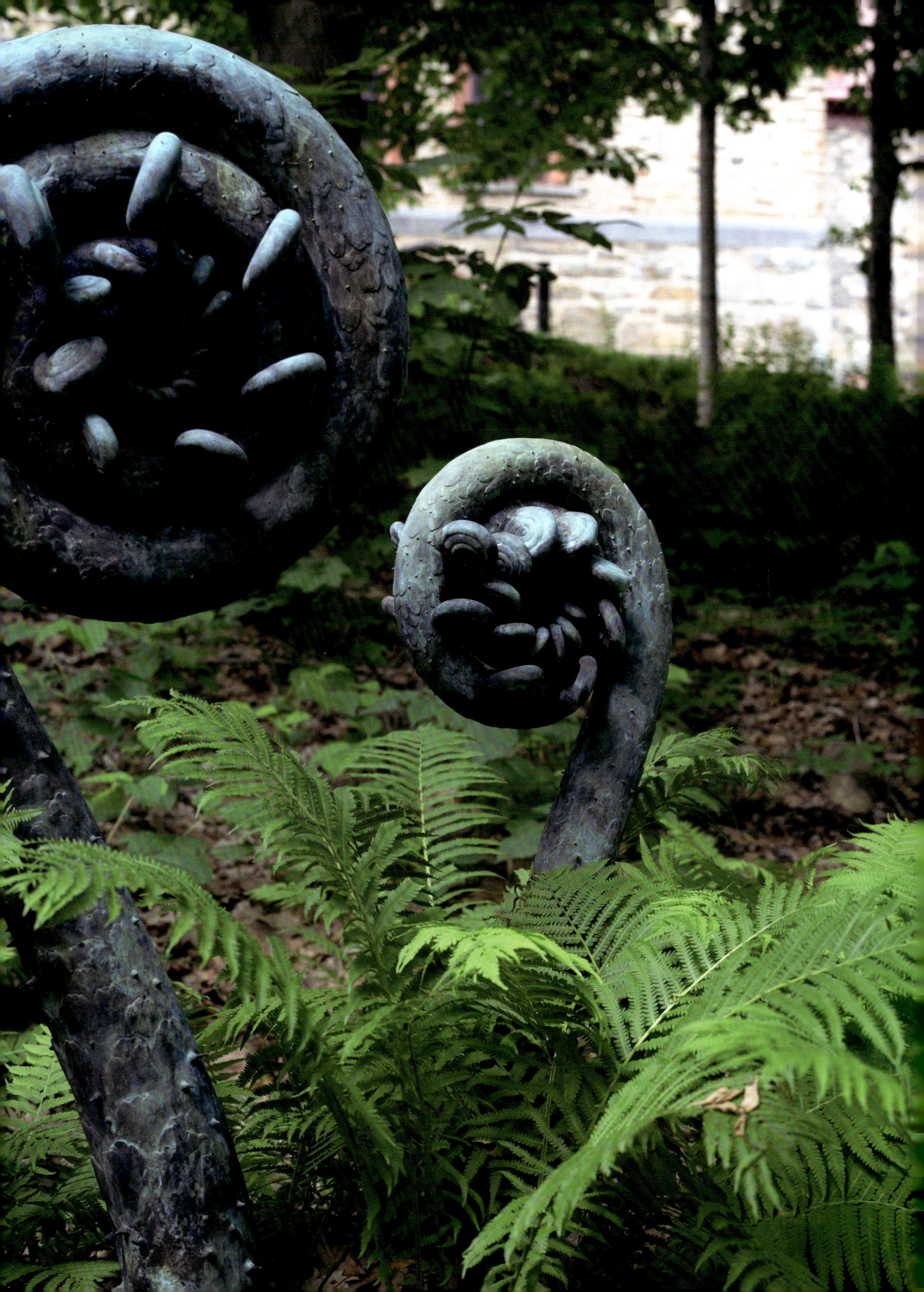

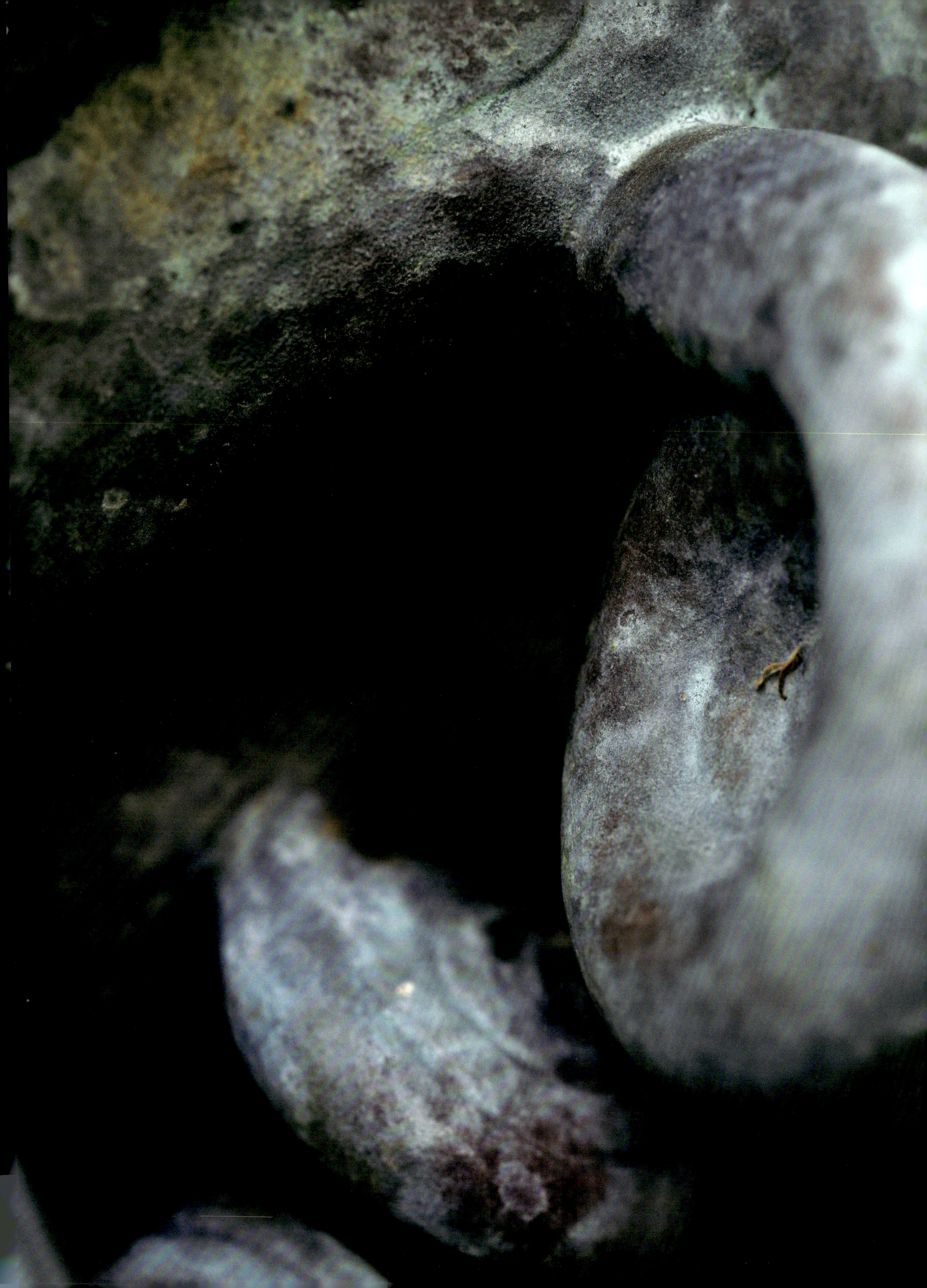

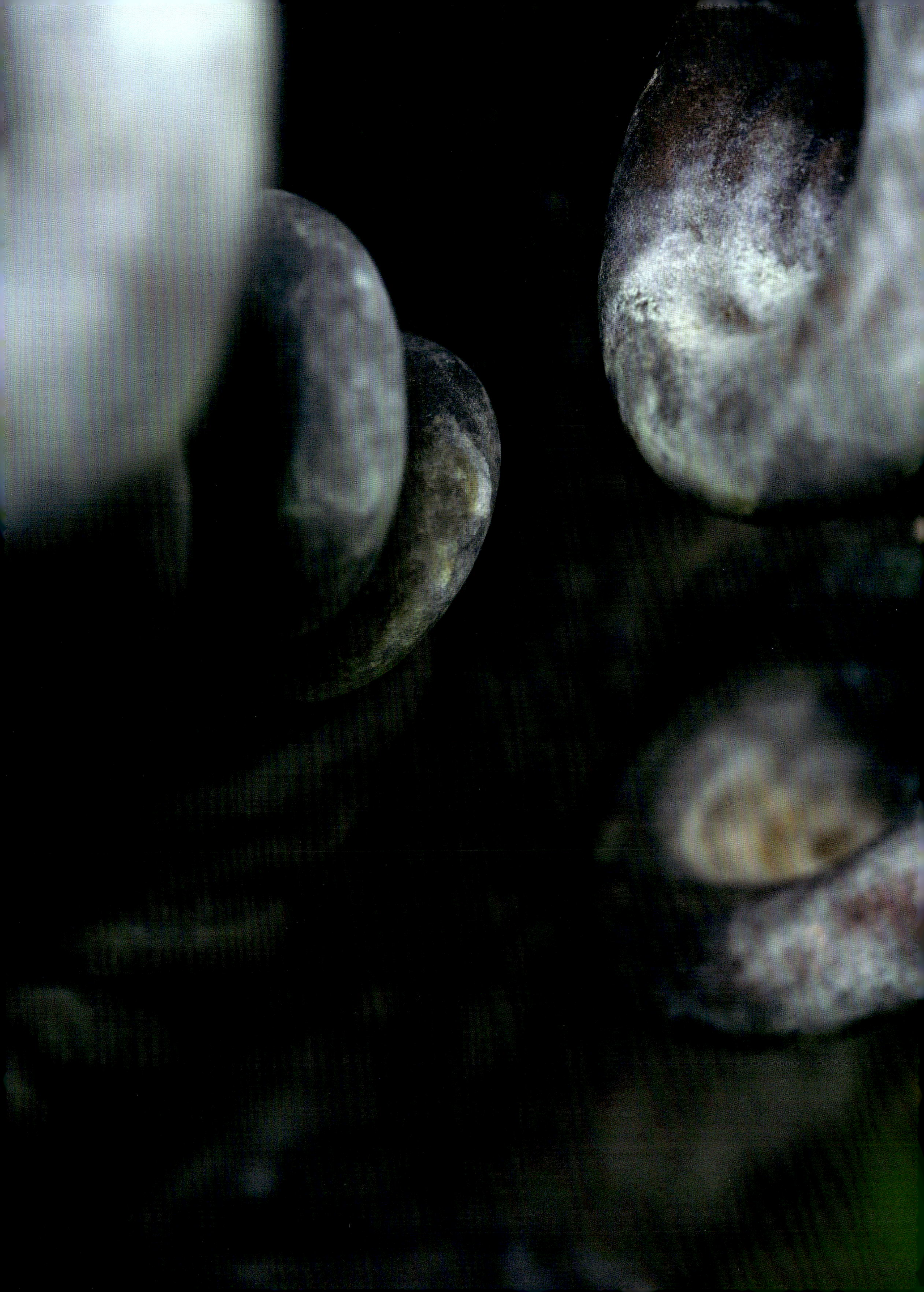

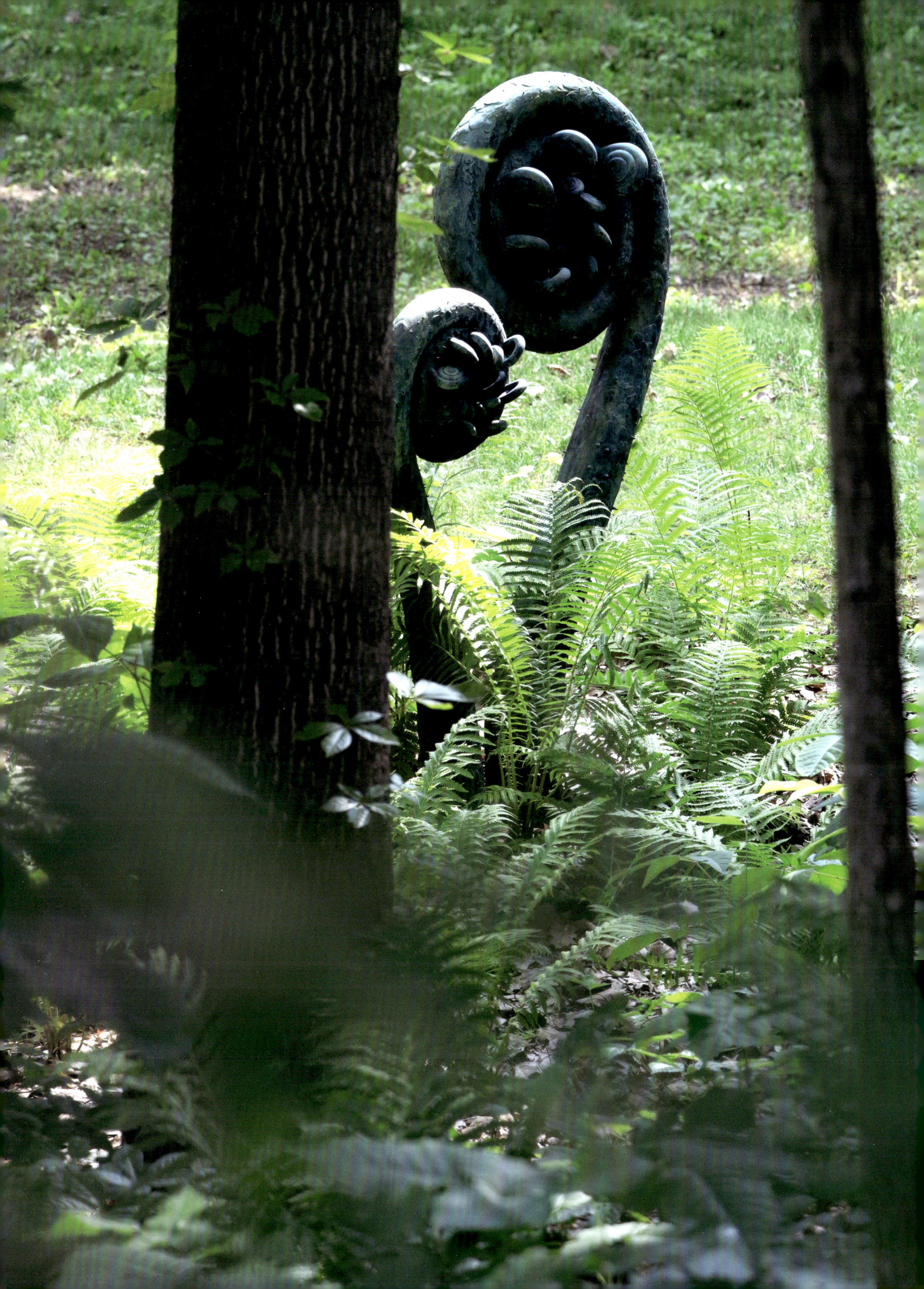

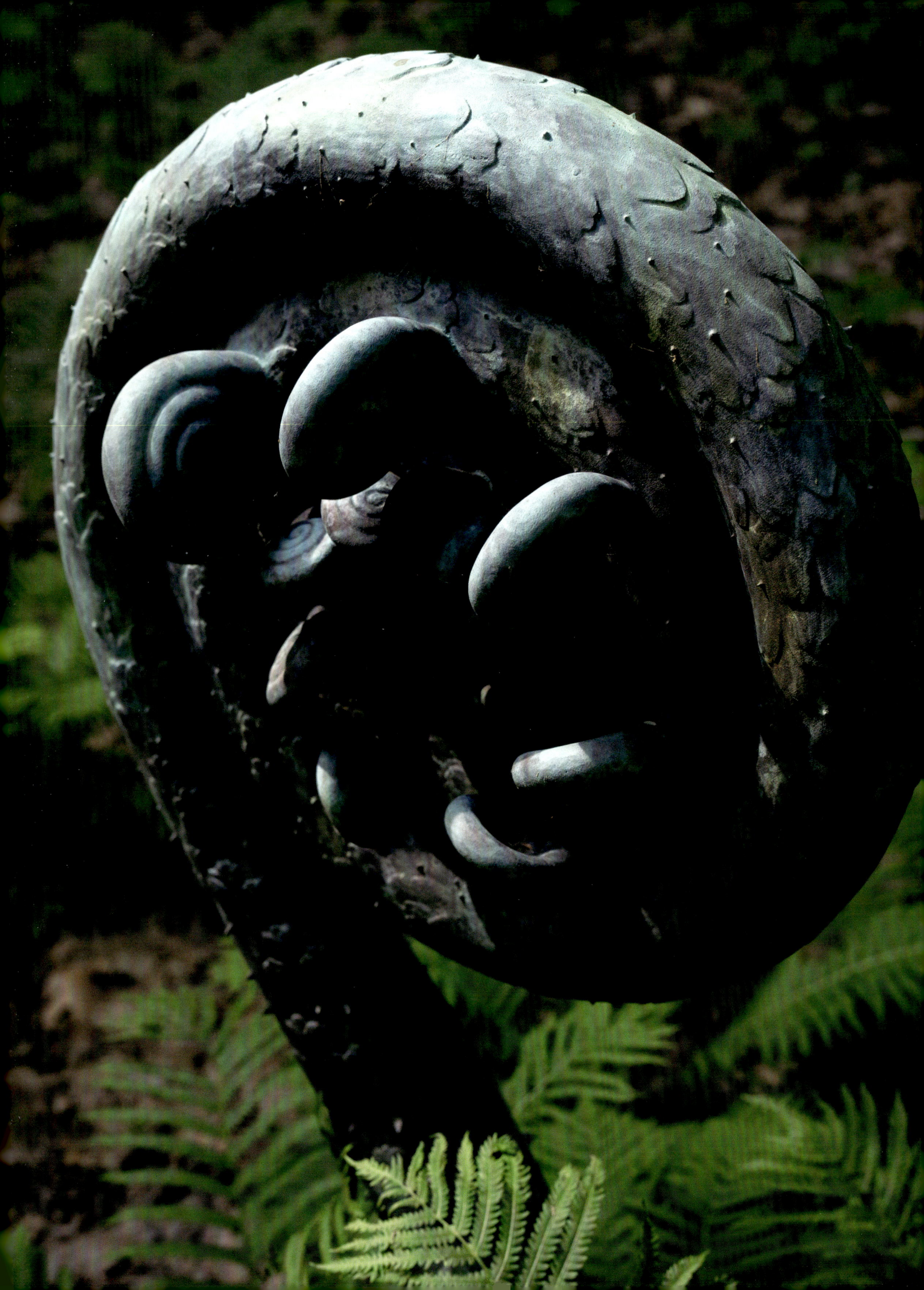

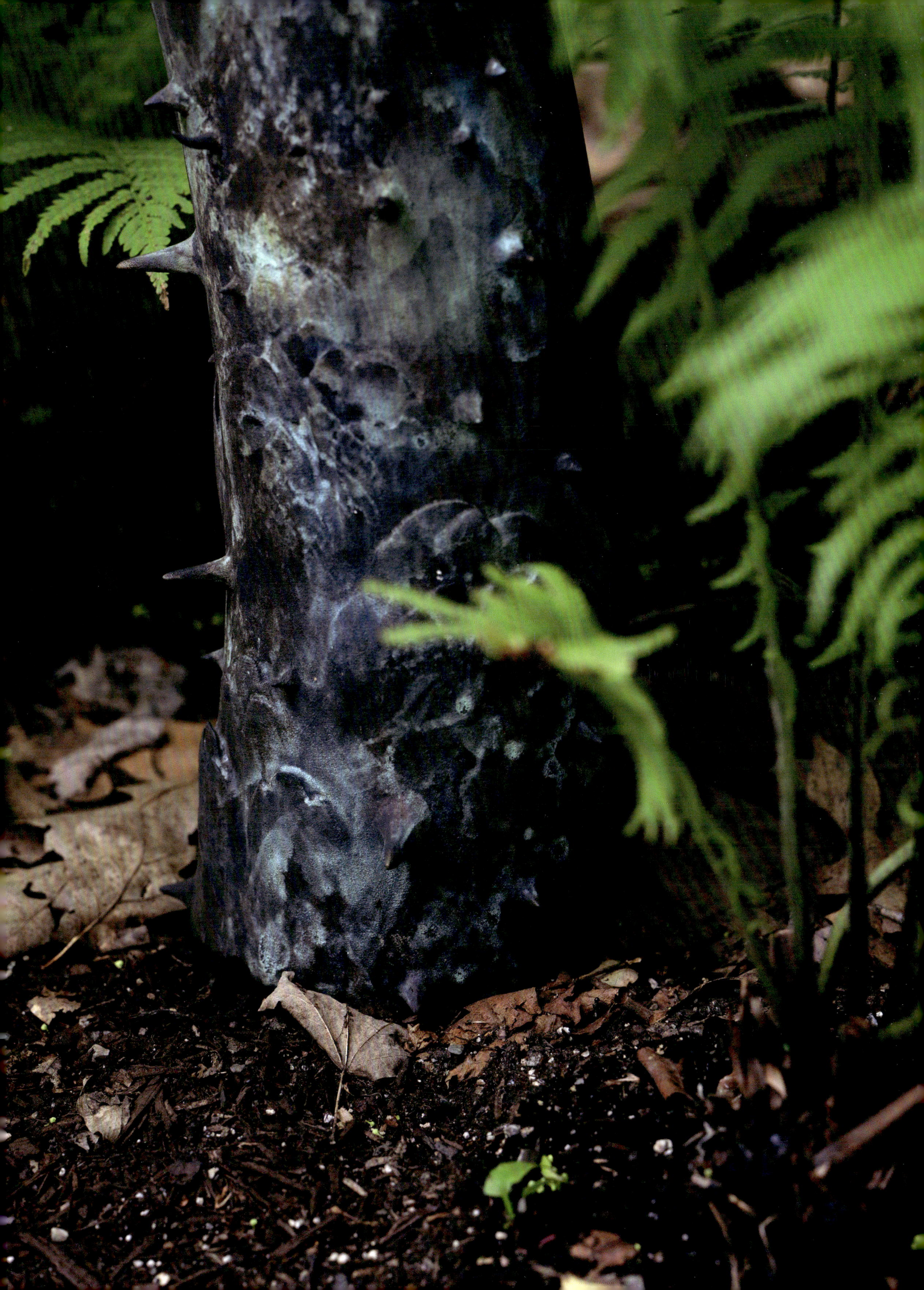

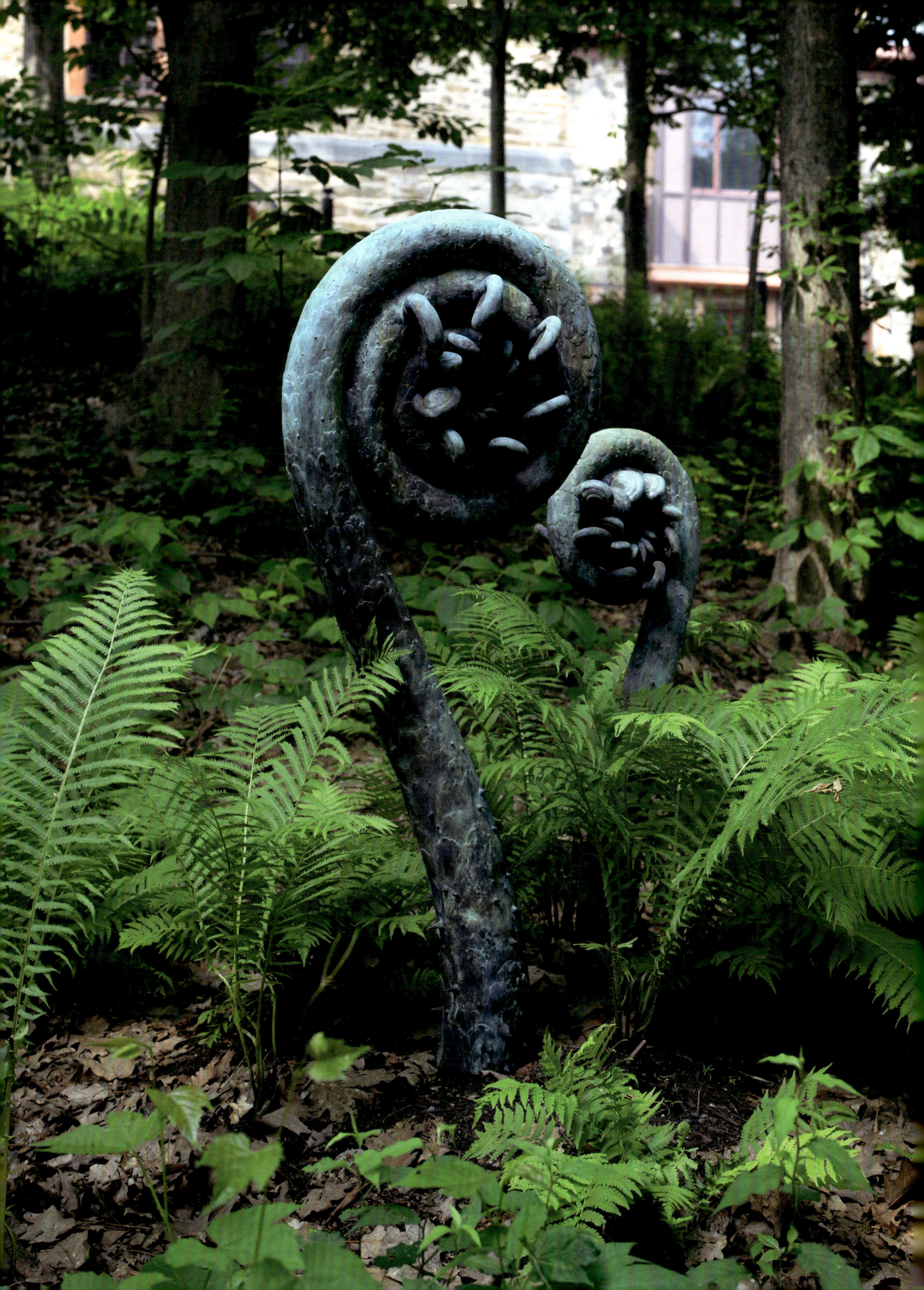

CONTRIBUTORS

William L. Coleman is the Wyeth Foundation Curator and Director of the Andrew and Betsy Wyeth Study Center at the Brandywine Museum of Art, with additional oversight of Wyeth Foundation initiatives at the Farnsworth Art Museum. As The Olana Partnership's former Director of Collections and Exhibitions, he served as co-curator with David Hartt of *Terraforming: Olana's Historic Photography Collection Unearthed.*

Corey Keller is an independent curator and historian of photography based in Oakland, California. She recently stepped down as curator of photography and acting head of the Photography Department at SFMOMA, where she was a member of the curatorial team from 2003 to 2021. She is currently at work on a book about Anna Atkins.

David Hartt is a visual artist and an Associate Professor in the Department of Fine Arts at the University of Pennsylvania. His work is represented by Corbett vs. Dempsey, Chicago; David Nolan Gallery, New York; and Galerie Thomas Schulte, Berlin.

TERRAFORMING

Published on the occasion of the exhibition
Terraforming: Olana's Historic Photography Collection Unearthed,
curated by David Hartt, and organized by The Olana Partnership in collaboration with the New York State Office of Parks, Recreation and Historic Preservation, and presented at Olana State Historic Site from May 14, 2023—October 29, 2023.

Published by
The Olana Partnership
P.O. Box 199
Hudson, New York
12534

www.olana.org

For The Olana Partnership
Sean E. Sawyer, Ph.D, Washburn and Susan Oberwager President
Mark Prezorski, Senior Vice President and Landscape Curator
Allegra Davis, Associate Curator
Ida Brier, Librarian and Archivist

Publication
Design: David Hartt
Digital models and renderings of *Specimen* by Mark Lyon
Managing editor and production: Todd Bradway
Copyedited by Dan Fox
Printed and bound by Faenza Printing SpA, Italy

Dimensions are stated in inches; height precedes width.

When possible, image titles follow the wording given on the original 19th-century photographic prints, including variations in place names and their spellings.

Unless otherwise credited, all photographs are reproduced from the collection of Olana State Historic Site, New York State Office of Parks, Recreation and Historic Preservation.

First edition, 2023
ISBN: 979-8-9876675-0-7

Printed and bound by Faenza Printing SpA, Italy.

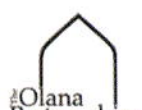

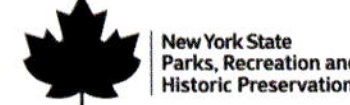

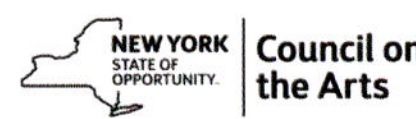

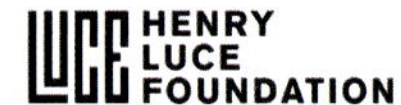

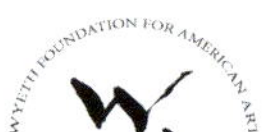

Support for this publication has been provided by the Wyeth Foundation for American Art. The associated exhibition has been made possible by a grant from the Henry Luce Foundation, support from the donors to The Olana Partnership's Novak-Ferber Exhibitions Fund, and in-kind contributions by the New York State Bureau of Historic Sites, Office of Parks, Recreation, and Historic Preservation. General support for The Olana Partnership's programs is provided by the New York State Council on the Arts with the support of the Office of the Governor and the New York State Legislature.

About Olana and The Olana Partnership: Olana is the masterwork of Frederic Edwin Church (1826–1900), the preeminent American artist of the mid-19th century, and the most important artist's home, studio, and designed landscape in the United States. Church designed Olana as a holistic environment integrating his advanced ideas about art, architecture, landscape design, and environmental conservation. Olana's 250-acre artist-designed landscape, with five miles of carriage roads and a Persian-inspired house at its summit, embraces unrivaled panoramic views of the Hudson Valley and Catskill Mountains and welcomes more than 170,000 visitors annually.

Olana State Historic Site, administered by the New York State Office of Parks, Recreation and Historic Preservation, is a designated National Historic Landmark and one of the most visited sites in the state. The Olana Partnership is the 501(c)(3) not-for-profit cooperative partner of the New York State Office of Parks, Recreation and Historic Preservation at Olana State Historic Site.

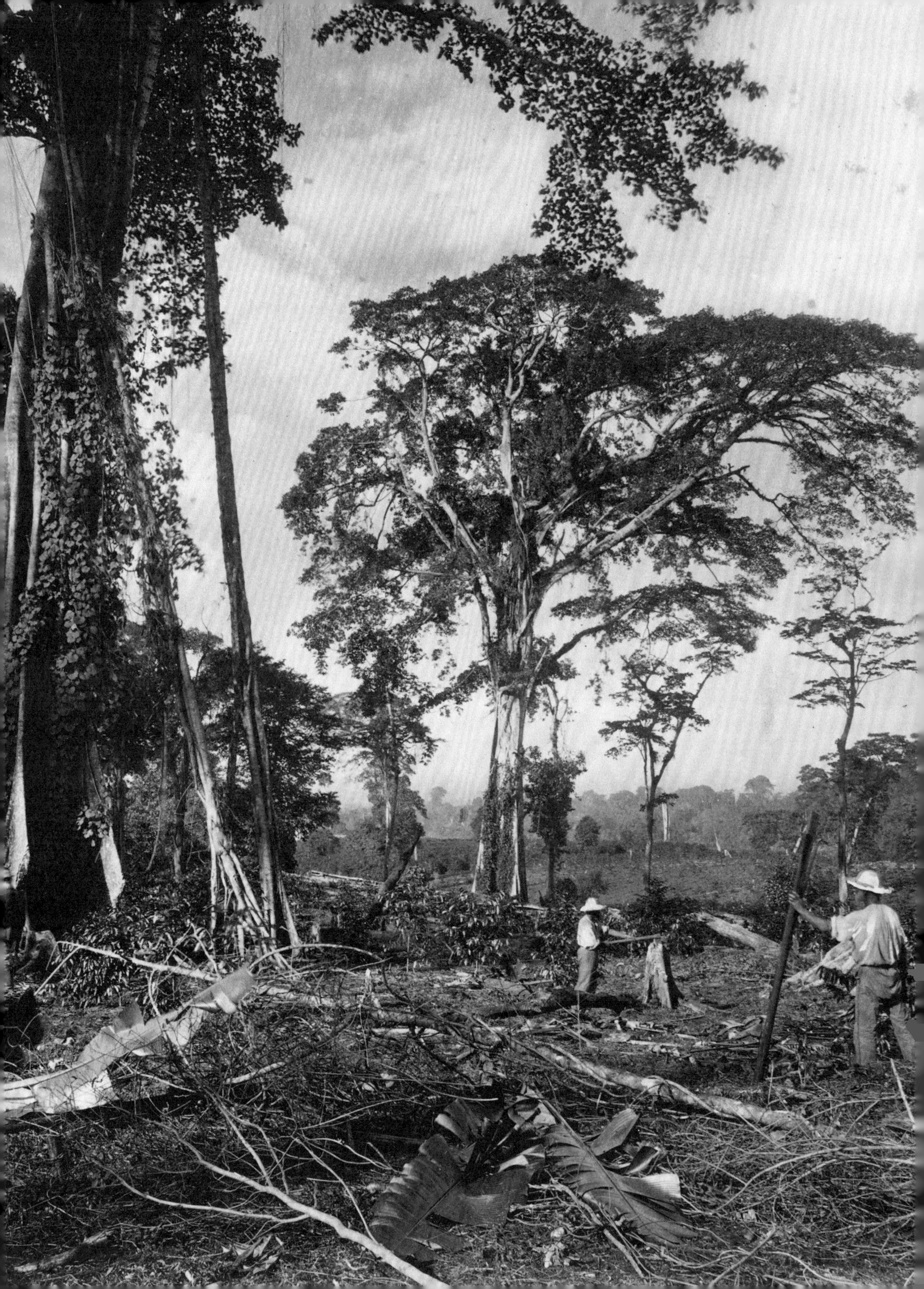

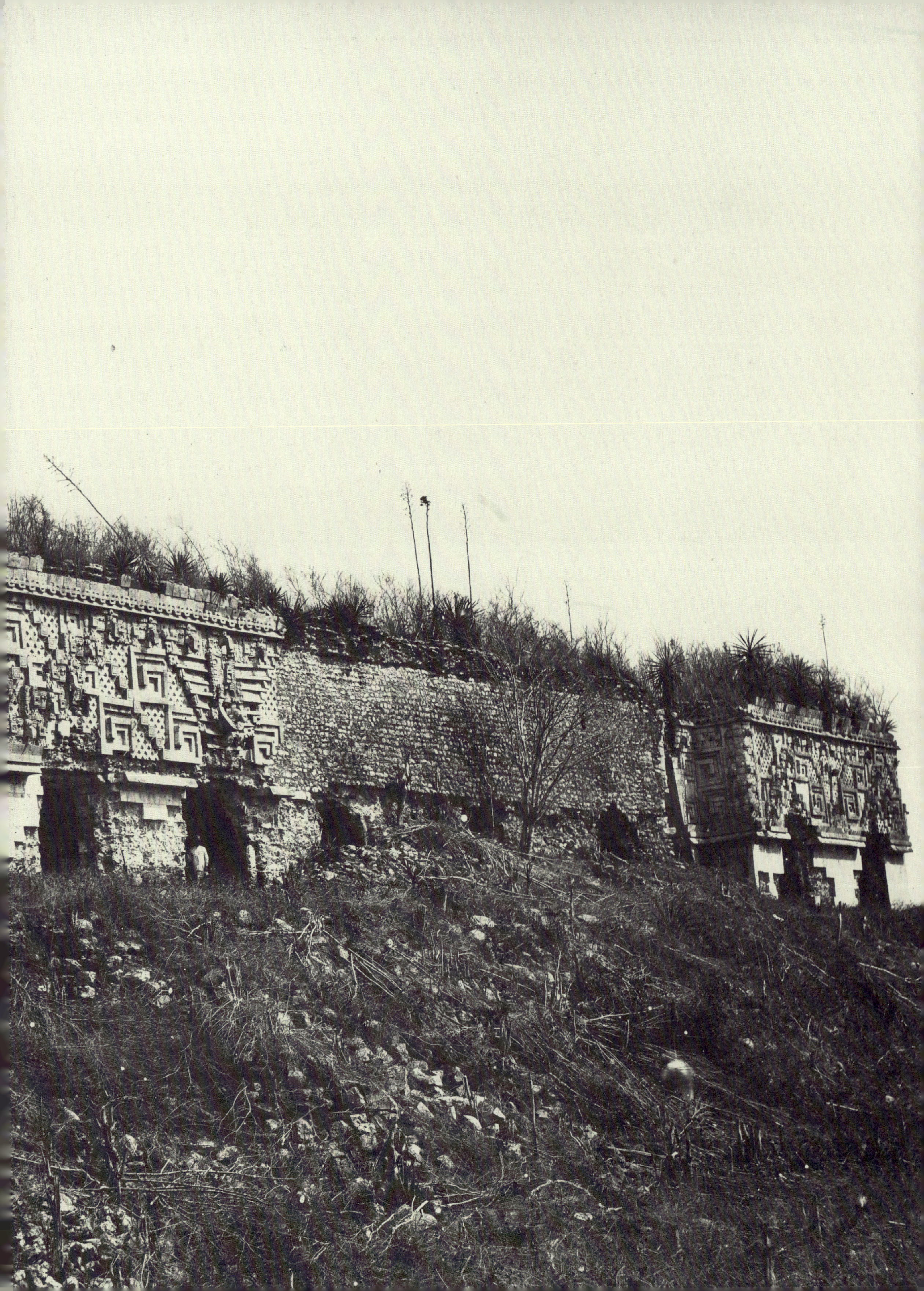